The Origin of God

Also by Laurence Gardner

Bloodline of the Holy Grail
Genesis of the Grail Kings
Realm of the Ring Lords
Lost Secrets of the Sacred Ark
The Magdalene Legacy
The Shadow of Solomon
The Grail Enigma

The companion book 'Revelation of the Devil' is due to be published by dash house in Spring 2011

Grateful thanks are due to dash house for their invaluable assistance in bringing this work to fruition

In loving memory of Laurence Gardner (1943-2010)

God standeth in the congregation of the mighty;
He judgeth among the gods ... 'Ye are gods; and
all of you are children of the Most High'.
Psalm 82:1,6

The Origin of God

Laurence Gardner

If the books of the Bible had never been written,
would we know about God from any other primary source?

dash house
Brockenhurst UK

First published in 2010 by dash house

ch

dash house
PO Box 394
Brockenhurst
Hants
SO41 1BP

The website address is: www.dashhousepublishing.co.uk

ISBN 978 0 9567357 0 6

A catalogue record of this book is
available from the British Library

Printed and bound in the Great Britain by
Lightning Source UK Ltd

CONTENTS

ILLUSTRATION AND MAPS

INTRODUCTION

Belief in the One male God of Judaism, Christianity and Islām can be traced back for something over 2,500 years to the time when the Hebrew scripture of Genesis was compiled in the 6th century BC. The narrative content of Genesis was clearly derived from older traditions but, on the face of it, we have no documentary evidence from any other source of a monotheistic culture in respect of this particular God from before that date.

Throughout the millennia thereafter, the image of God has evolved somewhat differently within the three primary One-God religions. But, despite the apparent variations in godly perception, it is nevertheless a commonly held view of each faith system that God is the merciful and benevolent protector of his followers. It is therefore inconsistent with this precept that these same followers have been subjected through the ages to a constant barrage of tragedy and disaster. Whether by way of natural calamities or purposeful tyranny, people in their millions have suffered pain and violent death to the extent that the supposed caring nature of God appears to have been either misconceived or is wholly lacking in effect. The opening first decade of this 21st century has proved to be no different in terms of the events themselves. But there is a very marked difference in that God's perceived role in such devastation and suffering is now being questioned as never before.

Whether referencing deliberate incidents such as the World Trade Center destruction in 2001, or naturally occurring phenomena such as the Asian Tsunami in 2004, a constantly asked question these days is, 'Where was God?' In the light of this, some churchmen and theologians have written books supporting God's position with given reasons for his otherwise inexplicable methods of divine judgement. Meanwhile, atheists and some humanists have published works that seek to establish an anti-religious dogma that there is no God whose motives can be called into question. Thus it is clear that, even after more than

2,500 years of scriptural and doctrinal tradition, there remains a dispute, fought at the highest levels of academia, over the very concept of God's existence.

For anyone reading literature from either side of the debate, it is plain from the outset that they are receiving commentaries based on particularly expressed viewpoints and opinions derived from individually vested interests. Although these books are popularly read by all and sundry, they are more inclined to appeal to readers who make their literary choices by virtue of their own personal leanings — either towards or away from a belief in God. The problem here is that a great many people are wholly or partially uncertain as to where they actually stand on the matter. A textual sermon from one camp or the other might well sway them if it is forceful enough in approach, but such writings leave little room for manoeuvre; they are specifically designed to persuade readers to adopt the various authors' personal points of view.

By contrast, *The Origin of God* is neither theistic nor atheistic. It is not contrived to weigh any balances by taking a calculated midstream approach, but takes the route of a documented biographical investigation with no design for any predestination or predetermined outcome. The objective is a headlong, impartial quest to trace the origin and evolution of God as a figure of belief by way of collating all demonstrable and circumstantial evidence in a chronological sequence of monotheistic development.

Where was God?

On 26 December 2004 the biggest earthquake for 40 years occurred between the Australian and Eurasian tectonic plates beneath the Indian Ocean. This rupturing of a seabed fault-line triggered giant tsunami waves that carved paths of destruction into the coastal communities of South and Southeast Asia, including parts of Indonesia, Sri Lanka, India and Thailand. The casualty toll was estimated at around 230,000 dead and missing. The tsunami event drowned people of every religion and none, whilst also destroying temples, mosques and churches. Thus, the question was soon raised: 'Where was God?'

Referencing this dilemma after the catastrophe, Dr Rowan Williams, England's Archbishop of Canterbury, declared, 'Of course this makes us doubt God's existence ... The question: How can you believe in a God who permits suffering on this scale? is therefore very much around at the moment, and it would be surprising if it were not'.[1]

Although accepting the legitimacy of people's concern about the nature of God's role in such adversity, Dr Williams could offer no conclusive answer on behalf of the Anglican Church. At best he quoted the words of a fellow churchman, stating, 'I have nothing to say that will make sense of this horror today. All I know is that the words in my Bible about God's promise to be alongside us have never lost their meaning for me'.

Beyond the Asian tragedy, nations were suffering from famine and oppression in various parts of Africa. In a later address, the Archbishop drew particular attention to the plight of those in Darfur, where around 200,000 had died in an ongoing conflict between the militias of the Sudanese government and the region's tyrannized black population. He claimed that the violence of brutal massacres targetted against whole communities is 'one of the greatest disgraces of the century'. Again, however, Dr Williams was unable to explain the incomprehensible nature of such tragedies occurring under the watchful influence of an ostensibly protective God. He stated only: 'We pray that God will help us keep our eyes open to the reality of injustice and of suffering'.[2]

In August 2005, not long after the Asian tsunami, the Atlantic hurricane *Katrina* (the third deadliest on record) formed above the Bahamas and swept over southern Florida to devastate much of the north-central Gulf coast of North America. Causing severe destruction across the Mississippi region into Alabama, the greatest loss of life and property occurred in New Orleans, Louisiana, which flooded as the low-lying city's protective levee system failed. More than 1,800 people died and, once again, the question was posed: 'Where was God?'

Many devout people were baffled as to how it was that in Cuba, where hurricane *Dennis* had destroyed 15,000 homes just a month before, only sixteen people had lost their lives. The bewilderment was enhanced by the fact that, although there are many religious residents in Cuba, the country had officially been proclaimed an atheist state from 1959, when around 80 percent of the Catholic priests were obliged to leave the country. The people asked, 'How could it be that the godless Cuban government spared no effort in moving a million people to safety, when the wrath of the Lord descended so violently on believers in the United States?'

The lost residents of New Orleans were mostly Christians, whereas the 1,400 killed by the Kashmir earthquake two months later, in October 2005, were mainly Muslims. The Muslim community had also been decimated when 30,000 people were lost to an earthquake that destroyed the Iranian city of Bam in 2003. Monotheistic believers across the globe could not comprehend why God had elected to wage such a continuous wide-scale war of retribution on his own followers, but numerous religious leaders were quick to take up the challenge. In their attempts to justify and support God's vengeance, they ignored weather patterns and natural phenomena, to lay their blame squarely on the very people who had suffered the dreadful results of catastrophe — especially that which had fallen upon New Orleans.

Without any consideration for those who were drowned or crushed beneath the rubble of collapsed buildings, and with no sympathy for their surviving relatives, friends and neighbours, Steve Lefemine, director of Columbia Christians for Life, pronounced that 'God judged New Orleans for the sin of shedding innocent blood through abortion'.[3] Pastor Bill Shanks of the New Covenant Fellowship of New Orleans even rejoiced that 'The hurricane has wiped out rampant sin'. Mohammed Yousef Al-Mlaifi, a director of the Kuwait Ministry of Endowment, blamed American foreign policy in the Middle East. He described the hurricane as 'a wind of torment and evil that Allāh has sent to this American empire'.[4] Louis Farrakhan, the controversial leader of African American Muslims in the United States, pursued the same theme, asserting that *Katrina* was God's judgment for America's war in Iraq.[5]

Shortly before this, from the pulpit of a Union Bethel church in New Orleans, President George W Bush had expressed the overtly Christian doctrine that faith was best served by the 'Miracle of Salvation'.[6] The United States *Constitution* specifically affirms that there is no tie between the State and any particular religion, and that America is, by definition, 'One Nation under God'. And yet, the President's address was phrased emphatically in the language of Evangelical Christianity — a clear indication of detachment from the constitutional ideal.

Rabbi Ovadia Yosef, the Jewish spiritual head of a right-wing Israeli religious party, claimed that America was punished by God because the Bush administration had pressured Israel into withdrawing settlers from Gaza.[7] The Christian journalist Stan Goodenough wrote for Jerusalem's *Newswire*, 'What America is about to experience is the lifting of God's hand of protection; the implementation of his judgment on the nation most responsible for endangering the land and people of Israel'. Michael Marcavage of Philadelphia's evangelical organization, Repent America, claimed that God flooded New Orleans because the city was about to host a Gay Pride event: 'We're calling it an Act of God'.[8]

One way or another, representatives of the Christian, Jewish and Muslim religions forged their various reasonings in order to exonerate God by claiming that his actions were entirely just, and that the people deserved the punishments received. Moreover, some Islāmic scholars characterized such disasters as 'blessings'. Pain and suffering were said to 'test the patience and submission of believers while encouraging non-believers to repent for their ungodly ways'. Christian, Jewish and Muslim clerics have all described natural catastrophes as being designed and inflicted by God in order to test fortitude and faith. An American evangelical group, The Community of Antioch Church, actually reckoned the tsunami in Sri Lanka to be an advantageous event, claiming that it provided a good opportunity to recruit new members since the survivors were now 'ripe for Jesus'.[9]

Explaining the manner of God's judgement by way of such disasters, Rev Alex McFarland of the Colorado-based Christian ministry, Focus on the Family, stated: 'When someone asks: Why do innocent people suffer? I will gently remind them that we are not really innocent ... After God judged human sin in Noah's flood, the weather patterns that we know today developed'.[10]

The Southern Baptist evangelist Billy Graham said of hurricane *Katrina*, 'It may be the greatest opportunity to demonstrate God's love in this generation'.[11] This style of argument remains common in a religious environment that ignores the dead to concentrate instead on the strangely pronounced 'good fortune' of the survivors − those whom it was deemed God elected to save by way of his unbounded mercy.

To bring this natural catastrophe section down to date at this present time of writing, the Caribbean island of Haiti was struck last week by a devastating earthquake on 12 January 2010. Measuring 7.0 on the Richter scale, Haiti's worst disaster for 200 years flattened the capital city of Port-au-Prince, along with surrounding towns and villages. The final toll has not yet been ascertained, but an estimated 270,000 people are thought to have died, and well over a million homeless and injured.

Bombs and Bullets

On 29 September 2001, four years before the *Katrina* disaster, CNN reporter Larry King hosted a television debate following the terrorist attack on the World Trade Center in New York on the 11th of that month. The debate was entitled 'Where was God?' Its objective was to ascertain the viewpoints of variously defined religious guests concerning God's role in the event. More than 2,750 lives had been lost when two scheduled airliners, hijacked by *al-Qaida* affiliate terrorists, had been flown into the twin towers, levelling them to the ground.

Suicide attacks of this type were not a new form of terrorism but, prior to 9/11, they had mostly been the internal product of occupied territories in faraway places. The New York event differed in that it was a warlike assault against a democratic nation at the behest of an outside foreign enterprise. The extents of death and destruction were also far greater than had occurred in other suicide attacks across the world, and it was not directed against any particular religious or political sect. It was an act of token aggression against innocent victims within buildings that represented a culture to which the instigators of the violence were opposed.[12] To enforce this point of opposition, Christians, Jews, Muslims and those of other faiths were killed and maimed with impunity. So, 'Where was God?'

Setting the scene for Larry King's CNN debate was Deepak Chopra, author of *How to Know God*, who described God as the Lord of 'infinite love and infinite compassion'. When Rabbi Harold Kushner was asked if God could have prevented the 9/11 disaster, he surprisingly answered 'No'. According to Kushner, God's intervention was not to be found in the terrorism, but in the courage of the rescue services. He explained: 'God's promise was that, even if life is unfair, we would not have to face it alone, for he will be with us in the valley of the shadow'. Bruce Wilkinson, president of Walk Through the Bible Ministries, asserted that there was no reason to question matters of faith since 'God was grieved in his heart because violence filled the Earth'.

Larry King then referenced a letter written by one of the 9/11 terrorists, who explained that he was a Muslim intent to enter Heaven as a God-given consequence of his violent actions. King asked Dr Maher Hathout, an Islãmic scholar, how the taking of human life could be reconciled with a supposed God of love and forgiveness. Hathout responded that 'God does not condone or accept that his creature could be destroyed in this way, and does not accept cruelty'.

The debate actually achieved very little, except to confirm that none of the participants wanted to associate God with the 9/11 atrocity. Unlike the opinions generated in terms of natural disasters, there was clearly a perceived difference when it came to violence inflicted by the hand of man. All admitted that God had, for some reason, allowed the event to happen, but there was no suggestion as to why this might have been the case. John

Macarthur, the pastor of Grace Community Church in Sun Valley, Idaho, summed up the general puzzlement, saying, 'I don't question what God chooses to allow. It's not a matter of my opinion'.

Meanwhile, other more extreme members of the Christian movement were expressly outspoken in their condemnation of those who suffered in New York. Rev Jerry Falwell of the Southern Baptists, and the televangelist Pat Robertson of the Christian Broadcasting Network, both claimed that the September 11th attacks were indeed 'God's divine retribution for paganism, abortion, homosexuality, feminism and the proliferation of liberal groups'.[13]

More recently, following severe public criticism of those such as Falwell and Robertson, right-wing Christians and others have been rather more guarded in their comments. This was especially the case after the shooting massacre at the Virginia Tech research university in Blacksburg. On 16 April 2007, the South Korean student Seung-Hui Cho shot and killed 32 students and staff, and wounded many others before committing suicide. Once again the same questions were raised: 'Where was God?' — 'Why did God allow this to happen?'

Dr D James Kennedy of Coral Ridge Presbyterian Church in Fort Lauderdale, Florida, addressed the question 'Where was God?' by stating, 'He is right here, in the midst of our suffering, enduring more of it than any of us ever has or ever will ... He gives us the power to bear our suffering'. Offering further insight, Kennedy said that God uses pain and adversity for good in our lives: 'Suffering is used by God to make us more compassionate to others'.[14]

Notwithstanding such opinion, the notion of compassion was clearly not on the agenda of the 9/11 terrorists or any other variously deluded perpetrators. On 22 October 2002, members of the extremist *Jemaah Islāmiyah* movement detonated three bombs in a tourist district of Kuta on the Indonesian island of Bali. A total of 202 people were killed (164 of whom were foreign nationals), and a similar number were seriously injured.

Not surprisingly in the wake of the New York and Bali attacks, along with other such acts of violent terrorism, a widespread fear was engendered between the world's Christian and Muslim communities. This was especially heightened when Western troops invaded the Islāmic state of Iraq in March 2003 — an action that was opposed by a great many Christians in Britain and the United States. In consequence, the previous fears of opposing religious groups resolved into outright hatred in many areas.

On 11 March 2004 terrorist bombs killed 191 people and wounded more than 1,800 on four Spanish commuter trains in Madrid. Following this, the British Government warned citizens to be vigilant in the face of likely attacks from fanatics on the unofficial fringe of Islām. Then on 7 July 2005 a series of four coordinated bombs hit London's public transport system during England's morning rush hour. The blasts killed 52 commuters on three underground trains and a bus, as well as the four suicide bombers, and a large number were injured.

Once again, Dr Rowan Williams, Archbishop of Canterbury, was quick to try and console the nation. 'We must take courage', he said in a BBC radio broadcast. Then, citing a biblical passage from St Paul, he concluded, 'We don't know how to pray or what to hope for sometimes. But the spirit of God is working with us, and even our wordless cries and groans become part of the Spirit's action'.[15]

As Primate of the Church of England and leader of the world-wide Anglican Communion, Dr Williams was seemingly addressing Christians with his message from the New Testament. But he was joined by Muslim colleagues in stating, 'We were all as one in our condemnation of this evil, and in our shared sense of care and compassion for those affected in whatever way'.[16] Meanwhile, in line with the stated clerical unanimity, the vast majority of everyday Christians and Muslims had absolutely no desire to fear or mistrust each other, but the seeds of suspicion had been sown. Above all, the most perplexing of all questions remained: 'Where was God?'

On 11 October 2007 it was announced that 138 of the most powerful Muslim clerics and scholars had come together to write an unprecedented letter to the world's Christian leaders. Addressed to the Pope, the Archbishop of Canterbury and the heads of the Lutheran, Methodist and Baptist churches, the letter called for peace between the world's Christians and Muslims. Signed by no fewer than 19 current and former grand ayatollahs and grand muftis from countries as diverse as Egypt, Turkey, Russia, Syria, Jordan, Pakistan and Iraq, the letter argued that 'the most fundamental tenets of Islām and Christianity are identical: Love of one and the same God, and love of one's neighbour'. David Ford, director of Cambridge University's Interfaith Programme, stated, 'I hope it will be able to set the right keynote for relations between Muslims and Christians in the 21st century, which have been lacking since September 11th'.

The letter was issued on the eve of *Eid al-Fitr*, the Muslim feast that marks the end of Ramadan. It was designed to rally Muslim moderates at a time when extremists appeared to have hijacked the faith for political purposes.[17] But, whatever religious banner terrorists might care to wave in presumed support of their actions, they have little in common with the views of their mainstream leaders, and are quite divorced from any moderate opinion. Until the leaders at all levels of the various belief systems get their individual houses in order, the high-level meeting of minds between religious groups will have no impact on street-level violence. Atrocities will continue, and the everyday moderate members of each faith will be left to ask the same questions about God's position in the scheme of things.

* * *

The net result of all this is one of apparent confusion. There is, in the first instance, confusion over what God instigates as against what he will allow. Secondly, there is confusion in respect of God's motivation in either case. Whether he is thought to be instigating or allowing some vicious atrocity, the perpetual question is always, 'Why?' It is perhaps natural that large-scale catastrophic events cause the question to hit the headlines from time to time but, on any given day, innocent children are struck by lightning or disease, or drown in frozen rivers, or starve in the drought-wracked desert. The question 'Why?' is rarely asked by the press and media on these individual occasions; it comes to the fore only when there are great calamities and people suffer in large number.

Either way, when people die violently before their naturally presumed allocation of time, it is reckoned by many religious communities to be the result of God's judgement. The problem is that, apart from certain maliciously directed accusatory statements as cited above, no one from any religious mainstream is able to explain why God would inflict or condone such atrocities if he is loving and merciful as the believers would have it. When pressed on the matter of God's unfathomable justice, Franklin Graham (head of the Billy Graham Evangelistic Association) side-stepped the issue in order to change the emphasis of ultimate cause. Responding to NBC after the Virginia Tech massacre, he stated, 'I tag this on the Devil. He's responsible ... He's the one who wants to destroy'.[18]

For a great many people, none of this makes any sense. The very idea of a vengeful and destructive God simply does not equate with a God who is supposedly benevolent and merciful. Thus, some far bigger questions emerge: 'How does anyone know that God actually exists?' Does he exist? Did he ever exist?

These are the questions that we shall endeavour to answer in *The Origin of God*. Beginning with documents that pre-date the Bible, we shall construct God's biography through the centuries to unravel the mysteries of a monotheistic culture which, through a series of evolutionary interpretations, has survived from ancient times to the present day. Our quest is to discover, from all available sources, what evidence there is, if any, to support the long-standing and widespread notion of God's existence. Is there a creative, supernatural, intelligent entity in the Universe — or is the concept just an abiding superstition?

Laurence Gardner
Exeter, 2010

God identifies the Tree of Knowledge
Lucas van Leyden, 1510

Part I

God of Creation

1

THE CREATION DEBATE

The Young Earth

On 28 May 2007 an expansive new state-of-the-art visitor attraction was formally opened in Petersburg, Kentucky, not far from the Greater Cincinnati International Airport. Located on 49 acres of designated land, incorporating a magnificent building complex covering 60,000 square feet, the $27 million facility has an impressive planetarium and a large special-effects theatre. Many of the high-tech displays were created by Patrick Marsh, a designer of the *Jaws* and *King Kong* scenic attractions for Universal Studios in Florida. The advertised purpose for visitors is to experience the Earth as it was at the very dawn of time. The features include a stunning forty-foot high glazed portico with a cliff wall, and there are 160 exhibits.

Amid an artificial forest, bubbling waterfalls and lush gardens with arrays of bright flowers, there are moulded turtles, lizards, hummingbirds and butterflies. At first glance, with animatronic dinosaurs roaming the staged sets, it appears rather like any other plasticized natural history theme park. But differences are soon encountered; the pastoral scene at the 'dawn of time' is richly cultivated, and children play among the dinosaurs. With a robotic crocodile from the film *Crocodile Dundee* guarding the birthplace of the world, the environment is supposedly representative of the Garden of Eden in the days of Adam and Eve.[1]

This is the Creation Museum — a project of the Answers in Genesis ministry, where every exhibited prehistoric bone, mineral artefact and fossil from millions of years ago is said to be no more than 6,000 years old. This is the place where estimated visitors of over 500,000 a year will be taught that the biblical flood of Noah occurred in the Grand Canyon of the Colorado River.

The Museum's co-founder Mark Looy told BBC News reporter James Westhead that 'Noah's flood breached its earthen dam; the water rushed in very quickly and carved out the canyon'. According to the Museum's brochure, visitors are taken 'on a fantastic quest to find the real purpose and meaning of life'.

Mike Zovath, another co-founder of the Museum, told Britain's Channel-4 television correspondent Jonathan Rugman, 'The Bible says that man was created on day six, and the animals were created on day six'. The overall message is that God created the Universe and everything on Earth within one very busy week in about 4000 BC, and the ministry's literature states: 'The days in Genesis do not correspond to geologic ages, but are six consecutive 24-hour days of Creation'. When asked about the archaeologically discovered fossilized remains of early man-like creatures from millions of years ago, Patrick Marsh told a British press reporter from *The Guardian*, 'There are no such things. Humans are basically as you see them today. Those skeletons they've found ... I've seen people like that running round the streets of New York'.[2]

The Museum's displays are said to be 'based on what the Bible says about dinosaurs' (not that the Bible makes any mention of dinosaurs). Despite the fact that dinosaurs became extinct around 65 million years ago, Mark Looy asserts that children had dinosaurs as pets. A Triceratops is even depicted wearing a saddle, and a Stegosaurus is shown aboard a scale model of Noah's Ark. To support all this, the Museum's introductory video claims, 'It is time to take up the sword of God's word'.

ABC News reported that 'some 35% of Americans believe such things to be literally true ... that the Earth and everything on it were created by God about 6,000 years ago'. Moreover, there are exhibits at the Museum which explain that 'not believing these things has led to moral breakdown and social ills such as abortion and pornography'. In one of the Museum's large-screen videos, a male teenager is shown at his computer looking at Internet pornography, and a female teenager speaks with a Planned Parenthood consultant about having an abortion. Both instances are blamed on the teenagers' ungodly beliefs that the Earth is millions of years old. 'The Bible speaks for itself at the Creation Museum', states the official literature. 'Be prepared to experience history in a completely unprecedented way ... Enter the Cave of Sorrows and see the horrific effects of the Fall of Man'. And, of course, 'don't forget to visit Noah's Café'!

Not surprisingly there has been a considerable backlash from the scientific community, along with demonstration rallies organized by moderate Christians who do not subscribe to such extreme fundamentalist views. Although one would not expect scientists to go along with the concept of a mere 6,000 year-old Earth, this particular area of dispute is not in itself related to any belief or disbelief in God. This is made evident by those many Christians who oppose the purpose of the Creation Museum. The opposition is specifically concerned with whether or not the biblical text should be interpreted literally. It is a debate not only about the age of the Earth, but of whether life was created by God in its present forms from the outset or, as determined by Charles Darwin (1809–1882) and subsequent scientific evaluation, evolved through time by a process of natural selection.

In this regard, the Creation Museum's own Mission Statement, prepared by the Answers in Genesis ministry, goes even further than supporting the notion of God's creation. By way of some unexplained non-biblical thought process, Jesus Christ is confused with the Old Testament's Creation account in Genesis. It is stated that the Museum's mission is 'to exalt Jesus Christ as Creator, Redeemer and Sustainer'. Also 'to equip Christians to better evangelize', and 'to challenge visitors to receive Jesus Christ as Saviour and Lord'. The Statement of Faith issued by Answers in Genesis states: 'Those who do not believe in Christ are subject to everlasting conscious punishment'.

To further antagonize scientists, the Museum's exhibitions are portrayed in a manner which asserts that the Bible is itself a work of provable science. Ken Ham, president of Answers in Genesis and director of the Museum, said, 'It's not a matter of Bible versus science', but that he and his team are putting up a successful scientific defence against the secular humanists who have ruled God out of all scientific matters.[3] A foremost precept of Answers in Genesis is that 'No apparent, perceived or claimed evidence in any field, including history and chronology, can be valid if it contradicts the scriptural record'.

In retaliation, the US National Center for Science Education issued the statement: 'We, the undersigned scientists at universities and colleges in Kentucky, Ohio and Indiana, are concerned about scientifically inaccurate materials at the Answers in Genesis Museum. Students who accept this material as scientifically valid are unlikely to succeed in science courses at the college level. These students will need remedial instruction in the nature of science, as well as in the specific areas of science misrepresented by Answers in Genesis'. The Museum's own research scientist Dr Jason Lisle, with a PhD in astrophysics from the University of Colorado at Boulder, gave a suitably hypocritical answer when questioned about how he managed to pass his exams. He stated, 'I answered from my knowledge of the topic, not my beliefs'.[4]

The most substantial fact in all this is that the Museum is not just anathema to scientists and atheists, but has emphasized a significant focus of disagreement within the Christian community of North America. Those who run and support organizations such as Answers in Genesis are classified as 'Young Earth Creationists'. By contrast to mainstream Christians, they apply a literal interpretation to every word in the Old Testament, as if the words were written or dictated by God himself. Not even the Jews, whose own Israelite scribes compiled the original Hebrew scripture, take such an extreme view. Geologist Greg Neyman, the Christian head of an alternative 'Old Earth' ministry known as Answers in Creation, states that 'Today, the church is comprised of many individuals who accept an old Earth'.

Rev Mendle Adams, pastor of St Peter's United Church of Christ in Cincinnati, Ohio, joined secularists and other Christians to protest at the Museum's opening, arguing that the concept will 'make us a laughing stock'.[5] Roman Catholic theologian John Haught, a research professor at Georgetown University in Washington DC, claimed that the Museum will cause an impoverishment of religion, stating, 'It is theologically problematic to me, as well as being scientifically problematic'. Summing up the problem which Young Earth creationism presents to the more rational Christian faith, Harvard graduate Michael Patrick Leahy, editor of the online magazine *Christian Faith and Reason*, says that the Museum 'makes all Christians who don't accept evolution look stupid ... It undermines the credibility of all Christians' and provides 'an easy opportunity to misrepresent all Christians as irrational'.

The Old Earth

Contrasting in every way with the Disney-like displays of the Creation Museum is the American Museum of Natural History in Manhattan, New York. Located in the 18-acre Theodore Roosevelt Park, the establishment, covering 1.6 million square feet, has 25 interconnected buildings housing 46 permanent exhibition halls, research laboratories, a world-renowned library and a collection of more than 32 million specimens, increasing on average by some 90,000 specimens and artefacts a year. The library, which contains over 450,000 individual works, also includes collections from the American Ethnological Society and the New York Academy of Sciences.

Founded in 1869, the Museum is chartered for the purpose of 'establishing and maintaining a Museum and Library of Natural History; of encouraging and developing the study of Natural Science; of advancing the general knowledge of kindred subjects and, to that end, of furnishing popular instruction'. Around 225 full-time scientific staff conduct research in astrophysics, zoology, genomics, palaeontology, earth sciences and anthropology. They also operate worldwide to survey and study biological diversity, and to mitigate threats to the Earth's ecosystems.

The Anne and Bernard Spitzer Hall of Human Origins (formerly the Hall of Human Biology and Evolution) opened at the Museum on 10 February 2007. This, by contrast to the 'Young Earth' theory, is the world of Charles Darwin, and is the premier United States presentation of in-depth investigation into human evolution. The original Hall was the first US facility to trace and examine the story of *homo sapiens*, the path of human evolution and the origins of human creativity. Now a truly impressive multimedia wonderland, the exhibits include life-sized dioramas of the human predecessors *Australopithecus afarensis*, *Homo ergaster*, Neanderthal and Cro-Magnon, showing each species in its habitat and demonstrating their behaviors and capabilities. Also displayed are casts of important fossils, including the 3.2 million year-old *Lucy* skeleton, the 1.7 million year-old Turkana Boy, and *homo erectus* specimens such as the Peking Man.[6]

* * *

Notwithstanding the dispute between science and the Young Earth protagonists concerning the age of the world (whether the planet was naturally formed 4.5 billion years ago, or created by God just 6,000 years ago),[7] there persists a more pertinent question about the matter of life itself. Was earthly life created by God, as stated in the Bible, or did it evolve from tiny molecules over billions of years, with humans emerging from the primitive anthropoids of 30 million years ago?

Many Christians of the 'Old Earth' persuasion, who might well accept the truth of the planet's own very distant origin, still have a problem in this regard. In whatever manner the six days of Creation (as given in Genesis) might be interpreted, it remains the case that God is explicitly stated in the Bible to have created the various life forms in an ultimately recognizable state. In the post 9/11 environment of this 21st century (as discussed in our Introduction) this has given rise in recent years to a fiercely fought battle within the world of education — a dispute over which version of life's origins should take precedence by way of teaching in schools and colleges.

Science and Religion

At the forefront of this educational conflict are the scientists and theologians of the United States. It has also been a subject of debate in Britain, where the line between religion and science recently became a hotly contested battleground. The Creation Debate is not a new tournament of wills; it has simply been heightened in this past decade because the very existence of God is being questioned as never before in the wake of so many natural disasters and acts of deliberate terrorism.

A test-case debate, concerning how children across the United States should be taught about the origin of the Universe, approached its climax in Ohio in March 2002. The 18-member school board, working on a new curriculum, was divided in opinion. While it was agreed that evolution would be taught, some members confirmed that they would also like to see the creative designer work of God included in the guidelines for teaching science. Given that this creationist objective relied on a religious interpretation rather than being based on scientific evidence, its connection with science teaching was disputed, and both sides predicted that the controversial issue would end up in court.

Meanwhile in England, a similar argument prevailed with regard to Emmanuel College in Gateshead. Sir Peter Vardy, the private financial sponsor of this otherwise State funded college was an evangelical Christian, as were many of the staff, and the headteacher, Nigel McQuoid, insisted that evolution and creationism stood equally as 'faith positions'. Several senior members of staff had published material on teaching creationism, and a school conference in March 2002 was to be addressed by none other than Ken Ham, the head of Answers in Genesis and eventual director of the Creation Museum in Kentucky.[8]

Scientists were quick to take a stand against the concept of public money being used to teach evangelical creationism in England. The resultant campaign was led by the eminent biologist Richard Dawkins FRS, Oxford University's Charles Simonyi Professor of the Public Understanding of Science. 'Any science teacher who denies that the world is billions (or even millions) of years old is teaching children a preposterous, mind-shrinking falsehood', Dawkins asserted; 'These men disgrace the honourable profession of teacher'.[9]

Following this and a great number of public complaints that taxpayers' money should fund matters of religious belief within a science curriculum, the Government's Office for Standards in Education (Ofsted) agreed to investigate the matter. But the Government had already afforded the Vardy Foundation certain rights to influence the ethos of the school in return for Vardy's considerable monetary sponsorship.[10] Thus it was that, a couple of months later in May 2002, David Bell, Her Majesty's Chief Inspector of Schools, announced that Ofsted would not pursue its inquiry into the teaching of science at Emmanuel College.[11]

Back in America, David Haury, the Associate Professor of Science Education at Ohio State University in Columbus, said that if Ohio allowed creationism to be taught, 'it would have a resounding effect across the country in terms of a wake-up call that there is a serious threat to scientific education'.[12]

In January 2005 a further round of argument erupted at a high school in Dover, Pennsylvania. The town's school board instructed biology teachers to preface lessons on evolution with an explanation that it was only a theory which carried no more weight than the scriptural concept of an intelligent designer. However, a Supreme Court decision in 1987 had banned the teaching of creationism on the grounds that 'it would violate the constitutional separation of Church and State'. Witold Walczak, a legal director of the American Civil Liberties Union, claimed: 'What these folks are proposing is to allow faith and miracles and supernatural creators to be considered as science'.[13]

Soon afterwards in a parallel case, Judge Clarence Cooper of the Federal Court ordered a school district in Georgia to remove stickers from its science textbooks which declared that 'Evolution is a theory, not a fact'. State law, he affirmed, prohibits the use of public money to aid religion.[14]

A few months later, in October 2005, the University of California at Berkeley was challenged for running a website called *Understanding Evolution*. Creationists (citing the same point of legislation which had been used against them) claimed that the website contravened the constitutional law of separating Church and State 'because it was linked to religious organizations which believed that faith can be reconciled with Darwin's *Theory of Evolution*'.[15]

It became a period of extensive press and media polling across the United States. Only one-third of people reckoned that creationism should replace evolution as a subject in schools, whilst more than half were in favour of offering both explanations in order to facilitate informed choice. In the midst of this, BBC News reported: 'In the state of Kansas they have succeeded in getting the science syllabus altered so that teachers can tell their pupils that God made everything in its present form'. This approach, according to the US National Academy of Sciences, 'would put the students of Kansas at a competitive disadvantage as they took their place in the world'.[16]

Meanwhile, in Dover, PA, things were going badly for the Creationists, and all eight Republican members of the school board, who had attempted to introduce the teaching of 'intelligent design' as an alternative to evolution, were ousted by Democrat challengers in the local elections. Then in December 2005, following a 6-week trial, Federal Court judge John E Jones ruled in favour of the parents' lobby, stating, 'Our conclusion today is that it is unconstitutional to teach intelligent design as an alternative to evolution in a public school classroom'. He added: 'In making this determination, we have addressed the seminal question of whether intelligent design is science. We have concluded that it is not'.[17] The verdict was immediately hailed as a victory by the American Civil Liberties Union. 'This will make the teaching of science a lot easier', said Eugenie Scott, the executive director of the National Center for Science Education.

Subsequently in Ohio, a similar ruling followed in February 2006 when the Board of Education handed victory to proponents of evolution by throwing out a model biology lesson which gave credence to creationism. A school district in California then cancelled plans to introduce a course on 'intelligent design', and State legislators in Indiana pared back their intentions to introduce creationism into the classrooms.[18]

Creationist opponents of the decisions claimed that the State authorities were waging a war against religion. But, in practice, all that had happened were rulings which did not permit religious beliefs to form part of a science curriculum. Religious studies were deemed a different subject in the same way that Albert Einstein is not discussed in Bible research. Nevertheless, teachers told the American Association for the Advancement of Science conference in St Louis, Missouri, that there were still school boards and some parents in the Midwest who insist that they abandon biology textbooks for biblical creationism or intelligent design. The executive director of the National Science Teachers Association, Gerry Wheeler, said, ' Some teachers feared losing their jobs if they taught evolution'.

Appeasement Declined

While all this was going on over the Atlantic, the people of Britain followed the progress of the US Creation Debate with a certain amazement and not a little amusement. *The Daily Telegraph* reported: 'The American Religious Right are increasingly turning to home schooling, lest their children be exposed to the evils of sex, drugs or — heaven forbid — Darwin!' Little did the British onlookers expect what was soon to end up in their own laps.

Immediately after the Ohio ruling, Muslim medical students in London, England, distributed leaflets that dismissed Darwin's theories as false. The leaflets, produced by the Al-Nasr Trust, a charity to promote Islām, were circulated among students at the Guy's Hospital site of King's College London as part of the Islām Awareness Week in February 2006. Seemingly quoting from the Koran, it was stated: 'God creates what he wills, for verily God has power over all things ... Man is the wonder of God's creation'. Some evangelical Christian students also became increasingly vocal in challenging the notion of evolution, and the Muslim-led creationist movement spread quickly to colleagues and supporters in other university colleges.[19]

In a surprising move that stunned people nationwide and ostensibly pandered to a minority whim of some radical students, the Westminster Government announced in the very next month that 'Pupils in England will be required to discuss creationism as part of a new GCSE [General Certificate of Secondary Education] biology course being introduced in September'. No one queried the fact that the creationist idea had long been discussed as a topic within religious education, but to include it in science lessons was more than most could tolerate. Even the Anglican Archbishop of Canterbury, Dr Rowan Williams, stepped into the controversy, saying that he does not believe that creationism (that God created the Earth and heavens in six days just 6,000 years ago) should be taught in schools. 'My worry is creationism can end up reducing the doctrine of Creation rather than enhancing it', he said.[20]

The national science academies of 67 countries, including Britain's Royal Society, issued a joint statement warning that scientific evidence about the origins of life would be 'concealed, denied, or confused' if creationism were introduced into main-stream education. The statement urged parents, as well as teachers, to provide children with the known facts about the origins and evolution of life on Earth.

Supporting the academies, Professor Richard Dawkins estab-lished the Foundation for Science and Reason (RDFSR) in an attempt to keep God out of the science classroom and 'prevent pseudo science taking over in schools'. His idea was to subsidise books, pamphlets and audio-visual material for teachers to fight what Dawkins described as 'an educational scandal' that had seen the rise of 'irrational ideas'. Meanwhile, in their efforts to adhere to the new Government guideline, some 59 English schools were already making use of DVDs and information packs produced by 'intelligent design' activists in the United States. The Government was quick to announce, however, that these packs are 'not appropriate to support the science curriculum ... Neither intelligent design nor creationism are recognised scientific theo-ries'.[21] This left teachers thoroughly confused about what the Department of Education actually wanted them to discuss with their pupils. All agreed that the Government's intention was decidedly ambiguous.

It transpired that 5,700 information packs (along with manuals and DVDs) had been mailed to every secondary school science department in Britain by an English creationist group called Truth in Science. The Royal Society's immediately published response was that creationism represents a move to 'distort or misrepresent scientific knowledge and understanding to promote particular religious beliefs'.[22]

On 27 November 2006, BBC commentator Jeremy Paxman interviewed Andy McIntosh, a professor of thermodynamics at England's Leeds University, on the *Newsnight* television programme. Professor McIntosh, a leader of the Truth in Science organization, had repeatedly stated that, in his opinion, the Earth was only 6,000 years old. He claimed in the interview that 'intelligent design' is itself a science which recognizes the influence of an intelligent designer. Paxman then asked McIntosh to name the specific designer — anticipating the answer to be 'God' — but no satisfactory answer was forthcoming. McIntosh said only that it was up to people to decide for themselves who their preferred designer might be.

Soon after the interview, Leeds University issued a formal statement that 'The University wishes to distance itself publicly from theories of creationism and so-called intelligent design, which cannot be verified by evidence'. Consequently, the Government wrote to schools (seemingly in contradiction of its original instruction), telling them that controversial teaching materials promoting creationism should not be used in science lessons. The education minister Jim Knight wrote: 'Neither intelligent design nor creationism are recognized scientific theories and they are not included in the science curriculum. The Truth in Science information pack is therefore not an appropriate resource to support the science curriculum'.[23] And so the embarrassing nine months of an ill-conceived governmental appeasement initiative came to an end in December 2006. Science was 'science' (a discipline based on experiment and evidence), and Religion was 'religion' (a matter of faith which requires no evidence). Henceforth, the subjects were to be kept separate in the classrooms as they had always been.

* * *

In the years since September 2001, when international terrorism struck the World Trade Center in New York with such a devastating result, there has been a significant questioning of matters concerning God. In the United States of America and Great Britain, along with many other countries, there has also been a sharp downturn in regular church attendance.

As we have seen above, and in our Introduction, religious devotees of all monotheistic religions have fought hard, and often objectionably, to support and sustain God's position against the weight of evidence which appears not to be in his favour. Equally, however, God's traditionally perceived role in many respects is now being questioned by a great number of faithful Christians, Jews and Muslims who find it difficult to reconcile with a persistent trail of tragedy and disaster across the world. Even the Creation Debate (provoked in the first instance by ardent believers in biblical and other holy scriptures) has fallen foul of competitive science to the extent that Creationists have no real support beyond the confines of their own movement.

It is evident from all the various discussions inherent in this debate that, outside 'belief' itself, there is no generally accepted proof of God's existence. And yet, despite all the questioning and areas of uncertainty, belief in God continues on a wide scale.

Our purpose now is to investigate why this belief exists, how it began and how it has survived through so many generations to the present day.

2

GATEWAY OF THE LORD

A Question of Identity

From as far back as can be traced by way of effigies and other cultural relics, people have believed in superior or supreme deities. In the art and literature of emergent sophisticated nations in Egypt, Greece and Rome, the gods and goddesses of variously determined pantheons live on today in the colourful adventures of the divine. But for all that, and while a fascination with these romantic figures persists within the realm of classical mythology, a large proportion of the world's religious population settled some while ago on the preferred notion of an omnipotent and everlasting, single male God.

Stemming from Judaic, then Christian and later Islãmic belief systems, this God is not perceived as a senior deity among other gods and goddesses, but is reckoned to be the 'one and only' God. In literary terms, his story begins in the Hebrew Bible — that part of the holy scriptures known to Christians as the Old Testament. But notwithstanding the religious dogma of One God belief, not even the Christian Bible stipulates that God was alone in his environment. Psalm 82 opens in the King James Authorized Version, for example, with:

> God standeth in the congregation of the mighty;
> he judgeth among the gods ... 'Ye are gods, and all
> of you are children of the Most High'.

From entries such as these, it becomes clear that there are elements of difference between the way the scriptures were written and the way they have come to be taught and understood. In Old Testament times, it was not so much a case of this God being the 'one and only', but that to his Israelite followers he was the most senior judge among the gods, and therefore the only one that mattered.

The fact is, however, that there was a recognized senior godhead for each of the parallel godly assemblies. So, was the God of the Abrahamic Hebrews one of these, who later became known to the Mosaic Israelites as Yahweh, or did he have a quite separate identity? If the latter, then what would be the case if the Israelite scribes had not introduced this God into their writings? Supposing the books of the Bible had never been written. Would we know about this particular God today from any other primary source?

Biblical Origins

During the 1st century AD, at the time of Jesus, there was no amalgamated Hebrew version of the Old Testament Bible in the way that we have come to know it. The word Bible comes from the Greek plural noun *biblia*, meaning 'a collection of books'. But, in the Gospel era, the various books which now make up the composite Hebrew Bible existed only as individual texts. A good example is the 23-foot (*c*.7 m) scroll of the book of Isaiah,[1] the longest of all the *Dead Sea Scrolls*. Within the overall collection, some 38 scrolls relating to 19 Old Testament books were found at Qumrân, by the Dead Sea in Judaea, between 1947 and 1951.

Judaea (or Judah as it was called before its Greco-Seleucid occupation in the 3rd century BC) was that part of the Holy Land which embodies the city of Jerusalem, and the Jews were so called by virtue of being Judaeans. The land to the north of Judaea was Samaria, and above that was Galilee. In the early days, prior to the mass Israelite settlement from the 14th century BC, the overall territory was called Canaan.

Dating from around 100 BC, the Isaiah scroll is the oldest, longest and most complete ancient Semitic biblical text discovered to date. Such lengthy manuscript parchments were treasured possessions held for use in synagogues, but were not available to people at large.

The first biblical documents to enter the general public domain appeared during the latter 1st century AD, especially after the fall of Jerusalem to the Roman general Titus who destroyed the city in AD 70. They were compiled in an endeavor to restore faith in Judaism at a time of social unrest. Their language, however, was different to that of earlier Hebrew texts such as the Isaiah scroll. Hebrew, at that stage of history, was primarily the language of the priestly schools, whereas the Jewish people generally spoke a form of Aramaic. This had been the language of the Aramaeans, who were established in Mesopotamia (Iraq) in the 13th century BC, and who spread northward and westward into Syria and Canaan some time later.[2] Hence, the biblical scriptures for common consumption in synagogues emerged in the Aramaic language and were called *Targums* (or *Targumim*), meaning 'translations').[3] They were recited, through to the Middle Ages, along with the Hebrew *Torah* — the opening five books of the Bible: Genesis, Exodus, Leviticus, Numbers and Deuteronomy.

The two most prominent *Targumim* were the *Targum Onkelos* and the *Targum Yerushalmi* (sometimes called the *Targum of Jonathan Ben Uzziel*). But there were differences between them, and indeed between them and the immediate Hebrew interpretation. That said, for all practical purposes the contents were consistent even if slightly variant in wording. For example, the now commonly rendered opening to the Bible (Genesis 1:1–2) reads:

> In the beginning God created the heaven and the earth. And the earth was without form, and void; and darkness was upon the face of the deep. And the Spirit of God moved upon the face of the waters.

The *Targum Onkelos* relates:

> At the beginning the Lord created the heavens and the earth. And the earth was vacancy and desolation, solitary of the sons of men, and void of every animal; and darkness was upon the face of the abyss, and the Spirit of mercies from before the Lord breathed upon the face of the waters.[4]

Although God is personally undefined in the Hebrew scripture, the *Targum Onkelos* (when describing the expanse of the sky) gives an impression of God's presumed enormity in those days: 'And the Lord made the expanse, upbearing it with three fingers, between the confines of the heavens and the waters of the ocean'.

It is not known how or why the first generally available compilation of individual books occurred, but the oldest known collection of amalgamated biblical texts was neither in Hebrew nor Aramaic; it was in Greek. The books were translated from Hebrew scrolls between the 3rd and 1st centuries BC, and began as a commission from the pharaoh Ptolemy II Philadelphus in about 250 BC. The work was conducted in Alexandria, Northern Egypt, and it is believed that 72 scholars were employed for the ongoing translations. This led to the compilation becoming known as the *Septuagint* (relating to 'seventy').[5]

Overall, the variously produced and, for the most part, mutually supportive scriptural texts, in Hebrew, Aramaic and Greek, constitute the definitive history of God in terms of religious understanding.

The fully consolidated Hebrew Bible (the *Tanakh*)[6] did not appear in its currently extant form until the early 10th century AD. Onwards from the 8th century, a group of Jewish scholars, who were known as the Masoretes, had appended the *Masorah* (a body of traditional guideline notes) to the earlier texts. The purpose of this was to ensure a continuity of rabbinical teaching, rather than have the scriptures (especially the *Torah*) subjected to different oral interpretations. The oldest existing copy of this Masoretic Bible comes from less than 1,100 years ago in AD 916 (soon after the reign of Alfred the Great in England). Unfortunately, the original manuscripts used by the Masoretes are presumed not now to exist; neither are there any known comparative texts. But the discovery of the *Dead Sea Scrolls* has provided some insight into their probable style and nature.

By any standard of reckoning, it seems inconceivable that prized and ancient manuscripts, which underpinned a whole culture of belief and would have existed in so many synagogues, if not also elsewhere, should have gone missing without a trace.

Accidents and carelessness might have occurred here and there, but not everywhere unless the documents were purposely destroyed. Maybe that was an implemented strategy in order to establish the pre-eminence of the Masoretic discipline. But the early works were regarded as being sacred, quite apart from their historical worth, so even that possibility is difficult to reconcile.

What is known, however, is that the individual books of the Old Testament were originally written between the 6th and 2nd centuries BC. They were commenced during the Babylonian captivity of the Israelites, and were concluded by subsequent generations back in Judaea — a series of separate accounts from Babylonian and other sources, whether previously documented or based on oral traditions. In historical terms, therefore, that does not make even the original Hebrew scriptures especially old. We are looking here at a writing period which corresponds to a commencement date as late as the 26th reigning dynasty of Egypt.

So, from where precisely did the Israelites of that era glean their knowledge of events and characters from thousands of years before — events which, following the brief account of God's earthly creation, begin in the book of Genesis with the story of Adam and Eve? Did the priestly writers, scribes and prophets invent God for some reason at that stage, or were there perhaps earlier writings about God? If so, what were they?

The Egyptians, Persians, Mesopotamians and others had been venerating numerous gods and goddesses for at least 2,500 years before Genesis was compiled, and we have a wealth of documentary evidence from these cultures. So why did the said One God of Creation make his literary appearance so very late in the day? Surely the Genesis writers of c.550 BC could not have been the first people ever to have heard of him.

The Seat of Life

From early times, it has been believed in some circles that the books of the *Torah* were dictated by God, and written by the hand of Moses in the 14th century BC. This view is still common among

Orthodox Jews, although there is absolutely nothing within the *Torah* to suggest that it was the case. Onwards from the first named mention of Moses in Exodus 2:10, he is referred to throughout in the third person.

Although much of Deuteronomy appears to emanate as if from Moses himself, the book explains in its own introduction: 'These are the words which Moses spake unto all Israel'. Eventually, Deuteronomy 34:5 records Moses' death, followed by the appointment of Joshua to succeed him as leader of the Israelites — things that Moses could not possibly have written about.

In respect of the authorship of Deuteronomy, the *Jewish Encyclopedia* states: 'It is the unanimous opinion of modern critics that Deuteronomy is not the work of Moses. It was probably written sometime after 621 BC'.[7] This date is based on the fact that Deuteronomy is thought to represent the Israelite *Book of the Law*, which 2 Kings 22:8 claims the high priest Hilkiah found in the Temple of Jerusalem during the reign of King Josiah of Judah (*c*.640-609 BC). Quite what happened to this original book after that is unknown. It was reckoned to contain the ordinances which had been conveyed by God to Moses but, soon after its said discovery, the Temple was destroyed and Jerusalem was laid to waste by Nebuchadnezzar of Babylon.

Deuteronomy is a somewhat anomalous book in that it does not follow the direct focus of its predecessors (Genesis, Exodus, Leviticus and Numbers), which are accounts of ancestral record. It is rather more concerned with constructing a framework of lore, which was to become law, and it takes little heed of certain aspects of the previous books of the *Torah*. In Exodus 20:13, for example, we have the Commandment instruction from God: 'Thou shalt not kill'. But, on various occasions in Deuteronomy, Moses gives the Israelites quite contrary orders when preparing to invade the land of Canaan. Referring to the Canaanites, Deuteronomy 20:17 states, 'Thou shalt utterly destroy them'. Prior to that, the Mosaic instruction in Deuteronomy 7:2 is 'Thou shalt make no covenant with them, nor show mercy unto them'.

There are many aspects of Deuteronomy which separate it from the other books of the *Torah*, not the least being that it is a wholly retrospective and reflective account. Written long after the events which it portrays, Deuteronomy looks back to the time of Moses in an attempt somehow to justify the Israelite invasion of Canaan under Joshua (c.1320 BC). But in this context, it actually expresses the concerns applicable when the Israelites were themselves being invaded by Nebuchadnezzar in a much later era (c.606–586 BC). The main point of difference that emerges from this comparison of time-frames is that God was seemingly on the Israelites' side when they were the invaders, but sided against them when they were themselves subsequently invaded.

In detailing why God allowed the Israelites to be taken into Babylonian bondage and servitude, the book of 2 Kings 21:3 explains that the Lord was angry with the Israelites because their long dead King Manasseh of Judah had erected altars to a competitor god. It mattered not that Manasseh's grandson, King Josiah, had since destroyed these altars with the people's blessing;[8] God took his revenge in any event, saying,

> I will wipe Jerusalem as a man wipeth a dish ... and deliver them into the hand of their enemies ... They have provoked me to anger since the day their fathers came forth out of Egypt.[9]

It is then explained that 'At the commandment of the Lord came this upon Judah, to remove them out of his sight for the sins of Manasseh, according to all that he did'.[10] The fact remains nonetheless that, had the captive Israelites never been taken to Babylon, the Bible would not have been written, for it was in Babylon that the early records of their ancestral heritage were found — the texts which enabled them to begin writing the *Torah* with the book of Genesis.

Whatever the Israelites might previously have known about their ancestral past, a bigger picture emerged for them in Babylon. They discovered from the Babylonian archive, and from subsequent research, that their ancestors had entered the land of Canaan (later Palestine and Israel) in two different periods and from two different directions. Moses and Joshua had led the tribes eastwards into Canaan from Egypt. But, around 600 years before that, Abraham (the revered patriarch of the Hebrew nation) had brought his original family northwards and westwards out of Mesopotamia. Ultimately, therefore, the Jewish heritage was Mesopotamian.

As one of the primary cities of Mesopotamia, Babylon was founded by King Ur-Baba in about 2000 BC. It was located on the east bank of the River Euphrates a little south of modern Baghdad, which was built long after in about AD 765. From the outset, the princes and rulers of Babylonia commissioned temples, palaces, city walls, bridges and quays. The city evolved to become a great centre of learning, and the magnificent Hanging Gardens of Babylon were one of the *Seven Wonders* of the ancient world.[11] The city's name derived from *Bāb-ilû*, which meant 'Gateway of the Shining Lord'.[12]

In 689 BC, Babylon was sacked by King Sennacherib of nearby Assyria in northern Mesopotamia, who levelled the city to the ground. Some years later, Nebuchadnezzar II (Nabû-kudur-uzur) of Babylon rebuilt and restored his capital to its former glory but, to expedite this, he needed architects, craftsmen and engineers, together with an ongoing supply of labourers. He chose to obtain these craftsmen and builders from Jerusalem. The Old Testament book of 2 Kings relates that, in 586 BC, Nebuchadnezzar laid siege to the city:

> He captured King Jechoniah of Judah and carried him off to Babylon along with all of Jerusalem, and the princes, and all the mighty men of valour, even ten thousand captives, and all the craftsmen and smiths; none remained save the poorest sort of people of the land.[13]

Through an ensuing period of some decades, the captives and their offspring worked to fulfil Prince Nebuchadnezzar's objective but, in the course of this, they found a wealth of ancient writings when reclaiming the old palace and temple libraries. Here, inscribed on numerous clay tablets (many of which have now been rediscovered), they found stories of the Creation, of Adam and Eve, the Great Flood and the Tower of Babel. Not only was Babylon known as the 'Gateway of the Shining Lord', but they also learned that Mesopotamia was considered to be the *Tin-tî* — the 'Seat of Life'.

God of the Bible Writers

From the very beginning of the Old Testament, it is generally accepted by scholars that there was more than one writer of the Hebrew *Torah* (variantly known in Greek as the *Pentateuch*, relating to a 'unit of five' books). There were not only different hands for penning these books and the Hebrew Bible in general, but the individual texts emanate from different scribal time-frames. In short, the Old Testament is a series of glued together accounts, which make their competitive presence felt from the outset.

In Genesis 1:27 it is related that God created Adam. Then, in Genesis 2:7 Adam is seen to be created again, thereby determining that the sequence is woven from the works of two different writers. Following the glorification of God by way of his bringing the Earth from the darkness of Chaos,[14] there are two quite distinct Creation stories in Genesis. The first is the work of a priestly writer of the 6th century BC, and concludes with the implementation of the Sabbath day of rest. The second is concerned with the institution of marriage. Both stories, however, detail that humankind gained dominion over the animals.[15]

In the original linguistic terminology of the amalgamated sequence, God is referenced individually by the priestly writer, but the other wrote more specifically about the *Elohim*. This was a Canaanite plural noun, the singular of which was *El* or *Eloah*, while in Mesopotamia the comparative singular godly distinctions were *El* or *Ilû*. These terms all related to Bright or Shining[16] — stemming from *êl* ('to shine') and *êllu* ('to be bright').[17]

The *Elohim* were the traditional gods of Canaan, but when the Old Testament was eventually translated for Christian Bibles and other Western-language renditions, the plural term *Elohim* was generally reapplied to relate to a singular concept of God. In some instances, however, the plural connotation remains — for example, near the beginning of Genesis where, in connection with the creation of Adam, God says, 'Let us make man in *our* image, after *our* likeness'.[18] Then later, God says, in respect of the Tree of Knowledge in the garden of Eden, 'In the day ye eat thereof, then your eyes shall be opened, and ye shall be as *gods*'.[19] This is followed by: 'The Lord God said, Behold, the man is become as *one of us*'.[20] Also, as we have seen, the Israelite God was said to have addressed an *Elohim* assembly of gods, referred to as the 'congregation of the mighty'.

In the Canaanite tradition, the principal deity of the *Elohim* was El Elyon, whose seat was at the headwaters of the Orontes and Litani rivers that rise above Canaan in the Beqaa Valley of southern Lebanon. The Orontes flows northward through Syria, and the Litani southward to the Mediterranean Sea. The headwaters location, where El Elyon would hold court, was a temple dedicated to his son Baal and known as Baalbek (*see* Map 3).

According to the Genesis account, it was Abraham who, in around 2000 BC, left his Mesopotamian homeland to bring aspects of his own religious heritage into Canaan. In this respect, it is significant to note that the God of Abraham did not use the style of Yahweh (*Yhwh*) as he became known in later Mosaic times. The Lord introduced himself to Abraham, saying, 'I am El Shaddai'[21] — a name which is used 48 times in the Hebrew Bible.[22] On 11 other occasions El Shaddai is alternatively called El Elyon.[23]

Notwithstanding these very distinctive nominal entries in the Hebrew scripture, the Christian Bible translators elected to ignore them by substituting *El Shaddai* with 'God Almighty'[24] and rendering *El Elyon* as 'the Most High'.

The Semitic word *shaddai* derives from the Assyrian *shaddu* which relates to a 'mountain'.[25] Hence, *El Shaddai* renders as 'Shining Lord of the Mountain'. It was the direct vernacular equivalent of *Ilû Kur-gal*,[26] by which distinction this same deity would have been known to Abraham in southern Mesopotamia. *Ilû Kur-gal* also means 'Shining Lord of the Mountain'.

As El Elyon, this mountain lord is featured extensively in ancient Canaanite texts as the 'Father of all gods'.[27] With his northerly court at the temple of Baalbek, his Canaanite seat to the west is described in Genesis (in accord with Canaanite tablets) as being at Bêth-El (House of El).[28] It was here that Abraham's grandson, Jacob, built an altar to commemorate his dialogue with El the Most High.[29]

* * *

To this point it is evident that, despite the strategic misapplication of *Elohim* (Shining Ones) in Christian Bibles — with a few noticeable exceptions where the plural 'gods' remains — the Hebrew scripture is clear enough throughout concerning the existence of (or belief in) a number of gods rather than a single God: e.g. 'Ye shall be as gods' (Genesis 3:5), and 'God stands in the assembly of gods' (Psalm 82:1).[30]

For the moment, however, we are only concerned with one of those gods — the one whose personal identifications were suppressed in Christian Bibles in order to present a consistent and uniform image for the relevant 'God Almighty'.

Fortunately, the old styles of identification have not been lost, and we already know the three that applied to the one deity referred to as the 'Most High' in the Abrahamic era:

o El Shaddai — the God of Abraham and his son Isaac.
o El Elyon — God as encountered by Isaac's son Jacob.
o Ilû Kur-gal — as El was called in Mesopotamia.

In terms of chronology for Abraham and his immediate offspring, we are in the region of about 2000 BC — close to 4,000 years ago. Our next chapter will confirm this by way of extra-biblical contemporary evidence. Also, in due course, we shall learn the reason for the 'mountain' aspect of El's distinction. As well as being biblically cited 48 times as the Lord *El Shaddai*, and 11 times as *El Elyon*, God is on 250 other occasions identified by the abbreviated style of *El*.[31]

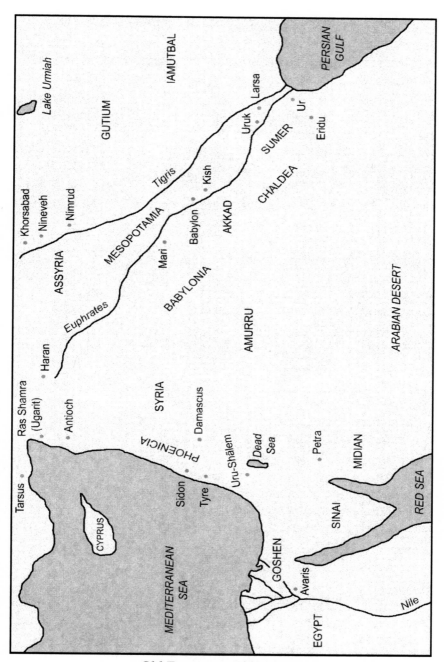

Old Testament Bible Lands

Emanating from that period, the godly identifications, as given above, appear in first-hand historical record, and their individual use is entirely dependent on the regional culture from which the records derive.

Eventually, however, in the days of Moses — more than 600 years after Abraham's time — a new form of godly identification appears in the scripture. We are introduced at that stage to Yahweh (*Yhwh*) as the supreme deity of the Israelites during their exodus from four centuries of pharaonic bondage in Egypt. In this regard, a question therefore becomes evident: Was the eventual *Yahweh* of the Mosaic Israelites the same *El* who had been the original God of the Abrahamic Hebrews?

If so, then a whole new complexion is placed on religious tradition, for Yahweh would not have been the exclusive prerogative of the Israelites as is customarily maintained. He would equally have been the supreme deity of the Canaanites and the Mesopotamians.

On the other hand, if Yahweh and El were not one and the same, then an equally contentious scenario is presented in that the God of Abraham and the God of Moses would not equate within what is supposed to be a continuous Hebrew-Israelite attachment to the One God.

One way or another, it is plain that only one of these long-promoted notions can survive close inspection; the other must necessarily be a scribal myth.

During the course of this investigation, we also need to confront another question. The Genesis scribes of the Babylonian Captivity in the 6th century BC would have been well aware of El's tradition in Abrahamic times. They had also discovered tablets of information concerning much earlier events in Mesopotamia, such as the garden of Eden, the great Flood and the Tower of Babel. But from where did they get the story that El (who in *c.*2000 BC held court at Baalbek and had another residence at Bêth-El) had somehow been the great Lord of all Creation?

It seems very likely that the opening Creation account in Genesis would have emerged from an ancient myth that had nothing whatever to do with El or Yahweh, but was presented for the sake of maintaining a consistent One God image. It has to be remembered as we progress our research that, although the Bible contains an amount of valuable historic record, its purpose was not that of a history book. It was specifically designed to underpin a monotheistic faith. There is no room in such a work for any breakdown in continuity as far as the attributes and involvements of its central One God are concerned.

In order to follow the biblical chronology of God from the scriptural outset, we must therefore soon join Adam and Eve, along with others of the formative cast in Mesopotamia. But since Abraham provides the essential key to understanding the literary evolution of God, it is with Abraham that we should remain for a while longer in order to cement him, if possible, into an historical context outside the Bible.

Part II

God of the Records

3

HERITAGE OF THE PATRIARCH

Formative Roots

Mesopotamia (meaning 'Land between the rivers') was technically the country between the Tigris and Euphrates in what is now Iraq. But historically the Mesopotamian boundaries enveloped these two rivers from the Taurus Mountains down to the Persian Gulf. In the days of Abraham, the primary regions of old Mesopotamia were Akkad (referenced in Genesis 10:10) in the middle reaches of the two rivers, and below this down to the Gulf were the rather more ancient city kingdoms of Sumer, where the concept of independent city-states evolved from about 3900 BC. Subsequent to Abraham's era, Akkad and Sumer became enveloped into the rising empire of Babylonia, while Assyria grew in the north, eventually to become the heart of another new empire.

One of the foremost cities of Sumer was Uruk (modern-day Warka), the first true city on Earth. It is from Uruk that the eventual name of Iraq derives. South-east of Uruk was the city of Ur. These days, the Persian Gulf sweeps below Iraq to Iran (Persia) from northern Kuwait, but in those early times the Gulf extended a good deal further inland, so that Ur was practically on the coast.

Municipal society with community councils had evolved in the region from about 5500 BC, when the farming *Halafans* of Tel Halaf introduced cobbled streets and drainage systems more than 3,000 years before Stonehenge is reckoned to have been constructed in England. One of the main *Halafan* communities was established as a delta settlement at Ubaid, a noted centre of metallurgy and pottery. And nearby emerged Sumer's most sacred city of Eridu. Other important cities of the era were Kish, Nippur, Erech, Lagesh and Larsa. Just as many of today's Western cities are distinguished by their great cathedrals, so were these highly cultural centres focused on richly decorated, temple-topped citadels called *ziggurats*. These enormous multi-storey constructions of mud-brick were built with rising platforms, consecutively reduced in size to form staged pyramids. With stairs leading from each level to the next, the perimeter terraces were planted with trees, shrubs and hanging gardens. The most famous of these terraces were those of the *ziggurat* of Babel on the Babylonian plain of Shinar.

Although Mesopotamia had long been a world leader in numerous fields of operation, there was a very marked advancement from about 4000 BC when southern Mesopotamia became identified as Sumer and the truly structured cities began to flourish. From that time they were formally recognized as city-states which flourished as individual kingdoms, and it is the amazing rise of Sumer which provides the thrust of the initial narrative in the Old Testament book of Genesis. This sudden cultural expansion was not simply a matter of general evolution; it was a mighty technological and academic revolution which has long baffled historical scholars worldwide.[1]

* * *

Around 4,000 years ago, Lord Ibbi-Sin of Ur governed the Sumerian Empire. He was revered as 'King of the Four Quarters of the World', and his dominion stretched way above the Persian Gulf, from the hills of Lebanon to the Iranian borders of Elam. The city of Ur (now an archaeological site called *Tell al Mugayyar*)[2] was on the western bank of the River Euphrates, near modern Basra. But Mesopotamia was no desert land in ancient times; it had long been a lush and fertile region with dark virgin soil and superb irrigation. Indeed, it was largely an agricultural domain, as revealed by the English anthropologist Sir Charles Leonard Woolley's excavations in the 1920s.[3] For about two millennia, Ur was the most influential city-state on Earth, but during Ibbi-Sin's reign, shortly after 2000 BC, the whole structure of the city's governmental administration collapsed:

Ur was verily granted kingship;
A lasting term it was not granted.
From the days of yore, when the country was first settled,
To where it has now proceeded,
Who ever saw a term of royal office completed?
Its kingship, its term of office, has been uprooted.[4]

The cause of disruption was a multi-tribal invasion which swept in from all sides: Akkadians from the north of Sumer, Amorite tribes from Syria, and fierce Elamites from the east (now Iran).[5] This led to a great exodus from Ur, and it is from the accounts of this mass emigration that the biblical story of Abraham emerged.

Some while prior to that, in a previous kingly reign, the scene had been set for a considerable weakening of the city and its defences when Ur, along with Uruk, Larsa and other neighbouring city-states, was said to have been 'devoured by thunders' and 'scorched with heavenly fire'. The *Lament Over the Destruction of Ur*, a 430-line account of the destruction, relates:

The country's blood now fills its holes
    like hot bronze in a mould.
Bodies dissolve like fat in the sun.
Our temple is destroyed.
Smoke lies on our cities like a shroud.
The gods have abandoned us like migrating birds.[6]

In recent times, the record of this disaster was discussed at the 1997 Cambridge *Natural Catastrophes* conference of the Society for Interdisciplinary Studies. Evidently, research into past cosmic activity had identified the possibility of an impact fireball striking the Gulf region in about 2345 BC.[7] Science correspondent Robert Matthews confirmed subsequently in the *Sunday Telegraph*, 16 November 2001, that satellite images of southern Iraq have revealed a two-mile-wide circular depression, which scientists say bears all the hallmarks of an impact crater. 'It lies in what would have been shallow sea 4,000 years ago, and such an impact would have caused devastating fires and flooding'.

Kingship From Heaven

The Sumerian system of kingly guardianship had been fully operational from around 3900 BC, when Sumer made its mark in
history as the 'Cradle of Civilization'. However, the *Sumerian King
List* (a series of 15 inscribed tables from the 3rd millennium BC)
details the kings of the region from long before that era. Relative
to the Old Testament accounts of Genesis, this comprehensive
record gives generational details of the rulers before and after the
great Flood, as referenced in the biblical story of Noah.[8] It begins:

> When the kingship was lowered from heaven, the
> kingship was in Eridu [a little south-west of Ur].

Translated in the 1930s by Professor Thorkild Jacobsen of the
Oriental Institute at the University of Chicago, the *Sumerian King
List* provides an uninterrupted record of kings from the very
dawn of monarchy down to the 18th century BC.[9] It names the
individual kings and their periods of reign, along with details of
their locational seats of kingship within Sumer.

A more ancient Sumerian tablet fragment, found at Nippur
and published by the noted Sumerologist Arno Poebel in 1914,
confirms the opening of the *King List* with the statement:
'Kingship had been lowered from heaven … The exalted tiara and
the throne of kingship had been lowered from heaven'.[10] Then, in
further confirmation of the *King List*, the very same city seats of
original kingship are given — those of Eridu, Bad-tibira, Larak,
Sippar and Shuruppak.

An overriding feature of these, and of all related tablets, is that
kingship was regarded as an institution of divine origin, introduced and implemented by supreme overlords known as the
Shining Ones. Moreover, there are indications that, in the earliest
times, the kings were themselves regarded as being somehow
semi-divine. Writing about this in 1948, Professor Henri Frankfort
(another eminent Sumerologist of the Oriental Institute) stated,
'There can be no question in Mesopotamia of kings who differ
necessarily and in essence from other men'.[11]

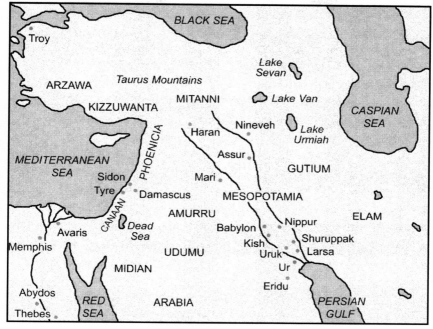

Ancient Mesopotamia

Light of the Magicians

Ur was situated within a Sumerian region that was later called Chaldea, where the people were known as Chaldeans.[12] This region, which swept upwards towards Babylon, was renowned as a land of great scholarship, and the Old Testament book of Daniel 1:4 relates specifically to the advanced learning and unique language of the Chaldeans. There is, however, a mistranslation in the English version of Daniel, in that the original text refers more specifically to the *Kasdim*,[13] rather than to the Chaldeans as a whole. The same mistranslation appears first in Genesis 11:28 and 31, where Abraham's family are said to hail from Ur of the Chaldees. In the more original texts this reads, 'Ur of the Kasdim'.

A long-standing Hebrew tradition relates that Abraham escaped from a fiery furnace instigated by a wicked ruler of Ur Kasdim. The fictional story varies somewhat in different versions, but it was based on the premise that *ur* meant 'light' (as in the Hebrew *uwr*) — whence it is assumed 'fire'. But, in Mesopotamia, *Ur* was an inherited Scythian word that meant 'Lord'.[14] Irrespective of this, Ur is given in Genesis 11:31 as being the home city of Abraham (Abram).

The municipal records of Ur date from 1,000 years before King Ibbi-Sin's reign, and the venerated scholars of Ur — astronomers, mathematicians and physicians — were those defined as the *Kasdim*. It was to this caste that Abraham appears to have belonged, and a Hebrew rendering of Genesis states that Abraham was of the *Uwr Kasdiy* — sometimes given as *Aur Kasdeems*, which means Light of the Magicians.[15]

When Sir Charles Leonard Woolley unearthed the once magnificent city of Ur, he noted in his journal, in reference to Abraham,

> We must revise considerably our ideas of the Hebrew patriarch when we learn that his earlier years were passed in such sophisticated surroundings; he was the citizen of a great city, and inherited the traditions of an ancient and highly organized civilization.[16]

But more than that, Abraham was seemingly of the royal blood of Ur. His male-line descent from Adam is given in Genesis, but the Hebrew *Book of Jubilees* (a Pharisee chronicle from around 120 BC)[17] also discusses Abraham's female ancestry. Jubilees 11:1–4 reveals that Abraham's great grandmother, Ora (the wife of Reu), was the daughter of Ur-Nammu, who reigned *c.*2113–2096 BC and built the famous *ziggurat* of Ur. King Ur-Nammu was the paternal grandfather of Ibbi-Sin,[18] which means that, if the *Book of Jubilees* is correct, King Ibbi-Sin and Abraham were related.

On that basis, it is hardly surprising that Abraham became such a universally influential figure. But even without the *Jubilees* scenario, it is to Abraham that the world's three major monothe-istic (One God) religions cling for the roots of their foundation. Abraham is, of course, the great father figure of the Hebrew nation via his second son Isaac. He is equally revered by Muslims, who claim a heritage from Ishmael, the first of Abraham's sons. And the Christian New Testament opens with Matthew 1:1 citing Jesus' genealogical descent from the patriarch Abraham.

If Abraham was of the *Kasdim* caste of Ur, as Genesis maintains, then he would have been a scholar of some notable merit. His family would have been wealthy and influential. Sir Charles Leonard Woolley was amazed when he unearthed the ancient houses of Ur. They were not the modest homes of primitive people, but two-storeyed villas with up to fourteen rooms. The walls were plastered and whitewashed, and there were wash-basins in the entrance lobbies. The inner courts were neatly paved, with staircases rising to the upper floors. All around, from the ground-floor and gallery, were the family and guest rooms — even indoor lavatory provision and drainage systems. These houses were built in the 3rd millennium BC, but they were mansions of considerable luxury.

From the Other Side

The Bible explains that, once settled in Canaan, Abraham was regarded as a 'Hebrew'. The term is referenced in Syrian texts as *Habirû*,[19] and derives from *Eber han-nahor*: from the 'Other side of the flood' [the River Euphrates][20] as explained in Joshua 24:3. Interestingly, the term *Eber* is given in Genesis as the name of Abraham's 6th generational ancestor,[21] whilst one of his brothers was called Nahor.[22]

On the other side of the Euphrates from Canaan was the northern Mesopotamian city region of Haran on the Syrian border. (Haran is mentioned in Genesis 11:27 as the name of another of Abraham's brothers.) The chief cultural centre of Haran was the royal city of Mari — now an archaeological site called *Tell Hariri* — where the great royal palace was excavated in 1934-36 by the French archaeologist Professor André Parrot of the Louvre Museum. It was to Haran that Abraham's family were said to have travelled northwards along the River Euphrates from Ur. According to the scripture, they were settled there for some time before eventually moving westwards into the land of Canaan, as Genesis explains:

> And Terah took Abram his son, and Lot the son of Haran his son's son, and Sarai his daughter-in-law, his son Abram's wife; and they went forth with them from Ur of the Chaldees, to go into the land of Canaan; and they came unto Haran, and dwelt there.[23]

In Abraham's day, the Palace of Mari would have been one of the greatest sights in the world — an architectural gem covering a full ten acres.[24] It is the largest and most impressive construction to be unearthed and, with a library of over 23,600 clay tablets, the complex housed one of the biggest single ancient document collections ever discovered. Everything was so well preserved that Parrot wrote, 'Even the kitchens and bathrooms could be put into immediate commission'.

Under the same roof had been various Government departments, including a Foreign Office and a Board of Trade, with residential quarters for all the ministers, administrators and their families. The palatial rooms housed the oldest mural paintings in Mesopotamia — 1,000 years older than those of Nineveh, Nimrud or Khorsabad — and their bright colours are all in splendid condition.[25]

To date, only a quarter of the Mari Palace texts have been published (in French) as a 25-volume set entitled *Archives Royale des Maries*. Of particular interest, however, are some of the personal names which they contain: Abram (Abraham), Terah (Abraham's father), Nahor (Terah's father), Serug (Nahor's father), Peleg (Serug's grandfather), Haran (Abraham's brother), and Laban (Nahor's son) — all in accordance with the Genesis family listing. This does not necessarily prove that the names relate to the same people, but it is certainly possible and is too coincidental to ignore. If nothing else, it confirms the authenticity of the names in those distant times. Given that some of the personal names were also the names of major cities, this might indicate that Abraham's family were city governors, known as *ensis*, and constituted a powerful dynasty. Indeed, Genesis 13:2 makes the point that 'Abram was very rich in livestock, in silver, and in gold'.

In addition to the Mari discovery, further excavations at a nearby location produced similar results in 1975. These were conducted by Italian archaeologists from the Roman University of La Sapienza, under the direction of Paolo Matthiae, at a site known as *Tell Mardikh*. Tablets from the same historical period as Mari (around 2000 BC) revealed the Abramu (Abraham) name once again, along with references to Israilu (Israel) — the name given to Abraham's grandson Jacob — and Esaum (Esau), Jacob's brother.[26] The texts also provide historical references to the Dead Sea city of Sodom — the destruction of which forms such an important part of Abraham's biblical story.[27] Additionally featured in the tablets are the cities of Ur and Haran.

The capital city that Matthiae had unearthed at the *Tell Mardikh* site was that of Ebla, whose kingdom incorporated seventeen city-states in Syria and Lebanon. Like Mari, Ebla was an agricultural domain — a land of barley, wheat, olives, grapes, figs and pomegranates. The people made the world's finest damask cloth, and were masters in metalwork. It was called the Kingdom of the White Stone.

Prior to the sacking of Ur, the kings (identified as *lugals*) were responsible to powerful masters known as the Shining Ones. Ancient tablets from Mesopotamia classify these overlords as the *Anannage* (Fiery great sons of An) or, as they were otherwise termed, *Anunnaki* (Heaven came to Earth).[28] They were said to have governed by way of a Grand Assembly of nine councillors — the Bible's Congregation of the Mighty. They had been responsible for establishing the city-states and introducing the office of kingship. But, when the city of Ur was overthrown in about 2000 BC,[29] these supreme governors were unable to withstand the onslaught. They organized a mass evacuation, whereby Abraham's family and others departed northwards for Haran, where Mari was a key caravan station for travellers into Canaan.

In terms of literary presentation, the *Anannage* lords appear to have been the first physical beings ever to be classified as 'gods'.

That is not to say the Sumerians regarded them as being wholly phenomenal, which clearly they were not. But the *Anannage*, whose ultimate place of origin is not specified in the texts, were substantially advanced (agriculturally, municipally and technologically) far beyond the recognized standards of the era.[30] Consequently, they were revered, obeyed and venerated.

Lord of Shālem

In Genesis 17:5, the name Abraham is said to have been changed from Abram. This constitutes a dialectic or orthographic variation, and is not an etymological progression.   In ancient Hebrew, Akkadian and Syrian texts, the name appears as Abiram, Abramu and Aburamu.[31] It is said, in Hebrew, to mean 'Father of a multitude', in which event the name is descriptive of Abraham's personal attainments and relies on the Semitic root *rhm* relating to 'multitude'. A more correct definition of Abram (reliant on *ram* [high place] rather than *rhm*) would, however, be 'Father exalted'.[32]

Apart from the biblical commentary concerning Abraham's wealth and status, his martial abilities are also made evident in Genesis following the kidnapping of his nephew, Lot, by King Chedorlaomer of Elam.[33] Having demolished Ur and swept through Mesopotamia, the Elamites launched an assault on Canaan under the command of King Khudur-Lagamar (Chedorlaomer, as he is called in Genesis 14).[34]

With his own troops, and those of other kings — namely Amraphel of Shinar (Babylonia), Arioch of Ellasar (Larsa) and Tidal of Goiim (a league of nations) — Khudur-Lagamar invaded the Dead Sea Valley of Siddim. Genesis explains that, on sacking the Canaanite cities of Sodom and Gomorrah, Chedorlaomer seized Lot, but Abraham was quick to respond. With an army of trained militia, he pursued the invaders northwards into Syria, where Khudur-Lagamar was slain and Lot was rescued.

Following this event, and with due thanks from the King of Sodom, the high priest Melchizedek blessed Abraham with an offering of bread and wine.[35] This is the first biblical reference to this time-honoured ritual — the same as eventually performed by Jesus at the Last Supper,[36] and as referenced in the *Messianic Rule* document of the Dead Sea Scrolls from around 100 BC:

> And when they gather for the community table ... and mix the wine for drinking, let no man stretch forth his hand on the first of the bread or the wine before the priest, for it is he who will bless the first fruits of the bread and wine.[37]

It was this very ritual of bread and wine that was later appropriated by the Christian Church for the eucharistic communion. Notwithstanding this, many classical artists have preserved the original Melchizedek tradition in their paintings,[38] with scenes of him and Abraham after the Battle of the Kings.

An intriguing fact about Genesis chapter 14 is that its content comes from a notably different source than the chapters which surround it. Genesis 14:13 refers uniquely, for example, to 'Abram the Hebrew' at a time when only non-Hebrews used the term. In such respects, the whole account is objective and impersonal. It appears to emanate from an isolated scribal source, and has a different personality from anything else in the Old Testament. In this chapter, Abraham is glimpsed incidentally through the eyes of an outsider. He is depicted as a resolute and powerful chieftain, as against his more familiar equable representation. This is of enormous significance, especially when connected with the records of Abraham's name at Mari and Ebla, since it tends to support the fact that he was indeed an historical character, and not just a nebulous literary figure.

Much of Genesis 14 has nothing to do with the patriarchal story. It is an insert — a documentary account of battles between opposing kingly confederations — and yet Abraham features personally in the latter stages. As stated in the comment attachments to the *Anchor Bible* (a translation from the Masoretic Hebrew), 'This is as close as we can as yet come to a direct epigraphic witness of the patriarch'.[39]

From the 1st century BC, fragments of the *Prince Melchizedek Document*, found in 1947 among the Dead Sea Scrolls at Qumrân in Judaea, indicate that Melchizedek and the archangel Michael were considered to be one and the same.[40] Similarly, the Qumrân *Damascus Document* confirms that the priestly styles of Zadok and Melchizedek were equivalent and mutually supportive. Given that *Zadok* (Righteous One) was the ultimate high-priestly distinction from the time of King David (*c*.1000 BC),[41] and since *Melchi* (or *Malchus*) meant 'King' in Hebrew, it is evident that the style of *Melchizedek* relates to the King of Righteousness. Melchizedek is also called the King of Shālem,[42] which is generally considered to mean King of Peace. But it does have another more original connotation.

Yurushalem (Jerusalem) relates, in Hebrew, to City of Peace, but the Hebrews did not name the city. Before coming under Israelite control in the 12th century BC, it had long existed as a Canaanite settlement with much the same name: Uru-Shālem. In this context it was the City of Shālem — and Shālem was a son of the biblically identified god, El Elyon.[43]

It follows, therefore, that since Abraham met Melchizedek in Canaan centuries before the Israelites moved into Uru-Shālem, making it their own holy city, Melchizedek's kingly status actually related to the god Shālem, and to the city which bore his name. In this regard, the case is firmly stipulated in Genesis 14:18, which confirms that Melchizedek was 'the priest of El Elyon'.

Information about the Canaanite god Shālem emanates from a collection of Phoenician tablets discovered in 1929 at Ras Shamra (the old city of Ugarit) in north-western Syria. These tablets identify various gods and goddesses related to the supreme lord El Elyon. Dating from a period between 1950 and 1400 BC, thousands of inscribed tablets were unearthed at the royal palace of Ugarit. The excavations were supervised by FA Claude Schaeffer, French associate curator of the Museum of National Antiquities at Saint Germain-en-Laye, near Paris.

Prior to that expedition, archaeologists did not know the exact location of old Ugarit. But in 1928 a farmer's plough struck a rock, which digging revealed as a tombstone, and more extensive digging revealed as a city. The tablets are written in a unique Phoenician Semitic script, which has now been dubbed *Ugaritic*.

Phoenicia was a narrow coastal strip in northern Canaan, with its heartland in the Mediterranean sea-plains of Lebanon and Syria. The Phoenicians were a great maritime nation, whose famed port cities included Tyre, Sidon, Byblos and Ugarit. In essence they were Canaanites (*Canaani*), but the Greeks called them *Phoiniki* (Purple Ones) because of the renowned purple and crimson textile dyes on which much of their trade was founded. Obtained from the Murex shellfish, the *phoenix* dyes became the favourites of royalty on an international scale. The Old Testament book of 2 Chronicles 2:14 references this when Hiram came to Jerusalem from Tyre to be King Solomon's chief Temple decorator. It states that Hiram was 'skilful to work in … purple, in blue, and in fine linen, and in crimson'.

The Ras Shamra tablets refer to El Elyon as the 'Supreme Almighty One, the Father of all the Gods … who is called the King and the Judge'. In Genesis 46:3, this same God speaks to Abraham's grandson Jacob, stating (prior to corrupted translations), 'I am El, the God of your father [Isaac]'. Previously, in Genesis 35:1, it is stated that the 'Elohim said unto Jacob … make thee an altar unto El'. It is further related that Jacob called the altar *El-elohe-israel* — an item that remains unchanged in many Bible editions today.[44]

Thus, it follows that if El Elyon, the God of Jacob, was also the God of his father Isaac — hence also the God of Isaac's father Abraham — then El Elyon and El Shaddai were indeed synonymous. Neither the Ras Shamra tablets nor the Bible leave any room for doubt that this was the case.

What then of Yahweh? Was he a separate entity? It would appear not. When Moses first spoke with God at Mount Horeb in Sinai, he asked for some identification, and was told '*Yhwh*'. With vowels added, the consonantal stem resolved as *Yahweh*, but this was not a name; it was simply a statement of fact, said to mean 'I am that I am'. Twice, however (in Exodus 3:6 and in Exodus 3:15), Yahweh made his identity perfectly clear to Moses, saying, 'I am the God of thy father, the God of Abraham, the God of Isaac, and the God of Jacob'. Then, clarifying the matter further in Exodus 6:3, he added, 'I appeared unto Abraham, unto Isaac and unto Jacob by the name of El Shaddai'.

Once again, therefore, we are dealing with precisely the same God as identified in the Ras Shamra tablets. The God of Abraham, Isaac, Jacob and Moses was the supreme Canaanite deity El Elyon, alternatively known to the Hebrews as El Shaddai, and to the Mesopotamians as Ilû Kur-gal.

4

GODS AND GODDESSES

Abraham's War

From the time that Abraham left Mesopotamia with his wife, father and other relatives after the destruction of Ur, the direct connection was biblically made with the *Anannage* figure of Ilû Kur-gal. Genesis 12:1 confirms that it was the Mesopotamian Lord who suggested that Abraham should 'Get thee out of thy country, and from thy kindred, and from thy father's house, unto a land that I will show thee'.

It was therefore at Ilû's bidding that Abraham moved from Mesopotamia to Canaan. When next they met, Ilû called himself El Shaddai, and said to Abraham, 'I am the Lord that brought thee out of Ur of the Chaldees'.[1] As previously ascertained, *Ilû Kur-gal* and *El Shaddai* were styles relating to the same character, and were direct linguistic equivalents for 'Shining Lord of the Mountain'.

Onwards from that point in Genesis , there was nothing more to be drawn by the priestly scribes from the Babylonian library archive. Abraham had left Mesopotamia and, nearly 1,500 years later, the scribes and other descendants of the Israelite captives of Nebuchadnezzar were themselves making the same journey — returning to Jerusalem in waves from about 536 BC.

Plainly, the book of Genesis would need a new reference source for information, at which point the Canaanite royal library of Ugarit (modern Ras Shamra), to the north of Israel, would have been the obvious choice. Unfortunately, the city had been destroyed by sea invaders 600 years earlier, but there were sufficient tablets from the old site in places of safe-keeping throughout Israel and Judah.

In Canaan, Ilû Kur-gal had been known as El Elyon. Along with his primary operational base near Baalbek (north of

45

Damascus), El was said to have maintained a more southerly residence at Bêth-El, a little north of Jerusalem, and this was perfectly suited to the literary continuation of his relationship with Abraham.

Not until as recently as 1929 was it in any way clear to what extent the Genesis scribes might have contrived their account of Abraham's life in Canaan. But when the old palace of Ugarit was unearthed, with thousands of inscribed clay tablets reclaimed from before the city's demise in about 1180 BC, Abraham appeared as a figure of some noteworthy historical record.

When discussing Abraham's arrival in Canaan from the 'other side of the flood', the Old Testament book of Joshua 24:2 makes the point that 'Terah, the father of Abraham ... served other gods'. Although Genesis 11:32 identifies that Terah had died before Abraham's final journey from Haran, one of the oldest Ras Shamra tablets (from around 1950 BC) tells of a battle which subsequently took place in Canaan between Abraham's followers (the Abramites) and his late father's supporters (the Terachites).

Abraham had moved into Canaan, seemingly as instructed by El Elyon, who subsequently promised,

> I will establish my covenant between me and thee
> ... I will make nations out of thee, and kings shall
> come out of thee ... And I will give unto thee, and
> to thy seed after thee ... all the land of Canaan, for
> an everlasting possession.[2]

It is not known whether this covenant address is in any way authentic as described, but the Ras Shamra tablet explains that, when Terachites arrived on the scene and endeavoured to seize tracts of territory in Canaan, Abraham took up arms.[3]

At that time, a certain Kereth was the King of Sidon on the Phoenician coast, and El commanded him to lead his troops against the disciples of Terah. With the need for two armies, led by Kereth and Abraham respectively, the hostile might of the Terachites must have been considerable. The tablet is not clear about the precise course of the battles that followed, but Kereth and the Abramites evidently won the day. Resultantly, tens of thousands of people were moved into distinctive clan settlements throughout Canaan, with the Terachite faction sectioned into the regions of Hebron and Beersheba.

The Shining Lord

The chances are that the Bible's said 'other gods', as served by Terah, were those affiliated to Ilû's nephew Marduk, who had been newly elected as president of the *Anannage* Grand Assembly to become the senior god of Babylon.[4] It was here, following the destruction of Ur, that the best-known biblical ziggurat was constructed on the plain of Shinar — the first Tower of Babel.

According to Genesis 11:4, the people said, 'Let us build a tower, whose top may reach unto heaven; and let us make a name lest we be scattered abroad'. The word 'name' in this English entry is actually a mistranslation. The original text stated that the people said 'Let us make a *shem* lest we be scattered abroad'. The word *shem* derives from the root term *shamah*, which means 'that which is highward'.[5] The Babylonians called this sanctuary tower the *Esagila*, meaning 'the structure with the utmost raised head'.[6] In later times, when Nebuchadnezzar II built the second ziggurat tower in Babylon (*c*.580 BC), he wrote, 'I have toiled hard to establish Esagila'.[7]

Following the disastrous events at Ur, the Babylonians had feared a similar fate of being routed and 'scattered abroad' if they did not cement their allegiance to Marduk with a monument in his honour, and thereby claim his protection. This veneration of his nephew greatly intrigued Ilû (El), and Genesis 11:5 tells of how he came to investigate the Tower of Babel project. Once again (without revealing who was being addressed), a plural terminology is used, and the Bible relates that, on approaching Babylon, God said, 'Go to, let *us* go down'.[8]

In respect of Babylon, the biblical story of this event relates: 'Therefore is the name of it called Babel, because the Lord did there confound the language of all the earth'.[9] But this is the result

47

of nonsensical interpretation. When writing of the Babel event, the Genesis scribes were themselves being held as the bonded servants of Nebuchadnezzar in Babylon. Perhaps not wanting to convey in their scripture that the name of their enemy's city derived from *Bāb-ilû*, which meant 'Gateway of the Shining Lord', the scribes rendered the name incorrectly as *Bâbhel* which, instead, meant 'mixing up' or 'confusion'[10] — the biblical 'confusion of tongues'.

There is, nevertheless, reason here to understand the nature of El's particular interest in the *Esagila* Tower project — perhaps even his anger as described, but not explained, in Genesis. The new dedication of Babylon to his nephew Marduk was, in effect, a usurping of his own authority. Until that time, El had himself been the master of Babylon — for he was the *Ilû* of *Bāb-ilû*. He was the 'Shining Lord' of the city's foundation. But the people had now changed their allegiance following the downfall of Ur — an event for which Ilû was held largely to blame. He, and others of the Grand Assembly had left the city unprotected, and the resultant citizens' *Lament* lived on to remind the residents of Babylon: 'The gods have abandoned us like migrating birds'.[11]

Where Art Thou?

Although, as has been stated, the Israelite scriptures represent the definitive history of God as we know it, he actually features very little for a great length of time in Genesis. Beyond the story of Adam and Eve, leading to the accounts of their sons, Cain, Abel and Seth, God's only appearances are in respect of the Flood and the Tower of Babel. Then, following an extensive genealogical listing, the text leaps forward to the time of Abraham in about 2000 BC.

Since all the early stories of Genesis came from the Mesopotamian archive, it is clear that the separate Mesopotamian and later-commenced Canaanite records were stitched together in order to set the Abrahamic scene. Thus, the essential purpose of the Genesis narrative is not so much to do with God, but is rather more concerned with Abraham and his immediate descendants, whose stories occupy nearly two-thirds of the 30 chapters in Genesis.

A popular biblical subject for pictorial artists over the years has been the dream of Abraham's grandson Jacob,[12] wherein he envisioned the angels ascending and descending a skyward ladder at Bêth-El:

> And behold, the Lord stood above it, and said, I am the Lord God of Abraham, thy father, and the God of Isaac.[13]

On waking from the experience, Jacob exclaimed in fear, 'This is none other but the House of God'[14] (Bêth-El = House of El).

The root of this Bible story lies in the Ras Shamra tablet records of El Elyon from the Abrahamic era. Unlike the now common perception of God's heavenly abode, El was said to live in a great house called the *Pavilion*,[15] located at a high place in his field at Bêth-El. Given the nature of the 'high place', El was said to reside 'below the heavens, above the earth'. By his corresponding name, Ilû, in Mesopotamia, it was likewise written that he lived in a high place, with a great house called the *E-gal*, 'where heaven and earth met'.[16]

To this point in the sriptural account of God — and with Jacob now some 21 generations removed from Adam — there have been numerous consistencies between the Mesopotamian and Canaanite tablets concerning El and his portrayal in Genesis. Not least among the similarities has been the aspect of mundane activity, with God as a physical presence who walked the Earth in those days.

Genesis 3:8 describes how, on one occasion in Eden, God was 'walking in the garden in the cool of the day'. Without explanation, he is said to have somehow lost Adam, who was hiding among the trees — and God called out, 'Where art thou?'[17]

Such entries are a far cry from the all-knowing, omnipotent God who evolved within later scriptural development. But they are entirely in keeping with the more temporal persona of El Elyon as he was recorded at the time. The very specific Genesis inclusion of the residence at Bêth-El (House of El) leaves us in no doubt that the biblical God, variantly called El Shaddai and El Elyon, was entirely synonymous with Ilû Kur-gal, who featured extensively in the contemporary annals of Abraham's Mesopotamia.

To complete the story, it is subsequently related that Jacob built an altar, which he called *El-Bêth-El*,[18] and his own name was changed from Jacob to *Isra-El* (Soldier of El).[19] Thus it was that the line of Abrahamic Hebrews from Jacob were destined to become known as Israelites — the 'children of Israel'.

The Family of El

Apart from El's son Shālem, whom we have already discussed, the most generally familiar members of El's family are his consort Ashtoreth, his senior son Baal, and his daughter Anath, distinguished as the Queen of Heaven. The Semitic scholar Dr Raphael Patai (a past lecturer at the Hebrew University in Jerusalem) maintains that the *Yahweh* acronym *YHWH*, as conveyed to Moses, was originally a consonantal reference to these four members of the godly family. He states that, in philosophical Judaism, *Y* represented the father; *H* was the mother; *W* corresponded to the son, and *H* was the daughter.[20]

Ashtoreth, progenitress of the gods and sometimes called Asherah, was also referred to as Elath.[21] Her seat was at the northern tip of the Gulf of Aqaba, and the town still carries her name to this day.[22] Whether styled as Ashtoreth, Ashtaroth or Asherah, the name of this goddess features no fewer than 44 times in the Old Testament.[23] She also appears in the *Tell el-Amarna* tablets (letters from Mesopotamia to the 18th-dynasty pharaohs of Egypt) and in the Canaanite texts from Ras Shamra.[24]

Baal (whose idols are biblically cited as *Baalim*)[25] also has numerous Old Testament references. His 'high places' are mentioned in Numbers 22:41, and there are various entries which state that, some time after the era of Moses, the Israelites were predominantly followers of Baal.[26] Biblical items concerning him elaborate by adding that Ashtoreth was the primary goddess of the Israelites in Old Testament times.[27]

It is clear therefore that, notwithstanding El's personal covenants with Abraham and Moses, El's wife and son were equally venerated thereafter by the emergent Israelites. Not until about 1060 BC (nearly 1,000 years after Abraham) is it stated that 'the children of Israel did put away Baal and Ashtoreth, and served the Lord only'.[28] But not long afterwards the Ashtoreth culture returned with the building of King Solomon's Temple. The scriptural book of 1 Kings 11:5 explains that Solomon worshipped Ashtoreth, and that she was an integral part of religious life in Jerusalem until the Israelites were carried off to Babylon from 586 BC.[29]

In her role as the Queen of Heaven, El's daughter Anath is featured a number of times in the Bible.[30] Entries such as Jeremiah 44:25 confirm that the Israelites of that period (c.610 BC) would burn incense, bake cakes and pour drink offerings to Anath. This was just before Nebuchadnezzar's invasion of Jerusalem, and it is evident that, even at that late stage of Israelite history, the One God culture had not yet become the common system of belief despite the attempted reforms of King Josiah a couple of decades earlier.[31]

Anath was regarded as the high goddess of love and war, and her seat was the town of Beth Anath (Anathoth),[32] north of Jerusalem. Now called Anatha, this was the birthplace of Jeremiah the prophet, son of Hilkiah the high priest.[33]

Just as El Elyon was identified by different appelations in different racial and regional situations, so too were the members of his family known by other names. Baal (meaning simply 'Lord') was, for example, known as Hadad in Phoenicia and, more originally, as Nergal in Mesopotamia. Ashtoreth's own tradition as the wife of Ilû Kur-gal was Sumerian and, along with other names, she was commonly identified as Nînlil, whilst in Babylonia she was called Ishtar. The Sumerian name for the Canaanite Anath was Inanna who, in Phoenicia, was known alternatively as Astarte.

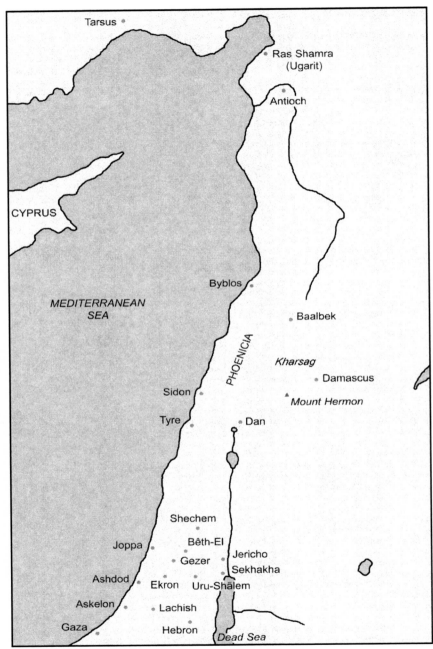

Canaan and Phoenicia

The Hebrew Goddess

Although Ashtoreth and Anath were the venerated goddesses of the Hebrews and Israelites through a biblically recorded period of some 1,400 years, the concept of a Goddess to accompany God did not persist into eventual mainstream Judaic teaching beyond about 520 BC. An element of the Hebrew goddess culture was preserved, however, within esoteric Judaism.

In the Jewish philosophical realm of Kabbalah (Tradition)[34] the figures of Ashtoreth and Anath were merged into a single spiritual entity — a consort of Yahweh known as the *Shekhina*. (The word was extracted from *sh'kinah*, a Hebrew abstract verb meaning 'to dwell'.) By the latter 1st century AD the *Shekhina* had become the Mother Goddess representation, as given in the *Targum Onkelos*,[35] an Aramaic version of the *Torah* which appeared soon after the lifetime of Jesus.

Rabbi Yehoshua of Siknin wrote in the 1st century that 'As soon as the Tabernacle was erected,[36] the *Shekhina* descended and dwelt among them [the children of Israel]'. The *Shekhina* was deemed to be the spouse and female representative of God upon Earth. Her original dwelling was said to have been the Tabernacle of Moses in Sinai,[37] and her later abode was King Solomon's Temple in Jerusalem.

The *Shekhina* was, in essence, a figurative portrayal of the Holy Spirit — the epitome of Wisdom (in Greek *Sophia*, and in Hebrew *Hochmah*).[38] She represented Yahweh, but was opposed to him in matters of retribution, as related by the Ashtoreth-based doctrines of Solomon — for example in Proverbs 24:29: 'Say not I will do unto the man as he hath done to me. I will render to the man according to his work'. This is contrary to the earlier 'life for a life, eye for an eye, tooth for a tooth' teaching of Yahweh in Exodus.[39]

When defining the *Shekhina* wisdom of the Holy Spirit, the Old Testament book of Proverbs 8:29–30 states, 'When he gave to the sea his decree ... then I was with him, as one brought up with him; and I was his daily delight, rejoicing always before him'.

The dilemma, as posed by the medieval Jewish philosophers, was that the spirit of the *Shekhina* had been lost. She had lived in the Temple of Jerusalem, but the Temple had been destroyed by Nebuchadnezzar. Although rebuilt in stages from around 520 BC, it was damaged yet again by Syrians, restored by King Herod in the 1st century BC, and ultimately demolished by the Romans in AD 70. Devoid of a home, the *Shekhina* was said to have moved into an unknown exile, and she never returned. Consequently, Yahweh was left to rule without the bride who was the source of his inspiration.

By the Middle Ages, the Jews had been persecuted for centuries by the papal Christian movement in Europe,[40] and Yahweh had not intervened on their behalf. Hence, there was a deep-seated requirement to reinstate the maternal aspect of their deity,[41] with a heightened leaning towards the *Shekhina*.[42] Only she could influence Yahweh, who had not been treating the Jews very kindly. He was their all-powerful tribal Lord, and had promised Abraham to exalt his race above all others — but their history had been full of hardship and misgiving. To better qualify the nature of the missing feminine element, the *Shekhina* was then given a more explanatory domestic style, and was henceforth termed the *Matronit* (from the Latin *matrona*, denoting a 'motherly lady').[43]

The Great Advance

As we have seen, the Ras Shamra tablets of Ugarit were not found until 1929. Sir Charles Leonard Woolley's discovery of Ur also took place in the 1920s. The Mari Palace archive was not unearthed until 1934, with the *Sumerian King List* published shortly after in 1939. The *Dead Sea Scrolls* were discovered at Qumrân between 1947 and 1951, and the *Tell Mardikh* tablets of Ebla were unknown until 1975. All of this has happened during the past century, and archaeological excavation of any note did not begin until the latter 1800s in any event. Prior to that time, our forebears and all their ancestors, through more than two millennia, had little knowledge of anything outside the Bible in terms of ancient documentary record.

From a century before the archaeological era, what the generations did have in their English library collections from 1759–66
was a 42-volume publication entitled *An Universal History from the
Earliest Account of Time*. It was issued by a consortium of London
booksellers and became greatly revered as an authoritative
account of the biblical era. It stated with considerable assurance,
however, that the Earth was created at 6.00 pm on 22 October,
4004 BC. Some theologians reckoned that 22 March was perhaps
the more likely date, but all agreed that the year was accurate and
it was generally accepted that (in accordance with Genesis 1–2)
there were only six days between cosmic nothingness and the
emergence of Adam.

The date of 4004 BC had been deduced initially by the Irish
Christian archbishop, James Ussher of Armagh, in his *Annales
Veteris Testamenti* of 1650. His method of calculation was very
straightforward, being based on the said ages of the early
patriarchs and the later kings when they fathered their respective
sons as given in the Bible's key succession. Subtracting the total
number of their years from a known historical date in the
9th century BC,[44] he arrived at 4004 BC as the date for Adam.
In comparison, the standard Jewish reckoning for the Creation
(on which the Judaic calendar relies for its emergent year) is
3760 BC — so there was not too much difference. Either way
(and based on our knowledge today), the main flaw in these
calculations was not so much about the possible date of Adam
himself, but rested in the notion that Adam was considered to be
the 'first man' on Earth, which (according to Genesis) had only
been created a few days earlier.

It is from precisely this 17th-century calculation that the lately
opened Creation Museum in Kentucky (as discussed in chapter 1)
takes its lead, and upon which the Answers in Genesis ministry
asserts that the Earth is no more than 6,000 years old.

For Adam to have appeared somewhere around the given
dates would put him notionally in the Bronze Age of his
Mesopotamian locality — a time when farming and agriculture
were substantially advanced. The temperate, moist conditions of
the period gave rise to extensive tracts of open woodland, and a

variety of long grasses had been developed to produce barley and wheat on a large scale.

Harvesting of cereal crops can be traced back to Canaan, southern Lebanon and northern Syria in about 9500 BC, and to Jericho and the Jordan valley by 9300 BC. As the cereal and grain cultures advanced by way of improved seeding, fertilization and ripening methods, so too were pulses and legumes (such as peas and lentils) cultivated. In this well-nurtured grazing environment, certain animals were tamed and herded, with gazelles and goats being the primary meat providers, whilst the latter were also used for milking. Sheep farming was additionally popular in northern Mesopotamia from about 9000 BC, subsequent to which pigs and cattle were likewise domesticated.[45]

Through a gradual process alongside the agricultural and farming pursuits, socially maintained villages and organized communities were established. By 5000 BC in southern Mesopotamia, there were operative municipal structures, complete with civic councils run by the Halafans of Tel Halaf. Westwards on the River Jordan, Jericho was an established urban residential centre from before 6000 BC. By 4000 BC, the plough and the wheel were in widespread use, and the sailing-ship was developed for effective service during this era.

None of these things need necessarily affect the possible mean date of 3882 BC for Adam; they serve only to confirm that, if this date is roughly correct, then he was certainly not the first man on Earth. Maybe Adam was simply the first of a kind in a newly established Sumerian environment. In this regard, and notwithstanding the particular methods used by the Jewish and Christian chronologists to calculate Adam's date, it is perhaps not unduly coincidental that his perceived time-frame fits precisely the c.3900 BC date which saw the sudden rise of the Mesopotamian city-states and caused Sumer to be dubbed the Cradle of Civilization.

Of particular importance to historical record is the fact that Sumerian script is the oldest sophisticated form of writing in existence, having first appeared in about 3500 BC.[46] It is neither crude nor primitive, and there is no other region which identifies any scribal concept that might have been its immediate forerunner.

It appeared as a complete and composite form in the style known as *cuneiform* (wedge-shaped). This was a series of angular phonetic symbols (*cuneates*), ostensibly abbreviated from the pictographs of the Sumerian temple priests.[47] This type of Mesopotamian writing dates back more than 5,500 years, and was first academically discussed in 1925 by the Oxford Assyriologist, Stephen Langdon, who had unearthed *cuneiform* tablets at Uruk in Sumer and at Jemdat Nasr, between Baghdad and Babylon.[48]

The facility which made the Sumerian script decipherable in the early 20th century was that comparative writings were also found in Akkadian texts from a later period, with footnotes relating to the Sumerian records from which they had been transcribed. This particular Akkadian language had a known Semitic base and could therefore be translated by the Assyrian and Babylonian scribal schools. With this done, they then set the comparative Akkadian and Sumerian texts side by side, and compiled bilingual syllabaries (dictionaries of symbols relating to syllables). By comparing the Akkadian words and phrases with the corresponding Sumerian symbols, it became possible to decipher the latter, even though the two scripts were as dissimilar as those of any two written languages could be.[49]

Not only was Mesopotamia a very advanced nation in numerous cultural respects, but the scribes were also recording their history far ahead of any other nation on Earth.[50] It therefore comes as no surprise that the most prominent stories of earthly beginnings — those later adapted for the Bible — emerged from that very region.

The first evidence of written Sumerian history came to light in the 1850s. This was followed twenty years later by some limited journal publication, but it was not until 1918 that the first translations were released into the public domain. As the archaeologists progressed their excavations beneath the Mesopotamian and Syrian deserts, ancient clay tablets and engraved cylinders emerged in their tens of thousands from the very Bible lands of Adam, Noah and Abraham, and they were in large measure contemporary with the Old Testament's patriarchal and dynastic eras. Some of these accounts were immediately familiar, and it soon became obvious that they were the models for stories written down in retrospect by the Israelite compilers of Genesis.

The ancient records should have been greeted with enthusiasm by all — but they were not. The historical accounts, characters and locations were all recognizable as being the Old Testament prototypes. But their literal emphases were so different from conventional biblical teaching that Church indoctrinated society and its governing authorities felt immediately threatened. Even now, the dogma of contrived scriptural history is still taught in our schoolrooms, whilst the original documents from which the scripture was constructed are substantially ignored. This is particularly unfortunate because the old compilations are far more explicit than the Old Testament in their detailing of the pre-patriarchal era. In these texts, the Bible stories are not only placed in a better chronological context, but their social and political relevance becomes far more understandable.

Delusive Substitutions

In summary of our findings to this point, the most pertinent discovery is that the Israelite God, commonly dubbed Yahweh from the time of Moses (c.1360 BC), was previously known to Abraham and his successors (from c.2000 BC) as El Elyon or El Shaddai. Alongside these styles of biblical recognition, he was known in Mesopotamia as Ilû Kur-gal.

We have also established that, despite all strategically designed religious veiling of the archive, the Old Testament refers throughout to the fact that the Israelites also had goddesses. In this context, it is evident from the frequent biblical mentions of Ashtoreth, along with citations of Anath, that the Israelites were wholly attached to the Canaanite culture of El Elyon whose name is biblically associated with God from the outset.

The Bible narrative is especially concerned with a Hebrew ambition to gain particular favour with El Elyon as his preferred 'chosen people'. Whether historically founded, or just a usefully inspired notion by the compilers of Genesis in the 6th century BC, the concept is established by the scribal introduction of El's territorial covenant with Abraham and his son Isaac:

> I will give unto thee, and to thy seed after thee ... all the land of Canaan, for an everlasting possession.[51] ... I will establish my covenant with him [Isaac] for an everlasting covenant, and with his seed after him.[52]

Notwithstanding that El Elyon was already the Shining Lord of the Canaanites, a presumed Abrahamic right to favour was built strategically into the biblical story by virtue of El seemingly having brought Abraham from Ur into Canaan.

Everything in terms of narrative purpose, through the balance of the Old Testament, hangs upon the threads of Abraham's personal relationship with El, and on the 'covenant' said to have been engendered by that relationship. Beyond the inclusion of these two key plot-points in Genesis, however, there is nothing in extra-biblical record to substantiate the historic validity of either premise.

When read as it was written, the Masoretic Bible is not in any way shy of presenting the Hebrew God, El Shaddai, as having been entirely synonymous with El Elyon. The veiling of the fact was perpetrated, in the first instance, by translators of the Old Testament for the Christian Bible. Regrettably, however, it is also the case that translations of the Jewish scriptures into English are now commonly issued as 'Revised Text' editions, thereby widening the scale of literary distortion to bring the content into line with what is felt to be more suitable in an integrated Judaeo-Christian environment.

As a particular exception to the general rule, the Catholic *Jerusalem Bible* does retain — whether by chance or design — an 'El Shaddai' reference in Genesis 17:1, which reads:

> When Abraham was ninety-nine years old, Yahweh appeared to him and said, 'I am El Shaddai. Bear yourself blameless in my presence and I will make a covenant between myself and you'.

Apart from that, other English-translated Bibles — including the 1611 King James Authorized Version (KJV) — have substituted *El Shaddai* throughout with 'Almighty God', have replaced most *El Elyon* entries with 'the Most High', and have rendered *El* generally as 'Lord'. The foremost objective has been to present God as being wholly unique to the Judaeo-Christian tradition and independent of any other past cultural association.

* * *

In order to progress our investigation from this juncture, we should now seek to discover the precise and correct personal name of this God, because none of the aforementioned styles (not El Elyon, El Shaddai or Ilû Kur-gal) is actually a name. They are all descriptive titular appellations.

5

IN THE BEGINNING

Six Days

Although we do not have access to any original form of Hebrew Bible, except for some individually produced scrolls, we do have the Greek text of the *Septuagint* from the BC years. More usefully perhaps, in terms of learning how the Jews of the Gospel era thought of the Bible historically, we have the complete 1st-century works of the Hebrew writer Joseph ben Mattathias, who is generally better known by his Romanized name, Flavius Josephus. His two major publications are entitled *The Wars of the Jews* (AD *c.*78) and *The Antiquities of the Jews* (AD *c.*92).[1]

Born in AD 37 (shortly after the crucifixion of Jesus), Josephus was descended from the 2nd-century BC Hasmonaean priest-princes of Jerusalem. He trained for the Pharisee priesthood, but entered military service when the Judaeans rose up against their Roman overlords in AD 66, and was appointed commander in the defence of Galilee. Subsequent to the unsuccessful Jewish Revolt, which ground to a halt after the Roman destruction of the Jerusalem Temple in AD 70, Josephus was instrumental in the city's surrender, and then travelled to Rome to become an historical writer. His books provide a comprehensive insight into the long and complex history of the Jewish nation from the time of the early patriarchs to the years of Roman oppression.

In his Preface to *The Wars* and *Antiquities of the Jews*, Josephus tells of the lengths to which he researched his subjects. But, having no other source for the more ancient histories, he states that these are 'as interpreted out of the Hebrew scriptures'. Thus, we know that, in matters of *Torah* interpretation, he put forward the details as they were taught and discussed in his own 1st-century era. This gives us a close insight as to the biblical texts that were available at that time and, in respect of the Creation, the *Antiquities* begin in much the same way as the book of Genesis does today: 'In the beginning God created the heaven and the earth'. A similar account follows of the six days of Creation and the 'formation of man ... called Adam'.

Whatever the Bible's *six days* represent in terms of universal and earthly creation, we now know that the Earth evolved through billions of years, and that the earliest primitive life-forms arose some four billion years ago. If we discount the entire evolutionary process from the most primitive anthropoids of 30 million years ago, we still end up with positive proof that Neanderthal man existed before 70,000 BC. This race became extinct after some 40,000 years, and in the meantime Cro-Magnon man had appeared by 35,000 BC, thus beginning the era of *homo sapiens* ('thinking man' — from the Latin *sapienta*, meaning 'wisdom') with his art, clothing and community structure.

Even though chronologically ambiguous, the Genesis text is in many respects seemingly quite accurate. Plainly, in the scribal era, no one had any archaeological knowledge of early life-forms, nor even of dinosaurs and other prehistoric creatures. But, in accordance with the latter-day research of Charles Darwin and others,[2] Genesis 1:11–25 relates that prior to man there were plants, fish, birds and animals — and these various life-forms are detailed in a scientifically logical progression, with humankind ultimately gaining the potential for dominion over the others.[3] Overall, the sequence of events portrayed in Genesis appears reasonably in line with geological and archaeological discovery, except for the reality of a more general long-term evolutionary process.

Intelligent Design

In the mainstream of thought, there are seen to be two opposing philosophies concerned with the origin of life. One is defined within 'religion' — that God created everything in its final form. The other is classified as 'science' — that all life evolved slowly by means of natural selection ('survival of the fittest'). Those on either side of this debate are generally defined as Creationists and Evolutionists. We saw in chapter 1 that the Creationists are associated with a concept of godly creation referred to as 'intelligent design', but in its wider context the notion of Intelligent Design can be seen to have a progressive, life-formulating aspect which is not necessarily related to God.[4] For example, the purposeful cross-pollination of plants and cross-breeding of animals to produce new strains are matters of 'design', and are biologically scientific, although not evolutionary and certainly not divinely created.

Intelligent Design maintains that certain features of living things are best explained by an intelligent cause, not by an undirected process such as natural selection. Its proponents assert that the conjecture stands on an equal footing with current scientific theories regarding the origin of life. In opposition to this, a majority of the scientific community views Intelligent Design as an invalid concept which is not proven science. Religious opinions are mixed.

Either way, the United States National Academy of Sciences has stated that the Intelligent Design theory and other 'claims of supernatural intervention in the origin of life are not science because they cannot be tested by experiment, do not generate any predictions, and propose no new hypotheses of their own'.[5] Although this is an accurate statement, it only achieves its accuracy by virtue of introducing the words 'supernatural' and 'origin'. But Intelligent Design does not necessarily stipulate anything supernatural. When considered in a broader context than the ultimate origin of life, it simply postulates the idea of purposeful intervention in aspects of the evolutionary process.

Alongside this, United States Federal courts have ruled as unconstitutional a public school district requirement endorsing Intelligent Design as an alternative to evolution in science classes because 'it is not science, and is essentially religious in nature'. But, in the field of practical education, even some overt Creationists claim that Intelligent Design is too vague to be considered religious because it does not necessarily attribute its premise to God.

When publishing his *Descent of Man* in 1871, Charles Darwin coined the expression 'missing link' in relation to anomalies in the human evolutionary chain. He detected an undeniable inconsistency in the supposed lineage, which at first seemed like a gap in the sequence. But he soon realized that there was no gap, simply an indefinable bridge. Over a century later, the precise nature of this 'missing link' has still not been resolved. For example, it is now known that the Cro-Magnon human strain and modern *homo sapiens* have not the slightest trace of DNA ancestry from the Neanderthalers.[6] The latest report from the Neanderthal Genome Project, as of August 2008, confirms that certain DNA similarities between the strains represent the last common female ancestor of around 660,000 years ago,[7] following which there was a complete divergence of species and no subsequent trace of any evolutionary process from Neanderthal to *homo sapiens*. Within the Darwinian *Theory of Evolution*, many aspects of 'natural selection' have now been proven beyond doubt, but not all, and there are still some unexplained grey areas.[8]

In practical terms, Intelligent Design (i.e. purposeful intervention in a natural process) is precisely what is going on right now in all forms of genetic engineering, from crops to animals and humans. What the Intelligent Design theory suggests, however, is that genetic engineering is not necessarily a new form of science, and that similar interventions might well have occurred in the distant past. As we shall see in the next chapter, this notion presents itself as rather more than a theory. It was documented and detailed by the Sumerians over 4,000 years ago, and this adds a relevant new category to the Creation Debate. It is not just a matter of science versus religion; we also have to consider aspects of recorded history.

In moving towards the contents of these old Sumerian texts, it would be particularly interesting if perhaps, along with discovering the Adam prototype in some pre-biblical account, we might also find a more original source than Genesis for the six-day Creation concept, with its seventh day of rest.[9] It is, therefore, with a view to such matters that we can turn again to the tablets of old Mesopotamia.

Babylonian Genesis

In the 6th century BC, when the Israelites were captives of Nebuchadnezzar II in Babylon, there was a standard recitation at the city's New Year celebrations. These annual festivals lasted through the first few days of *Nissan* (modern March–April), and the poem (more than 920 lines) was related in its entirety by the high priest, with parts of the story re-enacted.[10] Here, in this environment, the Israelites witnessed the story of universal creation being ritualistically played out before their eyes — and the opening theme for the biblical Genesis was born. In recent times, the poem has been dubbed the Babylonian Creation Epic, but it is more generally called *Enûma elish*, meaning 'When on high'.

The *Enûma elish* was first composed around 3,500 years ago,[11] and its title derives from the opening lines of the poem: *Enûma elish la nabû shamamu. Sha'litu ammatum shuma la zahrat ...*

> When on high the heaven had not yet been named,
> Firm ground below had not been called by a name ...[12]

The tablets were unearthed in the 1848–76 excavations of Sir Austen Henry Layard, from the library of King Ashurbanipal (*c.*668–627 BC) at Nineveh in Assyria. The transcripts were subsequently published by the British Museum in 1876 under the title *The Chaldean Account of Genesis*. Other tablets and fragments containing versions of the same epic were found at Ashur, Kish and Uruk,[13] and it was ascertained from imprints in the clay that an even older text of the epic existed in a more ancient language.

The poem does not tell that the Earth was created in six days, with a seventh day of rest (as explained in Genesis), but there is a thought-provoking similarity which might well have inspired the biblical concept. The readings and re-enactments of this Creation myth were conveyed at the festivals in daily stages through a series of six individual clay tablets, with a seventh-day tablet devoted to celebration and reverence for the god who shaped the heavens and the Earth, and created everything on Earth, including humankind. According to the pre-biblical *Enûma elish*, that god was said to have been Marduk, who became the great Lord of Babylonia.

The story recounts that, in the beginning, there was nothing but a watery dimension[14] in a veiling mist. This is not so different from the beginning of Genesis, which states that 'the earth was without form, and void, and darkness was upon the face of the deep'.[15] The *Enûma elish*, however, treats the watery dimension universally, whereas the Bible relates it solely to the newly created Earth.

In referring to the original salt waters of this dimension, the *Enûma elish* calls them *tiâmat* — just as the word translated to 'the deep' in Genesis was the Hebrew variant *tehôm*, which as a plural becomes *tehômot*. Semitic scholars, such as Raphael Patai of the Hebrew University, have asserted that the association between the Hebrew word *tehômot* and the Akkadian *tiâmat* was purposely suppressed in the biblical tradition for doctrinal reasons.[16]

Following the creation of the firmaments of the sky and the heavens, the *Enûma elish* states that Marduk established the Earth's solar orbit, thereby determining the earthly year, with the moon to make known the nights and the months. In just the same way, Genesis states that 'God said, Let there be lights in the firmament of the heaven to divide the day from the night; and let them be for signs, and for seasons, and for days and years'.[17] A particularly interesting feature of the Babylonian entry is the fact that, in those far-off days, the Earth's orbit around the sun was understood. And yet, 3,000 years later, the Catholic Church insisted that the Earth was flat and at the centre of the universe!

At length, the *Enûma elish* tells that Marduk, in conversation with another god, imparts the details of his final plan: 'Then will I create *lullû* — man'.[18] In Genesis 1:26, the biblical God is also depicted as if in conversation with a colleague, stating, 'Let *us* make man in *our* image, after *our* likeness'.

A key difference between Genesis and the *Enûma elish*, however, is that within such plural identifications from Genesis, along with God saying, 'Behold, the man is become as *one of us*',[19] the plurality of the scripture has been lost in the term *Elohim*, which is customarily mistranslated in the singular as 'God'.

The *Enûma elish*, on the other hand, not only discusses other gods, but even explains in its mythology how the gods were themselves created — beginning:

> No pasture had yet been formed; no marsh had yet appeared. None of the gods had yet been brought into being. Not one bore a name; their destinies were undetermined. Then it was that gods were formed in their midst.

In continuing the story from this point, the *Enûma elish* does at least attempt to answer one of the most asked of all modern schoolroom questions about the biblical Yahweh: 'If there was nothing before God created everything, then where was God before that? Where did he come from?'

The Babylonian difference is that its Creation Epic does not begin with 'nothing'. It begins with there already being a Chaos from which all things arose — a Chaos whose watery dimensions were *Apsû* (male: sweet waters) and *Tiâmat* (female: salt waters). It was out of their union that the gods were said to have been born and the realm of Creation (the subjugation of Chaos) began.

This is similar in concept to an old tractate from 3rd-century Alexandria, entitled *On the Origin of the World*. Unearthed in 1945 at the Egyptian settlement of Nag Hammadi, north of Luxor, it also deals with the original nature of Chaos. In this account, the 'first father', Yaldaboath, was brought out of the depths by the Holy Spirit, who was called Sophia, meaning 'wisdom'.[20] The Holy Spirit of Sophia was said (just as is related in Genesis 1:2) to have 'moved on the face of the waters'.[21]

Whilst the Babylonian *Enûma elish* pre-dates the writing of Genesis by more than 1,000 years, it was itself based on far more ancient records, and the earliest Sumerian Creation Epic discovered to date is more than 1,000 years older than the *Enûma elish*.[22] This again features the 'primeval sea' (called *Nammu*)[23] as being phenomenally eternal and uncreated, before any god appeared on the scene. The premise is that this watery dimension engendered the Heavens and the Earth, and from their union came Air, out of which came the Sun and the Moon. Then the Earth and Water united with the Air and the Sun, giving rise to Life (fish, plants and animals).[24] The Earth, Water, Air and Sun, then engendered their own Gods to personify superior Life, and the Gods created Man. This might well be a mythological concept, but its explanations (written around 4,500 years ago) have a more sequential base than the way the story is portrayed in the text of Genesis.

The Bible, in its true sense, exists in the form of the Jewish scripture. The New Testament is a separate compilation which was tagged on to the Old Testament for Christian Bibles in the late 4th century AD. It is therefore odd that certain fundamentalist branches of modern Christianity apply a more literal interpretation than do the Jews to the Creation account in Genesis. This is rather more evident in America than in Britain and elsewhere. Whereas the *Torah* is regarded as being literally true in Orthodox Judaism, its text is not accepted slavishly in the Jewish mainstream, wherein matters such as the Creation are constantly debated in an effort to rationalize the ambiguities of the scripture. Fundamentalist Christians insist, however, that the Genesis story is precisely the Word of God, that the Earth and Universe were created in just six days, and that Adam and the dinosaurs were coexistent.[25]

The Sumerian Archive

When the first Sumerian tablets were discovered in the latter 19th century, historians and linguists were completely puzzled by the strange *cuneiform* script. It was neither Semitic nor Indo-European; it bore no relation to Arabic, Hebrew, Canaanite, Phoenician, Syrian, Assyrian, Persian, Indian, Egyptian, nor to any language from the European, African or Asian continents. The symbols were eventually deciphered, and the Sumerian language is now understood, but scholars are still baffled by its origin, and indeed by the sudden, extraordinary emergence of the Sumerian people.

To quote the Assyriologist, Professor Samuel Noah Kramer (1897–1990), the Sumerian language 'stands alone and unrelated to any known language living or dead'.[26] In historical terms, the Sumerians (as against the Halafans and previous inhabitants of southern Mesopotamia) appeared, seemingly from nowhere, soon after 4000 BC.[27] But there is no doubt that, upon their emergence, they were already highly advanced to a cultural level far beyond that recorded or sustained in any place from where logically they could have emanated. The anthropologist, Sir Charles Leonard Woolley (1880–1960), wrote that they came 'whence we do not know'.[28] And the Iraq historian, Georges Roux (1889–1968), stated that the great wealth of texts and relics now discovered in Sumer, 'far from offering a solution, have made it even more difficult to answer'.[29]

Today's collections at the British Museum, the Ashmolean Museum, the Louvre Museum, the Berlin Museum, Yale and Pennsylvania University Museums, and elsewhere, hold a far greater wealth of documentary record from the Sumerians than has been obtained from the preserved archives of any other ancient culture. There are many tens of thousands of clay tablets and cylinder-seals containing everything from administrative and taxation records to essays and social history.

The tablets are of flattened, cushion-shaped clay, upon which the scribes wrote, while it was still soft, with obliquely cut reed stalks, before baking them hard in the Mesopotamian sun. Separately, the cylinder-seals are made of stone and, as their name suggests, they are cylindrical in shape. Their main difference in manufacture, as against the tablets, was that they were negatively engraved — that is to say, inscribed in reverse, as might be a printer's block or a royal seal. Containing either text or descriptive pictures, these hard stone cylinder-seals were used to roll positive images into soft clay, which was then baked. They facilitated a reproduction process for any number of impressions and, by virtue of this, were often used for decorative building reliefs or matching pottery designs.

At an administrative level, the Sumerians were highly educated and qualified. They introduced the first-known schools

— professional environments much like our business schools today, where clerks and secretaries were trained.[30] In a short time the scope of the schools widened and they became centres of advanced learning for doctors, agricultralists, historians, astronomers, mathematicians, lawyers and accountants.

One of the scholarly adepts of later times was King Ashurbanipal of Assyria, who wrote on a clay tablet in the 7th century BC:

> The god of the scribes has bestowed upon me the gift of the knowledge of his art. I have been initiated into the secrets of writing. I can even read the intricate tablets in Sumerian. I understand the enigmatic words in the stone carvings from the days before the flood.[31]

Lord of the Mountain

Where Sumerian history is concerned, we are looking at texts with far older roots than the earliest Egyptian records so far discovered. Text after text of Sumerian origin, whatever the subject matter, has a central overriding theme: the relevance in all things of the *Anannage* Shining Ones — the most ancient of all recorded gods whose Grand Assembly sat at Nippur.[32] This was the Court of the Most High — the Congregation of the Mighty as attended by Yahweh in the Old Testament Psalm 82:1.

The original president of the Grand Assembly was An (Anu), the most senior Lord of the Sky, who was said to have evolved from the primordial waters of *Apsû* and *Tiâmat*.[33] In some less esoteric writings, Apsû and Tiâmat appear more in the nature of real characters as the parents of An.

The nine senior councillors of the Assembly each represented a realm of duty and, in later times, the governors of these realms became known in Greek as the *Ennead* (a grouping of nine deities). In the later Norse tradition, the realms were called the Nine Worlds which, as in ancient Sumer, were each represented by a golden ring of office. In this context, the senior Norse god,

Odin, was said to be the ruler of the Nine Worlds of the Rings, having the ninth Ring (called the 'One Ring') to govern the eight others.[34] This tradition was a direct inheritance from the *Anannage* Grand Assembly and their rings of perpetually divine justice.

In cylinder-seal impressions, the *Anannage* Shining Ones are often seen holding their rings, along with another device known as the 'rod' or 'rule', with which the divine justice of the ring was measured. Those overlords who held the *rule* were called the 'rulers', which is from where the governmental term derives. It is not insignificant, therefore, that when JRR Tolkien (a linguistics professor at Oxford University) was asked in the 1960s about the Middle-earth environment of his famous novelistic trilogy, *The Lord of the Rings*, he said that he perceived its setting to relate to a time-frame of about 4000 BC.[35]

The early texts relate that An's consorts were his sisters: Ki (the Earth Mother) and Antu (Lady of the Sky)[36] — each of whom had a son by An. Ki's son was Enlil, Lord of the Earth and Air, and Antu's son was Enki, Lord of the Earth and Waters.[37]

Enlil's sister and wife was Nînlil who, among many expressions of popular endearment, was called the 'Lady of Life'.[38] Nînlil was also espoused to Enki, the father of Marduk who became the god of the Babylonians as featured in the *Enûma elish*.

The name by which Nînlil has become better known to Sumerologists is Nîn-kharsag — that is to say, 'Lady of Kharsag' — a particular distinction that we shall discuss, along with the extraordinary nature of Kharsag, in the next chapter.

Enlil, who had succeeded as head of the Grand Assembly when his father An died, was president of the *Anannage* Congregation of the Mighty, with the Earth subject to his governance, and the seas entrusted to his brother Enki:

> The gods had clasped their hands together,
> Had cast lots and had divided.
> An then went up to heaven.
> To Enlil the Earth was made subject.
> The seas, enclosed as with a loop,
> They had given to Enki.[39]

As the supreme leader of the *Elohim*, Enlil was the designated 'El Elyon' — the Most High. He was distinguished with the titular style of *Ilû*,[40] which signified the Shining Lord,[41] and was identified with a 'great mountain'[42] — the *kur-gal*.[43] Thus, his principal appellation was Ilû Kur-gal — 'Shining Lord of the Mountain'.

Identifying God

Ilû Kur-gal and *El Shaddai* (as given in the Bible) were linguistic variants of the same titular distinction. Emanating from ancient Sumer (southern Mesopotamia) and later Assyria (northern Mesopotamia) respectively, the *Anannage* appellations defined the 'Shining Lord of the Mountain'. The holder of the prestigious office was Enlil the *El Elyon*, whose principal court ('by the headwaters of the two rivers') was on the Beqaa Plateau, north of Damascus, at the Canaanite temple of Baalbek.

Within authentic biblical texts, prior to translatory corruption, these are the very titular styles by which the Hebrew and Israelite God (eventually to become known as *Yahweh*) is introduced in the *Torah* and is further referenced throughout the Bible. The personal figure of God can thus be identified historically as Enlil, president of the Grand Assembly lords of the *Anannage*.

o Enlil (*Ilû Kur-gal*) was the Lord of Ur biblically portrayed as having instructed Abraham to leave Mesopotamia for Canaan.

o When they reconvened in Canaan, the Genesis scribe (consulting the records of a different region) described the event using the local vernacular equivalent of the title. Enlil (*El Shaddai*) announced to Abraham: 'I am the Lord that brought thee out of Ur of the Chaldees'.[44]

o Confirming his identity, when establishing his covenant of kingship with the Abraham–Isaac line, Enlil (God) pronounced to Abraham, 'I am *El Shaddai* [Shining Lord of the Mountain]'.[45]

o When addressing Abraham's grandson Jacob at Bêth-El (the House of El), Enlil (*El Elyon*) announced by way of introduction: 'I am the Lord God of Abraham thy father, and the God of Isaac'.[46]

o In the city of Hamor, Enlil met Jacob again, asserting, 'I am *El Shaddai*. Be fruitful and multiply'.[47]

o Counselling Jacob — now renamed Israel (*Isra-El*) — before taking his sons to Egypt, Enlil confirmed his identity yet again: 'I am *El*, the God of your father [Isaac]'.[48]

o Arriving in Egypt, Jacob-Israel explained to his son Joseph that he met with God: '*El Shaddai* appeared to me at Luz in the land of Canaan, and blessed me'.[49]

o At the burning bush in Sinai, Enlil's voice was heard by Moses, claiming, 'I am the God of thy fathers, the God of Abraham, the God of Isaac, and the God of Jacob'.[50]

o Moses asked this God for identification, and was told, '*Yhwh* (I am that I am) ... the Lord God of thy fathers, the God of Abraham, the God of Isaac, and the God of Jacob'.[51]

o Curious about the *Yhwh* response, Moses requested further information. Enlil (*Yahweh*) duly explained: 'I appeared unto Abraham, unto Isaac and unto Jacob by the name of *El Shaddai*'.[52]

In the contexts of these pronouncements: 'I am the God of ... [your fathers, Abraham, etc.]', the Hebrew verb 'to be' is used, with *Ehyeh* becoming 'I am'. Alongside this, the term *Yhwh* — with its different spelling and pronunciation — is strangely linked to this verb and also reckoned, in translation, to relate to 'I am', which it clearly does not.[53] In fact, the term *Yahweh* actually has a rather more specific meaning, and a precisely defined route of derivation, as we shall see in chapter 12.

Notwithstanding all retrospective scribal entries relative to the term *Yahweh*, the word's first-known documentary appearance in history (discovered as recently as 1905) is entirely related to the era of Moses and the Israelite exodus from Egypt, long after the time of Abraham. Thus, although *Yahweh* became a popular identification of God from the Mosaic era, it had not previously been used at any stage by the Abrahamic Hebrews. Throughout the Genesis period, down to the 14th century BC, the descriptive terms for the High God's identification were:

o *Ilû Kur-gal* (Mesopotamian): 'Shining Lord of the Mountain'.

o *El Shaddai* (Assyrio-Hebraic): 'Shining Lord of the Mountain'.

o *El Elyon* (Canaanite): 'Shining Lord of the Height'.

Tablets of contemporary record, lately recovered from archaeo-logical sites in the regions concerned, now confirm that these styles of personal recognition were all applicable to one and the same character, and were used in accordance with the linguistics of the individually neighbouring nations. Although biblically associated in particular with the Abrahamic Hebrews for scrip-tural reasons, there was no Hebraic prerogative to the affiliation with the Mountain Lord — no historical indication that they were in any way a preferred 'chosen people'.

According to Genesis 15:7, El (Ilû) had brought Abraham from Ur into Canaan, in which event nothing changed concerning Abraham's personal allegiance. He simply carried his traditional culture from one land into another where that same culture was already flourishing. The High God of the Hebrews at that time was therefore equally the prevailing High God of the Mesopotamians and the Canaanites.

Hence we are now in a position to answer the question with which this book began: 'If the books of the Bible had never been written, would we know about this particular God today from any other primary source?'

The immediate answer to the question is that we would indeed have learned of him once the various tablet inscriptions were found and translated onwards from the late 19th century. Nevertheless, without the Bible to consider, we would have had no means of relative association, and the revealed character would have had no ongoing religious significance. Without the Bible, we would know little or nothing of Abraham, Isaac, Jacob or Moses, so the question of whether or not this was their God would never have arisen for asking. Thus, the considered answer to the question has to be 'No'. If the books of the Bible were not to exist, the cultural relevance of this God would be tied historically to a period in the distant past. Without the Bible we would know nothing about his adoption as a figure of perpetual veneration beyond the time-frame of the original writings.

Given, however, that we do have the Bible as a base reference, and since we now have so many unearthed tablets from the Genesis period with which to make comparisons, the personal identity of God becomes wholly evident. When considered in unison, the Bible and the tablets are mutually supportive, and neither the scriptures nor the ancient records give rise to any doubt in the matter. Whether defined as *Ilû Kur-gal, El Elyon* or *El Shaddai*, the God of Genesis was Enlil — president of the Grand Assembly of the *Anannage* (the biblical Congregation of the Mighty) — as first recorded long before the time of Abraham in the Sumerian archive of southern Mesopotamia.

Part III

God of the Enclosure

6

THE EDEN PROJECT

The Anannage

To this point in the story of God, there is little discrepancy between the manner of his biblical representation and those of the Sumerian, Akkadian and Canaanite tablets from which the Genesis portrayal derived. Where differences occur, they are not contradictory at this early stage, but there is much information in the source records which the Bible writers preferred to leave unstated.

In this respect, we shall see that, as with the Tower of Babel account, certain key Genesis sequences, such as related to the garden of Eden and the great Flood, are scripturally adapted versions of primary source material. But things are soon destined to change. From part-way into Genesis, through the book of Exodus and the rest of the Bible, God's image becomes increasingly a matter of retrospective scribal interpretation as the available body of original reference depletes and finally expires within a few hundred years of the Abrahamic era.

For the time being, whilst we are still in the realm of historical record, rather than expedient scriptural invention, it is worth comparing the biblical perception of God with the figure of Enlil. This is best done in terms of those aspects of his role which the Bible ignores in order to present a more illusive and less mundane image. By virtue of applying this religiously motivated requirement, the initially active God of Genesis is soon left without any literary purpose except to keep reiterating the terms of his Covenant to individual patriarchs in succession.

In complete contrast, every item of written and pictorial attestation concerning Enlil and his counterparts of the *Anannage* confirms that they fulfilled specific functions with designated community duties. They were patrons and founders; they were

79

teachers and justices; they were clinical technologists, agriculturalists and kingmakers. They were jointly and severally venerated
as governing masters, and were the very first beings to be documented as gods.

Since there are no historical records older than those from
ancient Sumer, we have no way of knowing anything of *Anannage*
involvement in other cultures before the emergence of *cuneiform*
writing. We have genealogical listings and accounts of their activities from the times when recorded, but their ultimate place of
origin remains an untold mystery. All we know is that the
Sumerian texts were the first (from well over 2,000 years before
the book of Genesis was ever conceived) to discuss matters of
origin and godly creation. Whoever the *Anannage* might have
been, and from wherever they might have come, the Sumerians
were absolutely sincere about their existence at a time when their
social, academic and technological cultures leapt forward way in
advance of any other region on Earth.

We are left, therefore, to wonder how a race of beings with no
evident background or historical provenance could otherwise
be so well documented. Ostensibly related, and functionally
disciplined within their family ranks, those such as Enlil, Enki,
Nîn-kharsag and Inanna must surely have been the product of a
very sophisticated culture. And yet, seemingly out of position in
time and place, these highly advanced individuals appear, like a
cast-remnant from Atlantis, to create the most impressive and
influential civilization of the era.

Whence they came?

Given that Sumerian texts refer to the *Anannage* as having
'descended' into the region, some researchers have deduced that
they were representatives of an alien race from another planet.
Foremost and pre-eminent in this regard is the noted American
scholar Zecharia Sitchin, an exponent of the Sumerian language,
whose *Earth Chronicles* books have investigated and upheld this
possibility with some considerable merit.

There is, however, another school of thought fast gaining ground in anthropological and agricultural studies, which supports the notion that the *Anannage* were the surviving descendants of an advanced earthly race which had persisted from very early times. In this context, their 'descent' is related rather more to a geographical high place (perhaps a mountainous region or more northerly country), rather than from the skies.

* * *

In the course of Sir Charles Leonard Woolley's Sumerian excavations in the 1920s, having discovered the lost city of Ur, he also unearthed the ancient ziggurat of nearby Eridu.[1] This place was later discovered by the Iraqi Directorate of Antiquities in 1946 to have been the residential seat of Enki,[2] the brother of Enlil. Here, at Eridu in the Euphrates delta, Enki was said to have pursued unique methods of seed cultivation, crop management and the domestication of certain animals. A related tablet concerning Eridu reads:

> The plough and the yoke he directed,
> The great prince Enki ...
> To the pure crops he roared.
> In the steadfast fields he made the grain grow.[3]

Within the numerous Sumerian *cuneiform* texts concerning the *Anannage*, a great deal of attention is drawn to matters of farming, agriculture and animal husbandry. Following a disastrous flood, which covered the land with silt and clay, the Sumerian grain crops had to be reinstated along with the herds of cattle and flocks of sheep. According to one fragmented tablet,[4] this was supervised by the goddess Ashnan and her brother Lahar.[5] They were given the task of preparing the ground, and of farming grain and cattle respectively, with sheep as a joint responsibility.

As we saw in chapter 3, the *Sumerian King List* identifies Eridu (modern Abu Sharain, near the Persian Gulf) as the very first seat of earthly kingship. The remains of the last Eridu ziggurat, as unearthed by Woolley, have been dated to about 2500 BC, but beneath this construction have been found seventeen temples, many of them very elaborate, with the oldest dating back to proto-historic times.[6]

The inference here is that, whilst the land of Sumer might well be dubbed the Cradle of Civilization by today's historians, there was plainly civilization in the area long before the generally understood Sumerian period from around 4000 BC. This naturally gives rise to the question of where else on Earth the same might have been the case. It is most unlikely that Eridu was somehow the world's lone pioneer region of organized settlement through thousands of years.

When considering the dates, as given in our previous chapter, for municipal and agricultural development in the neighbouring realms of Canaan, Lebanon, Syria and Mesopotamia, we are actually looking at a period onwards from around 10,000 BC. This was a time of emergence from the last Glacial Period and from the worst ravages of the associated Ice Age.[7]

What we have, in terms of conventional understanding, is a situation whereby (once the major ice-sheets of the hemispheres had reduced towards the poles) the 're-starting' of more normal human activity is perceived as the modern historical era with its own new beginning. But what of the inhabited world that existed before the glacial ice-sheets formed? Researching this question in particular, Food Energetics authority Steve Gagné, in his study of ancient agricultural development, concludes:

> With the advent of satellite imaging, NASA has recently discovered lost civilizations in Cambodia, South America and India. Man-made megalithic structures have also been found off the coasts of Japan and Malta. A recent discovery off the coast of Cuba reveals what appears to be a complex of temples and other structures resembling Mayan architecture. Because of their 2,000-foot depth, these ruins are believed by some researchers to have sunk around 50,000 years ago … If and when some of these new

discoveries prove accurate through current methods of dating technology, this will be further confirmation that human beings were building sophisticated cities and temples 50,000 to 60,000 years ago. And where there is civilization, there is agriculture.[8]

In attempting to determine what happened to humans before and during the last Glacial Period, two distinct theories have come to the fore, namely those of *Catastrophism* and *Cultural Diffusionism*. The first identifies a series of global catastrophes, perhaps caused by comet or asteroid impacts leading to tidal-waves, earthquakes and volcanic disruption. The second describes the cross-cultural exchange between highly advanced civilizations and the more primitive hunter-gatherer communities, as would doubtless be evident in the transient wake of major calamity.

Legends abound from various parts of the world concerning cataclysmic events that left harsh and brutal environments. It then fell to the more capable survivors to take responsibility for re-establishing civilization, and the stories tell of these tenacious 'culture-bearers' who arrived by sea, or descended from high mountains, to provide leadership and become venerated as benevolent gods.[9]

Soon after 10,000 BC, with the ice-melt under way, sea-levels had risen considerably. Survivors would naturally have been in search of higher ground, and extensive sea voyages were undertaken by the adventurous pioneers from the worst affected global regions.

In all aspects of portrayal, the *Anannage* overlords of ancient Mesopotamia are the best recorded of such pioneering 'culture bearers'. It is, therefore, entirely possible that they were intrepid colonizers from some other part of the world, who re-started agriculture and introduced community structure in a hitherto less advanced region than their own had been. In terms of documentary record, from the advent of *cuneiform* writing, we have a considerable archive dating onwards from the 4th millennium BC. Within this archive are texts which indicate that, prior to their Sumerian settlement, the *Anannage* were active in the more northerly realm of the Lebanese border country. It was here that agricultural development was actively revived in about 9500 BC. Subsequently, this development progressed southward through the Jordan Valley in Canaan, and eventually into the Persian Gulf flood-plains of Mesopotamia as the fertile land was reclaimed.

The recent discovery of semi-domestic emmer wheat at the site of Nahal Oren, by Mount Carmel in Israel, denotes that wild grain was in use as early as 14,000 BC. Nearby, the archeological site known as Ohalo II in Galilee has revealed specimens of wheat and barley dating from 23,000 years ago, long before the last Ice Age. In the light of such findings during the past twenty years, it emerges that many crops, previously thought to be wild progenitors, could actually be cultivars from a civilization predating the orthodox theory for agricultural origin.[10] Thus, the c.9500 BC date for suppose agricultural beginnings in the Canaanite region becomes more precisely related to a 'kick-start revival' of techniques that extended much further back into prehistory.

Collected specimens, from Canaan and elsewhere on the map, now support the contention that domestic agriculture emerged several times in numerous parts of the world during the past 20,000 years — possibly from as early as 50,000 years ago.[11] It is, therefore, now evident that the genetic tweaking of wild grass species to produce nutritious offspring during the *Anannage* era was no haphazard experiment. It was the competent work of those who already had the knowledge to create a vital and sustainable human food source during a period of urgent require-ment following the Ice Age.[12] Their similar expertise was then applied to extraordinary feats of engineering, architecture and general community development, to create an incomparable city-state environment for the indigenous people of Mesopotamia.

In England's post-Restoration days of Sir Isaac Newton and the scientific Royal Society of Natural Philosophy, Professor Charles Rollin (1661–1741), Principal of the Collège de Beauvais, published his multi-volume history of the ancient world, *Histoire Ancienne*. In this work, he discussed 'the manner in which arts and sciences were invented, cultivated and improved', stating:

The nearer we approach those countries which
were once inhabited by the sons of Noah, in the
greater perfection we find the arts and sciences ...
When men attempted to revive those arts and
sciences, they were obliged to go back to the
source from whence they originally flowed.

In 2004, the journal *Scientific American* concurred with the tablet
texts of old Mesopotamia in a study of crop genetics. Discussing
ancient intervention by those such as Enlil's wife Nîn-kharsag,
the article states: 'Comparing the genomes of major cereal-crop
species shows their close interrelationships and reveals the hand
of humans in directing their evolution'. The report continues:

As our ancestors domesticated these plants, they
were creating the crops we know now through a
process very much like modern plant breeding.
From the wild varieties, they selectively propa-
gated and cross-bred individual plants possessing
desirable traits, such as bigger grains or larger
numbers of grains ... The human modification of
cereal plants through selective propagation and
cross-breeding began in prehistoric times.[13]

Modern science has now proved this; Charles Rollin knew it
intuitively, and the ancient texts recorded it over 4,000 years ago.
Genetic engineering is not a product of the modern age; it is one
of the oldest sciences on record, and legitimately can be classified
as Intelligent Design ('the hand of humans in directing evolution',
as cited in *Scientific American*). Resultantly, some 99% of all
today's agricultural production stems from a base of just 24 plant
species developed from those early times. (This traditional form
of genetic tweaking by way of a 'one-stage process' must, of
course, be viewed as entirely distinct from today's genetically
modified organisms [GMOs] which destroy biodiversity and
create sterile land by eliminating vital micro-organisms and soil
nutrients, thereby decimating the natural genetic information

vital to a food's integrity. Neither is it comparable with today's insanely contaminated pseudo-foods, such as fruits and vegetables laced with animal DNA.)[14]

In line with the research of Professor Daniel Zohary of the Department of Evolution Systematics and Ecology at the Hebrew University in Jerusalem,[15] independent research by the UK Patrick Foundation has recently confirmed that DNA data reveals the domestication of crops to have been re-established in accordance with the *Chronicles of Kharsag*.[16] These ancient tablets and cylinder-seals of Sumerian record are the most revelatory of all documented testimonies concerning the *Anannage* foundation of Eden. (In some concordance Bibles the Sumerian term *eden* — a 'stepped pasture land' — has erroneously been associated with the Hebrew noun *eden*, relating to 'enjoyment'.)[17]

The high-ground location of the Kharsag Eden — settled about 9500 BC in southern Lebanon — is in due accord with the sea-level requirement of the era. Moreover, NASA satellite imagery conforms in all key respects with the ancient site description, including the great reservoir and irrigational watercourse positionings of the 'head enclosure' (the *gar-sag*).

Concurring with today's re-evaluated dating concepts (as explained above by Steve Gagné concerning situations of agricultural 're-start' during the glacial ice melt), Edmund Marriage, principal of The Patrick Foundation and the *Kharsag Research Project*,[18] explains:

> Following a global catastrophe, they were forced to seek a high elevation, favourable climate, a glacial refuge for wild grasses and plants suitable for domesticated agriculture (which included the pistachio and oak at this site), and the ability to irrigate their crops in a very fertile former lake bed. The choice of location at that time was perfect, close to what became a sub-tropical climate in the Dead Sea valley, where the fig was domesticated as early as 9300 BC near Jericho.

Fireball and Flood

In various of his books, notably *The Earth's Shifting Crust* (1958),[19] *Maps of the Ancient Sea Kings* (1966),[20] and *The Path of the Pole* (1970),[21] Harvard University historian, Charles Hapgood, speculated that the ice mass at one or both poles over-accumulates and destabilizes the Earth's rotational balance, causing slippage of all or much of the Earth's outer crust around the core, which retains its axial orientation. He argued that each shift completion took approximately 5,000 years, followed by twenty-thousand to thirty-thousand year periods with no polar movements.

In the context of this, and based on a *Sea Kings* map which appeared to show a partially ice-free Antarctica,[22] Hapgood postulated that a 15° pole shift occurred around 9600 BC at very much the time when the above-mentioned *Anannage* activity became evident in terms of substantial new agricultural development to the north-west of Mesopotamia.

Despite a glowing pre-emptive Foreword written by Albert Einstein in 1955 for *The Earth's Shifting Crust*, the likelihood of such a Pole Shift (a slippage of the Earth's crust from its axis) has since been challenged by the emergent geological understanding of Plate Tectonics. This science determines that the Earth's crust is not a cohesive solid, but consists of several plate layers that move laterally against each other at their boundaries, causing earthquakes, tsunamis and volcanic action.

Explaining the matter a little further, solar energy consultant Paul LaViolette describes that high-velocity cosmic rays, known as Galactic Superwaves, 'could deliver a powerful jolt to the Earth's crust and cause high ocean tides. A sudden crustal displacement of even a few metres would have triggered widespread earthquake activity'.[23]

Whatever the case, the c.9600 BC time-frame was pertinent to a major catastrophic event of some kind, and coincides with the *Anannage* establishment of a significant high-ground agricultural project very near to El Elyon's Baalbek court in southern Lebanon.

It transpires that 9600 BC is the very year attributed to the Earth's emergence from an intense cooling and drying era of global proportion known as the *Younger Dryas Period*, sometimes called the Big Freeze. This emergence was the most abrupt moment of climate change in the northern hemisphere, prior to which the summit of Greenland had been 15°C colder, and the mean average temperature of Britain was just 5°C.[24] Quite suddenly it was wetter and warmer. Where there had been thick glacial ice, there was now flooding on a monumental scale and, continent-wide, all but the high ground was submerged.

The initial cause of the preceding *Younger Dryas Period*, from about 11,000 BC, is reckoned by geologists to have been a significant impact event above or near the Great Lakes of North America, with coinciding impacts in Hudson Bay to the north, down to the Carolinas. Lethal reformations within an unusually resilient debris-wave from a long-past supernova explosion had penetrated the atmosphere at speeds up to 70,000 miles per hour.[25]

The likely central trigger was a massive detonating fireball known as a *bolide* (flashing missile), a generic term used to define a devastating projectile whose precise nature is inconclusive — whether, for example, a rocky or metallic asteroid, a cataclysmic comet, or whether it makes physical contact or explodes above the Earth's surface.

To achieve a Pole Shift that would tilt the Earth as a whole, the governing spin-axis would have to change its inclination along with the crust. Since a considerable and far-reaching redistribution of mountains, seas and other surface weight would be necessary to cause any such realignment, science maintains the notion as a near impossibility. Nevertheless, given the magnitude of deep-ice melt and the speed of global redistribution following the *Younger Dryas Period*, there are some geologists who do not dismiss the possibility at that time.[26] Referencing substantial surface redistribution in a particular study of permafrost deposits, Oxford palaeogeographer Derek S Allan asserts:

> The waters must have first rampaged unopposed across, not only hills and valleys of more distant areas extensive enough to have straddled several climatic zones — in the

process tearing up loose surface materials and carrying with it the assorted remains of entire forests and countless land creatures — but must have also invaded older lakes and seas (incorporating their waters within itself) and swept them and their natural inhabitants up into one gigantic churning maelstrom.[27]

Although conventional science repudiates the notion of an axis-tilting Pole Shift, it is intriguing to note that a pseudoepigraphical work from the 2nd century BC, known as the *Book of Noah*, does indeed suggest that this, or something similar, was traditionally thought to have been the case. Relating to the event, it states, 'In those days he saw that the Earth became *inclined* and that destruction approached'.[28]

On 24 May 2007, a session at the spring joint assembly of the American Geophysical Union in Acapulco, Mexico, was held to discuss what is called the *Younger Dryas Impact Event*, which marked the sudden demise of many North American large mammals, including camels, woolly mammoths, giant short-faced bears and numerous other species. On 27 September 2007, a resultant paper was published in the *Proceedings of the National Academy of Sciences*. According to the study, 'The Impact Event may have led to an immediate decline in human populations in North America at that time'.

The matter was subsequently discussed in March 2008 at the annual meeting of the Society for American Archaeology in Vancouver, Canada. Debated was the crucial evidence for the event — a widespread carbon-rich layer of extraterrestrial materials: nano-diamonds, magnetic grains, iridium, magnetic spherules, and fullerenes enriched in Helium-3. But, since the *bolide* appears to have exploded above the mile-thick Laurentide Ice Sheet, it was difficult to be conclusive about the actual nature of the missile itself.

Arizona-based geophysicist Allen West (with support from University of Cincinnati assistant professor of anthropology Ken Tankersley, and Indiana Geological Society research scientist Nelson R Schaffer) asserts that the wealth of rich deposits in the immediate and neighbouring regions indicates that 'an object from space (about 2k m to 3 km in diameter) exploded just above the Earth's surface, sparking a massive shockwave that set large parts of the northern hemisphere ablaze'.

So intense was the heat that the disintegrating fireball would have caused widespread melting to seriously disrupt environments as far afield as Europe and Asia.[29] In the course of this, unevaporated water from the land-mass glaciers poured deep fresh-water lids onto the oceans, which soon froze when the cometary fires expired. And so it remained for over a thousand years until the warming of 9600 BC when the fertile high ground of the Levant was finally accessible for domestic agriculture to be resumed by those with the preserved genetic knowledge of long-distant times.[30]

Chronicles of Kharsag

From the late summer of 1888, through to 1905, a series of five excavations were undertaken by the University of Pennsylvania at the great library mound of Nippur — the ancient shrine-city of Enlil, thirty miles to the west of Babylon. Directing the teams in succession were the Assyriologists, John Punnett Peters,[31] Clarence S Fisher,[32] Hermann V Hilprecht[33] and John Henry Haynes.

At a time when treasure-seeking explorers were learning to become professional archaeologists, the first expedition was violently opposed by angry locals, who managed to overwhelm the camp and capture the dig. John Peters was compelled to flee the scene, but not before he had shipped out some 40,000 ancient tablets and fragments from the library collection of King Naram-Suen. His magnificent palace and extensive library had been destroyed by the Elamite invasion of Kurdur-Nakhundi in 2285 BC, and had never been rebuilt. Over 4,000 years later, the 1901–02 *Annual Report* of the University of Pennsylvania Museum confirmed: 'Precious inscriptions of stone, dating back to Babylon's earliest rulers, were obtained. Gold, silver and bronze objects, seals and cylinders, images of gods and objects illustrative of the daily life of the people were secured'.[34]

Cuneiform writing was entirely baffling to linguists at the time. But colleagues of John Peters in Istanbul sent word of a rock in Iran that was inscribed in Old Persian and seemingly copied alongside in *cuneiform*. From these comparative texts it was determined that the Sumerian writing code was revealed — and to some large measure it was. But, in Pennsylvania, the translatory results were still subject to elements of interpretation, and the interpretation was itself subject to the religious preconditioning of those concerned. John Peters (whilst having become a pioneering archaeologist) was, in the first instance, a professor of biblical language at the Protestant Episcopal Divinity School. Clarence Fisher was a biblical antiquary. Hermann Hilprecht was an oriental theologian, and their linguist colleague, George Aaron Barton, was a professor of biblical literature at the Quaker foundation, Bryn Mawr College.

Each, in turn, added his own interpretive stamp to the translatory process, based on the erroneus notion that ancient writings must necessarily be religious. It is in this context that we now discover a flaw in the statement at the beginning of this chapter — i.e. that the *Anannage* 'were the very first beings to be documented as gods'. Actually, they were not — at least not by the Sumerians. The term 'gods' (by way of customary Western understanding) was applied for expedience in the early translations to define characters who, somewhat incomprehensibly to the university theologians, had been venerated historically beyond the extent of any everyday norm. With the precedent established, *cuneiform* translations continued likewise through the 20th century and, for reasons of ingrained familiarity, the same is the case today. In practice however, and as confirmed in the *Sumerian Lexicon*,[35] the word *diñgir* (constantly rendered as 'god') should, in all instances, have been translated more mundanely as 'great lord',[36] and *nîn-diñgir* as 'great lady'.

A particularly intriguing series of nine tablets and inscribed cylinders, brought back by John Haynes in 1888, was a collection of Enlil-related texts from around 2800 BC. Along with much else from Nippur, they lay in storage at the University Museum until discovered by George Barton, who translated them eventually for publication by Yale University Press in 1918. In doing this, Barton's Introductory Note explained the difficulties he encountered in tackling a hitherto little-known language:

> It need hardly be added that the first interpretation of any unilingual Sumerian text is necessarily, in the present state of our knowledge, largely tentative. Everyone familiar with the language knows that every text presents many possibilities of translation and interpretation.[37]

Notwithstanding such difficulties in translation, the broad picture of the inscriptions was perfectly clear in depicting Enlil and the *Anannage* as the foremost Lords of Cultivation, with specific references to their primary agricultural project at the place called Kharsag:

> The holy sceptre of Enlil establishes Kharsag.
> They give abundance.
> His sceptre protects
> The sprouts of the land
> In Kharsag, the garden of the lord.[38]

In 1948, the Oriental Institute at the University of Chicago joined forces with the University of Pennsylvania Museum to conduct further biannual excavations at Nippur. The University of Chicago then became the sole sponsor from 1965. Prior to this, Professor Samuel Noah Kramer of the Oriental Institute announced that, although much within the damaged Kharsag inscriptions had been largely unintelligible at the time of George Barton's translations, a good deal of reconstructive work had progressed in the meanwhile. He had also found nine additional fragments of tablet 9205, entitled *Enlil and Nînlil*.[39] With particular reference to the Kharsag foundation cylinder 8383, Kramer added,

> Much that was unknown or misunderstood at the
> time of its publication is now gradually becoming
> clarified, and there is good reason to hope that the
> not too distant future will see the better part of its
> contents ready for translation.[40]

During the 1970s, with Sumerian transcript technique having
been vastly improved since 1918, a revised translation of the
Kharsag collection was undertaken by Cambridge exploration
geologist Christian O'Brien, CBE. Then retired from heading the
International Oil Operating Companies in Iran, O'Brien had been
instrumental in the 1936 discovery of the *Tchoga Zanbil* ziggurat,
subsequently excavated in 1952 by the French *Délégation
Archéologique*. Aided in the Kharsag project by his wife, Barbara
Joy, the results were published in their 1985 book, *The Genius of the
Few*.[41]

Along with the textual reconstructions, the advancements
made in more than 50 years of *cuneiform* understanding proved to
be of considerable benefit as George Barton's 'tentative' rendering
expanded to become a colourful, in-depth account of *Anannage*
proceedings at the Kharsag agricultural enclosure — beginning
with the moment of their arrival:

> *gar-sag — an-ki-bi-da-ge — erim — an-ni*
> *dingir-anu — a-nu-na-[ge] — im-to-ne — es-a-zu*
>
> Kharsag, where heaven and earth met, the
> heavenly assembly, the great sons of An,
> descended, the many wise ones.[42]

This led ultimately to explaining a previously made translation of
a similar Akkadian (rather than Sumerian) inscription, which
maintained that the place settled for agriculture by Enlil was
known as Duranki.[43] But, in view of the positive Kharsag identification, it soon became clear that *Duranki* was not a place-name
at all. It was a purely descriptive word: *dur-an-ki* (*dur* = bond)
(*an* = heaven) (*ki* = earth). Thus, *Duranki* represents the spatial

and physical bond between heaven and earth — the place 'where heaven and earth meet' — just as described for Kharsag. The term *duranki* is also perfectly in keeping with the biblical references to God's House, called Bêth-El, which the Ras Shamra tablets describe as having been 'below the heavens, above the earth'.

Moving through the *Chronicles of Kharsag*, the story is very much as one might expect to find it in the context of Levantine settlement in the post Ice Age environment. Here is the full account of a large-scale agricultural and farming complex, set upon high ground with fenced enclosures and an impressively designed cultivation system. The assembly chamber is defined as the Mountain House, with Enlil being the overall Shining Lord of the Mountain — the *Ilû Kur-gal* — precisely as he is biblically described as *El Shaddai* (Shining Lord of the Mountain) or as *El Elyon* (Shining Lord of the Height) in Genesis.

Foremost in Enlil's team was his sister-wife Nîn-kharsag, an agricultural biologist. Also present was his brother Enki as operations manager, and his grandson Utu (Shamash) in charge of surveys and site allocations. Nîn-kharsag sets the *Chronicles* scene with an address concerning the most important aspect of the venture — irrigation:

> With this settlement will come prosperity. An enclosed reservoir — a water-trap — should be established ... This perfect *Eden* is full of water. It should be irrigated from a cascading watercourse ... This water should flow from the reservoir.[44]

This pronouncement by Nîn-kharsag (written about 2,250 years before the book of Genesis was begun) is the oldest known pre-biblical text to identify Kharsag as the location of *Eden*. It is likely, therefore, that it was the very account from which the Israelites' later perception of the garden derived.

Nîn-kharsag also spoke of building roads, a granary and a maternity centre, along with new methods of pest control, and the treatment of soil to produce the finest crops from the planted settlement.

94

In her capacity as Governor of the Garden, we learn that Nîn-kharsag was the designated *Gabri-Ilû* — a style related to agricultural estate management — with the root of *Gabri* being GBR, the same as for the later Latin *gubenator* (governor). Just as *Isra-Ilû* became *Isra-El* (Israel), an alternative rendering of *Gabri-Ilû* was *Gabri-El* (Gabriel) — subsequently adopted nominally for a male archangel ('shining consul') in biblical lore. In strict terms of the first instance, however, gender was not a factor of the Kharsag titular ranking.[45]

Regarding the locational site of Kharsag, it comes as no surprise to learn that it was very near to where the Ras Shamra tablets of the Ugarit palace explain that El Elyon had his principal court. As we have already seen, his seat was at the headwaters of the Orontes and Litani rivers that rise above Canaan in the Beqaa Valley of southern Lebanon. These waters emanate from the Beqaa Plateau, north of Damascus, close to the one-time Canaanite temple of Baalbek.

To be specific, the Kharsag enclosure — the original Eden Project[46] — was located in the south Rachaiya Basin, 8 miles (12 km) north of Mount Hermon at the south-eastern end of the Beqaa Rift Valley, which lies between the peaks of the Lebanon and Anti-Lebanon mountain ranges.[47] The town of Rachaiya is 25 miles (37.5 km) north of Damascus, and 35 miles (52.5 km) east from Beirut.

* * *

Although the book of Genesis is wholly unspecific concerning the geographical location of the garden of Eden, this is not the case in terms of Hebrew literature in general. The Hebrew Bible is, by its very nature, canonical scripture, with its inherently collated books selected for the purpose of underpinning a stylized belief structure that was consolidated during the last few centuries of the BC years. In view of this, a number of equally well-known writings did not suit the selection process and were sidelined to be deemed inappropriate — the books of Maccabees, the book of Jubilees, of Enoch, Tobit, Esdras, Judith, Baruch and so forth.

It is within the body of these works that a Kharsag equivalent is to be found within the *Book of Enoch*. Parts of this work in Aramaic were discovered in the Dead Sea collection at Qumrân, Judaea, in 1947. Known as Scroll 4Q201,[48] this *Enoch* copy was produced by Hasidim ascetics who occupied the first settlement at Qumrân in about 130 BC. Some Greek fragments of the text were previously found in Cairo in 1886, but the fullest rendition is a translation into Ethiopic that was discovered in Abyssinia in 1773. The date of the original work is entirely unknown, and there is no way to determine the extent to which the currently available versions were embellished or romanticized through the ages. But the principal narrative source is reckoned to have been very old and is credited to Enoch, an early descendant of Adam. As will be discussed in chapter 8, two Enochs are listed biblically in parallel Adamite descents, but the account in the *Book of Enoch* most likely relates to Enoch (Henôkh) the son of Cain. His brother Atûn is given in the Sumerian annals as King Etâna of Kish (*c*.3500 BC) — a kingdom in the Tigris-Euphrates valley, north-west of Ur.

The *Book of Enoch* (known as 1-Enoch) confirms that the 'planted highlands' of the *Anannage* were in the vicinity of Mount Hermon, near the old Canaanite settlement of Baalbek. Referring to the arrival of an auxiliary staffing contingent, *Enoch* relates:

> And they were in all two-hundred who descended, in
> the days of Jared, on the summit of Mount Hermon.[49]

The use of the name Jared in this English-translated passage is, in fact, anachronistic. The *word* 'Jared' — as given in the Ethiopic text of 1-Enoch — was not a proper name as the 19th-century translator assumed. It was an improper capitalized noun relating to 'Destiny', and should have been translated along with the surrounding text. The passage should therefore not read: 'In the days of Jared'. It should correctly read: 'In the days of Destiny'.

That apart, the *Enoch* entry is entirely in keeping with the Sumerian Kharsag annals, whilst emphasizing the locational arrival of an *Elohim* workforce as being at Mount Hermon, the highest point of the Anti-Lebanon range.

Other aspects of *Enoch* are equally supportive in an account of how Enoch envisioned a past-time visit to the *ha'shemin* (high places) to witness *Anannage* activities at the agricultural enclosure.[50] In the course of Enoch's narrative explanation, many themes of the Kharsag tablets are supported and confirmed, not least those concerning matters of irrigation and the reservoir:

> When the water is required from the reservoir, the angels responsible come and open the sluice and let the water out. And when it has dispersed over all the fields, it soaks into the ground.[51]

Through subsequent millennia and successive *Anannage* generations, the Eden project appears to have spear-headed farming and municipal development through the Jordan Valley region, centred largely on Jericho as a trading hub, and into the lands around.

Notwithstanding the extensive time-span, there is no record to suggest that the *Anannage* (the biblical *Elohim*) were uniquely immortal or exceptionally long-lived, although perhaps the latter might have been the case. They were plainly not invulnerable to physical attack, and there are several accounts referencing individual deaths by means of accident or violent intervention.[52] Maybe they were capable of extreme longevity by comparison with ordinary standards, but the concept of eternal existence was never a feature of their documented history. The archive suggests that there was always a supreme Enlil (El), just as there was always an Enki and a Nîn-kharsag, but the characters were not the same individuals throughout. Their nominal styles appear to have been heritable aspects of *Anannage* culture, bestowed — as are modern inherited titles — in accordance with rank and station as the generations progressed.

In biblical terms, Kharsag was 'the garden planted by the Lord in Eden'. It was the place of new beginnings and of globally unprecedented development for agriculture and husbandry. Kharsag became the model for organized settlement and the new birthplace of civilized community. It was founded on a benevolent ideal brought to the region, in an age of chaos, from an unknown realm where social and technological advancements had been preserved from pre-glacial times.

The last days of Kharsag were in about 6500 BC, when the *Chronicles* relate that the enclosures were devastated by dreadful storms, torrential rains and violent outbreaks of fire. At the same time, Jericho — the very first organized and fortified township in the modern world — was abandoned. Although re-established eventually at a nearby location, the archaeological site of Old Jericho still retains evidence of violent surface attack, and of storm-flood channels from this major break in the settlement.[53] There is, however, no record of any attempt to resurrect the first Eden project. The culminating words from the *Chronicles of Kharsag* are final in their reckoning, with detailed descriptions of the individual seats of destruction, whereby the cumulative result was one of complete devastation:

> The great shining house was destroyed by fire ...
> The great reservoir was destroyed ...
> The enclosure was totally destroyed ...
> The granary was cut-off and overthrown ...
> The settlement of learning ... became marshland.[54]

From that time, the whole operation was moved southwards through Mesopotamia and, by *c.*5500 BC, was re-established in the Eridu delta plains of Sumer. Management of the new Eden project was then assumed by the prevailing Enki and Nîn-kharsag, whilst the prevailing Enlil took up residence in Nippur.

It was the end of the formative era, but was also the beginning of Sumer's great rise to prominence on the world stage. The Eridu period, from which the models of advanced community structure and the city-states evolved, also marked the dawn of significant new biological advancement in fields of Intelligent Design. It is therefore to Eridu that our story now moves, opening the door to the biblically familiar continuation of civilized earthly renewal and the emergence of Adam and Eve.

7

DAWN OF THE EARTHLINGS

Lady of Life

As previously discussed in chapter 2, there are two quite separate Creation stories in Genesis. In terms of signifying an ultimate goal for each, the first story concludes with the institution of the Sabbath day of rest (Genesis 2:2–3), and the second concludes with the institution of marriage: 'Therefore shall a man leave his father and his mother, and shall cleave unto his wife, and they shall be one flesh' (Genesis 2:24). In the biblical context as scripturally portrayed, this is a somewhat anomalous statement since Adam did not have a father and mother to leave.

It has also been mentioned that Adam (identified simply as 'the man') is seen to have been created twice by God.[1] But there is also a third account of the man's creation (subsequent to the introduction of his wife) which places an unfamiliar connotation on the name Adam. Genesis 5:2 states: 'Male and female created he them; and blessed them, and called *their* name *Adam*, in the day when *they* were created'. Hence the definition Adam was applicable, in the first instance, to both the man and the woman.

We are separately informed that the man later 'called his wife's name Eve, because she was the mother of all living',[2] but we are still left with the fact that *Adam* was not a personal name. In fact, it was not a proper noun at all. As explained by Robert Alter, professor of Hebrew at the University of California, *adam* was a generic term applied to both men and women.[3]

Given that the Bible offers no explanation of the term *Adam* (as it does for the name Eve), it is commonly presumed that, since 'God formed man of the dust of the ground',[4] and the word for 'earth' was *adâmah*, then that must logically be the root of the presumed name. But in discussing this, Professor Alter has claimed that English mistranslations of the Old Testament have 'placed readers at a grotesque distance from the distinctive literary experience of the Bible in its original language'.[5]

Adding yet another dimension, Flavius Josephus stated in his 1st-century *Antiquities of the Jews*: 'This man was called Adam, which in the Hebrew tongue signifies one that is red'. Thus, he deduced that Adam was 'compounded out of red earth'[6] because the Hebrew word for 'red' was *adom* and, in the Akkadian language of Mesopotamia, *adâmatu* was a dark red earth. There is, however, an interesting entry in the Hebrew *Anchor Bible*, which explains that Adam was not made '*from* the earth', but was '*of* the Earth', and would more correctly be described as an 'earthling'.[7]

We saw in the *Enûma elish* that the Babylonian god Marduk referred to 'man' as *lullû*, which means quite literally 'one that is mixed'.[8] In this respect, the earlier Sumerian *Creation Epic* does indeed refer to the 'mixing' of *Anannage* blood for the making of man. In some translations it is reckoned that the blood was mixed with a type of clay, but this results from a linguistic misunderstanding. The Babylonian word for potter's clay was *tît*, but in the more ancient Sumerian language *tî-it* meant 'that which is life', while in Hebrew the word *tit* meant 'mud'.[9] According to the Sumerian text, the mixing of *Anannage* blood with the *tî-it* ('that which is life') to make the *lullû* (man) was done by Nîn-kharsag.

Nîn-kharsag's personal emblem (which is to be found on various tablet and cylinder representations) was a symbolic womb, shaped rather like the Greek letter *omega* (□).[10] It relates to her primary distinction as the *Nîn-tî* — the Lady of Life. She was also called the Lady of Form-giving, Lady Fashioner and Lady of the Embryo, while a text entitled *Enki and World Order* describes her as the 'Midwife of the Country'.[11] Likewise, her half-brother Enki was called the *Nudimmud*, meaning 'Image Fashioner', being the archetype of original form.

Evidently, there was a degree of friction between Enki and his brother Enlil by virtue of Enlil's perceived seniority as president of the Grand Assembly. Enki was unhappy about this because, although Enlil was the elder of the two, his mother (Ki) was their father's junior sister, whereas Enki's mother (Antu) was An's senior sister. True kingship, claimed Enki, progressed as a matrilineal institution through the female line and, by this right of descent, Enki maintained that he was the firstborn of the royal succession: 'I am the great brother of the gods. I am he who has been born as the first son of the divine Anu'.

In the midst of this struggle between the brothers, Enki's son Marduk made his own bid for supremacy, and partially usurped the Assembly decision by gaining a majority following among the people of Babylon. Consequently, Marduk is portrayed as the god of Creation in the Babylonian *Enûma elish*, in which he is credited with the concept of *lullû*: man'. In the much older Sumerian texts, however, the creator of the *adâmu* earthling was said to have been Marduk's father, Enki.

At the same time when University of Pennsylvania teams were excavating at Nippur, from where the tablets identified Kharsag as the formative 'Eden', another important discovery was made by Dr William Hayes Ward, president of the American Oriental Society. As director of the Wolfe expedition to Babylonia in 1884, he unearthed an Akkadian tablet listing the key cities in southern Mesopotamia — one of which cities, affiliated to Eridu, was *Sipar Edina* (Sippara of Eden), thereby confirming the *Eden* name for the continuing purposes of regional identification within Sumer.[12]

The Creation Chamber

The records tell that, following a devastating flood that wrecked Eridu and the surrounding delta country, the overlords had no time to waste after the waters had subsided. The once fertile land had become a bed of clay and the whole environment had been destroyed. The first priority was to make the ground habitable again, and to restore the farming enterprise. The grain crops had to be reinstated along with the cattle and sheep herds. However, the task was too great for the *Anannage* alone, and labour assistance was urgently required. Consequently, it is explained that others were brought in to assist, and the *Tablet of Ashnan and Lahar* details that 'for the sake of the good things in their pure sheepfolds, man was given breath'.[13]

101

These newly developed humans were stated (in Genesis-style terminology, by way of Western-language translation) to have been created 'in the image of the gods'. With this in prospect, Enki was instructed by his mother: 'O my son, rise from your bed ... Work what is wise. Fashion servants of the gods, and may they produce their doubles'.[14] To this, Enki replied,

> O my mother, the creature whose name you uttered, it exists. Bind upon it the image of the gods ... Nîn-mah [Nîn-kharsag] will work above you ... she will stand by you at your fashioning. O my mother, decree upon its fate; Nîn-mah will bind upon it in the mould of the gods. It is man.

We are not, therefore, looking here at the first humans, but at a particular new breed — 'the man that already exists' upon which would be bound 'the image of the gods'. Nîn-kharsag was then approached by Enki and the Assembly, and was formally requested to create a new type of man to bear the yoke of the *Anannage* in the garden[15] — just as the biblical Adam was placed in the garden 'to dress it and to keep it'.[16]

In political affairs, the relationship between Enki and his sister-wife Nîn-kharsag was rife with disagreement, and they appear to have spent a great deal of time drinking wine and quarrelling. Scientifically, however, all reports indicate a very professional partnership. Nîn-kharsag was a highly regarded anatomical specialist, and there are many accounts of her research. These include the laboratory saving of Enki's semen to be applied to the cross-fertilization of certain life forms.[17]

For such experiments within the Eridu project, they ran a documented 'creation chamber' called *Bit Shimtî* (House of Shimti). This stems linguistically from the Akkadian *sh-im-tî*, meaning 'breath-wind-life' — the place where the 'wind of life' was drawn as 'new breath'.[18] The descriptive concept from the *Bit Shimtî* archive was seemingly used in Genesis 2:7 to explain how God (having created man) 'breathed into his mouth and nostrils the breath of life'.

Following initial trials with animals, six organically different types of person were created before the first true success.[19] Eventually, an Akkadian text known as the *Atrahasis Epic* relates that, in response to instruction from Enki's mother, Enki and Nîn-kharsag created fourteen new infants soon after the flood (seven boys and seven girls), and that the clinical process involved the wombs of women who had survived the deluge.[20] The tablet is very fragmented and much of the text has been lost, but what remains describes how Nîn-kharsag made use of the 'seven and seven wombs', having prepared fourteen 'pinches of tî-it', to which Enki added his 'repeated incantation'. The wombs are called the 'creatresses of destiny', and it is related that they completed Nîn-kharsag's work by developing 'the forms of the people that she made'.[21]

* * *

The fundamental difference between the original Mesopotamian records and the later Genesis version of the creation of Adam and Eve by God is that the *Bit Shimtî* offspring did not emerge in a ready-made adult form. They were scientifically induced, with human ova ('that which is life': tî-it) fertilized by Enki, to be placed as cultured embryos into the wombs of mundane surrogate mothers. As a result, they were born quite naturally as babies:

> Nîn-kharsag, being uniquely great,
> Makes the womb contract.
> Nîn-kharsag, being a great mother,
> Sets the birth-giving going.[22]

Not only were these new custodians of Eden created at the *House of Shimtî*, but a whole new social structure was conceived with the genetically advanced humans, in their eventual adulthood, becoming their own governors — thereby having transferred to them certain administrative duties of the *Anannage*. The tablet continues:

Mother Nîntur [Nîn-kharsag], the lady of form-giving,
Working in a dark place, the womb,
To give birth to kings, to tie on the rightful tiara;
To give birth to lords;
To place the crown on their heads.
It is in her hands.

First of a Kind

In general terms, the 'creation chamber' enterprise was a resounding success, but a more advanced plan was conceived to produce the desired kingly strain. To facilitate this supreme aspect of Intelligent Design, it was decided to place a cultured embryo into Nîn-kharsag's own womb so that it was nurtured with *Anannage* blood and carried the divine imprint. Among her various titles, Nîn-kharsag was also known as *Nîn-ki* (Lady Earth), and it is by this name that she is recorded in a quotation from Enki that describes her surrogate role: 'Nîn-ki, my goddess-spouse, will be the one for labour. Seven goddesses of birth will be near to assist'.[23]

Nîn-kharsag duly bore the male child, having developed an embryo cultured from the ovum of a mundane woman, which had been clinically fertilized by Enki. The outcome of this successful experiment was recorded as the 'model of man' — the *adâmu* or earthling. When the man was grown to adulthood, Enki called him Adapa and appointed him as his personal delegate.[24] At Eridu, Adapa was placed in charge of Enki's temple in the Sumerian Eden, effectively to become the world's first ever priest.

As distinct from those people of the previous experiments, the *Adâmu* was truly considered to be of the 'divine blood' of his creators. The Hebrew word for blood was *dam*,[25] as in *goel ha dam* (the 'avenger of blood' in Deuteronomy 19:12). In Hebrew terms, Adapa the *Adâmu* was therefore *ha dam* ('of the blood') — to become construed and interpreted in Genesis as *Adam*.

Three of the four tablet fragments in this regard were discovered, along with the *Enûma elish*, in the Nineveh library ruins of King Ashurbanipal of Assyria. The other was found in the Egyptian archive of Pharaoh Amenhotep III, who reigned in about 1400 BC. They explain that Lady Earth's son, Adapa, was granted extraordinary powers of control, being anointed into kingship by Enki:

> Oil he commanded for him, and he was anointed.
> A garment he commanded for him,
>   and he was clothed ...
> His command was like the command of An.
> With wide understanding, he had perfected
>   him to expound the decrees of the land.
> He had given him wisdom,
>   but he had not given him eternal life.
> Of the wise one, no one treated his command lightly.[26]

Later, in a continuation from another fragment, the *Adâmu* is described not only as the high priest and an anointed king, but also as being of the 'royal seed'.[27] It is apparent that the great importance of Adapa was not that he was the 'first man' (as the *Adâmu* is portrayed in Genesis), but that he was the first man of the royal seed. As was the case with the extraordinary crop development of the preceding era, the tablets are consistent in setting a detailed scene for Adam being the product of Intelligent Design. Thus he is documented as the first earthly priest-king with the *Anannage* bloodline imprint.

In the period of *Anannage* transference of kingship to the anointed custodians, the *Sumerian King List* records a period of reign by seven interim guardians, who were succeeded by King Atabba of Kish.[28] He was the founding father of the new kingly race, with Atabba being synonymous with Adapa. He was regarded as an 'intercessor' — an *abûttu* with the ability to protect his flock.[29] The 'abba' aspect of the Atabba name moved into later Semitic use, and was adopted in the New Testament (with *abba* meaning 'father') to define God.[30] But it was originally a Sumerian word which determined the fatherly role of the earthly priest-king — the *sanga-lugal*.[31]

A direct parallel between the Adapa (Atabba) story and the adapted Genesis account occurs in an incident concerning the 'bread of life'. In Genesis 2:17, God warns Adam not to eat from the Tree of Knowledge, 'for in the day that thou eatest thereof thou shalt surely die'. Subsequently, however, both Adam and Eve eat the fruit of the tree,[32] but they do not die; they gain the wisdom of true awareness.

The original Sumerian story is similar to the Genesis portrayal in that Enki warns Adapa:

> When thou standest before An,
> When they offer thee the bread of death
> Thou shalt not eat it ...
> This advice that I have given thee, neglect not.

Subsequently, An (the father of Enlil and Enki) instructs the lords Dumuzi and Ningishzida to make such an offer to Adapa. But, in An's opinion, the bread is not related to death. In contrast, he considers it to be the food of life:

> Bring him that he may eat the bread of life.
> They brought him, but he did not eat ...
> An looked at him, and wondered at him.
> Why hast thou not eaten?
> Now thou shalt not live.

The result was that, by not taking the bread, Adapa lost any prospect of immortality,[33] just as Adam was similarly deprived in Genesis.

* * *

The name of Adam's biblical wife, Eve, was originally Khâwa (Ava) and relates in Semitic terms to the verbal root *hayah* ('to live').[34] Eve is given in Genesis 3:20 as representing the 'mother of all living'. This is repeated in the 1st-century *Antiquities of the Jews*, wherein Josephus explains: 'Now a woman is called in the

Hebrew tongue *issa* (she-man); but the name of this woman was Eve, which signifies the mother of all living'.[35] Hence, the name Khâwa was akin to the Sumerian *Nîn-tî* (Lady of Life) which, as we have seen, was a title of Nîn-kharsag.

When Nîn-kharsag's distinction was applied to her surrogate daughter and transposed to the name Eve, it was correctly interpreted by the Genesis compilers. But Eve's biblical origin from Adam's rib was wholly inaccurate and had nothing whatever to do with any original account.[36] The error occurred from the misidentification of a single small word. As in the distinction *Nîn-tî*, the Sumerian word *tî* related to 'life'. In fact, it meant 'to make live'. But the unrelated Sumerian word *ti* meant 'rib'.[37]

Adam and Eve's original state of nakedness — a feature of the Genesis narrative — was an initial reflection of their subordinate status in the prevailing environment. Their covering of themselves had nothing whatever to do with matters of sexual embarrassment as religious teaching seeks to imply. The Sumerian texts relate that it had to do with the fact that clothes were a prerogative of the masters, and cylinder-seal reliefs often depict the servants of the *Anannage* as being naked. The *Adapa Tablet* explains, however, that when Adapa was anointed to his high priest-kingly station, 'a garment was commanded for him, and he was clothed'.

In this regard, Adam and Eve (Adapa and Khâwa) would have thought nothing of their initial nudity, but when their 'eyes were opened' to the fact that they were beings of subordinate status, they were immediately struck with the reality of their situation.[38] Genesis explains that, in an attempt to remedy this, 'they sewed fig-leaves together and made themselves aprons'. There is no explanation of how these newly created people knew the technique of sewing, but it is subsequently related that God then made them 'coats of skins, and clothed them',[39] just as Enki had done for Adapa. This was the ultimate recognition that they were not inferior beings, but were regarded as people of high status in the ranks of the overlords.

8

RISE OF THE GUARDIANS

Tree of Life

It is commonly believed that the Christian term 'Original Sin', and the resultant Fall of Man, had something to do with Eve's sexual misbehaviour in the garden of Eden, but this is a Church-promoted absurdity. To the point where God banished Adam from the garden after eating from the Tree of Knowledge, there is no mention whatever of any physical contact between him and Eve. Their offspring were conceived in their new environment some time after Genesis explains they had left the garden. Notwithstanding this, it is made clear from the outset in Genesis 2:24 that Eve was the 'wife' of Adam, a fact which is repeated numerous times along with the instruction that the man 'shall cleave unto his wife, and they shall be one flesh'.

If Eve was perceived to have sinned, the notion could only relate to her eating from the forbidden tree along with Adam. In this regard, she accepted the serpent's advice that they would not die from the fruit, instead of heeding God's contrary warning that they would die.[1] The fact is, however, that God did not warn Eve against the tree; he warned only Adam at a time before Eve was even created.[2] It was for this reason that Adam alone was expelled from Eden — not because he had obeyed the serpent, but because he had 'hearkened to the voice of thy wife'.[3] Not until chapter 4 of Genesis do we discover that Eve followed Adam's footsteps out of the garden and, according to the Hebrew *Book of Jubilees*, they 'dwelt in the land of Elda'.[4]

It seems that, having eaten the fruit from the Tree of Knowledge, another of the garden's trees then posed a secondary problem: the Tree of Life. God is said to have banished Adam from the garden 'lest he put forth his hand and take also of the Tree of Life, and eat, and live forever'. Not content with this banishment, a revolving sword of fire was installed to prevent Adam's future access to the tree.[5] To complete the punishment, God said to Eve, 'I will greatly multiply thy sorrow and thy conception; in sorrow thou shalt bring forth children'. Then, even though Adam had not touched the Tree of Life, he was expelled and deprived of its benefits in any event.[6]

What the Genesis narrative concerning Adam and Eve achieves by virtue of the strangely contrived expulsion story is that it sets up women in general as being temptresses, and that Eve's said transgression was to have seduced Adam into her wicked ways. Thus the reasoning is used to establish a male supremacy that pervades the rest of the patriarchal scripture. For her misbehaviour with the fruit, and for daring to influence Adam against God's Will, Eve was told that, henceforth, 'thy husband ... shall rule over thee'.[7]

It is difficult to comprehend, in the context of the Genesis story, quite where the serpent came from. God had apparently created all the beasts and animals before he created Adam. But there is no mention of God making a serpent with the power to oppose him. We are actually told that he created 'everything that creepeth upon the earth', and he 'saw that it was good'.[8] Then, without any explanation, a vociferous serpent appears — an independent creature over which God has absolutely no control.

In order to explain the serpent anomaly, there is a consensus of religious opinion which identifies the serpent with Satan, but this does not emerge from anything written in Genesis. It derives from a much later Islāmic concept from the 7th century AD.[9] *Al-Qur'an* 2:35–39 relates that Adam was created by Allāh (the 'Only God') to be his deputy on Earth, and that the angels were instructed to bow before Adam. They all complied except for Satan, who lured Adam and his wife to eat from the forbidden Tree of Paradise — the tree of transgression.

Prior to the Koran, the Catholic Church Father, St Augustine of Hippo in North Africa (354–430 AD),[10] had pronounced the doctrine of 'Original Sin' which prevails to this day. It maintains that, owing to the transgression of Eve, all people are born in sin by virtue of having mothers! The resultantly inherited sin can only be redeemed by penance and the divine grace of God. The doctrine also holds that, although people have no choice in this, they are still personally responsible for their sinful natures, but can repent for individual sins and thereby gain Church absolution.

Some Calvinist and Lutheran Protestant movements claim that, as a result of the Fall, the ultimate sin of mankind is that of having 'free will' and the ability to choose whether or not to follow in the way of God. This element of 'choice' was confronted by the Catholic Church in its persecution of heretics from medieval times. The word 'heresy' derives from the old Greek *hairesis*, meaning 'choice'. Thus, a charge of heresy was a condemnation of the right of choice — a denial of individual free will.

In consideration of the serpent's Genesis identity (if not created by God), we are reminded of the fact that God was, of course, not alone among the *Elohim*. After Adam had eaten the fruit, God spoke to the serpent, cursing him for his actions,[11] and subsequently announced, 'Behold, the man is become as *one of us*',[12] thereby identifying the said serpent as another god. Given the persistent use of the plural term *elohim* (gods) in Genesis, and since we know that the primary God of Genesis was Enlil, then the chances are that the serpent was representative of his brother Enki. After all, it was Enki (not Enlil) who had actually created the *Adâmu* earthling and imparted to him wisdom and knowledge. The garden of Eden story therefore presents itself as indicative of the ongoing feud over seniority between the *Anannage* brothers. Enlil preferred that those who were created to toil in the garden should be maintained in scholastic ignorance,[13] but Enki was adamant that they should be educated.

The biblical term that became mistranslated to 'serpent' was *nahash*. Before the vowels were added, the original Hebrew stem was *NHSH*, which meant 'to decipher' or 'to find out'.[14] Hence, there was no serpent in the common snake-like sense of the word, and a better interpretation of *NHSH* would relate to a 'wise one'. In fact, this would have been the perfect definition for, in *Anannage* society, the sages were indeed classified as enlightened serpents.[15]

In the first instance, God endeavoured to prevent Adam from gaining any wisdom beyond his required servant status. He therefore warned him away from the Tree of Knowledge, claiming that he would die if he ate its fruit. But the 'wise one' asserted to Eve that this was untrue, and that they should partake of the knowledge: 'Ye shall not surely die, for God doth know that in the day ye eat thereof, then your eyes shall be opened, and ye shall be as *gods*'.[16]

In the event, the *nahash* (wise one) was correct. The man and woman did eat of the tree and they did not die, whereupon the disgruntled God warned Adam away from another tree — the Tree of Life. Then, although not challenged in any way, he still imposed his authority and sent Adam to till the ground as a punishment of servitude for his disobedience.[17]

Apart from being a mischievous scribal device to demonstrate the level of God's authority in any circumstance of his judgement being right or wrong, the only point in mentioning the Tree of Life was to clarify that Adam was denied immortality. It is perhaps significant, however, that the Tree of Life was a feature of the very oldest Sumerian tradition and perhaps too relevant to ignore. More than 2,000 years before Genesis was written, the Tree was mentioned in the foundation cylinder inscriptions of the *Chronicles of Kharsag*,[18] and it was clearly of some traditional relevance to the original Eden project. Eventually, when the second Eden project began at Eridu, the Tree of Life retained its symbolic importance as the sacred vine of dynastic inheritance.

According to the comprehensive *Assyrian Dictionary* of the Oriental Institute, the Tree of Life was recorded by King Etâna of Kish (*c.*3500 BC).[19] He was the second in regnal line from Atabba, and the brother of Henôkh (Enoch) in the Cainite succession. Etâna referred to the Tree of Life as the *Kiskanû Tree*, calling it also the Plant of Birth in the *Tablet of Etâna*.[20]

As we saw in chapter 6, the *Anannage* were not physically immortal, neither did they live for thousands of years as might sometimes appear to be the case. The notion of perpetual existence arose from the 6th-century BC Genesis scribal era, when it was applied to the Israelite God of the Bible. It was henceforth maintained that he is 'from everlasting to everlasting';[21] he 'will endure and his years will have no end'.[22]

By this literary means, the image of the forever-abiding 'one and only' God of Judao–Christianity was born; all competition was deemed cast aside, as was any personal synonymity with any other named god of the era. The fact is however that, by virtue of multiple-writer involvement in the scriptures, there was no cohesive strategy to cement the idea with any convincing finality. With constant regularity, God was presented in the biblical narrative as El Shaddai, El Elyon and El of Bêth-El, leaving absolutely no doubt as to his original identity.

It is fair to say that, throughout 2,500 years of recorded history from that time, there was no way for anyone to know the singular relevance of these titular appellations. But everything changed from the late 19th century when the long-concealed tablets of original Mesopotamian and Canaanite record were finally unearthed once again.

Was the living God who spoke with Adam the same character who met with Abraham 2,000 years later? Was Enki of Eridu the same Enki who had managed the estate at Kharsag 5,000 years earlier? The prospect in either case is extremely unlikely to the point of being beyond reasonable comprehension. The emblematic significance of the Tree of Life was one of seasonal regeneration, with new fruit to replicate and replace the former harvest. As an ever-growing vine, its twigs were reckoned to be the sceptres of succession,[23] and the attribute of its 'immortality' related not to individual perpetuity, but to the dynastic perpetuity of the *Anannage* bloodline. In this same respect, the English word 'clone' derives from the Greek *klon*, meaning 'twig'.

For the duration of the biblical period in question — from the time of Adam to the time of Moses (*c*.4000 – *c*.1400 BC) — there are comparative first-hand records concerning the figure of Enlil (El Shaddai/El Elyon), but they do not apply to the same persistent individual throughout. The dynastic tree remained constant, and the nominal appellations were retained through the generations, but the fruit (by way of successive title holders) was replenished as the generations advanced.

Everything from Nothing

To this point, we have seen that the Genesis scripture, from the Creation and through the account of Adam and Eve, was adapted from ancient Mesopotamian texts concerning the creative pursuits of the *House of Shimtî* and the Eden projects. Relative to what today's people at large believe about earthly creation in general terms, those dubbed Creationists adhere rigidly to Genesis as the absolute authority, whilst Darwinists consider a more natural long-term evolution to be the answer. The concept of Intelligent Design sits somewhere in between and, whilst recognizing the scientific evidence of evolution by way of natural selection, maintains that there are 'missing links' in the chain where aspects of some deliberate intervention are evident.

A variety of different, and at one time seemingly divorced, cultures around the world all have their respective Creation myths — stories of gods and dragons, floods and explosions that relate how everything came from nothing. But, as with the Genesis account, they still rely on the underlying fact that there was something 'at the beginning' (*b'rei-shêeth*), whether determined as God or simply an environment of Chaos. Even the scientifically evaluated Big Bang theory does not explain the beginning of everything — only what happened after the cosmic explosion of already existent matter. In this regard, the science journal *Nature* explains that evidence of heavy elements in the far distant universe indicates the existence of matter prior to the Big Bang.[24] In God-based religious terms, however, the Judaic and subsequently Christian interpretation of Genesis is not the only version of the Creation story. Others exist in Judaic texts outside the Bible and, although having the same central theme, are presented differently.

The *Haggadah*, which forms part of the rabbinical *Midrash* (Inquiry) and derives from the *Talmud* interpretation of Jewish traditions, relates that 'before the Heaven and the Earth, certain other things were created'. One of these is said to have been the *Torah* (the five books of Moses), which God wrote 'with black fire upon white fire' after inventing the alphabet. Other said creations were the divisions of Paradise and Hell, along with the celestial Sanctuary in which God placed his throne, an altar and a divine jewel.[25]

The *Torah* then becomes God's female source of inspiration, and he consults her about the creation of the world as described in the very text he had apparently written himself. *Torah* is not too excited about the idea, and she responds that men are too sinful to contemplate. But the *Torah* is already written, and God must adhere to the script; so he creates the world. But, in creating sinful mankind, God also introduces the notion of 'atonement' for those who are loyal to his decrees. We then discover that God and *Torah* are not alone; there are also angels in existence, and it is with their help that everything else, including the creation of Adam and Eve, is accomplished.

The Slavonic book of *The Secrets of Enoch* provides another Creation story. (This work is known as 2-Enoch, as distinct from the *Book of Enoch* [1-Enoch] that we have previously discussed.) It opens with God explaining: 'First I created all things from non-existence to existence, and from invisible into visible. And I have not informed my angels of my secrets, nor of their origins'.[26] The following narrative then moves disconcertingly into the strangest of all Creation lore, and to the introduction of an unfathomable character found in no other account. Explaining his secrets of Creation, God states:

> I commanded the great Idiol to come forth, having a great stone in his belly. And I spoke to him: 'Burst asunder Idiol, and let the visible be born from you'. And he burst asunder. A great stone came out of him, bearing all creation, which I had wished to create.

Sons of God

One of the most enigmatic entries in the Old Testament comes from Genesis 6:1–4, which states,

> And it came to pass, when men began to multiply on the face of the earth, and daughters were born unto them, that the sons of God saw the daughters of men that they were fair; and they took them for wives all of which they chose ... And there were giants in the earth in those days; and also after that, when the sons of God came in unto the daughters of men, and they bare children to them, the same became mighty men which were of old, men of renown.

Although this passage contains the specific definition of *nephilim* in the Hebrew scripture,[27] the word has been converted in English texts to 'giants'. This doubtless occurred because there was no single-word translation for *nephilim*, and the translators had been provided with 'giants' as a possible alternative by Flavius Josephus in his 1st-century *Antiquities of the Jews*. He explained that these godly sons (the *bene ha-elohim*) 'begat sons that became unjust on account of the confidence they had in their own strength; for the tradition is that these men did what resembled the acts of those whom the Grecians call giants'.[28] Josephus did not actually claim that the *nephilim* were giants. Referring to the mythological Titans, he said only that their strength resembled 'those whom the Grecians call giants'. The word *nephilim* actually relates to 'those who came down' or 'those who descended'.[29]

Given that the *bene ha-elohim* were reputed to have caused their own dishonour by consorting with earthly women, they were said in the *Book of Enoch* to have fallen from grace.[30] The word 'fallen' was perceived to be in keeping with the word *nephilim* (those who descended), and since the 'sons of God' had been identified as angels (*aggelos*) in the Greek *Septuagint*, a wholly new breed of beings emerged in writings outside the Bible. They were the 'fallen angels'.

The strangely isolated fragment of information in Genesis, concerning the *bene ha-elohim* and the daughters of men, is related to nothing that comes directly before or after it. But, as in the *Book of Enoch*, it was a theme taken up in non-canonical works. (Since *elohim* is a plural noun, *bene ha-elohim* actually means 'sons of the gods' — not 'sons of God' as given in the familiar Genesis translation.)

Because of the general ambiguity of the Genesis entry, it is not absolutely clear whether the *nephilim* and the *bene ha-elohim* were one and the same. Neither is it clear whether the *bene ha-elohim* were synonymous with angels as the *Septuagint* suggests. It is evident, however, that the *Book of Enoch* identifies them with a group of beings called 'watchers', who are also mentioned in the Old Testament book of Daniel. *Enoch* further explains that the watchers were indeed those same deiform beings who had mated with the earthly women,[31] while in Daniel we learn that the watchers were akin to the *nephilim* who 'came down':

> Behold, a watcher and an holy one came down
> from heaven.[32]
> The king saw a watcher and an holy one coming
> down from heaven.[33]

The Hebrew *Book of Jubilees* states that Enoch 'was the first one from among the children of men that are born on the Earth to learn writing and the knowledge of wisdom — and he wrote the signs of heaven'.[34] These signs are described as being the 'science of the watchers', which had been carved on a rock in distant times,[35] and the *Book of Enoch* explains that the watchers were the 'holy angels who watch'.[36]

The singular form of *nephilim* is *nephil*, and it is of interest to note that although the term — or at least its vowel-free Semitic root, NFL ('cast down') — was used in the Hebrew editions of Genesis, it is rendered as 'watcher' in Daniel (written around 400 years after Genesis, in *c*.165 BC).[37] Similarly, the books of *Enoch* and *Jubilees* both use the term 'watchers' instead of *nephilim*.

From the 1st century BC comes a text known as the *Damascus Document*, found among the Dead Sea Scrolls. In this manuscript, the fallen angel, watcher and giant classifications are all brought together:

I will uncover your eyes... that you may not be
drawn by thoughts of the guilty inclination and by
lustful eyes. For many went astray because of this
... The watchers of heaven fell because of this ...
And their sons as tall as cedar trees, whose bodies
were like mountains.[38]

Such notions as these are indicative of the way that original
concepts and meanings grew ever further removed from their
formative bases as the centuries passed. In the 6th century BC, the
exiled Israelites had written an adaptation of their ancestral
history from Babylonian records. Having also discovered an
ancient *Book of the Law* (as detailed in 2 Kings 22:8), they were
further enabled to cement the rules of their religious doctrine
from a fairly comprehensive literary base. By the 2nd century BC,
additional books were being compiled, not necessarily with
history in mind, but with a view to adding a mythological aspect
in keeping with the prevailing Greco-Alexandrian culture. This
was certainly a romantic age, but in adding the romance a good
deal of history became veiled so that the original *nephilim*
or 'watchers' (by whichever name) became misidentified as
heavenly angels fallen from grace.

In the first instance, they could not have been physically so far
removed (if indeed removed at all) from ordinary mortals, given
that they mated so easily with everyday women. And it takes
very little research to discover that the Watchers were simply an
order of craftsmen and surveyors, whose guild leaders were
admonished for allowing weapons to be brought into the Eden
agricultural settlement.[39] Being banished from a mountain
plateau is hardly the same as falling headlong from heaven.

Rule of Succession

From the opening sequences of Genesis, which detail the Creation
and the story of Eden, God becomes almost incidental for a good
while. Apart from his involvements with the Flood and the Tower

of Babel, Genesis is mainly concerned with documenting the saga of an earthly family descending from Adam to Abraham.

Continuing the story of Adam and Eve, Genesis 4:1–2 describes that, after leaving the garden of Eden, Eve bore two sons, namely Cain (Qayîn) and Abel (Hevhel). It is explained that Cain, the elder brother, was a 'tiller of the ground', and that Abel was a 'keeper of sheep'. Once again, however, we are in a realm of misinterpretation. The text should actually read that Cain had 'dominion over the earth',[40] and that Abel was 'a shepherd'.

The term 'shepherd' was customarily used in ancient Sumer to represent a princely status, as defined by the shepherd-king Dumuzi, a grandson of Enlil who reigned before the Flood. Earthly kingship was established by the *Anannage* as a hallowed employment, with the kings and princes being the designated 'guardians of their flocks' — Lugal-banda the shepherd, King Etâna the shepherd, and so forth.[41] The same terminology was biblically applied to God: 'The Lord is my shepherd' (Psalm 23:1), and to Jesus: 'I am the good shepherd' (John 10:11). As we have seen, however, the true course of kingly inheritance was reckoned to prevail as a matrilineal institution. Being the first son of Eve, Cain had the senior claim in this regard, and the entitlement to reign was deemed his as a birthright.

In Genesis 4:8–10 we read that when Cain and Abel were in the field, Cain 'rose up against Abel his brother, and slew him'. The word that led in translation to a concept of slaying was *yaqam*, but the text should convey that Cain was 'elevated' (raised or exalted) above Abel.[42] The *yaqam* terminology that Cain 'rose up' is correctly used in the English translation, but in quite the wrong context. In practice, he rose up 'above' his brother, not 'against' him. This misunderstanding fuelled the concept that Abel was slain, whereas it should read that he was 'shattered' by Cain's reaction.[43]

Abel's bloodright was junior to that of Cain in the same way that, in a subsequent generation, Jacob's inheritance was junior to that of his brother Esau. In this later instance, Esau sold his senior birthright to Jacob,[44] but Cain retained his right to succession, which exalted him above Abel. It seems, however, that Cain wanted both the kingly status and the accolade for his offering to the Lord. In anger for having his veneration rejected, he withdrew his brother's bloodright to fraternal protection, and 'The Lord said ... thy brother's blood crieth unto me from the ground'.[45]

As a punishment for his selfish action, God admonished Cain and exiled him to the land of Nod.[46] In this sequence, the relevance of Cain's high standing is again brought into play when the Lord explains that, should anyone slay Cain, 'vengeance shall be taken upon him sevenfold. And the Lord set a mark upon Cain lest any man finding him should kill him'. According to Professor Ephraim A Speiser, past Chairman of the Baghdad School of Oriental Research, the land of Nod (*nôdh*) was not so much a place as a state of being — an environment of wandering and restless uncertainty.[47]

The question might well be posed as to who the Lord feared might want to kill Cain, given that he and his parents were (according to biblical lore) the only living beings at that stage. Who could these potential enemies possibly have been? But the question only arises because of latter-day scriptural interpretation. In more ancient times the Eden symbolism would have been fully understood in the context of its Sumerian establishment.

As for the enigmatic mark placed upon Cain, this is reckoned to be the oldest recorded grant of arms in sovereign history. In the Hebrew and Phoenician traditions, the 'mark of Cain' is defined as being a centred cross within a circle. The same mark was placed on the foreheads of the righteous few of Jerusalem in Ezekiel 9:4–6.[48] It was, in principle, a graphic representation of 'the kingdom', which Hebrews called the *malkhut* (from the Akkadian word *malkû*, meaning 'sovereign').[49]

The Curious Wife

The story of Cain then takes an almighty leap in Genesis 4:17, when it is stated that he had a wife. Once again, this is contrary to the preceding account that there were no other people on Earth apart from the Adamite family. In reality, there were plenty of others around and, as we have seen, Adam and Eve were not the first people; they were only the first of a kind. In this regard, an important aspect of sovereign inheritance, which became a basis for widespread dynastic culture thereafter, was that a man could not be a king without a queen, and the queen had to be of the royal blood.[50] In Cain's situation — since his parents were the first of a kind — this could mean only one thing: his wife would need to be the offspring of at least one of them. This poses the question: Did Adam or Eve have a daughter?

Genesis 4:25 tells that Eve had a third son called Seth. Then, along with the mention of other sons, Genesis 5:4 does indeed state that Adam also had daughters independently of Eve.

Genesis does not give the name of Cain's wife, but the *Book of Jubilees*[51] identifies her as Awân.[52] A Syriac work entitled *The Book of Adam and Eve* additionally relates that Awân was called the *Luluwa* (meaning 'beautiful').[53] This now leads to another anomaly which contradicts the Genesis portrayal: If Awân's mother was not Eve, then who could she have been?

In the Hebrew tradition of the *Talmud* (a codification of Jewish law),[54] Adam's daughter Awân is said to have been a daughter of a demi-goddess called Lilith. This is an extraordinary revelation which provides a direct link to the original Sumerian pantheon. Lilith was a great-granddaughter of Enlil and Nînlil. Her name derives from the Akkadian *lilutu*, meaning 'wind spirit', and she is identified in the *Talmud* as Adam's first consort, before Eve. Hence, we now have further proof that the *Anannage* descent was indeed recognized by the Israelite scribes even though they veiled the information in their official scripture.

A Conflict of Names

The Genesis verses then move to the descendants of Cain and Awân, beginning with their son Enoch. This brings to light an intriguing series of duplications in the Bible's given descents from Cain[55] and from his younger brother Seth.[56] Beginning with Adam, the comparative biblical lists read:

Adam	Adam
Cain	Seth
Enoch	Enos
Irad (Jared)	Cainan
Mehujael	Mahalaleel
Methusael	Jared
Lamech	Enoch
Tubalcain	Methuselah
	Lamech
	Noah

There is, of course, no reason why popular names of the day should not appear in both lists, but they do conveniently both lead to a Lamech. In terms of the pre-patriarchal strain, it is the Sethian line which is subsequently progressed through Noah down to Abraham. But, apart from some reference to three sons and a daughter of Lamech in the Cainite succession, this senior strain of descent is sidelined thereafter in the Bible.

As related in the *Anchor Bible's* rendering of Genesis (a 1950s translation from the Hebrew text by Professor EA Speiser), the two lists were 'ultimately derived from the same distant source', and linguistic scholars are agreed that the Cainite and Sethian aspects of Genesis are by two different writers.[57] 'The entry of Methusael (*Mutu-sa-ili*) in the succession from Cain is distinctly Akkadian, and therefore much older than the Hebrew variant of Methuselah in the other list from Seth'. Speiser's report continues:

> It would thus appear that before they reached the Hebrews, these entries had gone through a secondary centre of dissemination, where they were transformed in accordance with local needs and conditions ... The biblical writers were intent on tracing the generations between Adam and Noah.

Under these circumstances, even if Seth's early descendants were entirely fictitious, as seems to be the case, it would have been

121

easier for the Genesis compilers to have dispensed with the brief Cain genealogy altogether. That way, the anomaly would not have become evident. Its importance, however, was in documenting Lamech and his son Tubalcain the artificer who could not be ignored.[58] Tubalcain's name was entrenched in philosophical lore as the founder of advanced metallurgy, and is still featured as such in Freemasonry to this day. Along with their ancestor Cain, Tubalcain and his brothers were revered as 'master craftsmen'. As the *Anchor Bible* explains, 'This line cannot be divorced from the *Sumerian King List*', and Tubalcain's father, Lamech (Amalek, Amalak or Akalam), was historically listed as King Akalem of Ur, *c*.3200 BC.[59]

Even if there were some genealogical merit to a parallel Sethian descent, the senior line from Cain was necessarily of far greater significance, descending through the kings of Kish to the kingdom of Ur. Nevertheless, although detailing the initial Cainite dynasts, the Bible writers then elected to ignore the continuing line by switching the biblical emphasis to a contrived parallel descent from Seth. Resultantly, Seth's line became the promoted ancestral strain of Abraham. But, as we saw earlier in chapter 3, Abraham was recorded as descending from King Ur-Nammu, whose own heritage was Cainite, not Sethian.

In consideration of a motive for taking this approach, the only reason for introducing the spurious line from Seth must have been to accommodate an entirely fictitious character whose name does not appear in the legitimate checkable listing. That being the case, then the primary candidate for scribal invention can only have been Noah. For all his seeming importance in the biblical narrative as a son of Lamech, Noah has absolutely no documentary provenance outside the Bible. Since his scriptural relevance is primarily concerned with the Flood, it is with this event that we should expect to find a major contradiction between historical record and the Genesis portrayal.

9

ANNALS OF THE DELUGE

A Final Test

For a while, as Genesis takes us through the early descendants from Adam, God does not feature too much in the narrative. But he is back with a vengeance at the time of Noah, following the entry concerning the sons of the gods and the daughters of men. From the way in which this anomalous Bible sequence is worded, it is difficult to imagine that the earthly daughters would have had much choice against the *nephilim*. The behavioural fault would appear to have rested squarely with these so-called 'giants' but, for some inexplicable reason, God then decided to punish all mankind. In a fit of unprecedented anger, he proclaimed that practically all the people, animals and birds on Earth must perish:

> And God saw that the wickedness of man was great in
> the earth ... And the Lord said I will destroy man
> whom I have created from the face of the earth; both
> man and beast, and the creeping thing, and the fowls
> of the air.[1]

Noah, his wife, their sons and their wives were then singled out to be the only human survivors of a devastating global flood. God instructed Noah to build a huge floating ark, into which he should herd seven male and female pairs of every clean animal and fowl, and two male and female pairs of every unclean beast.[2] Beyond these, God announced that he would 'destroy all flesh, wherein is the breath of life, from under heaven; and everything that is in the earth shall die'.[3]

No good reason is given as to why Noah and his family had been especially chosen to survive,[4] but the deluge came, and it rained for forty days and forty nights. The waters then prevailed for 150 days, at the end of which everyone else on Earth was dead. The ark was stranded upon the mountains of Ararat, and God said to Noah and his sons, 'Be fruitful and multiply'.[5] The suggested inference here is that, from that point in time, every person on Earth has been a descendant of Noah!

We know from the *Sumerian King List* that there were kings before the flood and after the flood. In fact, a good deal of Mesopotamian historical record is concerned with the separate antediluvian and post-diluvian periods, and there is no doubt that a major disaster did indeed take place on the Tigris and Euphrates flood plains. Even if not on a world scale as portrayed in Genesis, it was clearly of great consequence in the land of the two rivers, and was featured at length in subsequent *cuneiform* tablet epics from Sumer, Akkad and Babylonia.

In the knowledge that Noah (by virtue of the fabricated biblical line of his descent) was most likely a fictitious character, there is a chance here to test, as a measure of final confirmation, that Enlil of the *Anannage* and the God of Genesis were indeed one and the same.

The Confirmation

According to Genesis, God brought about the Flood purposely, and with foresight, as a means of mass annihilation because the people had offended him. We can therefore consult the Sumerian, Akkadian and Babylonian Flood records with a specific objective in mind: Might there have been a similar reasoning offered in respect of Enlil and the Mesopotamian deluge?

Given that the Noah account is very detailed in Genesis, the various records can be cross-referenced for other similarities, beginning perhaps with the most obvious of all questions: Was there, in the Mesopotamian flood accounts, an original Noah archetype who was instructed to build a boat of salvation? Was there a man whose identity could be lost to biblical history if he were supplanted by a fictional substitute? The answer to these questions is an unqualified 'Yes':

> Man of Shuruppak, son of Ubar-Tutu,
> Tear down thy house; build a ship.
> Abandon thy possessions, and seek thou life.
> Discard thy goods, and keep thee alive.
> Aboard the ship take the seed of living things.[6]

The 'Man of Shuruppak', as cited, was called Ziusudra. The *Sumerian King List* identifies that his father 'Ubar-Tutu reigned in Shuruppak when the flood swept thereover'.[7] The date was around 4000 BC, and it is evident that, unlike the probability for Noah, he was a real historical figure of ancient Sumer.

The oldest known direct reference to Ziusudra and the Flood comes from a Sumerian poem entitled *The Deluge*. Fragments of the 350-line tablet from the 3rd millennium BC were unearthed at Nippur in 1893, and are now held, along with the *Chronicles of Kharsag*, at the University of Pennsylvania Museum.[8]

Embodied within a compilation known as the *Eridu Genesis*, the verses explain that the Flood was decreed by certain overlords of the *Anannage* Grand Assembly:

> A decision that the seed of mankind is to be destroyed has been made. The verdict, the word of the divine assembly, cannot be revoked.

The incomplete tablet does not include the reason for the Assembly decision, but clarifies that it was individually pronounced by An and Enlil. In opposition was Nîn-kharsag, who was said to have deplored the idea. So too did Enki, who commissioned Ziusudra to preserve the 'seed of mankind' in a specially constructed boat.[9]

A later and more complete Akkadian text, called the *Atrahasis Epic*, offers rather more information concerning the decision to flood the land. A very distinct Genesis parallel is now evident in that the primary instigator of the Assembly decision is positively identified as Enlil.

The Ziusudra figure is now the *atra-hasis* (the 'extremely wise one') of Shuruppak, and the story is much as in *The Deluge* account. Enki suggests that Ziusudra should construct a boat to escape the flood planned by Enlil to destroy the seed of mankind. Just as God is said to have been offended in Genesis, it is explained that Enlil was similarly annoyed by the Sumerian people — not so much because of any wickedness, but because of their unruly behaviour and incessant noise.[10] Various disciplinary measures had failed and, in final desperation, Enlil decided that wholesale extermination by flood was the solution.[11]

Copies of *Atrahasis* have been found in Nineveh and in the Ugarit library of Canaan. Written by priests of Enki in denial of Enlil's fraternal seniority, the text is noticeably directed against Enlil in contrast to the generally benevolent image conveyed by the Nippur scribes of his own following.

The most complete and comprehensive version of the Flood saga comes from twelve Babylonian clay tablets, known overall as the *Epic of Gilgamesh*.[12] These were found in the middle 19th century among the Nineveh library ruins of King Ashurbanipal of Assyria. Since then, some older tablets have come to light in Ashur and Hattusas.[13] They relate to the mythical adventures of Gilgamesh, King of Uruk in about 2650 BC. In the course of his exploits, Gilgamesh travels back in time to meet with the long-dead Uta-Napishtim of Shuruppak (an alternative Akkadian name for Ziusudra), who gives him an account of the deluge.

The *Epic of Gilgamesh* Flood sequence was extracted from *Atrahasis* with numerous embellishments that transformed a regional calamity into a perceived global disaster. Other items, ultimately reiterated in the Genesis version, were also included — for example, the boat of Uta-Napishtim was said to have come to rest on a mountain. When the storm had abated, Uta-Napishtim sent forth a dove to check if there was any dry land beyond the mountain, but the dove returned. Eventually, when he sent out a raven that did not return, he knew that the flood-waters were subsiding. A near replicated version of this sequence with the dove and the raven appears in Genesis 8:7–12, thereby reinforcing the fact that the more lately written biblical story of Noah was adapted, with a newly devised central character, from the Babylonian text of the *Epic of Gilgamesh*.

Added to the Bible's regular use of Enlil's traditional appellations — El Shaddai, El Elyon and El of Bêth-El — we now have incontrovertible proof that the God of Genesis was indeed Enlil, president of the Grand Assembly of the *Anannage*. The scribal changing of Ziusudra's name to that of a fictitious Noah, in order to veil the fact, has succeeded through 2,500 years, but has achieved nothing in the ultimate long term. The formative tablets of ancient record, as consulted by the Bible writers in the 6th century BC, have now been rediscovered, transcribed, translated and placed on public display for all to see.

The Royal Seed

The original Sumerian *Deluge* saga has one particular feature which separates it entirely from the later 'animals in pairs' imagery of the Noah's Ark story. It does not portray Ziusudra as the saviour of a menagerie, but as the preserver of 'the seed of mankind'.[14] He was also instructed to take aboard his ship 'the seed of living things'. Similarly, the *Gilgamesh* account states that Enki had told Ziusudra (Uta-Napishtim) to build an enclosed ship in which he should convey 'the seed of living creatures'.[15]

In all instances, the operative word is 'seed' and, from the conjoined accounts, we learn that Ziusudra's boat (unlike Noah's Ark) was not a floating zoo for the salvation of living creatures. It was a clinical container vessel for the seeds of human and animal life in storage.

The ancient *Deluge* text relates that Ziusudra did take a few animals into his boat, but it specifies only an ox and a sheep, along with some other beasts and fowl. These were taken aboard for food provision, not to preserve the species. Indeed, the tablets identify that, although the flood was devastating in terms of land and property, there were plenty of survivors apart from Ziusudra.

What we have here is something that really cements the essence of the Genesis story of Adam and Eve into place once the Flood is viewed in its proper context. In all three portrayals of the characters involved in the event, the key opponents of the

Assembly were two of its most senior councillors: Enki and Nîn-kharsag. It was they who ran the *House of Shimtî* for genetic research within the second Eden project. It was the laboratory content of their work that needed the protection of Ziusudra's boat. And it was directly after the Flood that their most urgent and important *in vitro* fertilization work began, leading to the creation of Adam and Eve.

In this latter regard, we now discover another reason for the biblical switch of emphasis from Ziusudra to Noah. In the manipulated Genesis account, the Flood is set nine generations after Adam, rather than before his time as detailed in the Mesopotamian records. Had the story been conveyed in proper chronological sequence, there would have been no way for the Israelite scribes to assert that Adam was the first man on Earth.

* * *

By comparison with other scripturally identifiable stories within Genesis, a remarkable amount of space is given to the Flood, which occupies no fewer than 80 verses. Strategically placed, it constitutes a significant break-point in the early narrative by drawing a distinct biblical line under the Eden and Mesopotamian section before Genesis moves into a further genealogical sequence, leading to the story of Abraham's migration into Canaan.

The introduction of Noah and the lengthy flood story at this stage appears to have been a diversionary tactic by the Genesis scribes in order to break the generational sequence at a point where the line down to Abraham could be conveniently diverted through a spurious family succession. Following a total of four dramatic chapters devoted to tales of Noah and his sons,[16] it would be easy for the reader to forget the duplicity of the two different family listings down to Lamech.

It is expressly relevant that, when referencing the Cainite succession to Lamech and Tubalcain (*see* table in chapter 8), the descriptive commentary in the Hebrew *Anchor Bible* explains that this line cannot be divorced from the *Sumerian King List*.[17]

This being the case, then Abraham's own Sumerian royal descent from King Ur-Nammu (*c.*2113–2096 BC) — as detailed in the Hebrew *Book of Jubilees*[18] — falls into a more logical frame. Being a cousin of King Ibbi-Sin of Ur (as discussed in chapter 3), Abraham would undoubtedly have been of Cainite descent. So why would the scribes have attached him to a fabricated Sethian line that was contrived for the sole purpose of accommodating Noah in an untraceable genealogy? Why relegate the ultimate patriarch of the Hebrew nation to a position of heritable inconsequence when the truth is both traceable and impressive?

Philosophical Judaism suggests that the answer lies in the nature of scriptural understanding by way of linguistic intent. As we heard before from professor of Hebrew, Robert Alter, 'English translations have placed readers at a grotesque distance from the distinctive literary experience of the Bible in its original language'.[19] Do we read what the Bible says, or do we see what we expect it to say?

In the opening verse of Genesis 4, it is written that Eve said to Adam, 'I have gotten a man from the Lord'. Other translatory variants are: 'I have got me a man with the Lord', and 'I have acquired a man from the Lord'. The text then relates that this newly-begotten man (Eve's first son) was Cain. Subsequently, Eve gave birth to a second son named Abel, and then a third named Seth.

The Jewish *Midrash* (meaning Inquiry), a traditional commentary on the Bible, emphasizes the point, as stated, that Eve's first son was the 'son of the Lord', whereas the second son was the 'son of Adam'. When defining 'the Lord' in this instance, however, the *Midrash* invokes the name of Sāma-El (Lord of Sāma — i.e. Samael). This was a customary style, reckoned to identify the serpent who seduced Eve into transgression with the fruit of Eden. But more than that, Samael, by way of that seduction, was the father of Cain.[20]

From this reasoning, although Cain and Abel were both sons of Eve, only Abel and subsequently Seth were the sons of Adam. Since Adam, according to Genesis, was the 'first man' of God's creation, and the necessary progenitor of the patriarchal strain, then Abraham must be seen as a descendant of Adam. Thus, the spurious Sethian line was contrived to include both Noah and Abraham, whilst the Cainite descent from Eve and Samael was listed in brief (through Enoch, Lamech and Tubalcain), and then completely ignored thereafter. The implied reasoning was that the Cainite dynasty, fathered by Samael, was evil.

In terms of historical record, the underlying principle of the reckoning concerning Eve and Samael, might not be so far from the truth if, as previously discussed, the *nahash* ('wise one') of the garden was a figurative representation of Enlil's brother Enki. In fact, we are now in a position to assert that contention. Sāma was a kingdom to the east of Haran in northern Mesopotamia, and the Lord of Sāma (the Sāma-El) was indeed none other than Enki, whose Sumerian emblem was a coiled serpent.

It is entirely possible that laboratory development by Enki and Nîn-kharsag at the *House of Shimtî* was progressed beyond the point of Adam and Eve. If Eve's fertile ovum were further enriched by Enki's *Anannage* blood to result in the birth of Cain, then Cain would have emerged as the most advanced product of the royal seed.

A Line of Kings

In 1854, JE Taylor, a British Consul in Iraq, conducted an investigative mission for the Foreign Office at the great desert mound known as *Tell al Muqayyar* (Mound of Pitch) north of Basra. Discovered a little below the summit was an old building but, being archaeologically unqualified, Taylor and his digging gang managed to demolish completely the top tier of the structure before they realized what it was.

It was not until 1915 that the true significance of the site became evident when a British Museum official was stationed with Intelligence staff in Iraq during the First World War. It was he, R Campbell Thompson, who took another look at the mound and determined its considerable importance. Some very old texts, engraved on stone cylinders, had been brought back to England by Taylor, and one of these cylinder-seals had revealed the name of King Ur-Nammu, who had reigned around 2100 BC in Ur. In the light of this, it was considered that *Tell al Muqayyar* might well be the long-sought location of Ur — the biblical city of Abraham as identified in Genesis 11:31. Consequently, in 1923, the anthropologist Sir Charles Leonard Woolley, with a joint team from the British Museum and the University of Pennsylvania, set out to excavate the gigantic mound.

As Woolley's team struck deep into the hill, they discovered a series of large constructions, five of which were revealed to be temples, around which were various other buildings, including residential accommodation. Each of the fine houses had an integral paved court with surrounding rooms, and fountains fed by bitumen-clad water troughs were found intact, as were a variety of ovens and large brick tables. On rekindling one of the ancient ovens, Woolley wrote in his diary, 'We were able to light the fire again, and put into commission once more the oldest kitchen in the world'.[21]

The main temple shrine within the massive *Tell al Muqayyar* crowned a four-storey building with flat terraces surrounding the core constructions on each upper level. The rising platforms were consecutively reduced in size to form a staged pyramid, with outside stairs leading from one level to the next. Woolley had found the great *ziggurat* temple of Inanna on whose model the later Tower of Babel, with its magnificent hanging gardens, was based. It was ascertained that the earlier hanging gardens of Ur had been constructed upon gigantic arches, 75 feet (23 m) high, and were watered from the River Euphrates by way of a complicated mechanical system. The base wall of the Ur *ziggurat* stands about 50 feet high (around 16.5 m), and the whole tower reached about 75 feet as per the arches. The lower two sections were black, and the upper stage red, whilst the topmost shrine was faced with blue glazed tiles and crowned with a canopy of gold. These colours in a rising sequence represented the dark Netherworld, the habitable Earth, the sky and the sun.

Within the overall complex were found the preserved remains of offices, factories, warehouses, shops, hospitals, law courts and schools. Not only that, but a good deal of the old documentation was still extant: lawyers' records, taxation records, mill-owners' records, shopkeepers' records, educational records, medical records, even fashion-house records, all in the unique Sumerian style of wedge-shaped *cuneiform* writing. Additionally, mathematical calculators were found, including complex tables for extracting square and cube roots, and triangular formulae as manifest in the Alexandrian mathematics of Euclid, who lived some 1,700 years later.[22]

The Anglo-American excavations continued year upon year, and eventually the whole city of Ur began to appear within great walls of baked brick 26 feet (*c.*8.5 m) high and 77 feet (*c.*25.5 m) thick at the base. There were rows of impressive houses with streets between them − mansions of the utmost luxury, as described in chapter 3.

As if such monumental discoveries were not enough, there was more to follow. When the team investigated beneath the foundations of the 4,000 year-old *ziggurat* and its confines, they found the remains of another great *ziggurat*, and another buried city from even more ancient times,[23] with courtyard mud-bricks dating back to the 4th millennium BC. Also, there were graves and artefacts from around 3700 BC,[24] along with numerous archaeologically valuable items from a far more distant era. They even discovered a kingly burial ground, together with documentary records and cultural treasures unsurpassed in all Egypt before that time. Here was proof of the world's oldest and greatest civilization − a highly advanced culture which had existed for nearly 1,000 years before the ancient Egyptian civilization began.

Six years after beginning their excavations, Woolley's archaeologists found an intriguing complex of ancient graves dating to about 3500 BC, including a stone-built tomb of unusual significance. On entering the tomb, the men were confronted by treasures such as they had never seen.[25] There were golden goblets, fine ornaments decorated with red stones and *lapis lazuli* (a deep blue mineral), bronze tableware, silver jewellery, mother-of-pearl mosaics, and exquisite shell-decorated harps and lyres. There was a magnificent chariot with the golden heads of lions and bulls, along with vessels of silver, alabaster, copper and marble. They unearthed tools and weapons made of gold, and all manner of wonderful relics to equal the splendour of the Egyptian tomb of Tutankhamun from 1,600 years later.

Round and about, soldiers were buried with ornamental helmets, spears and shields of copper, silver and gold. And there were the remains of ladies in crimson robes, with ornate head-dresses, golden earrings and silver combs. These many attendants were the staff and guardians of the first tomb, which was found to be that of Queen Shub-ad, who reigned before the earliest dynasty of Egypt. Nearby was the grave of her royal husband Prince Abar-gi.

Abar-gi's remains had been badly wrecked in times long gone, but Shub-ad's were quite unmoved. She lay in state on a golden bier with a gold cup by her hand, and two maid-servants who had been kneeling at her side. Shub-ad's body had been lavishly adorned with a beaded cloak of gold, silver, *lapis lazuli*, agate, carnelian and chalcedony (types of quartz). On her arms were gold and silver amulets representing fish and gazelles, and her headdress was an exquisite wreath of golden beech and willow leaves.

In all, sixteen opulent royal tombs were found, one of which bore the inscription, 'Mes-kalam-dug, *lugal* [king]'. Another inscription, on a golden bowl within, identified him as the 'Hero of the Good Land'. Amid the fineries of his tomb was the most magnificent example of the ancient goldsmith's art ever found — a helmet of beaten gold, moulded to fit with cheek-pieces to protect the face. This relic, now well over 5,000 years old and held in the Baghdad Museum, is in the form of a wig, parted in the middle with locks of hair in wonderful relief, falling in wavy tresses and bound with a twisted fillet to form curls around the perfectly shaped ears. Even individual hairs are delicately engraved within the separated locks, and it is all made from one sheet of 15-carat electrum gold.

Here was not only a king from before the 1st dynasty of Egypt, but a king who, as explained in the *Sumerian King List*, reigned before the 1st dynasty of Ur.[26] But there was a more exciting discovery yet to come. An adjacent tomb was found to be the grave of Mes-kalam-dug's father, whose name was given on his cylinder-seal as 'Akalem-dug, *lugal'*. These two great kings of the world's oldest royal cemetery, buried along with their court treasures and courtiers, were more than just monarchs, they had been regarded as god-kings[27] and, as we saw in our previous chapter, King Akalem of Ur was the biblical Lamech (Amalek) in the Cainite succession.

The helmet of King Mes-kalam-dug is a unique example of the art of Tubalcain, the 'master craftsman' of Lamech's family, and this poses an intriguing possibility. According to the *Sumerian King List*, King Mes-[...] reigned for 36 years and was recorded as having been a 'smith'.[28] This is precisely what the name, or term, Cain (Quaîn) meant in biblical Hebrew: a 'smith' or metal-worker.[29] *Tubalcain* is not actually a name at all; it is a craft distinction relating to a metallurgical artificer or master metal-smith[30] and, since Mes-kalam-dug was the son of King Akalem, then he emerges most probably as the great Tubalcain himself.[31]

Discovering the Flood

At this stage, the archaeologists had excavated down to more than 1,700 years before the time of Abraham, and back more than 1,000 years beyond the supposed time of Noah, but so far they had come across no sign of any flood. Having found the royal burial ground, they continued to dig into the past, determined to discover what lay beneath. Shafts were sunk through dozens of feet of rubble until they came upon wood-ash and numerous inscribed clay tablets. They struck down still further, pulling up pieces of pottery and various household items until, at length, they appeared to have hit solid ground. They were at the very bottom — or so they thought.

Woolley then took himself into the depths of the pit, and there to his astonishment he found that he was not standing upon bedrock, but on solid clay — a type of clay that could only have been deposited by water.[32] His first thought was that, since Ur

was closer to the coast in olden times, this must be the accumulated silt of the early Euphrates delta. But a ground-study of the
surrounding area led to a quite different conclusion. Such a
concept was impossible for, even having dug down so deeply
through the mound, they were still higher than the river-bed of
the Euphrates. So they kept on digging. Down they went through
more than 8 feet (c.2.5 m) of clay, and then quite suddenly it
ended as abruptly as it had begun.

What they came upon was pure virgin soil — the kind that
would have been the perfect ground for irrigation when the land
was rich and fertile before turning into desert. Then came further
evidence of human habitation — pottery, jars, bowls and the like.
Beneath the great thickness of the water-borne clay belt was yet
another settlement, and when the clay was analysed it was found
to contain the fossils of marine life from a time when the sea had
flooded the whole area. The levels of strata were examined and,
like all geological structures, they provided their own calendar.[33]
The bed of clay had been laid down over the old settlement in
about 4000 BC, and Woolley sent a telegram to London: 'We have
found the Flood'.

Subsequently, other archaeologists conducted surveys in
various parts of the Tigris and Euphrates valleys and, a good way
north-west of Ur at Kish near Babylon, the clay was found
reduced to a thickness of 18 inches (46 cm), but it was still a
consistent layer. Overall, the flood was reckoned to have covered
an area of 400 miles (644 km) north to south, and 100 miles
(161 km) west to east.

The grave of Mes-kalam-dug was dated at around 3500 BC.
Some generations earlier, figures such as Ziusudra and Atabba
(the Adâmu) had been prominent in Shuruppak and Kish — and
the Mesopotamian flood layer was also from this earlier period.
But, according to Genesis, Noah lived nine generations after
Adam!

Clearly, as is already evident from The Deluge and the Epic of
Gilgamesh, Noah was not in any way connected with the region's
catastrophic deluge; he had been biblically grafted into the
context of a much earlier historical event. The Mesopotamian

texts place the Flood before the time of Adam, and it was as a result of the disaster that the *House of Shimtî* project was begun by Enki and Nîn-kharsag, leading to the emergence of Adam and Eve. As related in the *Atrahasis Epic,* the clinical process involved the surrogate wombs of 'women who had survived the deluge'.

Part IV

God of the Covenant

10

INTO CANAAN

A Nonsensical Curse

Following the lengthy flood saga, Genesis 9:8–17 relates that God established a covenant with Noah and his sons. He proclaimed that 'the waters shall no more become a flood to destroy all flesh', and decreed that he would establish his rainbow in the clouds as a mark of the covenant.

Without any preamble, we are then taken into a strange tale of how Noah became drunk and lay naked in his tent,[1] where he was discovered by his son Ham. His other sons, Shem and Japheth, then covered him with a garment. When awake and sober, Noah learned that Ham had witnessed his naked state and, because of this, he placed a curse of servitude on Ham's son Canaan, who was not even present at the scene.

The significance of this incomprehensible curse against an innocent grandson has never satisfactorily been explained. Neither is it made clear why Ham is at that stage called Noah's youngest son,[2] when he was hitherto portrayed as the middle-born son.[3] A distinction is drawn, however, between Ham and Shem, with Shem alone being granted access to God, whilst Canaan is denounced for no apparent reason: 'Cursed be Canaan; a servant of servants shall he be to his brethren … Blessed be the Lord God of Shem, and Canaan shall be his servant'.[4]

Albeit this confusingly portrayed sequence supplies more questions than answers, a strategically implied slur is directed against the future Canaanites who, according to Genesis 10:15–20, were descended from Ham's son Canaan. In this respect, the otherwise nonsensical curse paves the way for God's later granting of the land of Canaan to Shem's descendant, Abraham:

> 'I will give unto thee, and to thy seed after thee … all the land of Canaan, for an everlasting possession'.[5]

Plainly, there was no historical merit to any of this, but the Genesis scribes had given themselves an almost insurmountable problem from which they had to find a means of extrication. By virtue of the badly handled Flood episode, everyone on Earth was dead except for Noah and his family. Henceforth, the whole world population had to be spawned anew from this single family base! Meanwhile, the book of Genesis had come to a grinding halt in an ark at the top of a mountain.

By some means, future generations of friends, enemies and otherwise strangers had to be established scripturally from the sons of Noah before any more story could be told. The sons (now party to God's rainbow covenant) could not be set against each other to provide enemies. But if one of them had a son called Canaan from whom the Canaanites might have descended, that would at least provide a platform for conflict and the eventual second covenant with Abraham.

Overriding all this, of course, was the ever problematic fact that Noah was himself a product of scribal invention. In truth, there was no family — no Shem, Ham or Japheth, nor even Canaan, from whom the rest of the world could be born. But the poorly-crafted Flood story was left to stand, and various attempts were made from the 6th century BC to support Noah's individual credibility even if his given ancestral line was mythological.

From the time of Homer's epic Greek works, the *Iliad* and *Odyssey* (sometime before the 8th century BC), a new pantheon of romantically portrayed gods had emerged — Zeus and the Olympians, whose stories were heroic and adventurous. It was a very competitive literary period, especially from the 4th century BC,[6] when Greek mythology was enormously popular in the Mediterranean world. In the light of this, a body of original Hebrew literature was embellished and rewritten to suit the prevailing culture and, from this effort, emerged an Aramaic document which Israeli scholars have dubbed the *Genesis Apocryphon*.

Discovered in 1948 at Qumrân, the *Genesis Apocryphon* was not preserved in a sealed jar like the Dead Sea Scrolls unearthed at that time. Its sewn leather sheets were in very poor condition,[7] but some fragmentary extracts were salvaged and translated. Pseudoepigraphical in style, with characters like Lamech and Abraham appearing to convey their stories in the first person, the document endeavours to explain certain anomalies and questionable elements of scripture, not the least among which is the heritage of Noah.

The route taken in this regard was to revert back to the 'sons of God and daughters of men' Genesis entry that preceded the Flood, and to suggest that Noah was perhaps not the son of Lamech, but the enchanted son of a *nephilim* angel: a watcher.

The tale, in the supposed words of Lamech, relates that Noah was so pale and beautiful when born that Lamech doubted he was the natural father:

> Behold, I thought in my heart that the conception was from the watchers, and that from the holy ones ... And my heart was changed within me because of this child. Then I, Lamech, hastened and went to Bath-Enosh my wife, and I said to her, By the Most High, by the Lord of greatness, by the King, tell me in truth with no lies.

With the suggestion of Noah's angelic status now made, the notion then seems to fall apart when Lamech's wife responds negatively:

> When Bath-Enosh my wife saw that my face upon me was changed ... then she mastered her emotion and spoke to me, and said, 'I swear to thee by the great Holy One, by the King of Heaven, that this seed is truly from thee, and this conception is truly from thee, and this childbearing is truly from thee, and from no other; neither from any of the watchers, nor from any of the sons of heaven'.[8]

At first glance, it would appear from this that the object of the exercise was defeated in the telling, but the subsequent wording is clever in that the reader is not necessarily left doubting

Lamech's suspicion. Women are the temptress daughters of Eve, and the reader is actually left to wonder if Lamech's wife can be trusted.

The doubt was well enough cast to prompt another work on the subject, the *Book of Noah*. This manuscript of which fragments are preserved in Ethiopic, makes rather more of Lamech's dilemma, stressing the angelic possibility even further by explaining that the baby Noah was 'whiter than snow, and redder than the flower of the rose; the hair of his head whiter than wool, and his eyes like the rays of the sun'.[9] How, it was asked, could such a child possibly be the son of an ordinary family? Surely this was why God chose him to be the new progenitor of the human race. The problem was, however, that such a concept divorced Noah from the line of Adam, and it was scripturally necessary for Abraham (listed as a descendant of Noah) to be of the Adamite succession. Either way, the book of Genesis was already written, so nothing very much had been achieved and Noah remained in the spuriously devised line from Seth.

Mother of Nations

After relating details of the Tower of Babel and listing the regional tribes (formally known as the *Tables of Nations*) in eventual descent from Noah's three sons, Genesis brings us to the story of Abraham (then called Abram) and his migration into Canaan from Mesopotamia. From this juncture, God becomes more regularly featured in the narrative for a while. But, at the same time, it is increasingly evident that, although the Bible is the foundation document for information about God, it is not actually a book about God. It is the ongoing story of a descendent family, whose individual members have various experiences of God. We, as readers, are positioned to follow the generational trail as their story unfolds.

An anomaly which immediately becomes apparent is the matter of Abram's age. Genesis 11:26 explains that Terah was aged 70 when his son Abram was born, and that Terah lived on to the age of 205.[10] This would make Abram 135 at his father's death. But we are then informed that Abram was 75 years old when he departed from Haran after the death of Terah.[11]

There is little point in dwelling on this, except to treat it as an example of how matters of personal ages and chronology in general are thoroughly confused throughout the *Torah*. Even in matters of tense there are some perplexing entries as a result of the original style of writing. When the early books of the Old Testament were written, the Hebrew language treated matters of time with complete abandon, and did not distinguish between past tense variables. There was only one past tense and it referred to events that 'happened', 'have happened' and 'had happened' with equal relevance. Linguistically, there was no difference between what took place a thousand years ago and what occurred yesterday. Moreover, words such as 'day', 'week', 'month' and 'year' were used with unconstrained flexibility, which made translation into languages with more precise ideas of time very difficult.[12]

Some extraordinary ages are given for certain characters in the pre-patriarchal era, with the ultimate example being Methuselah, who was said to have lived for 969 years.[13] The longevity claims settle into some normality, however, once we are into the patriarchal descent from Abraham. In fact, the confusion over his own age actually represents the scriptural turning-point in this regard.

Genesis 12:4–5 relates that, having travelled from the Sumerian city of Ur as directed by God, Abram — with his wife Sarai and nephew Lot — entered Canaan, where they became known as Hebrews. Lot was then kidnapped by the kingly alliance, subsequently to be rescued by Abram's army, and (as discussed in chapters 2 and 3) El Shaddai (God) covenanted all the lands of Canaan to the posterity of Abram.

Apart from being entirely without justification or satisfactory reasoning, this territorial Covenant now becomes the mainstay of the Abrahamic narrative through four generations. Thus, when it is said, as above, that God becomes more regularly featured for a while, the operative word is 'featured', as against his being especially relevant or active. Henceforth, the scribal objective was to convince the reader at every opportunity that the land of Canaan (later Palestine and Israel) was the property of the incoming Hebrews because God (whose words they were scripting) had decreed it was so.

Historically, the unworkable nature of this concept was that, although the Hebrews were supporters of God as the *El Shaddai*, he was also the supreme Lord of the Canaanites as the *El Elyon*. The retrospective Israelite scribal effort from the 6th century BC was therefore presumptuous in its assertion that the Hebrews were of some better worth to El than were the Canaanites.

* * *

Above all things, Genesis is a book of generations, whose primary objective is to list genealogical descent through a period of more than 2,500 years from the time of Adam. By contrast, the rest of the Old Testament deals with a period of just 1,200 years. It is therefore not long before the scriptural 'begetting' begins again, and we move to the sons of Abram and their descendants. In the course of this, the covenant of circumcision is established;[14] Abram's name is changed to Abraham,[15] and his wife Sarai becomes Sarah, denoting a 'princess'.[16]

Sarah is said to have been barren during the early years of her marriage.[17] This is not an uncommon feature in the accounts of this family. Rebekah, the wife of their eventual son Isaac, was also described as initially barren,[18] as was Rachel, the wife of Isaac's son Jacob.[19] It is with regard to such entries that the biblical ages suggested for these women must be disregarded. It was both common and customary in those days for very young girls to marry before childbearing age, and it is to the infertile periods of their early married lives that the old texts generally refer.

Sarah's story is, nonetheless, strangely told. First we are informed that she cannot conceive, but also that Abraham is to be the founding patriarch of a great nation.[20] Sarah then presents Abraham with her Egyptian companion, Hagar, 'to be his wife', saying, 'I pray thee, go in unto my maid; it may be that I may obtain children by her'. But when Hagar conceives she is

chastised by Sarah as if her condition were somehow unex-
pected.[21] In due course, Ishmael, the first son of Abraham, is born
to Hagar, but it is then announced that his senior inheritance is to
be superseded by a forthcoming son of the erstwhile barren Sarah
— a son who will be named Isaac.[22]

At Sarah's behest, Hagar and Ishmael are banished, with some
bread and water, into the wilderness of Beersheba. When their
water has expired, Hagar fears the worst, but an angel directs her
to a convenient well. Additionally, the angel states that 'God has
heard the voice of the lad [Ishmael]', and will 'make of him a great
nation'.[23]

God (calling himself El Shaddai) now informs Abraham that
Sarah will be a 'mother of nations', and that 'kings of people shall
be of her'.[24] This switch of emphasis from covenanted territory to
the prospect of future kingship is designed to ring like a
prophecy. But we are of course in the literary realm of the Israelite
scribes and their latter-day knowledge of what would ultimately
be the case. With the words written into his mouth, God therefore
makes his pact with the unborn Isaac: 'I will establish my
covenant with him for an everlasting covenant, and with his seed
after him'.[25]

Genesis 15:18 also contains God's promise that Isaac's descendants will inherit the forthcoming Egyptian empire 'from the
river of Egypt, unto the great river, the river Euphrates'. No such
promise is made, however, in respect of Abraham's eldest son
Ishmael, nor for Abraham himself or his six other sons by his later
wife Keturah.[26] Abraham was somewhat bewildered by this and
asked about Ishmael's prospects, to which El Shaddai replied that
he would 'make him fruitful', and he would beget twelve princes
of a great nation, but 'my covenant will I establish with Isaac'.[27]

This secondary covenant makes it perfectly clear that,
although Ishmael was the elder of the half-brothers, Isaac was to
be recognized as the progenitor of the future kings. The questions
arise, therefore: Why, in Genesis 22:1–6, did Abraham later
concede to God's command to slay the young Isaac with a knife
and burn him as an offering upon the altar at Moriah? And why,
when putting a stop to the slaying, did the angel refer to Isaac as

Abraham's 'only son',[28] when we already know that he had previously fathered Ishmael?

All of the foregoing (from the initial Covenant to the near sacrifice) presupposes of course that God was actually involved in some or all aspects of the sequence. But there is nothing to corroborate or suggest this in any document beyond the scripture that was written some 1,200 years after the period concerned.

In practical terms, nothing of any consequence concerning God happens during this Covenant episode. It is no more than a series of prophetic assertions of how the Abrahamic family eventually will rise to govern the Canaanite lands and others beyond. This is reckoned throughout to be the covenanted Will of God, whereby the Hebrews are scribally portrayed (whether or not with any historical merit) to have been a uniquely chosen race. In this regard, the Covenant episode is noticeably propagandist for the consumption of a down-the-line audience in much later times.

During those later times of the latter 6th century BC, the Jerusalem priests were the regulators of society, perceived as the contact bridges between God and people at large. To disobey the priests was to disobey God. What better than to conclude the sequence with an example of how even the patriarch Abraham (the exalted father of the Hebrew nation) was willing to display unquestioned obedience to the Lord with the ultimate sacrifice of his son.

The Law Code

The ruling in respect of Hagar's substitute motherhood stems from an ancient practice in Mesopotamia that was qualified in the *Law Code of Hammurabi*, the Amorite King of Babylonia (*c.*1792–1750 BC).[29] These laws, as expressed by Hammurabi, were taken from the preceding *Law Code of Ur-Nammu* (*c.*2100 BC), Abraham's own ancestor, the King of Ur in Sumer.

The Hammurabi decrees specified the conditions for such an arrangement to be permissible. The most common-case scenario was that of a marriage between a male citizen and a wife serving as a priestess (a *naditum*) whereby, during her term of service, she was prevented from bearing children. In such cases, she was entitled to bring a handmaid to bear children for her husband. *Laws 144-145* make it clear, however, that such a decision was the wife's prerogative, not the right of the husband. It is also stipulated that the pre-eminence of the primary wife must be safeguarded, and that if the surrogate wife attempted to make herself equal, the senior wife had the right to assert her position.[30] These are the regulations that lie behind the expulsion of Hagar and, in response to Sarah's complaint, Abraham conceded, 'Thy maid is in thy hand; do to her as it pleases thee'.[31]

There is a particular entry concerning this custom in a clay tablet from *c.*1520 BC. It is one of around 4,000 tablets unearthed in 1925-31 at Nuzi in north-eastern Mesopotamia, near Haran. The account relates to a man called Shenma, whose wife Gilimninu was barren.[32] It states that Gilimninu was permitted to provide her handmaid as a second wife in order to produce children for her husband. Mesopotamian law stipulated, however, that if the first wife should subsequently bear a son, then that son would rank in succession above any son previously born to the substitute wife.

The 282 Babylonian laws of the *Code of Hammurabi* are inscribed on a large black diorite stela that was unearthed in 1901 at Susa in Elam.[33] The French expedition was led by Father Vincent Scheil, who translated the inscriptions in the following year. Although not entirely unique, the 7.5 foot stela (*c.*88 cm) remains the longest set of ancient laws yet discovered, and is currently on display at the Louvre Museum in Paris.[34] At the head of the stone, King Hammurabi is depicted receiving the dictated laws from the *Anannage* lord Shamash (grandson of Enlil) who holds the rod and ring of divine justice.

It becomes evident from the implementation of the wifely custom that, although Abraham and Sarah had become residents of Canaan, they were still following the lifestyle guidelines of their native Mesopotamia and the regulatory procedures as laid down by the *Anannage* guardians. In this respect, the *Law Code* begins with Hammurabi's own tributes to 'An the sublime, king of the *Anannage'*, to 'Ea [Enki], the god of righteousness', and to Marduk of Babylon 'who sent me to rule'. It is thus made clear, once again, that Abraham was a product of his Mesopotamian origin, and that the *El Shaddai* god culture of his family in Canaan was a direct continuation of the *Ilû Kur-gal* culture of Ur.

My Sister, My Wife

Researchers have long debated the ambiguity of El Shaddai's covenant, wondering in particular why the kingdoms of Egypt should be promised by God to the successors of Isaac. This would only make sense if the eventual compilers of Genesis knew from some record that a line of descent from Isaac had indeed become Kings of Egypt. Another anomaly which has long baffled historians is the introduction of circumcision at this particularly early stage of the Hebrew saga.

Herodotus, the Greek cultural writer dubbed as the 'father of historians', visited Egypt in about 450 BC and recorded that circumcision, a custom 'inherited by the Hebrews', was originally performed only in ancient Egypt. This has been confirmed from examinations of excavated mummies,[35] and by a bas-relief at Karnak which details the surgical procedure.[36] In his 1st-century work entitled *Against Apion*, the Jewish historian Flavius Josephus recorded that the inhabitants of Canaan learned about circumcision from the Egyptians.[37] That being so, then not only did God's covenant of kingship with Isaac promise future dominion from the Nile to the Euphrates,[38] but the covenant of circumcision introduced a hitherto unique Egyptian custom into the Hebrew culture from the days of Abraham. Why would that have been the case?

The only connection with Egypt that we are told about is Sarah's entry into the household of the pharaoh who wanted her for his wife. At that point Abraham denied that Sarah was his own wife, and claimed instead that she was his sister.[39] Then, a little later, we are informed that Abraham and Sarah were both offspring of Terah, and Abraham explains, 'She is my sister; she is the daughter of my father, but not the daughter of my mother, and she became my wife'.[40]

In the Syriac *M'ārath Gaze* at the British Museum, Terah's wives are given as Yâwnû (mother of Abraham) and Naharyath (mother of Sarah),[41] who is identified with Nfry-ta-tjewnen, a future wife of Pharaoh Amenemhet I (*c.*1970 BC),[42] Her son by this marriage was the succeeding Pharaoh Senusret I — the very pharaoh who claimed Sarah for his wife. This is not surprising, since Sarah would have been Senusret's maternal half-sister (as well as being Abraham's paternal half-sister), and it was common practice for Egyptian pharaohs to marry their maternal half-sisters in order to progress the kingship through the female line.

In the Qumrân *Genesis Apocryphon*, Abraham dreamed of his wife Sarah as a 'palm tree', and himself as a 'cedar tree' about to be cut down.[43] His fear was that the pharaoh was ready to cut down the cedar in pursuit of the palm, and Abraham recognized a significant threat to his life for having married the rightful sister-wife of Senusret. (In the most ancient of Sumerian liturgies, and on royal seals, the fallen cedar tree was the symbol of a dead god. The goddess Inanna was said to have 'raised up the noble cedar' when she resurrected her beloved husband Dumuzi.)

The *Apocryphon* account proceeds to relate, in some detail, the great beauty of Sarah in the eyes of the pharaoh and his vizier Horkanosh, and of how they sought to have Abraham killed. He was saved only by the pleas of Sarah herself when she became the pharaoh's wife and remained with him for the next two years.

The English translation of Genesis 12:19 quotes the pharaoh as saying to Abraham, 'Why saidst thou, She is my sister, so I might have taken her to me to wife?' But this is not what the Hebrew Bible states. The same entry translated directly from the Hebrew reads, 'Why did you say, She is my sister, so that I took her for my wife?' There is a distinct difference in terminology here, and the Israelite writers were quite explicit in detailing that Sarah and the pharaoh were actually married for a time.[44]

All things considered, there is a clear possibility that Isaac was not the son of Abraham after all, but the son of Sarah and Senusret. In that event, the details of the covenant would fall neatly into place if a future descendant of Isaac were to marry back into the Egyptian royal line. (This is something we should keep in mind as we follow the generational succession.) It would also explain why Sarai (Sarah) gained the distinction of 'princess', and why Isaac's family were said to have adopted the Egyptian custom of circumcision at the time when God had said of Sarah, 'She shall be a mother of nations; kings of people shall be of her'.[45]

Mysterious Guests

Before the narrative settles into the continuing story of Isaac, God moves once again into vengeful mode, intent on destroying the cities of Sodom and Gommorah, where the people's decadent lifestyle is offending him. He might well have promised Noah that there would be no more floods to devastate mankind, but he had not mentioned any other possible means of violent mass annihilation.

The scene, as portrayed, is a further example of El Shaddai's physical presence as an 'on-the-ground' figure, beginning when 'the Lord appeared unto him [Abraham] in the plains of Mamre; and he sat in the tent door in the heat of the day'.[46] Accompanying the Lord in Abraham's tent, 'three men stood by him'. Abraham served food to the mysterious guests, then addressed God personally: 'My Lord, now I have found favour in thy sight, pass not away, I pray thee, from thy servant'.[47]

Following a brief discussion about Sarah's impending motherhood, the men looked out towards Sodom, and God said to them, 'Shall I hide from Abraham the thing which I do?'[48]

In the next scene, God remains with Abraham to debate the pros and cons of his intended hostile action, and the others have gone to Sodom, where they are now classified as 'angels'. At this stage, the three attendants have become only two, but the Hebrew text adds a little more clarity, explaining that God was himself one of the original three — not that there were three others with him in the tent.[49]

When the two angels reach Sodom, Abraham's nephew Lot (a resident of the city) greets them.[50] He feeds them and even offers them his two daughters, 'which have not known man ... and do ye to them as is good in your eyes'. Then, in contradiction of this, the husbands of the two said virgin daughters become part of the action, and the angels advise Lot to take his family from the city because the Lord is about to destroy it.[51] So Lot leads his family to safety, and the Lord rains down 'brimstone and fire'.

Ignoring the angel's warning not to look back, Lot's wife turns for a last glimpse at her home and is transformed into 'a pillar of salt'. With Sodom, Gomorrah and all their inhabitants totally demolished, and the daughters' husbands not in the escape party for whatever reason, Lot ends up in the mountains with his two daughters. They then decide, 'Let us make our father drink wine, and we shall lie with him, that we may preserve the seed of our father'. Resultantly, the daughters each bear a son, and Lot had apparently been so drunk that he had not the slightest recollection of any of it.[52]

Historically, it is not known what happened at Sodom and Gomorrah on the Dead Sea plain. An earthquake, with a massive eruption of underground petroleum gasses, is the most commonly suggested cause of the disaster.[53] There is, however, an intriguing entry in an old Egyptian document called the *Paraphrase of Shem*.[54] Discovered in 1945 at Nag Hammadi, near Luxor, the Coptic tractate[55] depicts Sodom not as a centre of wickedness (as related in Genesis), but as a city of great wisdom, where the inhabitants 'bear witness to the universal testimony'. It is further prophesied that 'Sodom will be burned unjustly by a base nature'.[56]

As for the location of the cities, it seems that Sodom and Gomorrah were probably one and the same place. The *Gospel of the Egyptians* (another Nag Hammadi tractate) refers to Sodom as 'a great pasture which is Gomorrah'.[57] A final clue comes from the Bible's New Testament book of The Revelation 11:8, which refers to the place 'which spiritually is called Sodom and Egypt'. At that time in the 1st century AD, *Sodom* and *Egypt* were terms used by the tribal order of East Manasseh to identify the settlement of

THE ORIGIN OF GOD

Qumrân, where the Dead Sea Scrolls were eventually found.[58] On that basis, it is likely that Sodom once stood near to the eventual Qumrân location.

In his *Antiquities of the Jews*, Flavius Josephus made numerous mentions of an asphalt lake situated in Judaea, some 300 furlongs (37.5 miles) south of Jerusalem.[59] Greek and Roman writers also recorded this now non-existent geographical feature and its noxious gasses.[60] In 1848 the American explorer, WF Lynch, took a team into the region to investigate the biblical Vale of Siddim, which Genesis 14:3 states is the 'salt sea' (the Dead Sea).[61] From this and subsequent expeditions, it has been ascertained that the asphalt lake now lies beneath a Dead Sea that extends far beyond its original southern boundary.

Lying on the Jordan Valley Fault, the Dead Sea has lengthened considerably, north to south, over time in a series of earthquake subsidence events. There are still craters from extinct volcanoes, stretches of lava and deep layers of basalt in the fault, and it is likely that volcanic eruption would have caused the Bible's 'brimstone and fire', as seemingly rained down by God. Writing in about 1400 BC, the Phoenician scholar Sanchuniathon explained that 'the Vale of Siddim sank and became a lake that was always steaming and contained no fish'.[62] Everything points to the probability that Sodom was enveloped in a rain of burning pitch and, in the greater course of time, the resultant asphalt lake was submerged as the land further subsided beneath the expanding waters of the Dead Sea.

There is no way of knowing what interpretation might have been placed on the ultimate cause of the destruction in Abraham's day. It is plain however that, by the 6th century BC, when the priestly Israelite scribes recounted their version of the incident in Genesis, they were of the opinion that it was a purposeful act of God's vengeance. Such monumental disasters set powerful scenes for demonstrating the extent of God's displeasure and retribution when not obeyed to the letter. It did not matter how natural were the catastrophes since God was reckoned to control Nature in any event. Earthquakes with unseen beginnings were not so conducive to the explanatory process but, when heavenly fire and brimstone rained, God's fearsome weaponry was deemed evident.

Although fault eruption might well have ignited the underground pitch, it is possible (as discussed in chapter 3 for the disaster at Ur) that the Vale of Siddim incident, with its high level of above-ground activity, had a more visibly provocative instigator. In a study of such 'heavenly fire' events as related to religious scriptural lore, Bruce Masse, an environmental archaeologist with Los Alamos National Laboratory, has therefore deduced: 'It appears from these passages that the Sodom and Gomorrah story encodes the observation of a terrestrial impact'[63] — either a meteoroid or comet fragment that exploded a few miles above the Earth's surface.

11

STRATEGY OF SUCCESSION

Shaping Destiny

In philosophical and theological terms, the stories of the Old Testament, especially those of the *Torah*, have different aspects of emphasis in accordance with a variety of different teachings. To some people they are chronicles of history; to many they are pure religious scripture, and to others they are superficial parables with hidden meanings beneath. To the Christian fraternity, the Hebrew Bible is generally perceived as the religious history of God — a scene-setting precursor to the New Testament. To the Jewish community, the Bible forms the basis of cultural law, whether specifically or loosely defined. In this latter regard, the interpretations of academic Judaism move within a range that can be wholly definitive or thoroughly esoteric.

Although the *Torah* is considered to embody the written law, there is also a good deal of orally transmitted law within Judaism, and there have been many centuries of rabbinical discussion about the applications of each. Debates have long ensued about laws, ethics, customs, traditions, histories and legends. In works such as the *Midrash, Talmud* and *Zohar*, millions of words have been written in a quest for a greater understanding of the philosophies behind the Jewish faith. In consequence, there is far more information about key biblical characters within these works than exists within the Bible itself and, as the grand patriarch of the Hebrew nation, Abraham is extensively treated as a figure of constant investigation.

As we saw in chapter 3, Abraham was said to have been of the learned Sumerian caste of *Ur Kasdim*. On leaving Mesopotamia, he was regarded as having gained access to a unique series of ideograms revered as a testament of 'all that mankind had ever known, and of all that would ever be known'.[1] To the Sumerians, the original tablet which gave rise to Abraham's cipher was known as the *Table of Destiny*.[2] It was said to have been held in the sequential guardianships of Enlil and Enki, along with their sons Ninurta and Marduk, and was in the form of an inscribed seal worn against their breasts. Jewish tradition relates that the tablet was called *Raziel ha Malach* — a collection of universal secrets, said to have been embedded in sapphire[3] and given to Adam by the angel Raziel.[4] In this tradition, the cipher was subsequently passed down through Lamech to Abraham, and constituted the Signs of the Watchers as referenced in the *Book of Enoch*.

In the wisdom culture of Kabbalah, the enigmatic codes are said to have been deciphered and re-authored by Abraham, to become known as the *Book of Formation (Sefer Yetzira)*. The ideograms are reckoned to have been as brief and simplistic as Albert Einstein's $E=MC^2$ — the five characters that help define and mathematically explain the mysteries of time, space, energy and matter.[5] In much the same way, the various formulae applicable to the tables of *Formation* and *Destiny* were said to be immediately understandable to the initiated, but required lengthy explanation for those not versed in the art.

According to Isaac Newton's *Third Law of Motion*, 'For every action, there is an equal [in size] and opposite [in direction] reaction'.[6] Forces always come in pairs, with the reaction being the resultant 'destiny' of the action. Kabbalistic philosophy maintains, therefore, that elements of destiny can be predetermined by one's actions in order to achieve the desired reactions. Hence it is said that, in terms of human response, destiny is not necessarily an uncontrolled fate, but can be shaped by way of appropriately designed actions.

Stemming from the Hebrew verb *laykabbel* (to receive), Kabbalah describes the motive of actions as 'the desire to receive', with an emphasis on the receipt of enlightenment. It is in this context that Abraham's departure from Mesopotamia into Canaan was perceived by the scribes as something more than just a routine expedition of several hundred miles. It is presented as being the start of a journey in search of spiritual truths — a quest for an ideal that marks the true beginning of the biblical process.[7]

It is, therefore, with Abraham (c.2000 BC) that the Bible story changes from its Mesopotamian archival thrust to become the narrative story of a descendent family in Canaan. In the course of this, the scriptural driving-force remains constant, and we are presented with an epic saga of how this family, from which emerged the Israelite nation, was permanently torn between a belief in one God or many gods. Regrettably, unlike the early sections of Genesis, there is very little contemporary evidence of the family during the post-Abrahamic era.

The biblical accounts for the period after Abraham were written in retrospect, based on oral traditions and possibly derived from some written records that are no longer available. In some respects, there are historic chronicles that support the Bible's environmental portrayals (the stage on which the generational story is enacted). But, with certain exceptions, the scriptural players are not personally evident in these writings. It is clear however that, to whatever extent their individual stories might have been factual, the overriding purpose of the biblical text is to relate the evolution of the eventual One God faith of Israel.

Son of the Covenant

A key item which soon becomes obvious is that El Shaddai's covenant with Isaac did not come to fruition in his lifetime. Isaac did not inherit the kingdoms from the Nile to the Euphrates, nor did his immediate descendants. It is logical to wonder, therefore, why the Genesis scribes of around 550 BC would have written about something that had no historical foundation and which could so easily be proved untrue. What would be the point of inventing such an important prospect, a specific decree of God, if it is not seen to produce an equally impressive result?

The likelihood, then, is that there was an element of truth in what they wrote — something which might well have been known in the era when written, but which has since become lost

156

to mainstream understanding. With this as a possibility, we should now look for Egyptian kingly connections as we progress through the biblical narrative from the time that Isaac was married and his descendent line commenced. Meanwhile, we know from history that the conjoined kingdoms to which the prophetic covenant of God referred (i.e. the Egyptian empire) did not emerge until more than 500 years after Isaac's era, in the pharaonic reign of Tuthmosis III. Right now though, and following Sarah's marital episode with the pharaoh, any further association with Egypt appears to be out of the question, with Genesis 26:2–3 explaining that El Shaddai, said to Isaac, 'Go not down into Egypt; dwell in the land which I shall tell thee of ... and I will be with thee'. Quite why Isaac might have considered going to Egypt is not explained, but it would perhaps have been a natural inclination if he were indeed the son of Sarah and Pharaoh Senusret.

Genesis 24:3–4 relates that, on advice from El Shaddai, Isaac's wife was not selected from the women of Egypt or Canaan, but from Abraham's own family stock back in Mesopotamia. In order to choose a suitable wife for his son, Abraham sent his eldest servant, along with some men and ten camels, 'to Mesopotamia, unto the city of Nahor'.[8] Apart from its references to Ur and Chaldea, this is the Bible's first specific mention, by name, that 'Mesopotamia' was indeed the original country of the Abrahamic Hebrew race.

The servant is traditionally reckoned to have been Abraham's steward, Eliezer of Damascus. Although not stated as such in the account, his name is mentioned some while earlier, at a time before Isaac was born.[9] Nahor, to whom Eliezer's city of destination was attributed, was Abraham's own brother.

On arrival at the city of Nahor, Eliezer took his camels to drink at the well, and decided that the woman who would gladly fill her own pitcher for him would be the chosen wife for Isaac. Before long, a young woman did indeed draw water for Eliezer and his camels, and she turned out to be none other than Nahor's own granddaughter Rebekah. The servant duly gave her golden bracelets and an earring (presents from Abraham), whereupon

Rebekah's brother Laban took Eliezer to meet with their father, Abraham's nephew, Bethuel. He then gave his consent for Rebekah to travel back to Canaan with Eliezer, and to become the wife of Isaac.

By this time, Abraham's wife Sarah had died,[10] and we are subsequently advised that Abraham became married to a woman named Keturah, who bore him another six sons before he also died.[11] Additionally, we learn that Ishmael (Abraham's first son by Hagar) had twelve sons who became 'princes of nations'.[12]

Pivotal to the plot in Eliezer's story are the camels for whom the prospective wife of Isaac was required to draw water from the well. This concept is indicative of so much retrospective biblical writing in that, although camels were employed for desert travel when Genesis was written, they were not used until several centuries after the time of Abraham.[13] There is no mention of tame camels in Egyptian, Syrian, Canaanite or Mesopotamian record prior to about 1200 BC,[14] and their appearances in Genesis are mistranslations which should, in fact, denote donkeys.[15] Another common English mistranslation, in the King James Bible and elsewhere, is the mention of an earring for Rebekah, whereas the Hebrew text specifically denotes a golden nose ring.[16]

Birthright and Blessing

Next on the genealogical agenda in Genesis 25 are Isaac and Rebekah's twin sons, Esau and Jacob. The firstborn, Esau, was said to have been 'red all over like an hairy garment'.[17] From this, he acquired the alternative name Edom (a variant of *adom*, denoting 'red'),[18] by which definition his descendant Edomites became known.[19] We are told, however, that Esau became 'a cunning hunter, a man of the field'[20] and, in this context, his 'hairy' definition is entirely reminiscent of Enkidu, the 'man of nature' in the Babylonian *Epic of Gilgamesh*.[21]

As previously cited, Esau's name (E-sa-um), was discovered in 1975 on ancient tablets at *Tel Mardikh* (the old city of Ebla) in Syria, along with references to Abraham (Ab-ra-mu) and Israel

(Isra-Ilû)[22] to which the name of Esau's brother Jacob was changed by God at Bêth-El.[23]

Whilst Esau became a skilled hunter, Jacob was said to have been 'a plain man, dwelling in tents',[24] or more precisely from the Hebrew text, the 'indoor type'.[25] Then follows an account of how, when Esau was faint with hunger and wanted some of Jacob's stew, Jacob would only consent to the request if Esau would sell him his birthright in exchange for the bowl of lentil pottage — a bargain to which Esau duly agreed.[26]

There is a very similar account of a birthright sale, and possibly the original source material for the Genesis version, in another of the Mesopotamian *Nuzi Tablets*. It details an incident in which a man transferred his birthright to his brother for a grove of three sheep.[27] What Genesis does not make clear, however, is the precise nature of the birthright granted by Esau to Jacob. As far as we are made aware, there was no property or titular entitlement to consider and, since both were the sons of Isaac, the only apparent birthright would have related to the El Shaddai covenant that a race of kings would ensue from their father.[28]

This is very much a repeat of the situation that applied to Cain and Seth. Cain had been the original senior successor in the Eden story, but the scripture switched the heritable emphasis to Adam and Eve's later son Seth. Then, some generations later, the *Babylonian Law Code* of Hammurabi was invoked to dismiss Abraham's senior son Ishmael in favour of his younger half-brother Isaac. And now we have Esau (the senior successor to Isaac and Rebekah) handing his birthright, literally on a plate, to his junior twin Jacob. There appears to be little doubt that the Genesis scribes manipulated the continuing generational record by side-switching senior lines of inheritance between brothers in order to create a smooth descent that suited the patriarchal purpose of their scriptural endeavour.

Meanwhile, Isaac's story continues with an account of how he and Rebekah went to live in Gerar, where Abimelech was a king of the Philistines.[29] The term Philistines is anachronistic in this context, since there were no Philistines in Canaan at that time.[30] They arrived many centuries later, at around the time of Moses.

God then promised Isaac that he and his offspring would inherit this place and 'all the countries' in accordance with the covenant made with his father. But all that follows are details of how the men of Gerar lusted after Rebekah and kept filling Isaac's wells with earth. This caused him to move out of the area to Beersheba, with El Shaddai saying, none too helpfully, 'I am the God of Abraham thy father; fear not'.[31]

Eventually, when Isaac's eyesight was failing in his old age, we have the strangest tale of how, when he was due to bless Esau (his eldest son), Rebekah contrived to disguise Jacob as his brother so that he received the paternal blessing instead. When Isaac discovered his error, he condemned Jacob and Rebekah's deceit, but was unable to grant the blessing of senior inheritance again, whereupon Esau declared that he would have to slay Jacob.[32]

Lords of Edom

There is an amount of confusion in Genesis concerning the eventual wives of Esau and their various fathers.[33] It is explained, however, that his wife Bashemath (a daughter of Ishmael)[34] bore a son called Reuel.[35] He, in turn, had two prominent sons: Nahath, Lord of Edom (Idumaea), and Shammah, also a Lord of Edom.[36] Along with the sons and grandsons of Bashemath's other generational offspring, and those from Esau's other wives, there were many resultant Lords of Edom. Despite their listing in the Bible (only to be sidestepped in favour of pursuing a junior course from Esau's brother Jacob), these powerful lords are still given an amount of temporary prominence, being cited as 'the kings that reigned in the land of Edom [north-east of Sinai] before there reigned any king over the children of Israel'.[37]

Scholars of Hebrew literature make the point that, in listing the Lords of Edom in the original senior line from Esau, the Genesis compilers defined twelve individual princedoms, equivalent in number to the twelve tribes of Israel which descended eventually from Esau's brother Jacob.[38] Given that two daughters of Ishmael (Bashemath and Mahalath) are named as being wives of Esau, this corresponds to some limited extent with El Shaddai's promise to Abraham that Ishmael's line would beget princes of a great nation.[39] But it does not necessarily prove the historical reality of the promise itself since the biblical accounts were written with hindsight long after the events to which they refer.

Mount of Witness

The main thrust of the continuing section of Genesis focuses on Jacob. Notwithstanding three generational switches between brothers (Cain to Seth, Ishmael to Isaac, and Esau to Jacob), it was Jacob who, by virtue of God changing his name to Israel, became the eventual patriarch of the descendent Israelite nation — or as Genesis 32:32 originally calls them, 'the children of Israel'. From this point in the narrative, the senior-line descendants from Cain, Ishmael and Esau are conveniently forgotten, and God is said to have been allied with Jacob.

To escape the wrath of his brother, whose inheritance he had usurped, Jacob set out for his mother's home in Haran (Nahor), to the north of Mesopotamia. There, he intended to find himself a wife from the daughters of Rebekah's brother Laban. On the way, he rested at Bêth-El of Luz, where he saw the vision of a stairway reaching to heaven, and El Shaddai told him, 'I am the Lord God of Abraham thy father, and the God of Isaac: the land whereon thou liest, to thee will I give it, and to thy seed'.[40]

At this stage, we are two generations removed from Abraham, with Isaac having inherited absolutely nothing, and his son Jacob is now presented with the same non-eventful carrot of territorial inheritance. As we shall discover, there is no such legacy coming his way either, and it is beginning to look very much as if the covenant story is a scribal myth in the way it has been portrayed. Maybe we shall find something that satisfies the godly promise in due course, but it does rather seem that the prophetic introduction of that promise at the time of Abraham was nothing more than a spurious insertion by the Genesis writers — something to create an ongoing suspense in the story-line. If so, then the suspense is now wearing thin to the point that the constant said reiterations by God are becoming wearisome, and his lack of other involvement is noticeably disconcerting. Meanwhile, we are left to follow Jacob into Mesopotamia in his search for a wife and, ultimately, we learn how the twelve Tribes of Israel were formed.

On his journey into Haran, Jacob met conveniently with Laban's daughter Rachel, and decided that she was the one to marry. But her father preferred that Jacob should marry Rachel's elder sister in accordance with the custom of marriage by way of seniority. They came to an arrangement, however, that Jacob would work seven years for Laban, at the end of which he would be allowed to marry Rachel. But, on their wedding night, Laban secreted Rachel's elder sister Leah into Jacob's bed, thereby constituting wedlock. Displeased with this subterfuge, Jacob complained, and was then allowed to marry his cousin Rachel as well, so long as he served Laban for another seven years.[41]

Jacob then ended up with two wives, but Rachel proved to be barren and so the *Babylonian Law Code* was invoked once again when she allocated her handmaid, Bilhah, to bear children for her husband. Meanwhile, Leah produced four sons, but then stopped conceiving, so she also granted Jacob her own handmaid, Zilpah.[42] Both handmaids produced sons for Jacob; then Leah began producing again and, finally, so did Rachel.

At this juncture, God said to Jacob, 'I am El of Bêth-El ... Rise, leave this land, and return unto the land of your birthplace',[43] whereupon Jacob, along with the four women and their sons set out for Canaan. For some unexplained reason, before leaving, Rachel stole her father's household 'gods' (deiform idols known as *terafim*),[44] and Jacob made off with some of Laban's livestock, which he considered rightfully his because he had bred them. The point is made here that, although Jacob had become a servant of El Shaddai, Rachel's family had not yet conceded to the monotheistic concept, and Laban duly gave chase after his property. He caught up with Jacob's party in the high country of Gilead, but Rachel kept the idols hidden and Laban did not find them. Eventually, Jacob and Laban made a pact for the future that neither would trespass, east or west, beyond that place in search of the other. They erected a pile of stones on the spot and called it *Galeed*, the 'mount of witness'.[45]

Soon afterwards, Rachel died in childbirth; Jacob patched up the succession dispute with his brother Esau, and El Shaddai changed Jacob's name to Israel (*Isra-El*: Soldier of El). By virtue of two different writers, whose accounts were amalgamated in the telling, this event is twice recounted (Genesis 32:28 and 35:10), with the Lord relating the words of his covenant yet again: 'Be fruitful and multiply; a nation and a company of nations shall be of thee, and kings shall come out of thy loins'.[46] The net result of Jacob-Israel's relationships with the four women was that he had a daughter, Dinah, and twelve sons from whom emerged the twelve Tribes of Israel.

Rape and Destruction

Dinah, the daughter of Leah, is relegated to little but a statistical entry in the ensuing narrative, with the exception of one brief story which is included to remind us of the importance of circumcision in the Abrahamic heritage. Genesis 34:2 relates that Dinah was defiled in Canaan by Shechem, the son of a certain Prince Hamor. Jacob's sons were enraged by this, especially when they discovered that Shechem was an uncircumcised Hivite. Shechem subsequently announced that he loved Dinah and wished to marry her, and Jacob's sons said they would consent to this if Hamor had all the men of his city circumcised.

Hamor and Shechem conceded to the request, 'and every male was circumcised'.[47] But Dinah's brothers, Simeon and Levi, were not content:

> They took each his sword, and came upon the city unopposed, and they killed every male. And Hamor and Shechem his son they killed by the edge of the sword ... and took that which was in the city, and that which was in the field, and all their wealth, and all their little ones and their wives they took captive, and they spoiled even all that was in the house.[48]

With so many documentary records now available, such an event as portrayed would undoubtedly have shown up in one historical account or another, but nothing even remotely similar has ever been found. It is in any case unlikely, if not inconceivable, that two young brothers could have sacked and slaughtered every male in a city, even if they were all suffering discomfort after their mass surgery. Quite what this story attempts to prove is impossible to determine, except perhaps to postulate a reason why, some three generations after Abraham, the said covenant of God (that the family would inherit all the land) had not yet come to fruition. In this regard, the story ends with Jacob saying to his sons, 'Ye have troubled me to make me stink among the inhabitants of the land ... and I shall be destroyed, I and my house'.[49]

To this point, despite all the promises by El Shaddai, the family had acquired no territory of any note in Canaan, and there has been no mention of their involvement in Egyptian affairs since the days of Abraham. We are told that the descendants of Abraham's son Ishmael, via his Egyptian mother Hagar, achieved some high estate in Edom,[50] and it is entirely possible that Sarah's son, Isaac, was actually the son of Pharaoh Senusret. But, apart from these imponderables, all we have really learned is that the wives of Isaac and Jacob were of Mesopotamian stock, and that squabbles over rights of seniority prevailed within the family.

Whether or not El Shaddai's covenant of Egyptian territorial dominion has any historical merit is something yet to be determined. But since it was the Genesis scribes who brought the matter to our literary attention, it is within the balance of Genesis that we should expect to find some indication of the covenant taking effect.

A Coat of Many Colours

Of all his recalcitrant sons, there was one whom Jacob-Israel favoured above the others. That son was Joseph, the firstborn of Rachel and, in view of this, his father 'made him a coat of many colours'.[51] Actually, this is a corrupted English translation from the Hebrew which denoted simply an 'ornamented tunic' — the *ketonet pasim* — and made no reference whatever to colours.[52] The *ketonet pasim* is later referred to in the book of 2 Samuel 13:18, and is again wrongly stated to be 'of divers colours' in English translations.[53] On this latter occasion, the gown was worn by a virgin princess and, in ritualistic practice, it was a unisex garment indicative of royal status. The origin of this gown was the Mesopotamian ceremonial robe of the *Anannage*, known as the *kutinnû pisannu*, with *pisannu* relating to appliqué ornaments sewn onto costly vestments.[54]

In view of the princely nature of the *ketonet pasim*, we might justifiably wonder what right Jacob had to present such a royal garment to one of his sons. The answer is that Jacob had no more entitlement to present it than Joseph had to wear it. In practice, the chances are that the story of this coat is yet another scribal myth — but a myth perhaps with a strategic purpose. What it does is to alert us to the fact that maybe the El Shaddai covenant is coming close to taking effect, and that Joseph is the man to watch. In real terms, we should expect now to be following the story of Jacob's senior son, Reuben. But instead, by way of the *ketonet pasim*, we are diverted into the tale of Joseph, a junior son of the line.

Genesis explains that, by virtue of the fact that Joseph was prone to ambitious dreams, his brothers conspired to kill him in the fields of Dothan.[55] The story, as told in Genesis 37, is somewhat chaotic since it is another amalgamation of accounts by two different writers, one of whom refers to Joseph's father as Jacob, whilst the other calls him Israel.[56] The 'Jacob' writer introduces Reuben as the one brother who endeavoured to protect Joseph from the rest, whereas the 'Israel' writer cites Judah (another son of Leah) as being the protective brother.

Initially, the eleven brothers are said to have removed Joseph's coat and thrown him into a pit with intent to kill him. But then, through a change of heart, they sold him to a passing caravan of Ishmaelites. Afterwards, some Midianite traders arrived on the scene, whereupon they (the Midianites) pulled Joseph from the pit and sold him to the Ishmaelites. It is therefore not clear who pulled him out and made the sale (either the brothers or the Midianites) but, one way or another, Joseph ended up with the Ishmaelites, who carried him into Egypt.[57]

Finally, we have another Egyptian link in the story-line, but there is now a further confusing element for it was not the Ishmaelites who arrived in Egypt with the seventeen year-old son of Jacob-Israel, but the Midianites. Whatever the case, they then sold him to a high chamberlain (*sar hatabahim*) named Potiphar.[58] In the interim, the brothers had dipped Joseph's coat in goat's blood and returned it to their father, claiming that 'an evil beast hath devoured him'.

Genesis then leaves us wondering what might have happened next to Joseph in Egypt. But, disregarding him at that point, the narrative then moves instead to the story of Leah's son Judah. Of all the brothers, Judah is ultimately the most significant in patriarchal terms, since it was his line that was said to have descended to King David and onwards through the Royal House of Judah. But this was not the reason why the Genesis scribes placed an interlude in the Joseph story at this stage. Their diversionary stratagem had a far more explicit purpose, as we shall see in the next chapter.

An Illicit Heritage

Earlier, we learned about the dream of Abraham, wherein he envisioned his wife Sarah (the princess) as a palm tree. The distinction of the royal palm was essentially Arabic, and the great palm oasis south-east of Sinai, beyond Aqaba, was called Tehâma[59] from the vehement heat of the region's sand.[60] From this derived the Hebrew female name Tamar.

There are a number of Tamars in the Old Testament, not the least of whom was a daughter of King David who also wore the *ketonet pasim*.[61] Absalom, one of David's sons, had a daughter called Tamar,[62] as did the later King Zedekiah. The original biblical Tamar was, however, the daughter-in-law of Jacob and Leah's son, Judah, and there is a bizarre story in Genesis 38:1–30 of how she conceived of her father-in-law who was said not to have recognized her.

We are told nothing of Tamar's heritage — only that Judah had selected her to be the wife of his firstborn son Er. But when Er died unexpectedly, Tamar was passed to his younger brother Onan, who was also prematurely slain. The Genesis writers attributed both these deaths to the Will of God, and then told of how the twice-widowed Tamar was accosted at the roadside by her father-in-law Judah, who seemingly mistook her for a harlot, pledging a kid from his flock in payment. No reason is given for Tamar's failure to announce her identity, but in due time she gave birth to twin brothers, Pharez and Zerah.

Yet again, as with Esau and Jacob, we are presented with another dispute over seniority. The scripture relates that, in the course of Tamar's birthing, a single hand first emerged, and the midwife placed a red thread around the wrist. The first boy to be fully delivered was Pharez,[63] but it was the hand of Zerah which had first entered the light of day and which bore the red thread. The dilemma, therefore, was in deciding which had actually been the firstborn son. It should have been Zerah, but Pharez had breached his way into position, and thereby was deemed to have gained the senior inheritance. Quite to what extent this account was literally contrived is unknown, but the details were hardly worth mentioning unless there was actually a point to be made in cementing Pharez as the primary inheritor of Judah.

In real terms of primogeniture, Judah (the father of Pharez) was not himself Jacob-Israel's senior heir in any event. That distinction rightfully belonged to Leah's firstborn son, Reuben. His four sons are listed in Genesis 46:9, but are totally ignored thereafter in respect of the El Shaddai covenant. Irrespective of any true right of succession, Judah's junior branch was strategically brought to the fore because it was from him that the eventual Davidic line of kingship ensued — albeit having commenced with Pharez, the illegitimate son of an illicit liaison between Judah and Tamar.

Part V

God of Tradition

12

YAHWEH THE INEFFABLE

A Generational Stratagem

Moving now to Joseph in Egypt — the story with which the book of Genesis concludes — we have something that we can actually check against the Egyptian annals. Genesis 45:8 quotes Joseph as saying, 'God hath made me a father to pharaoh, and lord of all his house, and a ruler throughout all the land of Egypt'. Quite suddenly, we have a major change in the family's fortune, and a junior member of the line has emerged inexplicably from slavery into a position of great prestige. So the question to be asked is: Was there a Joseph who ruled in Egypt, fathered a pharaoh, and who (as related in the Genesis narrative) would have ridden in the king's second chariot?[1]

The answer to each of these questions is 'Yes'; there was indeed an Israelite Joseph to whom these statements can all be applied. But it was not the same Joseph as in the Bible; their stories are four centuries apart, although the history of the latter was biblically grafted back onto the former to make them appear one and the same.

In consideration of this, we discover precisely why the book of Genesis ends with its account of Joseph in Egypt, whilst the following Old Testament book of Exodus begins with the story of Moses and the Israelites in much later times. It also becomes evident why (from the list of Jacob-Israel's twelve sons) there was never a Tribe of Joseph. Instead, the twelfth tribe was seemingly formed as a combination of Ephraim and Manasseh, who were said to have been Joseph's sons by Asenath, the daughter of Potiphar, a priest of the city of On.[2]

From evidence in the Egyptian records, it emerges that Joseph, the biblical son of Jacob, was moved literally from the company of his brothers by the writers of Genesis in order to link him with a prominent nobleman called Joseph (Yusuf) in Egypt some twelve generations later. In this regard, the introduction of Potiphar was conveniently suited to identifying the biblical Joseph with his later namesake who, at the age of thirty-three, did indeed marry the daughter of Poti-phera (*Pa-di-pa-ra*: 'Gift of the god Ra').[3]

An interesting aspect of the biblical scenario is the story of Joseph's attempted seduction by Potiphar's wife.[4] (The wife of the historical Poti-phera of later times was said to have been called Zelekah.)[5] When the biblical Joseph refused to submit to her wiles, the woman ripped his garment from him and presented it to her husband, claiming that she had narrowly escaped being assaulted by Joseph. Until a few decades ago, there appeared nothing untoward about this discreet little tale. But then Egyptologists translated a hieroglyphic document called the *Orbiney Papyrus* from 19th-dynasty Egypt (*c*.1250 BC). In this transcript they discovered the story's original prototype within the romantic lore of Egypt.[6] It recalled the unfortunate experience of a young man called Bata, and had nothing whatever to do with Joseph or Zelekah.

Attaching the dubious story of Potiphar's wife to the biblical Joseph, with the result that he was cast into prison, enabled the Genesis scribes to relate how (visited in his cell by the pharaoh's cup-bearer) Joseph became known as one who could decipher dreams. This led not only to Joseph's release, but to his interpreting dreams of the pharaoh, which prophesied a great famine. Consequently, Joseph was placed in charge of laying-up preparatory stores and received high promotion within the royal court. This brought his literary status to the strategically required level for association thereafter with Joseph the Vizier of much later times.

Genesis explains that eventually, as a result of the famine, which spread into Canaan, Jacob-Israel and his family — numbering seventy in all — came to seek Joseph's aid in Egypt. He established for them a settlement in the Nile delta country of Goshen,[7] and God qualified the words of his covenant with some additional information: 'Fear not to go down into Egypt, for I will there make of thee a great nation'.[8] Henceforth, these erstwhile

Hebrews and their descendants in Egypt became known as Israelites, or 'children of Israel'. Meanwhile, back in Canaan, the Hebrew legacy continued in parallel with the descendants of Ishmael and Esau becoming notable lords in the region.

The Grand Vizier

Eighty miles (*c.*129 km) south of modern Cairo is the town of Medinet-el-Faiyûm, where a 200-mile (322 km) canal has long transformed the desert into a lush garden paradise of fruit groves. Originally a meandering branch of the Nile with a deep lake depression called the *Payûm*, work began in the reign of Amenhotep III (*c.*1405–1367 BC) to transform it into a functional waterway for irrigation. To the local residents (the Fellahin) and throughout Egypt, the ancient waterway is traditionally known as *Bahr Yusuf* (Joseph's Canal), and was named after Joseph the Grand Vizier.[9]

In cementing the scriptural link between the two Josephs, Genesis 41:39–43 tells how the biblical Joseph was made Governor of Egypt:

> And Pharaoh said unto Joseph ... Thou shalt be over my house, and according unto thy word shall all my people be ruled; only in the throne will I be greater than thou ... And he made him ruler over all the land of Egypt.

It is also stated in the very last verse of Genesis that, when Joseph died, he was embalmed like a pharaoh — and this was precisely the historical case with Yusuf the later Vizier, who was indeed mummified and entombed in a fine sarcophagus in no less a place than the royal burial ground: the Valley of Kings at Western Thebes (modern Luxor).

Yusuf was the principal minister for the 18th-dynasty pharaoh Tuthmosis IV (*c.*1413–1405 BC), and for his son Amenhotep III. Yusuf's tomb was discovered in 1905, along with that of his wife

Tjuyu, and their mummies are now among the very best preserved in the Cairo Museum.[10]

It came as a great surprise to Egyptologists that anyone from outside the immediate royal family should have been mummified and buried in the Valley of Kings. Clearly, this couple were of tremendous importance in their day. Yusuf's funerary papyrus refers to him as 'The Holy Father of the Lord of the Two Lands' (*it ntr n nb tawi*), as does his royal funerary statuette. The style 'Lord of the Two Lands' was a pharaonic distinction relating to the kingdoms of Lower and Upper Egypt,[11] and it is plain that Yusuf was not only the viceroy and primary State official, but was also the father of a pharaoh (just as attributed to the biblical Joseph). He even held some personal kingly status, as determined by his own equally pharaonic designation: 'One trusted by the good god in the entire land'.[12]

The family of Yusuf was very influential, holding inherited property in the Nile delta, and he was a powerful military leader.[13] Anen, the elder son of Yusuf and Tjuyu, also rose to high office under Amenhotep III as Chancellor of Lower Egypt, High Priest of Heliopolis and Divine Father of the Nation. But it was their younger son, Aye, who held the special distinction, 'Father of the God',[14] and became Pharaoh in about 1352 BC.

Not only was Yusuf of individual royal significance, but so too was his wife Tjuyu. She held the special distinction of *Asenath* (*iw s-n-t*) — a style which derives from an 18th-dynasty Egyptian dialect, and means 'Belonging to the goddess Neith'.[15] Tjuyu was the daughter of Poti-phera, a priest of Heliopolis and, according to the *Corpus of Hieroglyphic Inscriptions* at the Brooklyn Museum, she was the designated King's Ornament (*kheret nesw*).

Albeit by a strategically fashioned scribal manipulation of time-frames (with two Josephs nearly half a millennium apart), it seems that we are now discovering the Egyptian aspect of the Bible's two-part covenant prophecy — for it was indeed Asenath, the daughter of Potiphar, a priest of On (Heliopolis), whom Genesis 41:45 spuriously identifies as the wife of the biblical Joseph more than four centuries earlier.

A Myth of Remembrance

The British anatomist, Grafton Elliot Smith, who examined Yusuf's mummified remains after their excavation, reported that 'his head shape is by no means a common one in the pure Egyptian'.[16] He was ultimately of Israelite descent — hence his Hebrew name Yusuf (Joseph). It had therefore been possible for the Bible writers expediently to close up the time-gap between him and the much earlier Joseph, son of Jacob-Israel.

The pharaohs in descent from Yusuf and Tjuyu have become known as the Amarna Kings; they were Akhenaten, Smenkhkare, Tutankhamun and Aye. Their short reigns were consecutive (c.1367–1338 BC) and, although the two Josephs were separated by 400 years, it is possible that they were genealogically connected, with the latter in descent from the former. If so, the Amarna Kings would certainly fit the prophesied El Shaddai covenant of Egyptian kingship made with Abraham and Isaac. It is rather more likely, however, that the biblical Joseph — if he truly existed by that name — never went to Egypt. It must be remembered that, of all Jacob-Israel's twelve sons, Joseph is the only one not to have had a Tribe named after him. From their latter-day knowledge of Yusuf the Vizier, however, the 'Joseph' name would have been well suited for use by the Genesis scribes in order to cover an inconsequential period of Israelite history and move swiftly from the time of Abraham to the time of Moses.

From the 18th-dynasty campaigns of Pharaoh Tuthmosis III (c.1490–1436 BC), the land of Canaan had been placed under Egyptian rule, and remained so into the era of the Amarna Kings. The American Egyptologist, James Henry Breasted of the Oriental Institute, referred to Tuthmosis III as the 'Napoleon of Egypt',[17] and the empire (from Syria to Western Asia), established by him and his son Amenhotep II, was indicative of the kingly domain promised to the descendants of Isaac, 'from the river of Egypt, unto the river Euphrates'.[18]

From the outset of Yusuf's sarcophagus discovery, Egyptologists were intrigued by its unusual hieroglyphics. In one way or another, Egyptian tomb inscriptions were generally related to the godhead under which the occupant was placed in life, revealing such deiform names as Ra, Amen, Thut and Ptah. But Yusuf's identification did not relate to any known god of Egypt. Instead, it was obscure, seemingly conveying a name such as *Yawa* or *Yuya*.[19] It even became common practice to refer to Yusuf himself as Yuya, and he is often referenced as such today.

With knowledge of Yusuf's Israelite heritage, the mystery of *Yuya* was ultimately revealed in the records of Yusuf and Tjuyu's daughter Tiye. She had married Pharaoh Amenhotep III to become a Queen of Egypt and, as we saw in chapter 7, it was in the unearthed library of Amenhotep III that a Mesopotamian *Adapa Tablet* concerning Enki, Nîn-kharsag and the creation of Adam was discovered in 1917.

Tiye's influence on Amenhotep III was great and, upon her marriage, the ancestral god of her Israelite culture was brought into the Egyptian pantheon. Yuya, it transpired was none other than El Shaddai who, after 400 years, had become known to the prevailing Israelites of Goshen as 'He who lives'. Stemming from the verbal root, *hayah* ('to live'), he was referred to as *Iouiya* or *Yaouai* — phonetically, 'Yahweh'.

At this stage of Israelite history in Egypt, we are just one generation removed from Moses. Thus it was that, when Moses led the exodus into Sinai, the godly heritage that travelled with them was that of Yaouai, and the identification of God by the style of 'Yahweh' moved into common usage beyond the confines of Egypt from that time.

In venerative terms, Yaouai was referred to by Israelites as the *Adon*, a Semitic word meaning 'Lord',[20] equivalent to the Egyptian *Aten*.[21] It is for this reason that, onwards from the time of Moses, the godly distinction of 'Adon' appears with some frequency in the Hebrew Bible alongside the more commonly expressed 'Yahweh'. It is as Adon that Moses first refers to God in Exodus 4:10, when negotiating the possibility of bringing the Israelites out of Egypt.

Upon his marriage to Tiye, Amenhotep III gave her the frontier city of Zarw in the delta land of Goshen, and made her the chief of his wives, even above his first wife, Queen Sitamun. At Zarw, he built the first 'Temple of the Lord' (the House of Aten) and excavated an enormous lake on which he placed his royal barge, called *Tehen Aten* (Aten Gleams).[22] The fortified settlement of Zarw was built on the site of the ancient city of Avaris. In later times it was reconstructed to become known as Pi-Rameses in the reign of Rameses II, who had been a mayor of the city.[23]

The essential difference between Aten and the indigenous gods of Egypt was that Aten did not have a personality that Amenhotep could ascertain. There was no associated mythology, no indication of character, nor any romantic lore that could be applied. But for Tiye and the Israelites the perception was somehow different in that Yaouai was deemed to live, albeit that through the period of sojourn his image had dissolved into its own myth of distant remembrance. Nonetheless, Amenhotep's representation for the Lord emerged as a glorious solar disc with downward rays terminating in hands. Ra was the great sun-god of the Egyptian nation, and the State god was Amen but, during the reign of Amenhotep III, the Aten disc of Yaouai was introduced as being the Light in which they prevailed.

The Genesis Players

Having now reached the end of Genesis with the death, mummification and burial of Joseph, we also emerge from the most colourful and engaging episode of the book. Albeit the story of Joseph was contrived as a personal fiction, it was inspired by a true account of Israelite history to provide a soundly grafted example of racial integration at the highest level, as was applicable in much later times. In parallel with this, however, the retained *Yaouai* tradition of the Israelites (as has recently been identified from the records of Yusuf, Tjuyu and Tiye) indicate that, even four centuries from the time of Abraham, the Israelite culture in Egypt was still largely Hebraic. Despite the individual professional rise of Yusuf-Yuya and those of his aristocratic circle, however, it is evident that the Israelites were mainly confined to the delta region of Goshen and were treated very much as a lower-ranked society by the Egyptian governors.

* * *

In scriptural terms pursuant to our investigation that the Bible is the foremost literary source of information about God, we discover once again that the text is not so much about God as might be imagined. Through 600 years of Genesis, from the time of Abraham (*c.*1960 BC) to the time of Moses (*c.*1360 BC), God has not played any physically active role, nor had any direct influence within the narrative. His last corporeal appearance was in the tent at Mamre and, as becomes evident in the ensuing book of Exodus, God has now disappeared from the reckoning as a personal entity, never to return as an 'on-the-ground' figure in the manner of his formative portrayal. Henceforth, God (by whatever name) becomes illusive and inscrutable, appearing only as an ethereal presence embodied within variously defined representations of natural and supernatural phenomena.

As for the male lead players of Genesis, we have witnessed a succession of fraternal disputes and a number of literary tactics to manipulate the descending line of seniority. In a process of scribal skulduggery, Cain's descendants have been sidelined in favour of those from his younger half-brother Seth. Ishmael has been disregarded to the benefit of his younger half-brother Isaac. Esau has lost his birthright to his younger twin Jacob, and Reuben has been bypassed to bring his third younger brother, Judah, to the fore as the progenitor of the eventual Davidic royal line in Jerusalem. Meanwhile, Joseph (one of Reuben's junior half-brothers) has been anachronistically characterized as the inheritor of a key aspect of the El Shaddai covenant.

Some of the more entertaining stories of Genesis, such as the Tower of Babel, the Mesopotamian Flood, and Joseph in Egypt, are now known to have been lifted wholesale from unrelated historical accounts whose stories were transposed to give weight to the biblical characters. Other than that, from the time of Abraham, the descendent patriarchs, Isaac and Jacob-Israel, emerge as a pretty uninspiring pair, who (as far as we are made aware) achieved very little. By contrast, the more impressive strains of the family were those descended from Cain, Ishmael and Esau, who appear to have gained some notable prominence in Mesopotamia, Edom and Canaan, but whose individual stories have been substantially ignored.

In the midst of all this, the women have not been presented in the best of lights. Eve was traduced and made subordinate to Adam because she proffered opinions of her own. Sarah was shunted between husbands, namely Abraham and Senusret. Hagar was banished with her son into the desert wilderness. Lot's daughters slept with their incognizant father. Rebekah duped her husband, Isaac, by disguising their younger son as his own older brother. Leah cheated Jacob into enforced wedlock. Rachel stole her father's household property. Dinah was raped and, finally, Tamar pretended to be a roadside harlot in order to conceive by her father-in-law. It will be interesting, therefore, to look closely at how other front-line women are portrayed as we progress through the balance of the Old Testament.[24]

Missing Years

The book of Exodus begins with a short account of Egyptian concern over the high level of Israelite procreation before leaping forward through the centuries to the birth of Moses. This becomes positively disconcerting, since the Joseph and Moses stories are portrayed as if they are linked together with hardly any time between them. It is especially disturbing, therefore, to read in the book of Numbers that, when Moses led the Israelites out of Egypt, the said seventy members of Jacob-Israel's family[25] had somehow multiplied to about two-million people, including an army of 603,550 male warriors aged over twenty.[26]

In historical confirmation of the Israelites' sojourn in Egypt, the annals of Pharaoh Rameses II (c.1304–1237 BC) make reference to Semitic people who were settled in the delta region of Goshen, but it does not specify them alone as Israelites. In reality, the

Semites of the region included other races from Syria, Phoenicia and Mesopotamia.[27] Apart from mentioning Semitic people in Goshen, these records (and those of Rameses' predecessor, Seti I) also refer to the town of Asher in Canaan.[28] But, Asher (as referenced in Joshua 17:7) was named after one of the Tribes of Israel who returned to Canaan with the Mosaic exodus,[29] thereby indicating that the exodus must have taken place before, or during, the reign of Seti (c.1333–1304 BC).

Genesis 47:11 states that, whilst in Egypt, Joseph's relatives were settled in the 'land of Rameses', while Exodus 1:11 claims that they actually built the city of Rameses (Pi-Rameses). However, Rameses I did not reign until c.1335 BC, and Rameses II not until c.1304 BC. In fact, it was quite impossible for Jacob-Israel and his family to have settled in the 'land of Rameses' because they arrived in Egypt many centuries before the Ramesside era. These incongruous biblical statements began to puzzle historians in Victorian times, but it has since been recognized that the comments relating to Rameses are anachronisms. They arose because the Old Testament compilers referred to the Egyptian delta settlement by the name known to them in the 6th century BC when that part of the Nile delta was called the 'Land of Rameses' and remained so-called until the 4th century AD.[30]

The Israelite exodus appears to have progressed in protracted waves from the time of Moses, and it seems that many Israelites remained in Egypt following the departure of the main body.[31] A reasonable guide to the timing of events was established in 1997 when cereals from the old archaeological layer at Jericho were carbon-14 dated to be about 3,311 years old.[32] This dates them to the early 14th century BC, which means that the exodus Israelites, who demolished the city when crossing the River Jordan into Canaan, had not arrived there at that time.

Additionally, the science journal *Nature* has identified the volcanic ash from the eruption of Mount Santorini in the Mediterranean with the biblical plague of darkness in Egypt, thereby wholly disassociating the event from the Moses timeframe as it is presented in Exodus.[33] The effect in Egypt of this volcanic disaster and its accompanying earthquake (geologically dated to 1624 BC) is related in the *Ipuwer Papyrus* acquired by the Museum of Leiden in 1828. This multi-page 19th-dynasty document, copied from an earlier source, tells of a series of devastating events in Egypt, in keeping with the plagues of Exodus, and it states that the fire and ash which consumed the land 'fell from the skies' some 300 years before the time of Moses.[34]

For a biblical perspective on the matter (so as to cover the centuries between the books of Genesis and Exodus), the duration of the Israelite sojourn in Egypt is claimed in the Hebrew scripture to have been 'four hundred and thirty years'.[35] In the King James Authorized Bible, the corresponding Exodus verse similarly states, 'Now the sojourning of the children of Israel, who dwelt in Egypt, was four hundred and thirty years'.[36] If this calculation is roughly correct as stated, from the days of Jacob-Israel, then the initial wave of Israelite departure into Sinai with Moses would have occurred around the middle 14th century BC.

The Terror of God

For all the grand *ziggurat* temples of their Mesopotamian heritage, and the temples which existed in Egypt, never once do we have Abraham, Isaac or Jacob even mentioning the temple concept in Canaan. At best, all we have are a few references to their individual constructions of primitive stone-heaped altars in the hills and wild places,[37] where they made offerings of drink and oil,[38] and performed animal sacrifices.[39] In terms of anything that might be likened to religious veneration in the form of prayer, the only reference occurs in Genesis 20:17, when Abraham requests that El Shaddai might somehow aid King Abimalech and his wife to have children. It was not until the time of Moses, 600 years later, that the idea of a religious priesthood emerged as an Israelite concept based upon the Egyptian model. The first related temple was the Tabernacle of the Congregation, constructed during the Mosaic exodus at Mount Horeb in Sinai.[40]

Following his said eradication of Sodom and Gomorrah, we see a fast decline in God's personal activity, much of which had, in any event, been entirely destructive. In the post-Abrahamic era, God's enterprise becomes quite secondary to the family orientated thrust of the scriptural narrative. He changes Jacob's name to Israel and reminds the patriarchs, with some regularity, that their descendants will become a great nation. But God is otherwise incidental to the ongoing saga. In a way this is not surprising because, as the Mesopotamian records ceased to be relevant to accounts of the new homeland, there was a limited supply of source material for the Genesis writers until they found the Canaanite texts concerning El Elyon's family, his Court of Assembly at Baalbek, and his *Pavilion* at Bêth-El.

The godly figure of El is cited 250 times in the Hebrew Bible,[41] with a number of specific references to God as El Elyon[42] and 48 mentions of him as El Shaddai.[43] These entries all denote that the God of Abraham, Isaac and Jacob was indeed the supreme Lord of the Canaanites — previously known to those such as Adam and Lamech as Enlil (Ilû Kur-gal) in Mesopotamia. Also, notwithstanding the singular application of the word in translations, the plural term *Elohim* (Shining Ones) is used no less than 2,570 times,[44] although wholly ignored in Christian Bibles.

God, by whatever name, appears to have been feared and revered by Abraham's successors, but had not yet moved into the realm of what might be termed a formally religious environment. On two occasions he is referred to in Hebrew as 'the Terror',[45] a figure that was both awesome and frightening.[46] This image was personified by his amazing powers of destruction, whether evident as floods, tempests, earthquakes or heavenly fire. The difficulty in understanding the situation from a readership perspective results from the lack of contemporary Hebrew literature from the period in question. We have only the scriptural opinion of what had been the case, penned by the hands of indoctrinated priestly writers in much later times. We do not know whether they were 'reflecting' the Abrahamic image of God as they truly understood it, or whether they were 'creating' the Abrahamic image of God to suit the mood of their own era. Either way, since the Genesis writers had the freedom to convey very much what they wanted, the likelihood is that we are presented with a retrospectively applied concept based on attitudes concerning God in their own period of writing. At that juncture, a great many Israelites had been in Babylonian bonded service for some decades. As far as the Israelite community was concerned, God had allowed this, and had obviously condoned it. He was therefore acknowledged as being harsh, judgemental, egocentric and expressly intolerant — a perception that is made very evident in the *Torah* book of Leviticus:

> If ye will not hearken unto me, and will not do all these commandments … I will even appoint over you terror, consumption, and the burning ague, that shall consume the eyes, and cause sorrow of heart: and ye shall sow your seed in vain, for your enemies shall eat it.[47]

Previously, in Exodus 20:5, it is stated:

> I the Lord thy God am a jealous God, visiting the iniquity of the fathers upon the children unto the third and fourth generations of them that hate me.

The Israelites believed they had been taken into captivity by Nebuchadnezzar of Babylon because their kings were not always wholly committed to a monotheistic doctrine.[48] Upon their eventual return to Jerusalem, they assumed every reason to fear the further retribution of Yahweh if they did not adopt an attitude of unquestioned subservience. This led to the subjugative mood in which the Hebrew Bible was written and, consequently, to a very insensitive and dictatorial portrayal of a God who had never been depicted in such a way by the earlier chroniclers of Canaan or Mesopotamia.

Change of Perception

From that time in the 6th century BC, 'Yahweh' became the most commonly used term for identifying God, even to the erroneous extent of it being deemed an actual name. Given that the term had sprung from an Israelite origin in Egypt, it was felt that God would approve. But, even then, a certain trepidation prevailed: Would God perhaps take exception to hearing his name spread abroad by everyday people in public? Consequently, when the rebuilt Temple of Jerusalem was completed in c.520 BC, a ruling was introduced to circumvent the risk. Henceforth, the name of God was considered generally to be 'unutterable'. Only the High Priest of the Temple was permitted to say the name 'Yahweh' as a once-a-year privilege on the Day of Atonement. The utterance was restricted to the inner sanctum of the *Holy of Holies*, and had to be whispered by the priest beyond the earshot of others.[49]

Two thousand years later, in AD 1518,[50] Christian interpreters of the Lutheran Reformation hit upon the idea of revising the 'Yahweh' name for the new Protestant movement. This was accomplished by a substitution of vowels within the stem *YHWH* added to phonetic assimilation ($j = y$ and $v = w$), with the resultant hybrid being 'Jehovah'. Whilst absolutely meaningless in terms of any original context, the name was readily accepted and gained four entries in the King James Bible.[51] Although essentially the corrupted product of anti-Semitic culture in Western Europe, the provocative *Jehovah* terminology (which should have been abandoned long ago) is still emphasized by some fundamentalist and otherwise non-mainstream denominations of the Christian movement today.

As well as the name 'Yahweh' being unutterable by Jews from the period of the Second Temple, it was also the case that God himself became an altogether mysterious character. Somehow, during the untold 400 missing years within the book of Genesis, the perception of God (at least in the minds of the eventual *Torah* writers) was changed from being that of a physical entity to one of spiritual and miraculous presence — from the natural to the supernatural — in the way that he is still perceived today.

One thing of which we can be sure is that, if there were any historical record of God having a physical presence after the exodus (as was the case in earlier-written Mesopotamian and Canaanite tablets), then the Bible writers would have seized the opportunity to recount any available instance. As it transpired, they completely changed the literary and doctrinal nature of the deity to that of an ineffable God in an unfathomable environment — an inscrutable overlord without an image. Moreover, the making of any image became strictly forbidden[52] — an edict that is still observed in the Jewish and Islāmic faiths. All artistic depictions of the widely familiar heavenly Father, as the ever-watchful Ancient of Days, come from the Christian interpretations of a much later era and bear little comparison to the vengeful, jealous and dictatorial God portrayed in the Old Testament.

In the light of this, a question now arises in that we have travelled through a period of roughly 3,000 years from the time of Adam and Eve in the garden, and more than 600 years from the days of Abraham. Had this one God, by whatever name, actually prevailed in character for such a length of time? Is he really 'from everlasting to everlasting' as claimed in the scripture?[53] Is it truly the case that 'He will endure and his years will have no end'?[54]

If the answer to any of these questions can possibly be 'Yes', then such an answer can only relate to a spiritual perception — a notion of immaterial dimensional endurance. Whatever the case, we are still left with the fact that, whilst God was moved into the realm of incorporeality from around 1400 BC, he was undeniably recorded outside the Bible (whether as Enlil, Ilû Kur-gal, El Elyon or El Shaddai) as a material presence prior to that date. The last of the Ras Shamra tablets (produced through a term of some 500 years) emanate from precisely that time, around 1400 BC, indicating that God's 'on-the-ground' tradition still prevailed at Bêth-El in Canaan. But that was the last of it; there are no such records coming forwards from that date.

Whilst considering the overall concept of extreme longevity, even to the point of eventual culmination, we should remain aware that, as we saw in chapter 6, the *Anannage* establishment was heritably dynastic. There was always a supreme El (along with those of other titular office), but different individuals carried the distinction in successive generations. Thus, irrespective of the *c.*1400 BC deadline for recorded material presence, it is necessarily the case that the El who walked in the garden with Adam would not have been the same El who sat in the tent with Abraham.

There is no specific reference to the God known as El having perhaps died or vacated the earthly domain in about 1400 BC, but all available first-hand records suggest that his active dynasty expired around that time. This, of course, gives rise to the question of whether God's presumed existence from that date, down to the present day, is purely a matter of continued superstitious belief rather than being an aspect of historic reality.

From a base of ancient Mesopotamian understanding, the quest for immortality was treated as the initial driving force behind the *Epic of Gilgamesh*. It was the objective that caused Gilgamesh to seek out his ancestor Uta-napishtim who, although actually long dead, is envisioned as being accessible in an eternal abode. Uta-napishtim explained, nevertheless, that the Gilgamesh search was in vain, for even the gods were not immortal. At best, he revealed the secret of a miraculous plant that could 'turn an oldster into a child again' so that, by repeatedly eating from the plant in old age, one could keep returning to childhood. But this was not what Gilgamesh was seeking; it was not the same as a progressive eternal life. What he ultimately learned from Uta-napishtim was that immortality is not an aspect of physical potential; it is a purely relative matter. It is obtained by way of lasting achievement — worthwhile deeds that outlive one for posterity, as exemplified by the great city walls of Uruk.[55]

* * *

Moving our sights from the book of Genesis, the next event with God playing a major scriptural role (although not actually in person) occurs in the book of Exodus around 600 years from when last encountered with Abraham at Mamre. On this occasion, Moses hears his voice from the midst of a burning bush in Sinai. At this stage, God is identified as Adon, but tells Moses that he is 'El Shaddai, the God of Abraham, Isaac and Jacob', further explaining that he is *Yaouai* (He who lives), which is biblically interpreted as 'I am that I am'.[56]

In the course of various Sinai incidents which follow in Exodus, we have a series of apparent communications between

Moses and God on the mountain — the presentation of the Ten Commandments and so forth. But we are not given the impression that God and Moses are necessarily in face-to-face contact. We read such comments from God as, 'Now, therefore, if ye will obey my voice',[57] and 'I come unto thee in a thick cloud, so that the people may hear when I speak'.[58]

In Exodus 24:10 it is given that beneath the Lord was a pavement like sapphire stone, 'as it were the body of heaven'. Then, in Leviticus, is the mention of another godly image, but it is still not a personal presence — only that 'the glory of the Lord appeared unto all the people'.[59] Later, in Numbers, it is stated that the Lord 'came down in a pillar of cloud' to the door of the tabernacle, where he announced that he might make himself seen 'in a vision' and would speak to any prophet 'in a dream' — after which 'the cloud departed'.[60]

Just as El Shaddai had become a myth of distant remembrance to the Israelites in Egypt, so too was he now a Mosaic-era reminiscence as far as the Bible writers were concerned. They could so easily have perpetuated a literary tradition of continued earthly presence for the purposes of a more forceful scripture, but they did not. In accordance with all contemporary evidence, the scribes elected to explain (even putting the words into God's own mouth) that henceforth Yahweh would be experienced only in visions and dreams.

13

THE MOSES REVELATION

A Basket of Rushes

Moving forwards through the centuries, from the time that Jacob-Israel and his sons were said to have joined the biblical Joseph in Egypt, we enter the book of Exodus in the days of Yusuf the Vizier. In taking this scribally concealed leap through 400 years, the two ends of the tale are linked by way of a man 'of the house of Levi' and his wife, 'a daughter of Levi'.[1]

Given that Levi was reckoned to be one of the biblical Joseph's brothers, the inference is that the 'daughter of Levi' and her husband were contemporary with that era. But we are actually in a new time-frame with Amram and Jochebed,[2] descendants in the Levi succession.

We have also now entered a new biblical phase wherein the patriarchal period of the Abrahamic Hebrews is over. Concentration from this point, and through the rest of the Bible, is on the descendants of Jacob-Israel alone. Henceforth, we follow the path of the Israelites, with Yaouai now regarded as the God of Israel.

The book of Exodus does not stipulate the particular pharaonic era of its scriptural opening, but we are in the reign of Pharaoh Amenhotep III, with the scene in readiness for Moses to emerge as a champion of the Israelites in Egypt. Amram and Jochebed are said to be his parents and, on joining Moses at the time of his birth, we are advised that the palace authorities had instructed that all newborn Israelite sons should be cast into the river and drowned. Although fabricated by the scribes for story-line purposes, this supposed blanket sentence facilitates the telling of yet another biblically grafted tale which, for all its practical irrelevance to Israelite history, has become a popular mainstay of the Mosaic tradition.

The biblically given reason for the edict is that the Israelites had 'multiplied, and waxed exceeding mighty, and the land was filled with them'.3 But when Jochebed has a son, he is secretly kept alive and placed by his mother in an ark of bulrushes daubed with pitch, which she hides among the water-reeds.4

Despite the illogicality of this action, the story then becomes even more implausible, for along comes the pharaoh's daughter, who discovers the baby and begins conversing with the boy's sister, who just happens to be standing nearby. The sister then returns the baby to its mother, who is paid by the princess to nurse him. Hence, the boy is back where he began, and any fear of the death threat seems conveniently to have been forgotten. Eventually, the princess adopts the boy as her own son and calls him Moses, with no one levelling any query about the child's natural parents. That is the extent of the biblical story of Moses' childhood, and in the very next verse he is portrayed as a grown man.5

Like so many of the more colourful Old Testament stories, the tale of Moses and the ark of rushes was adapted and reapplied from a much older Mesopotamian original. In this instance the prototype was the *Legend of Sharru-kîn*, who became Sargon the Great, King of Akkad (2725–2671 BC). An Akkadian text relating to Sargon reads:

> My changeling mother conceived me; in secret she bare me. She set me in a basket of rushes, and with pitch she sealed my lid. She cast me into the river, which rose not over me. The river bore me up, and carried me to Akki, the drawer of the water.6

The definition 'drawer of the water' is significant because, according to Exodus 2:10, Moses was given his name by the pharaoh's daughter who 'drew him out of the water'. In Hebrew, the name Moses is rendered as *Mosheh*, and is generally reckoned to derive from the Hebrew word *mosche*, which means 'the drawer out',7 from the verb *m-sh-a*: 'to draw'.8 It is very doubtful, however, that an Egyptian princess would have been aware of such Hebrew etymology. Had the story been factual, she would more likely have used an Egyptian name for the boy she adopted. Either way, it is clear that the nominal root, as explained in Exodus, was purposely structured to conform to the role of Akki, the 'drawer of the water', in the *Legend of Sharru-kîn*.

In researching the origin of Moses' name, James Henry Breasted (founder of the Oriental Institute at Chicago University in 1922), along with Sigmund Freud and others, discovered that it actually derived from the Egyptian word *mose* (Greek: *mosis*), which related to an 'offspring' or 'heir'[9] — as in Tuthmose (Tuthmosis): 'born of Thoth', and Amenmose (Amenmosis): 'born of Amen'.[10]

Following the story of the princess and the ark of rushes, we are soon with Moses in his adulthood with a wife called Zipporah of Midian.[11] A strange inconsistency then creeps into the text, with Zipporah's father being called Reuel in Exodus 2:18–21, whereas only five verses later the man's name has inexplicably changed to Jethro.[12] This exemplifies how the Old Testament compilers skipped, not very cleverly, through the centuries from Reuel, the son of Esau,[13] to his eventual descendant Jethro, the Lord of Midian.

We then learn that Moses became 'very great in the land of Egypt, in the sight of pharaoh's servants, and in the sight of the people'.[14] Meanwhile, and in apparent contrast to the story of his Israelite birth, we have been advised in Exodus 2:19 that Moses was actually 'an Egyptian'. In this regard, he was discussed by name in *The Aegyptiaca* by Manetho who, in about 300 BC, was an adviser to Pharaoh Ptolemy I. Manetho recorded that Moses had been an Egyptian priest at Heliopolis,[15] and the 1st-century Jewish chronicler, Flavius Josephus, subsequently wrote that Moses commanded the Egyptian army against the Ethiopians, and had married an Ethiopian princess called Tharbis.[16]

Despite the fact that we know the 'ark of bulrushes' tale came from the Mesopotamian folklore of Sharru-kîn, we could ask if there is perhaps something similar in Egyptian record — maybe the story of a boy under sentence who was saved in the era of Yusuf the Vizier. At the same time, we might enquire if such a boy was raised at the royal court as a noble heir (a *mose* or *mosis*), and was later associated with the priests of Heliopolis, eventually to become 'very great in the land of Egypt'.

This is actually quite a lot to ask in respect of one individual in a particular generational time-frame but, as we shall see, there was indeed a prominent figure to whom all these things can be attributed. At the same time it becomes wholly evident why Yusuf the Vizier was so important to the biblical narrative.

A Faceless God

As already determined, Yusuf was chief minister to the pharaohs Tuthmosis IV and Amenhotep III. When Tuthmosis died, his son Amenhotep married his infant sister Sitamun (as was the pharaonic tradition) so that he could inherit the throne. In line with the originally established principles of *Anannage* kingship in Mesopotamia, it was common practice for the pharaohs to marry their sisters in order to progress the kingship through the female line. These wives were generally the pharaohs' half-sisters, born of their mothers by different fathers.[17] It can be seen from genealogical charts of the era that, although Egypt had many successive kingly dynasties, the houses were only historically renumbered when a pharaoh died without a male heir. The important thing was that his senior queen had a female heiress (whether by her husband or preferably by some other man), and it was upon that daughter's marriage into another male line that a new reigning dynasty began. In essence, although individual successions were based on a father-to-son inheritance, the kingly bloodline itself was reckoned to be matrilineal.

Given that Sitamun was very young, Amenhotep also married Tiye, the adult daughter of Tjuyu and Yusuf the Vizier. It was decreed, however, that no son born to Tiye could inherit the throne and, because of the length of her father's governorship, there was a general fear that his Israelite relatives were gaining too much power in Egypt. It was also the case that, since Tiye was not the recognized legitimate royal heiress, she could not

191

represent the State god Amen.[18] So when she became pregnant, there were many at court who felt that her child should be killed at birth if a son.

Security arrangements were therefore made with Tiye's Israelite relatives at Goshen. She had a summer palace there, on the lakeside at Zarw, where she went to have her baby. The royal midwives then conspired to have the boy wet-nursed by Tiye's sister-in-law Tey, a woman of the house of Levi.

Tiye's son, another Amenhotep (born c.1394 BC), was later educated at Heliopolis by the Egyptian priests of Ra, and lived at Thebes during his teenage years. By that time, his mother had become more influential than the senior queen Sitamun, who had never borne a son and heir to the pharaoh, only a daughter who was called Nefertiti. Since young Amenhotep was precluded from any dynastic inheritance, Nefertiti was the direct matrilineal heiress to the throne, and the next pharaoh would, therefore, be the man that she married.

Amenhotep III then suffered a period of ill health and, since there was no direct male heir to the royal house, the restrictive law was relaxed in favour of Tiye's son. Young Amenhotep was permitted to marry his half-sister Nefertiti in order to rule as co-regent during this difficult time and, when their father died, he succeeded as Amenhotep IV.[19] Were it not for this marriage, the 18th dynasty would have expired at their father's death.[20]

Notwithstanding his time with the priests in Heliopolis, the new pharaoh, Amenhotep IV,[21] could not accept the Egyptian deities and their myriad idols. His upbringing had been greatly influenced by his mother's Israelite model and that of her father Yusuf, the Grand Vizier, whose traditional God, Yaouai, had been acknowledged and promoted as the *Aten* by his own father Amenhotep III. Resultantly, Amenhotep IV progressed and developed the *Yaouai* concept, even changing his own name from Amenhotep (Amen is pleased) to Akhenaten (Glorious spirit of the Aten).[22] Taking his ideal to the extreme, however, he closed all the temples of the Egyptian gods and became very unpopular, particularly with the priests of Ra and those of the traditional national deity, Amen.

It was the world's first major example of religious intolerance at a State level — a strict monotheism foisted upon the people with a preclusion of any choice.[23] This somewhat discordant concept of the One God in Egypt prior to the Mosaic exodus inspired the related 1930s research of the Moravian psychoanalyst Sigmund Freud. In line with a previous Oriental Institute investigation by James Henry Breasted, it was determined that 'Moses' (whether as *Mose, Mosis* or *Moses*) was not a Hebrew name at that stage; it was a distinctive appellation of an Egyptian royal heir. This led Freud to associate the biblical Moses directly with the reign of Pharaoh Akhenaten.

Not surprisingly, there were plots against Akhenaten's life, and threats of armed insurrection if he did not allow the traditional gods to be worshipped alongside the faceless God of the Israelites. But Akhenaten refused and was eventually forced to abdicate in short-term favour of his cousin Smenkhkare, who was succeeded by Tutankhaten, Akhenaten's son by his deputy queen, Khiba.

On taking the throne at the age of eleven, Tutankhaten was obliged to change his name to Tutankhamun, thereby denoting a renewed allegiance to Amen (Amun) rather than to Aten. But he was to live for only a further nine or ten years. Akhenaten, meanwhile, was banished from Egypt in about 1361 BC,[24] although to his supporters he remained the rightful monarch. He was the living heir to the throne from which he had been ousted, and was still regarded by them as the royal *Mose*, or *Moses*.

The Cult of Amarna

Prior to his departure from Egypt, Akhenaten had been persuaded by his mother, Tiye, to move from Thebes into a safer environment. Resultantly, he established his newly-built centre of Akhetaten (Horizon of the Aten)[25] at El Amarna — now called *Tell el-Amarna*. Hence it was that he and the 18th-dynasty pharaohs who reigned after him became known to historians as the Amarna Kings. In addition to his father's *House of Aten* temple at Zarw, Akhenaten also built his own temples to honour Yaouai at Amarna, Karnak and Luxor.[26]

Although Yaouai was relegated to a listed position within the Egyptian pantheon during the reign of Tutankhamun, the Israelite God was not banned by the young pharaoh. This is confirmed by the magnificent gold and inlaid back panel of his throne, which depicts him and his wife, Ankhesenpa-aten, together with the Aten disc. Tutankhamun did, however, move the royal capital from Akhetaten (El Amarna) to Memphis.[27]

When young Tutankhamun died in 1352 BC, the crown was transferred back up the family line to his great-uncle Aye. As we saw in the previous chapter, Aye was the son of Tjuyu and Yusuf the Vizier. He held the special distinction 'Father of the God' and was the brother of Akhenaten's mother, Tiye. Thus, when we read in Genesis 45:8 that the biblical Joseph was 'father to a pharaoh', it is to this eventual father/son event of Yusuf and Aye that the manipulated citation refers.

Pharaoh Aye was also the husband of Tey, who had nursed both Akhenaten and his half-sister Nefertiti. This now brings us full circle to the details of Moses' birth at the beginning of Exodus, where we learned that his parents were known as Amram and Jochebed.[28]

The nominal distinction of 'Amarna', which defined the kings of the Akhenaten family strain, derived from *Im-r-n* (*Imran*),[29] which denoted a 'People's Highness'.[30] In its Semitic form, the equivalent was *Amram* (the root being *ram* or *rama*, meaning 'height'). In patriarchal terms, the designated Amram of the era was Akhenaten's uncle Aye. (It was in his tomb that Akhenaten's famous *Hymn to the Aten* was discovered — the hymn which provided the model for the Bible's Psalm 104.)

There is no immediately obvious reason why Exodus 6:20 should claim that Aye the *Amram* was the father of Akhenaten the *Moses*, but he was of course the husband of Tey, who had wet-nursed Akhenaten and was therefore his 'feeding mother'. Her birth-name, however, was Yokâbar (Jochebed), a descendant of the house of Levi, just as biblically explained.[31] Her separate identification as Tey was a customarily bestowed grant by royal prerogative, being a variant of Tiye for whom she had nursed the royal heir. In this respect, Tey was called 'the great nurse, nourisher of the god, adorner of the king'.[32]

Aye, the ageing son of Yusuf the Vizier and Tjuyu the *Asenath*, was the last to reign of the Amarna line. He was succeeded by his son-in-law, Horemheb, an Egyptian traditionalist who refused to acknowledge Yaouai and terminated the Aten cult altogether. Moreover, he forcibly excised the 18th-dynasty Amarna Kings (Akhenaten, Smenkhkare, Tutankhamun and Aye) from the official *King List* and destroyed numerous monuments of the Amarna period.[33] It was for this reason that the discovery of Tutankhamun's tomb by Howard Carter in November 1922 came as such a welcome surprise, for so little was known about him or his family before that time.[34]

The Burning Bush

Following his deposition, and as explained in Exodus, Akhenaten (now recorded as the *Moses*) fled to the land of Midian, east of the Sinai peninsula.[35] There he married Zipporah, the daughter of Lord Jethro, and she bore him two sons, Gershom and Eliezer.[36]

At length, in the vicinity of Mount Horeb in Sinai, a burning bush halts Moses in his tracks. The bush is enveloped in a fiery light, but is not in any way consumed,[37] and an angel appears from its midst. A voice is then heard from the bush, claiming to be the voice of El Shaddai, 'the God of Abraham, the God of Isaac, and the God of Jacob'. God explains to Moses that plans should be made to bring the Israelites out of Egypt into Canaan. Baffled by this, and with no allegiance to any god but the *Adon*, Moses asks for better identification. He is told in reply, '*Yaouai*' (He who lives) — or, as rendered in Hebrew, '*Yhwh*', said in translation to mean 'I am that I am'.[38] The Hebrew Bible later adds the more explicit response: 'I appeared unto Abraham, unto Isaac and unto Jacob by the name of El Shaddai'.[39]

Whatever the historical provenance of the burning bush sequence, the incident was well used by the biblical scribes to assert the fact that El Shaddai of the Abrahamic Hebrews and Yaouai of the Goshen Israelites were considered to be one and the same God.

By that time, after the premature death of Tutankhamun and the subsequent death of Aye, Egypt had come under the harsh new rule of Pharaoh Horemheb, who eradicated the Amarna legacy and placed the Israelites of Goshen in bonded service. Horemheb had no royal blood in his veins, and had previously been a commander in the Egyptian army, but gained his kingly position by marrying Smenhkhare's sister Mutnogjme, the daughter of Aye and Tey.

Moses asks Yaouai how he will prove to the Israelites that he has the power and ability to free them, whereupon three instructions are given by the voice from the burning bush.[40] He should first cast his rod to the ground, where it will become a serpent, but will be reinstated as a rod when lifted. Secondly, he must place his hand on his breast, where it will become white and leprous, but will return to normal when the act is repeated. Then he should pour river water onto the land, at which it will turn to blood.

Moses seems content enough with the plan, but confesses that he is 'not eloquent', being 'slow of speech, and of a slow tongue', intimating that he is not well versed in the Israelite language. It is therefore arranged that his brother Aaron, who is more fluent, will act as an interpreter.

Until this point in the story, only an unnamed sister of Moses has been introduced (the sister who spoke with the princess when the ark of rushes was discovered). But now a brother called Aaron makes his scriptural appearance,[41] and with a somewhat baffling aftermath. Moses journeys back to Egypt, where he meets with Aaron, but it is before the Pharaoh, not the Israelites, that the magic of the rod and serpent is performed. Moreover, it is not performed by Moses, but by Aaron.[42]

This sequence is of particular importance because it serves to indicate that Aaron held his own pharaonic status. The rituals of the serpent-rod and the withered hand were both aspects of the rejuvenation festivals of the Egyptian kings — ceremonies wherein their divine powers were said to be heightened.

The pharaohs had various sceptres (rods) for different occasions, and the sceptre of rejuvenation was a rod topped with a brass serpent. It was also customary for the king to place his right arm limply across his chest, whilst supporting it with his left hand.[43] A preparation for this ceremony is pictorially shown in the tomb of Kherof, one of Queen Tiye's stewards, and the scene depicts her husband (Moses' father) Amenhotep III.

So, did Akhenaten the *Moses* have a brother who was himself a pharaoh, whose fate is unknown and who, like Akhenaten, is similarly recorded as having disappeared rather than dying? Indeed he did — at least he had a feeding-brother whose own mother was Tey, the Israelite wet-nurse of Akhenaten. As we have seen above, his name was Smenkhkare (*Smenkh-kare*: Vigorous is the soul of Re).[44] Given that Re (Ra) was the State sun-god of On (the Heliopolis House of Light), Smenkhkare was also *Smenkh-kara-on*, from the phonetic ending of which derives the name Aaron.

It is under this very name of Aaron that Smenkhkare appears in the Gaelic annals of old Ireland. It was his daughter (known in the West as Scota) who married Niul, a Black Sea prince of Scythia, and took her family to Eire-land.[45] During Smenkhkare's reign, Niul was the Governor of Capacyront by the Red Sea,[46] and in this regard the Irish annals state that 'Niul and Aaron entered into an alliance of friendship with one another ... at the time when Moses began to act as leader of the children of Israel'.[47]

Tombs and Exiles

When Akhenaten first left Egypt, the pharaonic crown had been transferred to Smenkhkare. Nefertiti appears to have died a short while before this and, although her remains have not yet been unearthed, a cartouche bearing her name was discovered in the 1930s in the royal tomb at El Amarna. In fact, sixty-seven cartouches have been found with her name, in contrast with only three for her husband, Akhenaten.[48] His royal cartouches were mostly destroyed or defaced by Pharaoh Horemheb.

Prior to that, Smenkhkare had married Merytaten, a daughter of Akhenaten and Nefertiti, in order that he could succeed to the throne. For a while he reigned as co-regent alongside Akhenaten, but his later individual reign only lasted a few months, during which period his wife, Merytaten, died. Then not long after Akhenaten's departure, Smenkhkare also disappeared from Egyptian records and his remains have never been found. This left Akhenaten's young son, Tutankhaten, to succeed as king thereafter, which he achieved by marrying Merytaten's sister, Akhesenpa-aten.

A tomb over which controversy prevails in respect of Akhenaten is not at El Amarna, but that numbered KV 55 in the Theban Valley of Kings. This tomb was discovered, unfinished and water damaged, in January 1907. It has only one burial chamber and the body within was identified as a female. At first it was thought that it was perhaps Akhenaten's mother, Queen Tiye, but this was only a guess since there were no cartouches to indicate the occupant's name. There were, nevertheless, remnants of Tiye's gold-overlaid sarcophagus. Subsequently, another female body was found in the nearby tomb KV 35 (the tomb of Amenhotep II) and this is now reckoned to be the body of Queen Tiye.[49]

In the wake of this discovery, the body from tomb KV 55 (which is not mummified, just a badly preserved skeleton) seems mysteriously to have changed sex, and was then claimed to be that of Akhenaten himself.[50] Recognizing, however, that the body was actually female, some writers even suggested that perhaps Akhenaten was really a woman masquerading as a man — completely disregarding the fact that he and Nefertiti are known to have had six daughters.[51]

Akhenaten's formally planned tomb site has since been separately located at El Amarna, where it appears to have been cut from the rock in about year-six of his 17 year reign. Also found is the outer of his three destined mummy casings (the main sarcophagus), but there are none of the inner casings that would have been used to house his eventual mummy; nor are there any items of funerary furniture. The tomb was never used, and there is not a shred of evidence concerning his death.[52] Akhenaten the *Moses* simply disappeared from the land along with his second wife, Khiba (the mother of Tutankhamun), and they were soon followed into oblivion by Akhenaten's feeding-brother Smenkhkare. At much the same time, however, three prominent characters emerged in the pages of biblical history as notable exiles from Egypt; they were Moses, Miriam and Aaron.

A Realm of Belief

At this stage of the biblical narrative, Exodus 12:40 advises that we are 430 years from when Abraham's grandson, Jacob-Israel, took his sons into Egypt. We are around 500 years from when El Elyon addressed Jacob from the stairway at Bêth-El, and approaching 600 years from when El Shaddai visited Abraham's tent at Mamre.

Not once in all that time has God played any part in the scriptural proceedings. Not a word was written about his involvement throughout the Israelite sojourn in Egypt, and we have learned nothing of his activities meanwhile back in Canaan or elsewhere.

If the Bible is the definitive work concerning the Judaeo-Christian God, which necessarily it must be since there is no comparative volume, then it is proving to be remarkably uninformative. At no stage has there been any attempt to prove, nor even to explain, the existence of God; his reality is simply taken as read from the outset. But this was not for the want of scribal access to original source material. As we have seen, there is a wealth of very ancient documentation to support the Bible's variously named identifications of God as a figure of record from long before Genesis was compiled. Fortunately, much of this comprehensive archive has become accessible again within the past century. But, had the recent tablet discoveries not been made, we would have only the Bible from which to draw any conclusion, and it is far from adequate in this regard.

There is nothing especially odd about this textual inadequacy when one considers that, in the first instance, the books of the

Bible were written *by* Israelites and Judaeans *for* Israelites and Judaeans in the late centuries of the BC years. They believed in God; his reality was taken for granted, so there was no need to encumber their scriptures with unnecessary attempts at proof or explanation. Such things were not required. What is perhaps odd is that, for more than 2,000 subsequent years, people other than Israelites and Judaeans, on an extraordinary worldwide scale, have accepted these same inadequate texts, without question, as providing a sound enough base on which to establish formally operative religions whose unelected hierarchy, by way of self-opinionated laws, have thereby controlled and regulated society through the ages.

If there are biblically given laws worthy of application in any latter day or modern mainstream environment, then some might be found among the commandments and ordinances of the *Torah* — precepts and principles as conveyed to Moses and the Israelites at Mount Horeb in Sinai. For a number of reasons, that will unfold as we progress into this scene, the events in Sinai constitute the most important narrative sequence in the whole of the Old Testament. It is undoubtedly the most historically provable scene and, as will become evident, gives rise to the most impressive biblical discovery ever made.

In preparation for the exodus events at Mount Horeb, the approaching scene has been heralded by the enigmatic incident of the burning bush. Following 600 years of God's personal irrelevance to the ongoing Israelite family saga, he is now back, answering to the style of *Adon* and confirming, by the use of two nominal distinctions, that he is 'El Shaddai the *Yaouai'*.

As a literary device, the burning bush is distinctly memorable by virtue of its conceptual imagery. It also appears to be unique in that there is no known counterpart or more original version of the scene as exists for so many other Old Testament depictions. It is the case however that, although presented as a close quarters, ground-level event, with Yaouai's voice in direct conversation with Moses, Yaouai actually remains unseen. In this respect it constitutes the first of a series of situations whereby God's hitherto physical presence is lost to a realm of wrappings within variously defined natural and supernatural phenomena. It paves the way for a whole new perception of God's presence, moving from corporeal to spiritual, and it is doubtless more than coincidental that this occurs at the same time when the extra-biblical tablets concerning him expire.

The Canaanite royal palace of Ugarit was demolished by invaders in about 1180 BC, and yet the now unearthed hoard of Ras Shamra tablets, inscribed with contemporary information concerning El Elyon through some 500 years, do not progress forward beyond about 1400 BC in the Mosaic era. There is no explanation as to what happened, to where the prevailing El and his family might have gone, or why.

Notwithstanding the possibility of a straightforward locational move, the Bible writers (when faced with a cessation of archival record) elected to portray a dimensional shift with God henceforth existing in a mysterious parallel realm whilst retaining communicative engagement with the mundane world. It was not to be long after the Sinai episode, however, that the phenomenal godly wrappings of clouds and fires also disappeared, from which time Yaouai's voice is no longer to be heard as he moves entirely from communication and is deemed henceforth to reside in Heaven. He then appears only through individual imaginations in the dreams of certain prophets and seers, and it is explained: 'The word of the Lord was precious in those days; there was no open vision'.[53]

As previously deduced, and in contrast perhaps to general understanding, the Bible is not so much a book about God as might be imagined. It is rather more the story of the Israelite nation and of how God was perceived by the priestly scribes to have adopted the Israelites as his own chosen people. Crucial to this premise was the covenant with Abraham and Isaac that their kingly descendants would inherit the land of Canaan. To facilitate this, the Israelite leaders, their communities and their armies have to be brought out of Egypt. Moses and Aaron are now positioned to lead the great exodus into the Promised Land. Following El Shaddai's lengthy absence from the scripture, he now re-emerges, newly identified as Yaouai, ostensibly to direct the longest running sequence of his involvement in the Bible. Whether his participation is historically accurate as described is not strictly relevant to an otherwise authentic account, since it is at this point in the narrative that Israelite support for Yaouai is seen to resolve into a formal religion. As such, we are led into a realm of 'belief' rather than recorded fact — the same realm of belief that has persisted from the time of the Bible writers to the present day.

Part VI

God of the Exodus

14

NO OTHER GOD

Sea of Reeds

As we have discovered, the fiercest opponent of the Amarna succession was Pharaoh Horemheb, an erstwhile military career officer who, by way of a tactical marriage to Aye's daughter, declared himself King of Egypt. Upon his death without an heir, all previous rules governing succession to the throne were abandoned, and the 19th dynasty began with a vizier named Rameses (Paramessu), who had no marital or other connection with the royal family. He achieved the throne by default since there was no one left with any claim to inheritance, and Rameses was the most experienced State official.[1]

At that time, in about 1335 BC, God said to Moses, 'Go, return into Egypt, for all the men are dead which sought thy life'.[2] And so he returned, ostensibly to aid the Israelites in Ramesside bondage, and more specifically to attempt a restoration of the Amarna dynasty. By performing the pharaonic rituals of the serpent-rod and the withered hand, Moses and Aaron were clearly challenging Rameses' right of succession. But Rameses controlled the Egyptian army and this proved a decisive factor in the power struggle.[3]

It would appear that Moses succeeded in establishing a core community of Israelite supporters at Zarw, although unsuccessful in his attempt to regain his pharaonic position. The biblical story relates, nevertheless, that Rameses was intimidated by various plagues and pestilences, which God brought to bear on the people of Egypt. Ultimately, Rameses conceded to let the Israelites go with Moses and Aaron,[4] but apparently followed them to the Red Sea.

God now features in the story again, having adopted a new guise. The Bible tells that he led the Israelites into Sinai as a pillar

THE ORIGIN OF GOD

of cloud by day and a pillar of fire by night, and caused the waters of the Red Sea to divide for their safe passage. Once they were across, the waters returned, flooding down on the pharaoh and his 600 charioteers, and 'there remained not so much as one of them'.[5]

Rameses I did not survive until the end of his second regnal year, but his death does not equate with the Bible's implied death of the pharaoh in pursuit of the Israelites. There is nothing on record of such a devastating event in respect of Rameses or any other pharaoh. But soon after his actual demise, and even before his mummification,[6] his son Seti I launched a campaign into Sinai and Syria, taking his troops in a swift military assault into Canaan.[7] The very fact that the 'land of Israel' is mentioned by name in a contemporary account of this campaign proves that the Israelites were in Canaan by that time. Outside Egypt, prior to the exodus, there were plenty of Hebrews in Canaan,[8] but there were no Israelites (the Egyptian-born descendants of Jacob-Israel) and there had been no land of Israel.

The troublesome Hebrews of Canaan had been documented some while before the Israelite exodus from Egypt, especially during the reigns of Amenhotep III and Akhenaten. This came to light in 1887, when a peasant woman, searching the ruins of *Tell el-Amarna*, unearthed a cache of inscribed clay tablets which proved to be diplomatic correspondence between various Canaanite rulers and the pharaohs of the 18th dynasty. The *cuneiform* writings, lately known as the *Amarna Letters*,[9] revealed that parts of the Egyptian empire were in serious decline, and the ruler of Jerusalem, Abd-khiba, had appealed for Akhenaten's help against incursions by marauding tribes of the *Habirû* (Hebrews).[10]

The information concerning Seti's campaign comes from a large granite stela discovered in 1896 by the British archaeologist Sir WM Flinders Petrie. It was found in the Theban funerary temple of Pharaoh Merneptah (*c.*1236–1202 BC), and its inscribed record had been commenced in the reign of Akhenaten's father, Amenhotep III. Merneptah (the grandson of Seti I) had brought the history down to date on the reverse of the stela, and in the fifth year of his reign he spoke of the Israelite residents of Canaan (part of which was then also known as Palestine). The *Israel Stela*, as it is called, is now in the Cairo Museum, and within the context of Merneptah's record are details of anti-Israelite campaigns which Egyptologists have dated to the reigns of his predecessors, Seti I and Rameses II.[11] 'Israel is devastated,' states the stela; 'Her seed is no more; Palestine has become a widow of Egypt'.[12]

It can be ascertained from this documented sequence of events that the Israelite exodus from Egypt began during the year of Rameses I's death — the first year of Pharaoh Seti I (*c.*1333 BC). However, in studying the Old Testament account of the exodus and the dramatic crossing of the Red Sea, whose waters parted to become 'a wall unto them on their right hand and on their left',[13] we find there was actually no sea for the Israelites to cross. The triangular Sinai peninsula sits to the north of the Red Sea, between the Gulfs of Suez and Aqaba.

We are told that Moses led the children of Israel out of Avaris (Pi-Rameses) in the Nile delta plain of Goshen, from where they travelled into Sinai on a route towards Midian.[14] The journey, as described, traversed the country above the Red Sea, and the original scripture refers more precisely to the Israelites crossing the 'Sea of Reeds': the *Yam Suph* (Papyrus Marsh), not the Red Sea. This was a swampy terrain near Lake Timsah above the Gulf of Suez,[15] where the wetland region had several fords. It is now cut across by the 103 mile (165 km) Suez Canal, which was opened in 1869.

A Female Bloodline

On the Israelites' biblical arrival in the Sinai peninsula, the sister of Moses appears once more on the scene. We learn that her name was Miriam, but she is treated very sparingly in the *Torah*, which relates only that she danced and played a timbrel, was shut out of the camp when she became ill,[16] and eventually died in Kadesh.[17] For what little she is mentioned, it seems hardly worth bringing Miriam into the story. But she is enigmatically called 'the prophetess' and, in the book of Micah 6:4, she is referenced along with Moses and Aaron as being a leader of the Israelites. This seems to indicate that, for some reason, Miriam was perhaps the subject of literary editing within the Sinai episode of Exodus, Leviticus and Numbers.

As suggested in our previous chapter, the historical Miriam was very likely Akhenaten's second wife, Khiba (Kiya) — and this is a concept now worth exploring. Not only was Khiba a wife of Akhenaten, but she was also his half-sister — the daughter of Amenhotep III and a Mesopotamian princess called Gilukhiba. Khiba was styled 'the Royal Favourite'[18] and was the deputy of Queen Nefertiti, whom she outrivalled in many respects — not least because she was the mother of Akhenaten's male heir, Tutankhamun.

Khiba's mother, Gilukhiba, was the daughter of King Shutarna of Mitanni (north of Assyria), and the name Khiba derived from the Mitannian goddess Khiba. As we saw above, it was the Jerusalem governor, Abd-khiba (Servant of Khiba), who appealed for Akhenaten's military assistance in one of the *Amarna Letters*. At that time, the Mitannian dynasts were very powerful, and their heritage was so steeped in the Mesopotamian lore of the *Anannage* that, when Khiba's female cousin Tadu-khiba visited Egypt, her brother King Tushratta of Mitanni wrote, 'May Shamesh and Ishtar go before her'.

In order to seek an identification of Khiba with the biblical Miriam, we need only check the etymology of the name Miriam. Although much used as a later name in Hebrew, it has its equivalent in the Greek variation, Mary. Originally, however, the name was Egyptian, arising from the epithet *mery* meaning 'beloved' — as in the name of Akhenaten's daughter, *Merytaten* (Beloved of Aten). In this regard, the name Miriam equates with *Meryamen* (Beloved of Amen),[19] a style that was applicable to Khiba, the daughter of Amenhotep III (Amen is pleased).

By virtue of her mother's marital alliance with Amenhotep III, Meryamen carried a dual royal legacy from the Kings of Egypt and Mesopotamia. Not only did she and Akhenaten have a son, Tutankhamun, but they also had a daughter. As a result of the destruction of Amarna records by Pharaoh Horemheb, the name of this daughter was expunged wherever it appeared in Egypt.[20] But her cartouche remnants convey that it was *Mery[...] tasherit* — most likely Meryamen-tasherit (with *tasherit* meaning 'the younger').

Progressing this into the Bible's genealogical listing, we should anticipate an encounter with this daughter in the book of Exodus. By whatever name the *Torah* writers might have called her, she should appear as a daughter of Moses, or as a daughter of Amenhotep IV whose equivalent name in the Hebrew scripture was Aminadab. Indeed, such a daughter does appear precisely on cue by the name of Elisheba ('Oath of El'). She is said to have been the daughter of Aminadab, and became the new wife of Aaron in Sinai.[21]

The Encampment

The Sinai peninsula — a mountainous desert landscape with scattered copper and turquoise mines — fell to the supervision of two primary Egyptian statesmen at that time: the Royal Chancellor and the Royal Messenger in Foreign Lands. During the reigns of Amenhotep III and IV, the Royal Messenger was a State official called Neby, who also happened to be the mayor and troop commander of Zarw in the predominantly Israelite region of Goshen. Moses (Amenhotep IV) was personally acquainted with Neby, and knew that he had no military garrison or resident governor in Sinai.

The position of Royal Chancellor was traditionally retained by the family of Pa-Nehas, and the current Panahesy, who joined the Mosaic exodus, had been the Chief Servitor at Akhenaten's temple of Amarna.[22] Biblically recorded as Phinheas, Moses conferred on him the 'everlasting priesthood' of the new Israelite religion.[23]

Across the river from El-Amarna was the city of Malleui, where the Levite high priest of the Amarna temple had been Merari.[24] He was another to whom Moses granted the new priestly status in Sinai, settling the Order of Yaouai firmly in the line of Levi — the line of his Israelite feeding-mother Tey (Jochebed). Thus, in the latter 14th century BC, the long-standing culture of El Shaddai was finally transformed into a structured religion with a formal priesthood attached. Henceforth, the supreme God of the Israelites gained the common identification of 'Yaouai' in accordance with the time-honoured custom of the Israelites in Egypt.

The book of Exodus spares no drama in relating this ultimate high point in world religious history. Against the soaring back-drop of Mount Horeb, amid thunder, lightning and desert storms, hundreds of thousands of Israelites are encamped as Lord Jethro pronounces the laws and ordinances of the community. The mighty Tabernacle is erected as the Temple of Yaouai; the Ark of the Covenant is constructed for the *Table of Testimony*; Moses burns the Golden Calf; the holy *manna* sustains the multitude, and the *Ten Commandments* are etched upon tablets of stone.

Foremost among the decrees said to have been instigated by Yaouai, and scribally recorded as if in his own words, is the clarification that the premise of monotheistic faith was never about the Israelite God (eventually, the Judaeo-Christian God) being the 'one and only'. It was about acknowledging the exis-tence of other gods whilst electing to support one in particular. In the instance as given, the pronouncement by Yaouai concerning 'other gods' is asserted rather more as a dictate than a matter of choice. But it remains nonetheless an authentic representation of a reality that is largely ignored by today's religious establishment:

> I am the Lord thy God ...
> Thou shalt have no other gods before me.[25]

The Forbidden Sanctuary

As a pertinent adjunct to this, it is of particular note that in 1904, when the explorer Sir WM Flinders Petrie was unearthing a previously unknown temple site at Mount Horeb in Sinai (the biblical mountain of Moses), he was surprised to find a green-stone Amarna statuette head of Akhenaten's mother, Queen Tiye. Preserved at the Horeb sanctuary, out of reach from the Horemheb destructions, and now in the Cairo Museum, it is one of the most striking of all Egyptian portrayals. Petri wrote, 'It is strange that this remotest settlement of Egypt has preserved her portrait for us, unmistakably named by her cartouche in the midst of the crown'.[26] Also discovered was the sculpted head of an unknown Egyptian princess (perhaps Meryamen-tasherit), which is not of Egyptian origin and is thought to have been made on site in the wilderness of Sinai.[27]

It is evident from the 1904 Sinai discoveries of Sir WM Flinders Petrie that the location of the biblical events was of considerable importance. At a height of 2,600 feet above ground at Mount Horeb, he found an expansive Egyptian temple. Upon his discovery, Petrie wrote: 'There is no other such monument known which makes us regret the more that it is not in better preservation. The whole of it was buried, and no one had any knowledge of it until we cleared the site'.[28]

Built on a sandstone plateau, with an extension cut back into a mountain cave, the complex had been in use from the 4th dynasty of Egypt, through a period from the days of Pharaoh Sneferu (who reigned about 2600 BC) until the latter Ramesside era of the 19th dynasty. Relief wall carvings, standing stones and a wealth of inscriptions depicted individually named pharaohs and aspects of ceremonial ritual through a term of some 1,500 years, with references to various gods and goddesses. Given that the temple was in use at the time of Moses, there is little doubt that he knew precisely to where he was leading the Israelites.[29]

Although strangely located in the midst of a windswept desert, far from the main Egyptian centres, the Horeb temple was an operative house of the gods. This place, now called *Serâbît el Khâdim* (Prominence of the Guardian) by the Bedouin, had been a department of Akhenaten's temple at El Amarna, and was under the supervision of the Mosaic levitical priest Panahesy (Phinheas), who was also Akhenaten's Royal Chancellor in Sinai.[30] The temple and its confines would have provided a very safe haven since there was no Egyptian garrison anywhere nearby. Moreover, it was a designated holy place and, whoever Moses might have consulted there, whether Lord Jethro or El Shaddai, he would necessarily have needed to climb to the temple height as explained in Exodus.

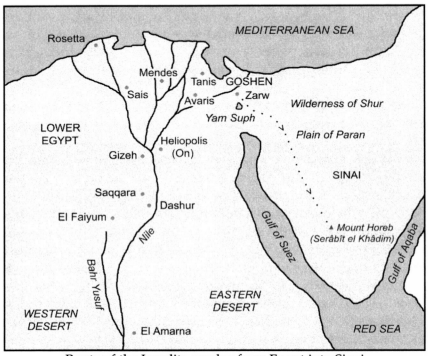

Route of the Israelite exodus from Egypt into Sinai

Following his monumental discovery in 1904, Petrie ran into trouble with the Christian Church authorities. His archaeological report was in contradiction of their long promoted view that the biblical mountain of Exodus was situated much further south in the peninsula. Back in AD 385, an order of Greek monks had founded the mission of St Catherine's Monastery on another mountain, and had dubbed the place *Gebel Musa* (Mount of Moses). It is clear, however, that this was an inaccurate conclusion since it does not comply with the Bible's geographical references. The book of Exodus explains the route taken by Moses and the

Israelites when they departed from the Egyptian delta region of Goshen, travelling towards the land of Midian (north of present-day Jordan) across the desert regions of Shur and Paran to the location found by Petrie. Notwithstanding this, the Church still clings to the notion of Mount Sinai (the biblical Mount Horeb) being at their alternative site. The main reason for the reluctance to change opinion in 1904 was that the temple of *Serâbît el Khâdim* added a material reality to the story of Moses and spoiled the doctrinal concept of God's miraculous presence on the mountain.

The Horeb temple complex actually housed a sizeable work-shop, which helps us at least to understand some of the goings-on in the Exodus account. It was here at the mountain that Moses was said to have organized the construction of the enormous Tabernacle (the 'tent of meeting') with its extravagent furnishings and richly devised adornments of bronze and gold. It was also where the ornately designed golden coffer of the Ark of the Covenant was made — all as described in great detail throughout Exodus 25-27 and 36-39. Given that we are presented with nothing more than a wild and empty desert location, seemingly in the middle of nowhere, it is hard to imagine from where all the necessary materials would have been found, and where the work might have been conducted if there were no workshops to facilitate the enterprise. But the temple — which extends over some 230 feet (*c.*70 m) outside the cave, with a good deal of additional space inside the mountain — even housed its own furnace and was the perfect base for such an operation. In our knowledge of this, various aspects of the biblical portrayal now make a lot more sense as we read them again with a wholly new insight. For example, when discussing the mountain: 'And the smoke thereof ascended as the smoke of a furnace'.[31]

15

THE WILDERNESS YEARS

God on Our Side

Whether or not historically accurate, we are presented with the scenario that, at the time of Moses, the acknowledgement of God as an awesome entity, by whatever name, took a major step towards what was eventually to become a widespread venerative religion. Since religion is, in practice, a system of 'belief', this is a good opportunity to examine the nature of the character to whom the Israelites were being directed to entrust their belief.

We are advised in Exodus 34:5–6 that Yahweh (Yaouai) came to Moses in a cloud and proclaimed that he was 'The Lord God, merciful and gracious, longsuffering, and abundant in goodness and truth'. Maybe so, but to this point the description bears no resemblance to the God we have been reading about. This does not sound like the same character who said, 'If ye will not hearken unto me ... I will even appoint over you terror, consumption, and the burning ague'.[1]

How and when did the God, who was reckoned to have drowned everyone in Mesopotamia and exterminated the inhabitants of Sodom, change to being merciful and gracious? According to Exodus 15:13, this concept relates to the fact that he brought the Israelites out of Egypt: 'Thou in thy mercy hast led forth the people which thou hast redeemed; thou hast guided them in thy strength unto thy holy habitation'. Meanwhile, though, his otherwise dictatorial nature is still seen to be the mainstay of the divine portrayal, and the book of Deuteronomy lists no fewer than 82 restrictive edicts of things which the Israelites 'shalt not' do in his judgement.

What seems to be the case here is that, following their escape from pharaonic bondage, the Israelites were persuaded that much would be granted to them if they settled into a cultural system of

214

total obedience. Being now a wandering, homeless people, their hoped-for prize was the land of Canaan — the Promised Land that 'floweth with milk and honey'.[2] In this regard, they were told:

> The Lord thy God shall have brought thee into the land which he sware unto thy fathers, to Abraham, to Isaac and to Jacob, to give thee great and goodly cities which thou buildedst not, and houses full of all good things which thou filledst not, and wells digged which thou diggedst not, vineyards and olive trees which thou plantedst not'.[3]

From Sinai, the Israelites were about to embark on a military invasion in which they were promised success in seizing the territory of others. But the price of that success was an obligation of absolute subservience:

> Thou shalt fear the Lord thy God, and serve him, and shalt swear by his name ... lest the anger of the Lord thy God be kindled against thee, and destroy thee from off the face of the earth.[4]

There is no way to know whether Yahweh or Moses ever uttered such words, but the writers of the *Torah* clearly believed it to have been the case. All those who lived in the lands to be invaded were now presented as enemy nations that must be overthrown — the Hittites, Girgashites, Amorites, Canaanites, Perizzites, Hivites, and Jebusites: 'And when the Lord thy God shall deliver them before thee, thou shalt smite them, and utterly destroy them; thou shalt make no covenant with them, nor show mercy unto them'.[5] Then, to set the final scene for the Israelites' presumed right of martial conquest, it was said: 'For thou art an holy people ... the Lord thy God hath chosen thee to be a special people unto himself, above all people that are upon the face of the earth'.[6]

Whether these statements were items of some historical merit, or simply wishful thinking by the biblical scribes, is a matter of debate. Either way, there is nothing merciful or gracious being stated here. What leaps from the page is the first literary example of the 'God on our side' principle. Then, in order to emphasise the point, this entry is followed shortly afterwards by: 'When thou goest out to battle against thine enemies ... be not afraid of them, for the Lord thy God is with thee'.[7] This concept has since been adopted on so many occasions by Jews, Christians and Muslims alike. It has fuelled religious antagonism and racial intolerance through the ages, with fear of retribution becoming confused with loyalty: 'Ye shall overthrow their altars, and break their pillars, and burn their groves with fire'.[8]

The Israelites might well have been the first to claim that they were God's specially 'chosen people', but they were not the last to do so. Notwithstanding all the imperious dictates of Yahweh, however, it does rather appear that the Mosaic intention to create religious and racial disunity was as unsuccessful in Canaan as it had been with the Aten impositions in Egypt. As we shall see, there were indeed battles that followed in the invasion campaign, but so too was there a wide-scale social integration by the Israelite immigrants. They were plainly not so aggressive and naïvely subservient as had been anticipated:

> And the children of Israel dwelt among the Canaanites, Hittites, and Amorites, and Perizzites, and Hivites, and Jebusites. And they took their daughters to be their wives, and gave their daughters to their sons, and served their gods.[9]

The mention of other 'gods' is of particular significance in this passage. It indicates once again that Yahweh was not alone in his environment, and was not perceived to have been alone by the Old Testament scribes of later times. There are a number of other such related comments in the scripture — for example: 'Thou shalt have no other gods before me'.[10] And, in the words of Moses, 'I know that the Lord is greater than all gods'.[11]

Later, in Judges 2:13, we are told that the Israelites 'forsook the Lord, and served Baal and Ashtaroth' —the son and consort of

El Elyon in Canaan. In essence, therefore, nothing had changed in 600 years since the days of Abraham. The deiform family is still seen to exist in the Israelite culture, along with the same internal rivalry that had begun with the *Anannage* factions of Enlil and his opposition relatives in Mesopotamia.

Write these Words

In the context of the Sinai episode in Exodus, the word 'write' is mentioned for the first time in the Bible. It occurs at a point when there was no water for the Israelites to drink, and the Lord said to Moses, 'I will stand before thee there upon the rock in Horeb; and thou shalt smite the rock, and there shall come water out of it'.[12] Having performed this feat with his staff, Moses subsequently found the device useful when his people were attacked by Amalekites. He discovered that, when he raised the rod aloft, 'Israel prevailed; and when he let down his hand, Amalek prevailed'. Moses' military commander, Joshua, was very impressed that the battle was won because Moses kept the Lord's staff held high and, to remind them of the event, God was said to have instructed Moses: 'Write this for a memorial in a book'.[13] The word 'write' is used again shortly afterwards in respect of the *Ten Commandments*, when God said to Moses, 'Write thou these words'.[14]

The fact that writing is first mentioned in connection with Sinai is especially interesting since it was at the Mount Horeb temple that the best examples of alphabetical development have ever been found. Not only was the workshop in operative use for around 1,500 years, but it was in a remote place where the workforce came from different regions, many of them leaving inscribed messages in the stones. Sir WM Flinders Petrie had numerous of these copied and brought back to England, but it was not until ten years later that they were deciphered by the noted linguist and hieroglyphics exponent Sir Alan Gardiner.

Working initially from some Hebrew characters, Gardiner discovered that the Canaanite goddess Baalath was synonymous with the Egyptian goddess Hathor, to whom the Sinai temple was dedicated.[15] Subsequently, by comparing scribal developments — from pictographs and hieroglyphs, through Phoenician and other languages which could be transposed into ancient Greek and beyond — a direct graphic route from individual diagrams was found to the alphabet of today. A horned bull's head was eventually upturned to form the letter 'A'; a barred gate became 'H'; wave-crested water evolved to become 'M', and so forth.

It is often considered (mainly by virtue of Christian artwork) that the *Ten Commandments* were somehow blasted into large stone slabs by the finger of God, but this is not indicated in the scripture. It is explained that Moses climbed the mountain to speak with the Lord, who sent him back down to deliver his commandments to the people.[16] Moses then informed the Israelites that 'God spake all these words, saying I am the Lord thy God ...', following which the commandments were verbally recounted[17] along with numerous ordinances which continue through Exodus chapters 20–23. Subsequently, it is reported that 'Moses wrote all the words of the Lord'.[18]

After that, God said again to Moses, 'Come up to me into the mount ... and I will give thee tables of stone, and a law, and commandments which I have written'.[19] On that occasion Moses was given full instructions on how to manufacture the Tabernacle, its furnishings and the Ark of the Covenant, along with details of priestly vestments and aspects of temple ritual. It is not for another seven chapters (forty days later) that eventually we read: 'He gave unto Moses ... two tables of testimony, tables of stone'.[20]

When Moses came down from the mountain, he discovered that Aaron had made a Golden Calf for the Israelites to worship as an idol in his prolonged absence. He became so angry that he cast the tablets of God's testimony to the ground and broke them.[21] Afterwards, God said to Moses, 'Hew thee two tables of stone like unto the first: and I will write upon these tables the words that were in the first tables, which thou brakest'.[22] But God did not then write on these tablets. Instead, he said to Moses, 'Write thou these words', whereupon Moses 'wrote upon the tables the words of the covenant, the ten commandments'.[23]

What the Israelites ended up with were not tablets written by God, but tablets apparently dictated by God and written by Moses. As for the broken tablets, previously said to have been given to Moses by God, they are never mentioned again in the scripture. Even if fragmented, they would still have been holy relics for posterity if they had actually existed as described. But, in contrast to the biblical account, the *Book of Jasher* maintains that Moses received the commandments and laws from Lord Jethro of Midian, not from Yahweh.[24] The chances are, however, that the *Ten Commandments* (as against other ordinances) were not only written down by Moses, but were actually implemented by Moses as aspects of his former royal court tradition in Egypt, thereby having nothing whatever to do with Yahweh.

The Commandments were, in fact, newly stated versions of pharaonic disclosures from an item entitled 'Negative Confessions' in the Egyptian *Book of the Dead*. This now exists as the oldest complete book in the world, emanating from Akhenaten's own 18th dynasty.[25] For example, the confession 'I have not slain' was transposed to the biblical commandment, 'Thou shalt not kill'; 'I have not stolen' became 'Thou shalt not steal'; 'I have not uttered lies' became 'Thou shalt not bear false witness', and so on.[26]

As for the *Yhwh* distinction of the Lord (originally *Iouiya*), it is evident from local texts that this derives from an Arabic terminology — hence its use by Yusuf-Yuya in Egypt before the time of Moses. From the 14th century BC it appears not only in Egypt, but also in the lands of Edom and Midian, where Jethro was the supreme overlord.[27] This might account for the nominal discrepancies between the books of Exodus and Jasher, and could mean that Lord Jethro was himself the governor of the Horeb temple. If so, this would perhaps sideline El Shaddai from the sequence wherein the laws and decrees of the land were presented to the incoming Israelites.

An item of particular note is that Hathor (*Hwt-hor*), the Egyptian goddess of the Horeb temple, was referred to as being the 'Gold of the Gods'.[28] She was customarily portrayed as a nursing mother with cow's horns, and was said to give birth at each sunrise to a 'golden calf'. It was for this reason that Aaron made a golden calf to worship at the site, although was not a form of idol that was relevant to any earlier period of Israelite history. In fact, with around 14 generations (430 years) of descent from Jacob-Israel having passed in Egypt (the same as from Tudor England to the present day), the Israelites would have been influenced significantly by the Egyptian culture. Thus, a golden calf would have been the most natural of all idols to make at the Horeb temple of Hathor in Sinai.

A Period of Wandering

Having lingered at Mount Horeb for a time, the Israelites set out towards the land of Canaan, with their next destination being Kadesh (*Ain Qedeis*). This was north-eastwards across the Sinai peninsula to the north of the Gulf of Aqaba. In the course of the journey there is said to have been much dissent among the people, who complained and constantly blamed Moses for the hardships of desert life, especially the lack of water: 'Wherefore have ye made us come up out of Egypt, to bring us in unto this evil place?' Moses, therefore, struck water again from a rock at Meribah, near Kadesh.[29] But neither Moses nor Aaron gave God credit for the miracle, and resultantly were told that they were henceforth superfluous to his requirement. So too, it seems, was Miriam, who died at that place.

Aaron was duly stripped of his priestly vestment at the summit of Mount Hor, and died immediately,[30] subsequent to which God told Moses that he would not live to take the Israelites across the border into the Promised Land. Shortly afterwards, Moses also died on Mount Nebo in the land of Moab.[31] His primary office as leader of the Israelites was then taken by Joshua, his erstwhile military commander, and Aaron was succeeded by his son Eleazar.

Apart from the Akhenaten references at the Horeb temple of *Serâbît el Khâdim*, there is no archaeological record to confirm the forty years that some hundreds of thousands of Israelites were said to have taken in their wanderings across the wilderness of Sinai.[32] As previously discussed, Pharaoh Seti I launched his campaign into the Canaanite land of the Israelites quite soon after the exodus from Egypt, whereas forty years later Seti had died and his son, Rameses II, was on the throne.

Not only were the Israelites said to have wandered in Sinai for forty years but, after that, God evidently became so fed up with their constant complaining that he delivered them into the hands of the Philistines for yet another forty years.[33] It is clear from the *Dead Sea Scrolls*, however, that there was a particular significance to the biblical term 'forty years' since it defined the term of a royal generation. Today's generation standard is reckoned at 30 years or so, but the dynastic standard in Bible times was determined at 40 years.[34] It was considered to be the correct period between a royal father's maturity and his son's inheritance, and denoted the optimum length of a kingly reign.

When eventually we arrive at the reigns of the Israelite kings in Israel and Judah, we see the notion of this principle in action. 1 Kings 2:11 states: 'And the days that David reigned over Israel were forty years'. Subsequently, with regard to his son King Solomon, 1 Kings 11:42 states: 'And the time that Solomon reigned in Jerusalem over all Israel was forty years'. Moving on to Solomon's descendant King Joash, 2 Kings 12:1 continues: 'And forty years reigned he in Jerusalem'. The true periods of their reigns did not appear to have concerned the Old Testament scribes. What they knew was that forty years was the accepted generational standard between one dynast's maturity and the next, and they ascribed this term to the kingly reigns of particular importance. Precisely the same was done by the New Testament Gospel writer of Matthew. In detailing the male-line descent from King David down to Jesus (between Solomon and Joseph — spanning about 1,000 years), he listed 25 generations of 40 years each.[35]

In writing the *Torah*, the compilers appear to have used the 'forty years' terminology to identify the future kingly nature of the line from Isaac in order to make a dynastic association with El Shaddai's covenant. We read, for example: 'And Isaac was

THE ORIGIN OF GOD

forty years old when he took Rebecca to wife ... and Rebecca his wife conceived'.[36] In respect of their son Esau it is then stated: 'And Esau was forty years old when he took to wife Judith'.[37] With regard to the forty years in the Sinai wilderness, the inference is that, during the Israelites' journey, a royal son reached his age of majority in the primary line of descent from Judah — the line that would, in time, lead to King David.

From what few records exist, everything points to the fact that the number of Israelites who made the journey was far fewer than claimed in the Bible, and that their Sinai crossing was much swifter than biblically conveyed. One way or another, it is clear that Moses, Aaron and Miriam did not complete the journey, and their individual deaths are very poorly explained. In fact, God's sudden change of attitude towards Moses and Aaron is so unsatisfactory as to be nonsensical, and it could well be that Moses (Akhenaten), Aaron (Smenkhkare) and Miriam (Meryamen) never actually left the Horeb sanctuary with the Israelites. With not a shred of extra-biblical evidence to back up the wanderings between Horeb and the Canaanite border, it rather looks as if the long-term portrayal of this sequence is entirely mythical. Even the story of Moses' death (just like the Sharru-kîn legend of his birth) is related back to Babylonian mythology.

By using the fictitious locational name of Nebo for the mountain of Mosaic demise,[38] the *Torah* scribes referenced the story of the *Anannage* god Marduk, whose shrine at the temple of Babylon was also called Nebo (from *nabu*: 'to proclaim').[39] In Mesopotamian lore, Nebo was said to be Marduk's inheritor as the guardian of the *Table of Testimony* — the 'tablet of destiny'[40] that was reckoned to have been copied by Abraham before he journeyed into Canaan. It might be that this was the very 'testimony' that was passed into Moses' hands at Mount Horeb, and which he subsequently placed in the golden Ark: 'And he took and put the testimony into the ark'.[41] It is for this reason that, throughout the book of Exodus, the Ark is always referred to as the 'Ark of Testimony'. Only from the book of Numbers 10:33 (when the Israelites began their onward journey from Sinai) was it literally restyled to become known as the Ark of the Covenant.

Ark of the Lord

The Ark of the Covenant is said to have been made in Sinai by Bezaleel,[42] the son of Uri Ben Hur and a craftsman in cunning work:

> And Bezaleel made the ark of shittim wood; two cubits and a half was the length of it, and a cubit and a half was the breadth of it, and a cubit and a half the height of it. And he overlaid it with pure gold, within and without.[43]

The Ark receives its first biblical mention in Exodus 25:10-22, when the Lord was said to have defined the specifications for its manufacture. With the measurements of the main coffer given in cubits, and using 18 inches as a cubit standard, it resolves at around 45 inches in length, 27 inches in width, and 27 inches in height (about 113 x 68 x 68 cm).[44] The box construction was of 'shittim wood'. This is generally reckoned to have been acacia, but translates from the old Greek language of the *Septuagint* as 'incorruptible wood'.[45] It was plated inside and out with pure gold, and was adorned around its upper perimeter with a rectangular gold crown. At each end of the long sides was a permanently fixed gold ring — four rings in all, to house the two carrying staves which were also made of shittim wood overlaid with gold.

A device called a 'mercy seat' is said to have been placed on top of the Ark — its dimensions being precisely the same as the outside edges of the open box: 2.5 x 1.5 cubits. It was, in effect, a lid which was prevented from slipping by the coffer's crowned outer rim. There was, however, no wood in the lid; it was reckoned to have been a slab of pure gold, which must have been quite thick to avoid bowing. The relevant Hebrew word for the 'mercy seat' (*kapporeth*) translates more precisely to a 'cover', while the *Septuagint* specifies a 'propitiatory' — a place of appeasement. Atop each end of this lid was a solid gold cherub, and they faced each other with wings that stretched inwards above the mercy seat. At length, it is related that God would commune with Moses from the space above the lid, between the cherubims. (These descriptions are all repeated in Exodus 37:1–9, which tells of Bezaleel making the Ark in accordance with this specification.)

The main difficulty in envisaging the Ark is the nature of the cherubims, because the Lord had previously issued a directive that 'Thou shalt not make unto thee any graven image, or any likeness of any thing that is in heaven above, or that is in the earth beneath, or that is in the water under the earth'.[46] If the cherubims were angelic representations, as is the popular artistic portrayal, then the divine regulation of the commandment would have been broken at its outset. Not long before this manufacturing project, Moses (upholding the commandment) had admonished Aaron for making the Golden Calf of Hathor[47] It is therefore inconceivable that he would then have asked Bezaleel to make a couple of golden angels.

The popular angelic use of the word *cherubim* was developed by the later Judaeo-Christian establishment as a plural form of *cherub*. This means that 'cherubims' (according to the Old Testament translations) constitutes a double plural. The error is partly corrected in places — as in Exodus 25:18–19, which refers to 'two cherubims' with 'one cherub' at each end. The same is said in Exodus 37:8. However, the *Septuagint* Bible and other old texts do not make the error; they refer generally to 'cherubs' rather than cherubims.

For the best clue as to the nature of the cherubs, we should consider the early use of the word. In biblical terms, we first encounter it in Genesis 3:24, when (seeming more like armed chariots than angels) cherubims and a revolving sword of fire were used to protect the Tree of Life. Quite unrelated to the Bible, the Alexandrian tractate, *On the Origin of the World*, tells of a ruler named Saboath who 'created a great throne on a four-faced chariot of cherubim'.[48]

The term 'cherub' evolved from the old Semitic *kerûb*, meaning 'to ride'.[49] Hence, 'cherub' is a noun rendered from a verb, and is correctly pronounced 'qerub'. It is consequently of some significance that, wherever forms of identification for cherubs or cherubim appear in the Bible, they are in all cases depicted as chariots or mobile thrones. They are certainly not portrayed as creatures in their own right. Such particular identification occurs many times in the Old Testament. In their accounts of the Lord on a rescue mission, both 2 Samuel 22:11 and Psalm 18:10, state: 'He rode upon a cherub and did fly'. Also, Ezekiel 9:3 refers to God on a cherub, stating, '[He] was gone up from the cherub whereupon he was, to the threshold of the house'. Likewise, 1 Chronicles 28:18 directly associates the cherub guardians of the Ark in Solomon's Temple with 'chariots'.[50] Flavius Josephus maintained in the *Antiquities of the Jews* that 'Nobody can tell, or even conjecture, what was the shape of these cherubims'.[51]

In philosophical Judaism, chariot lore is intermixed with mysticism within a study cycle known as *Merkabah*.[52] It is related to the 'throne' aspect of the Ark, and is particularly inspired by the visions of the prophet Ezekiel — a Jerusalem priest who, in 596 BC, was deported to Babylonia: 'And when I looked, behold the four wheels by the cherubims ... And when the cherubims went, the wheels went by them'.[53] On another occasion, Ezekiel related: 'And upon the likeness of the throne was the likeness as the appearance of a man ... This was the appearance of the likeness of the glory of the Lord'.[54]

The Oxford Word Library[55] specifies that the fundamental root of 'cherub' is obscure, but was nevertheless based on a notion of transport. In the term *kerûb* we have a direct association with 'Choreb', as the holy mountain of Moses was called in the *Septuagint* before its corruption to Horeb in later texts. As for the association of cherubs with thrones, the Bible certainly relates that, on occasions (although unseen), the Lord sat on the mercy seat of the Ark: 'He sitteth between the cherubims'.[56] It is also stated that he communed with Moses from this throne: 'He heard the voice of one speaking unto him from off the mercy seat'.[57]

Onwards from the book of Exodus, and through much of the Old Testament, the Ark of the Covenant is prominently featured as playing an important role in the Israelites' conquest of Canaan.[58] In the course of its history, the Ark killed without warning if the rules of its handling were not obeyed,[59] and the fury of its unleashed power caused tumors on a plague-like scale.[60] Two of Aaron's sons, Nadab and Abihu, were killed by the fire which leapt from the Ark,[61] given in the Hebrew *Talmud* as bolts 'as thin as threads'.[62] And when Uzzah the carter attempted to stay the Ark on its swaying conveyance, he was struck dead the moment he touched it.[63]

When not on its cart, the Ark had to be carried with independent staves, which were slipped through fixed rings, and close proximity was afforded only to the levitical priests, who were garbed in a very particular fashion. They had large amounts of gold in their specially designed apparel — golden breastplates attached to golden rings, chains and various other fixtures around their bodies.[64] They were instructed to remove their shoes and wash their feet 'that they die not' when approaching the Ark.[65] Similarly, those who bore the Ark on its staves were instructed to walk barefoot.[66]

* * *

The Tabernacle (the first Temple of Yahweh) is customarily regarded as an elaborate sanctuary to house the Ark of the Covenant. This extravagant construction is, however, confined to the entries of a priestly *Torah* writer known to scholars as 'P'. It does not conform to the much simpler Tent of Meeting described elsewhere in the text by another writer classified as 'E'.[67] Regarding the smaller construction, it is stated: 'Now Moses took the tabernacle and pitched it without the camp, afar off from the camp'.[68] There is no apparent similarity between this straightforward tent, pitched outside the Horeb camp site, and the mighty Tabernacle situated in the centre of the camp with its army of attendants and Levite guardians.

Apart from all its richly described furnishings, hangings, rings and adornments, the walls of the large Tabernacle were constructed of upright boards 13.5 feet high and 27 inches wide (*c.*4 m x *c.*69 cm).[69] There were more than four dozen wide planks, with additional corner pieces, in an overall 3:1 ground ratio of 45 feet x 15 feet (*c.*13.7 x *c.*4.6 m) and 15 feet in height.[70] This was all covered and draped in heavy linen and goatskins, while curtained within was the Sanctuary of the Ark, contrived as a 15-foot cubic space. It has been suggested that the said definition of 'boards' is perhaps a mistranslation for 'frames', but the old technical terms are obscure, so it is difficult to tell which is the more accurate.[71] Either way (even though frames would be lighter than solid boards), we have something here which was far from portable, as we are led to believe was the case.

The Tabernacle was set within a 150 foot by 75 foot enclosure: the Court of the Dwelling (c.45.6 x c.22.8 m) — about the size of an Olympic swimming pool. This was boundaried by 60 pegged wooden poles with bronze bases, and some 450 feet (137 m) of weighty curtaining to a height of 7.5 feet (c.2.28 m). For transportation, the dimensions, volume, and weight of all this would have been enormous, if indeed factual as portrayed. It is not surprising that the Tabernacle (Hebrew, *mishkan*: 'dwelling place') is diminished in the narrative reckoning soon after the Israelites' onward journey from Sinai is under way. It is further mentioned in Joshua 18:1 as being erected at Shiloh after the battle of Jericho, and 1 Kings 18:4 relates that it was eventually in Jerusalem when the Temple was consecrated.[72]

According to the book of 2 Chronicles 3:1, the Jerusalem Temple was built by King Solomon on the site of Mount Moriah, where Abraham had offered his son Isaac as an altar sacrifice to El Shaddai 1,000 years before. It was the place where an angel of the Lord had covenanted with Abraham: 'Thy seed shall possess the gate of his enemies'.[73] And so it was that, when the Israelites entered Canaan under the leadership of Joshua, they were headed ultimately for the Moriah site in Jerusalem — the gate of the Lord's enemies. At this place they anticipated the establishment of their own kingdom in accordance with the original covenant of El Shaddai. They also planned to build a great temple to house the Ark in its holy sanctuary, and had pre-empted this by constructing the Tabernacle of the Congregation in Sinai.

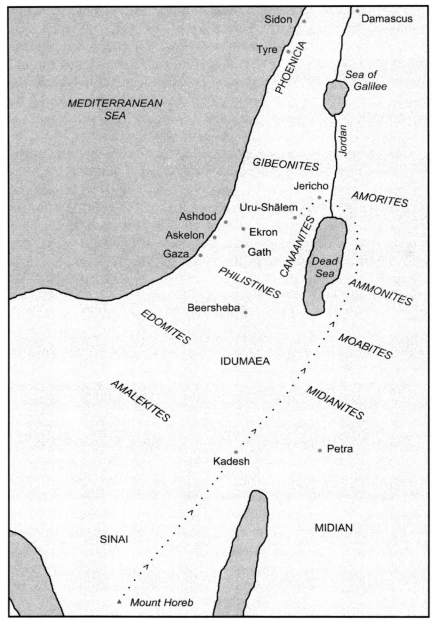

Route of the Israelite conquest of Canaan from Mount Horeb

Part VII

God of the Battles

16

THE CONQUEST

A Merciless Warlord

Apart from the Israelite incident against the Amalekites, when Moses raised his staff to win the battle, he is reported to have seen an amount of further action before he died. One particular occasion, which seems contrary to Moses' son-in-law relationship with Jethro, Lord of Midian, was the Israelite campaign against the Midianites:

> They slew the kings of Midian beside the rest of them that were; slain ... And the children of Israel took all the women of Midian captives, and their little ones, and took the spoil of all their cattle, and all their flocks, and all their goods. And they burnt all their cities wherein they dwelt, and all their goodly castles, with fire.[1]

After that, as they travelled, the Ark of the Covenant was sent on before them, with Moses calling, 'Let thine enemies be scattered, and let them that hate thee flee before thee'.[2] But their experience was not without some self-inflicted injury, and on one occasion an accident caused the Ark to blaze its fire in their own midst, killing some of the Israelites.[3]

The plan was for the army to move northwards out of Sinai, with an incursion into the Canaanite land west of the Dead Sea and the River Jordan. But there were five Philistine fortresses guarding the southern route to Moriah, in view of which it was decided to swing up eastwards of the Dead Sea, so as to come back across the Jordan and enter Canaan from the north. This meant crossing the frontiers of the Edomites, Amorites, Moabites, and Ammonites, which they appear to have done without too many problems. Soon the Israelites were the masters of Transjordan, and made their way northwards to move back across the river above the Dead Sea at Jericho.[4] It was at this stage, whilst surveying Canaan from across the water, that Moses was said to have died.

Moving now from the five books of the *Torah*, we come to the book of Joshua. This is essentially a document of battles, as the Israelites — henceforth portrayed as invading tribes — make their way into Canaan under their new leader. Compiled in about 450 BC, *Joshua* relates to a period more than eight centuries earlier, but the source of the information therein is unknown. We know from the *Israel Stela*, however, that Israelites were settled in Canaan during the Egyptian reigns of Seti I and Rameses II. Also, archaeological excavations at the old Canaanite city of Lachish, south of Jerusalem,[5] and at Hazor in northern Galilee,[6] both indicate that they suffered from Israelite incursion some little while after Joshua's initial assault into the country.

The main difficulty for theologians in reconciling the book of Joshua is that it portrays God throughout as a merciless warlord, intent on the complete annihilation of the native Canaanites. This image sits particularly hard with Christian commentators whose vision of God is one of love and compassion. Whatever the case, it is a fact that there is absolutely nothing on record outside the Bible to indicate that the Judaeo-Christian God, or any other deity, was in any way involved in the invasion, except in the minds of those who wrote about the campaign in the scriptures. These later writers were confronted with an especially violent period of land acquisition in their history, and it is most likely that they invented God's instigation of the hostilities in order somehow to justify the genocide for posterity. In doing this, one of the Old Testament's most glaring anomalies is posed since we know, from many affirmations in the *Torah*, that El Elyon of the Canaanites and El Shaddai of the Israelites were one and the same. The scribal attempt in the book of Joshua is to create a literal divide to the extent that El had forsaken the Canaanites by choosing the Israelites as his own special people. But this is in no way confirmed, nor even suggested, in any Canaanite text.

Unfortunately for the indigenous tribes of Canaan, the Israelites were not their only concern during that era. They were also being invaded by other plunderers who came in from the Mediterranean Sea. With a trail of destruction behind them in Crete, Cyprus and Asia Minor, they arrived on the Canaanite coast to become the greatest of all the Israelites' adversaries. The Egyptians called them *Pelestia*, which in Hebrew was *Peleshti*.[7] In biblical history they became known as the Philistines, and their subsequently extensive Canaanite territory was called Palestu, or Palestine.

In all their years as troublesome marauders, only Pharaoh Rameses III ever defeated the Philistines (Palestinians) on both land and sea.[8] Claiming a stretch of coast in southern Canaan, these maritime warriors established the five city kingdoms of Askelon, Ashdod, Ekron, Gaza and Gath. These were the five great fortresses which, as mentioned above, guarded the southern Gaza Strip route into the country, and caused the Israelites to move northwards through Transjordan to the east of the Dead Sea. This eventually led to the Israelites taking the north of Canaan, while the Philistines held the south-west. But they each had their sights set on the occupation of the whole.[9]

Since the Philistines' fortified centres were in existence when the Israelites arrived, it is evident that the Philistines were the first to lay claim to Canaanite lands in the southern coastal region which became Palestine. The Israelites subsequently moved downwards into Canaan from Jericho, so that the northern territories became known as Israel. Neither of them, at that stage, occupied Jerusalem, which sat in between and remained in Canaanite control. Notwithstanding the continued struggle, which persists between the Israelis and Palestinians over the same territories today, the fact remains that, in that era, they were both unwelcome invaders.

In terms of immediate descent, the Philistines hailed from Caphtor,[10] which is called Kafto in the Ramesside inscriptions.[11] This was a coastal region of southern Anatolia (modern Turkey), whose capital was Tarsus. It was the land of the Luwians,[12] who had arrived in about 2000 BC, bringing an Akkadian language and script from Mesopotamia. The Israelites were Egyptian descendants of the Abrahamic Hebrews (the *Habirû*) — the people from *eber han-nahor*: the 'other side of the flood', as explained in Joshua 24:3. Abraham had also come out of Mesopotamia in about 2000 BC, at the same time as the Luwians. This indicates that, in earlier times, the Israelites and Philistines were of related ancestral stock, with mutual origins in Mesopotamian Iraq.

The Walls of Jericho

Joshua's leadership commenced with one of the best known incidents in Old Testament history: the siege of Jericho. With the Ark at the head of their army, the Israelites prepared to cross the River Jordan into Canaan.[13] Joshua advised all but the Levite bearers of the Ark to stay well behind by about 1,000 yards/metres.[14] Then, with a biblical repeat of the parting of the Red Sea story (thereby establishing Joshua's scriptural position as a worthy leader), the Ark was said to have parted the River Jordan to make possible their crossing.[15] In real terms, the river is quite narrow at that point and has always been very fordable in places. Even when in full spate from its upper reaches, debris will cause it to dam, and chronicles of the past six centuries record the Jericho stretch as being dry for up to 24 hours at a time.

Once across the river, an armed contingent, along with seven priests blowing rams-horn trumpets, preceded the Ark to compass the city of Jericho once a day for six days. On the seventh day, they made seven circuits, whereupon a final blast of the trumpets and a shout from the Israelites brought the city walls tumbling down.[16] With apparent ease, they then took Jericho by storm, killing every man, woman, and child except for the family of the harlot Rahab, who had aided their advance scouting party.[17] The Israelites were then firmly on the soil of Canaan, which they regarded as their own 'promised land'.

Plainly, no amount of shouting or trumpet blowing could actually bring down stout city walls such as at Jericho. Excavations in the 1900s revealed that there were two parallel constructions of about 27 feet high (*c*.8 m), with the main inner wall being 12 feet thick (*c*.4 m).[18] By virtue of the extensive damage to the massive mud-brick fortification, it has been suggested that an earthquake was perhaps responsible, but that would have affected the Israelites outside as well as the residents within. It is more generally held that the destructively powerful Ark was somehow instrumental in aiding the demolition.[19]

With a foothold secured west of the Jordan, Joshua then formed an alliance with locally suppressed Gibeonites and set his sights towards a Canaanite settlement at the place called Ai. Like Jericho, Ai was strongly fortified,[20] but the battle was won by contriving a feint retreat after an initial assault. This drew the military guard of Ai out after Joshua's men into a strategically laid ambush,[21] while other Israelites swept down from the hills to set the city ablaze. Subsequently, further key settlements were taken and, in the course of this, the Israelites overran and annexed traditionally sacred places of the Canaanites, such as Hebron, Shechem, and Beersheba.

Tyranny of the Lord

Throughout the Jericho siege and afterwards, God is seen to have been constantly behind Joshua's actions: 'Be strong and of a good courage ... for the Lord thy God is with thee whithersoever thou goest'.[22] In towns and villages alike, the people of Canaan are said to have been vanquished with swords, fire and stones, until Joshua 'left none remaining, but utterly destroyed all that breathed, as the Lord God of Israel commanded'.[23] The conquered areas of Canaan were then subdivided into individual ownerships of the Tribes of Israel, and this was finally reckoned to have fulfilled El Shaddai's covenant that the seed of Abraham would inherit the land.

What began in the book of Genesis as a story about God and his relationship, person by person, with a particular family, has now evolved into a much wider scenario. He is now portrayed as the supreme warlord of a whole tribal nation. The scripture has changed to become a documentary record of battlefield triumphs under the auspices of a God who is presented as hating everyone but those who obey his dictates without question. At this stage (c.1300 BC) we have travelled chronologically through about 2,700 years from the time of Adam and Eve, but we have still not met with the God who is reckoned in the modern tradition to love everyone. Given that (as with the books of Genesis and Exodus) there are close to 400 years missing between the Old and New Testaments of the Bible, we are now left with only 800 years in which to discover a change of godly personality in the Hebrew scripture. But we already know in advance that this will not happen. In the final event, God even turned against the Israelites, subjecting his supposed hitherto 'chosen people' to bondage in Babylonia, saying,

> I will forsake the remnant of mine inheritance, and deliver them into the hand of their enemies; and they shall become a prey and a spoil to all their enemies because they have ... provoked me to anger since the day their fathers came forth out of Egypt, even unto this day.[24]

It is beginning to look, therefore, as if the God of love and deliverance who emerged in the New Testament was a newly conceived figure — a different character altogether. Outside the *Dead Sea Scrolls*, which emanate mostly from the 1st century BC, we have no real evidence of what transpired religiously in the period between the Testaments. There are some Hebrew writings such as the books of the Maccabees — a Hasmonaean family who ruled Jerusalem from 166 BC until the Roman occupation in 63 BC. These books were included in an updated version of the Greek *Septuagint*, but were excluded from the Hebrew Bible because they were 'primarily concerned with the affairs of man, and not with the affairs of God'. It is by virtue of this missing aspect of the authorized canon that the Gospel stories of Jesus emerge in a Roman environment which is quite divorced from the Old Testament scriptures.

Jesus appears in the New Testament as a type of latter-day Joshua (even with the same name in its Greek form)[25] who, instead of taking repossession of the land by force of arms, attempted to bring about a united kingdom through the peaceful application of his teaching. It is clear from the Gospels, however, that Jesus' opponents were not only the Romans, but also the Pharisee and Sadducee priests of the Temple along with the grand council of Jewish elders known as the Sanhedrin. But why would they object to Jesus, a Jew like themselves, promoting peace and harmony in the land? Because, if the Israelite scriptures are to be believed, at no time in previous biblical history had Yahweh ever promoted peace and harmony. From the Flood of Noah to the invasion of Canaan and beyond, his constant portrayal was that of a tyrannical destroyer.

God and the Judges

Back with the original Joshua, we are told that, once settled in their various parts of Canaan, the Israelites appointed judges to rule over them. Thus, after the death of Joshua, we move into the Old Testament book of Judges, which contains some of the best remembered stories in biblical lore: Deborah and Barak, Gideon and the oak, Jephthah's daughter, and Samson and Delilah.

Although not yet ready to establish a new kingdom, the Israelites did have a need for some overall management as their disparate tribes began to operate independently of one another. They settled on the concept of militarily empowered magistrates: judges who would control the regional groups until a monarchy was constituted. During this period, it is evident that the Israelites were in no way united in matters of religion. At Shechem, they had been gathered by Joshua to give their allegiance to Yahweh,[26] but after their leader's demise they also began to worship Canaanite deities such as Baal and Ashtoreth.[27] This is hardly surprising since Baal and Ashtoreth were the son and wife of El Elyon, who was synonymous with Yahweh. Without the harsh dictates of Moses and Joshua to consider, it would have been quite natural for the descendent Israelites to fall into the ways of their new homeland, where the culture supported the idea of a deiform family rather than a lone male godhead.

Not only were the Israelites of that era polytheistic, just as their forebears had been, but they were also wayward and violent in their social conduct. The rape of the maidens at Shiloh provides a good example.[28] Having butchered and slaughtered all the men, children and married women of Jabeshgilead, the single men of the Benjamin tribe saved for themselves 400 virgins to take as wives, but they were still 200 short of requirement. So the men hid in the vineyards of Shiloh at festival time. They pulled their maidens of choice from among the dancers into the vines, after which they carried them away from the township. As stated in Judges 17:6: 'Every man did what was right in his own eyes'.

The major Israelite judges of the colonizing years were Othniel, Ehud, Deborah, Gideon, Jephthah, Samson and Samuel. It is made clear throughout that, during this period, the Israelites were not cohesive as a unified nation, but had become settled into autonomous regional groups. Hence, the judges were not overall regulators, and those cited in the Bible are just representative examples from different regions, presented in the manner of legendary folk heroes. Although biblically identified as following one another in their posts, their stories actually relate to different geographical areas within Canaan, and to an overall time-frame of about 250 years.

Of Othniel and Ehud there is little to tell except that respectively they saved groups of captive Israelites from the clutches of two local kings. Ehud achieved his objective by visiting King Eglon of Moab on the premise of having a gift for him. 'I have a message from God unto thee', said Ehud, at which the king duly stood to receive his guest, and was immediately stuck and killed with Ehud's dagger.[29]

After that, and quite out of keeping with the Bible's general attitude towards women, arose Deborah the prophetess — the first female leader since Miriam, and a veritable Boudicca figure. She was said to have held her court beneath a palm tree near Bêth-El, where the Israelites would receive her judgement.

Prominent among the judges, Deborah and her commander-in-chief, Barak, instigated and led the most major offensive since the days of Joshua. This resulted in their defeat of the formidable Canaanite charioteers of King Sisera at the battlefield of Har Megiddo (Armageddon), thereby gaining the Valley of Jezreel for the Israelites, as well as their previously occupied high ground in the Galilean hills. Archeological discoveries determine that the event took place in about 1125 BC,[30] and its story was preserved in the evocative *Song of Deborah*, which she is reckoned to have sung to the assembled throng after the battle.[31]

Israel's next major triumph came under the leadership of Gideon when they were challenged by hordes of Midianites mounted on camels — nomadic warriors from a neighbouring land who had entered Canaan to pillage and plunder.[32] This must have come as some surprise to the Israelites and Canaanites alike, for tame camels were very new to the ancient culture, receiving no mention in any historical record prior to that date.[33] (As we have seen, all previous Old Testament references to camels are mistranslations, which should in fact denote donkeys.)[34] In the face of these unwelcome marauders, Gideon was visited by an angel of the Lord as he sat beneath an oak tree in Ophrah. Addressing Gideon as a 'mighty man of valour', the angel advised him that he would be the one to defeat the Midianites. Following that, we have a series of conversations between God and Gideon in order to test the man's loyalty before endowing him with the legacy of a national champion.

In confronting the Midianites, Gideon (like Joshua) resorted once more to the use of trumpets — this time 300 of them, blown in unison at night, whilst pitchers were broken and lamps were fired around the sleeping enemy's encampment.[35] In essence, Gideon fought his surprise war against the camels, rather than against the men, and the animals fled in terror, with their riders running after them.

Next in the legendary cycle comes the story of Jephthah, the son of a prostitute, who became an Israelite leader in Gilead and was persuaded to launch a campaign against the Ammonites.[36] In the first instance, Jephthah endeavoured to negotiate with the

King of Ammon, but there was no agreement over the disputed territory, and Jephthah took in his army. A few Ammonite towns were seized, but Jephthah was not confident in the hope of final success and, in a moment of uncertainty, he vowed to God:

> If thou shalt without fail deliver the children of Ammon into mine hands, then it shall be that whatsoever cometh forth of the doors of my house to meet me when I return … shall surely be the Lord's, and I will offer it up for a burnt offering'.[37]

And so Jephthah was victorious but, on arrival home in his triumph, the first to come from the house to greet him was his own daughter. She was afforded two months grace to bewail her fate, after which her father's vow to the Lord had to be honoured and she was duly sacrificed.[38] There is a similar story in the legends of Alexander the Great, wherein an oracle told him to sacrifice the first living thing he encountered on leaving a city. The first person he met was a man driving an ass, but the man had the presence of mind to save his own skin by pointing out that the animal had actually met Alexander first.

The story of the redoubtable judge Samson is well known, but the important aspect of his legend is that it is our first major introduction to the most intimidating of all Israel's enemies, the Philistines. Samson was born in the typical Old Testament manner from a mother who was barren, but received a divine revelation that she would conceive, whereupon Samson's personal greatness was foretold.[39] In time, he inflicted great punishment on the Philistines through exceptional feats of strength, such as slaying 1,000 men with the jawbone of an ass,[40] and he carried away the city gates of Gaza on his shoulders.[41]

The Philistines knew that Samson admired a local woman called Delilah, so they offered her a substantial reward if she would discover the secret of Samson's strength in order that they might overpower him. She asked a number of times, only to receive false answers, but Samson eventually confided that his great strength emanated from his long hair. On learning this secret, the treacherous Delilah received her payment and brought in a man to shave Samson's head while he was asleep.[42] The Philistines then seized Samson, put out his eyes and took him captive into Gaza, where they chained him between the internal pillars of the temple of Dagon. But Samson prayed for one last burst of strength and, on being granted his wish, he pulled down the support pillars, killing himself and everyone within as the whole temple collapsed.[43]

It is doubtful that any of these stories are entirely true as presented. They are each based on different aspects of cultural folklore in the heroic style of lowly-born figures who rise to become great deliverers. The point is made throughout, however, that their individual attainments of greatness occurred because of their obedience to the Lord, even to the extent of Samson losing his life and Jephthah being required to sacrifice his daughter.[44] It is also evident in this cycle of stories that the religion of Israel was in a state of flux and confusion. There is no overall veneration of Yahweh in this sequence, and each story begins with a statement such as 'The anger of the Lord was hot against Israel'.[45] Despite the teachings of Moses, as later upheld and implemented by Joshua, the tribes are still seen to have been more interested in day-to-day matters of home-life and agriculture, as against giving religion any priority in their lives. Irrespective of Yahweh or the judges, 'Every man did what was right in his own eyes'.[46]

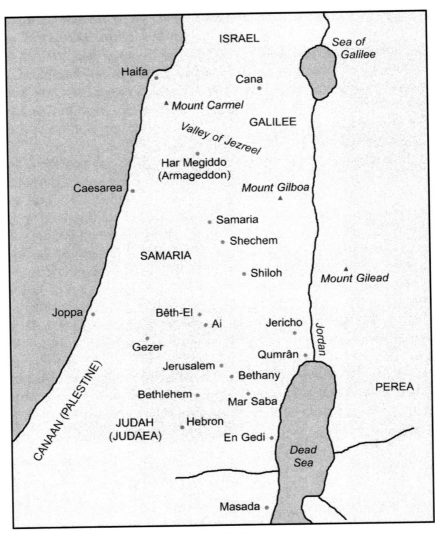

The Israelite Lands

17

THE ROAD TO MORIAH

A Strategic Digression

At length, with the book of Ruth, the scripture finally reverts back to Pharez, the illegitimate son of Judah and Tamar, who was born before Jacob took his family into Egypt. It was from the line of Pharez that the eventual King David was said to have descended and, in the book of Ruth, we meet with David's great-grandfather Boaz.

In a time-frame just three generations before David, we are in the 12th century BC during the latter period of the Israelite judges. Pharez had been born around 700 years prior to this, but (in view of the missing period between Genesis and Exodus) the book of Ruth gives only an abbreviated list of just six generations in the descent from Pharez to Boaz:

> Pharez begat Hezron,
> And Hezron begat Ram,
> And Ram begat Aminadab,
> And Aminadab begat Nahshon
> And Nahshon begat Salmon,
> And Salmon begat Boaz.[1]

This sequence of names is found only in the Bible; it does not appear in any contemporary text of the era yet discovered, so we cannot determine the historical accuracy. What is evident, however, is that we have seen a couple of these names before: Ram (Amram) begat Aminadab (Amenhotep), whose daughter Elisheba married Aaron. Looking back to the relevant entry in Exodus 6:23, we see that Elisheba had a brother called Nahshon, and this is confirmed in the above list from the book of Ruth:

'Aminadab begat Nahshon'. We can cross-check this in the book of 1 Chronicles 2:10–11, which confirms that 'Ram begat Aminadab; and Aminadab begat Nahshon, prince of the children of Judah'. And Nahshon begat Salma, and Salma begat Boaz'.[2]

What emerges here is that the ancestor of Boaz was Aminadab, whom we have already established was Amenhotep the *Moses* (His Israelite nursing mother was Tey [*Yokâbâr*], whose husband was Aye the *Amram*.) It is quite remarkable that these few generations are given such little space in the Bible, for they hold the key to the royal succession that was said eventually to have settled upon King David:

> Boaz begat Obed,
> And Obed begat Jesse,
> And Jesse begat David.[3]

So much scribal effort had been afforded to a series of generational side-switches between brothers in the patriarchal descent, in order to contrive the line from Judah and Tamar as the key succession, which actually it was not. And yet, having achieved this end in literary terms, the Bible writers were then obliged to ignore the final importance of the line down to David in order to veil the Egyptian heritage of the eventual Royal House of Judah. They achieved this by way of a tactic that was quite out of keeping with the scriptural norm and, instead of emphasising the male descent in the usual patriarchal style, they focused readers' attention towards a woman called Ruth. She is a complete newcomer to the plot, and we learn nothing of her heritage, but the digression of her involvement was deemed crucial enough to produce one of the canonical books in her name. God does not feature directly in this book, except by way of some passing references.

The book of Ruth is comparatively short by Old Testament standards, and consists of only one story. It is romantic enough, however, to have inspired numerous artists, and it certainly creates a sufficiently charming diversion from the male line of succession by way of a tale that concerns three women. By this strategy, the need to relate accounts of the men was circumvented and, consequently, the forebears of Boaz are rarely discussed in biblical studies.

The tale begins with a woman called Naomi and her husband Elimelech, who had two sons, Mahlon and Chilon. When Elimelech died, the sons married Orpah and Ruth, two young women of Moab. But soon afterwards Mahlon and Chilon also died, and the three women were left alone. Orpah went back to her parents, but Naomi and Ruth travelled to Bethlehem, where Ruth gained employment in the field, gleaning the crop at the time of the barley harvest. It transpired that the field was owned by Boaz of Judah, a kinsman of Naomi's deceased husband, who fell in love with Ruth and they were subsequently married.

The narrative is so well constructed that Naomi's distress and the romance of Boaz and Ruth divert us totally from the thrust of the surrounding scripture. This diversion is more noticeable in the Christian Bible, which places the book of Ruth between those of Judges and Samuel. In the Hebrew Bible, although actually out of context with the generational progression, it is inserted later after the Song of Solomon. Either way, for a few brief chapters in the family's history, we are moved from battles and heroic legend into the realm of a gentle nursery tale. In the course of this, Aminadab, Nahshon and Salmon are completely sidelined, and all we remember at the end is that the lovers, Boaz and Ruth, had a grandson called Jesse of Bethlehem, who was the father of David.

The sons of Moses (Aminadab) by Zipporah of Midian are given as being Gershom and Eliezer,[4] but we still have Princess Tharbis of Ethiopia to consider. As mentioned in chapter 13, she was the woman referenced by Josephus, in the *Antiquities of the Jews*, as an earlier wife of Moses. Numbers 12:1 indicates that Miriam and Aaron were angered in Sinai by some aspect of this marriage,[5] and it is likely that a son of Moses and Tharbis was making his presence felt at that time. On the basis of the veiled information tucked into the strategically anecdotal book of Ruth, it appears that this son was Nahshon, whose half-sister Elisheba became the second wife of Aaron.[6] According to Numbers 2:3 and

1 Chronicles 2:10, Nahshon was not only a tribal commander, but was regarded as a 'prince' of the children of Judah. The rabbinical *Midrash* even refers to Nahshon as a 'king', thereby confirming the royal status of his heritage in scholarly Judaism.[7]

It is apparent that if Nashon was of the tribe of Judah, then his father Aminadab (Amenhotep) was also of descent from Judah via his mother Tiye, the daughter of Yusuf-Yuya and Tjuyu the *Asenath*. Since there were no Israelite princes at that stage, the fact that Nashon was regarded as a prince is indicative of his being the son of a pharaoh of Egypt and a princess of Ethiopia — a son who, by the 40-year rule, had reached his majority. Thus we have a situation whereby Moses (Amenhotep) was not incidental to the Davidic bloodline, but was very much a part of it. In biblical terms, Moses is personified as the liberating champion of the Israelites, and is revered equally in Judaism with the patriarch Abraham. But his true significance was strategically lost in the scriptures. His ancestral role in the dynastic story was completely veiled in a scribal endeavour to separate the Israelite God concept of 'Yahweh the Adon' from the cult of 'Yaouai the Aten' in Egypt.

Scourge of the Philistines

Having moved through the Ruth digression, the scripture then gets back on track with Samuel, the last and most influential of the judges. At the same time, we are reminded that the Ark of the Lord is still very relevant to the story, which now centres on the Israelite conflicts with the Philistines.

In practical terms, the Philistines were far better equipped than the Israelites, having up-to-date military technology, horses, chariots and weaponry from their experience in more advanced lands.[8] They had also introduced iron-smelting into Canaan after learning the techniques from the Hittites, so their hardware and armour were far more efficient.[9] But what they did not have was the Ark of the Covenant and, despite all their potentially winning might, they knew they would have to seize the powerful device if they were to defeat their Israelite adversaries.

THE ROAD TO MORIAH

Samuel's story is linked from the outset with an old Canaanite sanctuary at Shiloh, where the Ark was ritually housed when not carried into battle. The problem was that, with the Philistines operating from five strategically placed key centres, the Israelite troops were necessarily split into separate units so they might protect their borders, and the Ark of the Lord could not be everywhere at once. As a result, the tribal factions became autonomous and disunited, in the course of which the Philistines managed to outwit the unit concerned and seize the Ark.[10] They took it to their citadel at Ashdod, but the residents were smitten by its emissions and fell victim to terrible infirmities. And so the Ark was taken to Gath, and then to Ekron, but the results were the same and there was 'deadly destruction' in the cities. Those who were not killed by its rays, suffered dreadful afflictions, so the Philistines decided that the Ark should be returned to the Levites at Bethshemesh.[11]

Given that Samuel was a priestly seer, rather than a warrior as previous judges had been, reprisals against the Philistines were taken up by the strongest and bravest of the Israelites — a Benjamite named Saul, who was installed as King in the field. Setting up his court at Gibeah, Saul managed to unite the tribal factions against the enemy for a while. But he was no diplomat and soon alienated his own priests, scores of whom he put to the sword for their lack of allegiance.[12] Whereas Saul felt he was the chosen King, to be succeeded by his son Jonathan, the majority viewed his status as being purely military and temporary. As far as Samuel the judge was concerned, the true King-elect was David, the son of Jesse, who was Saul's harpist and armour bearer.[13]

There is a confusing anomaly at this stage of David's story in that the following chapter takes no account of his already cited position in Saul's court, but depicts him as a stranger to the King. This occurs, as in previous instances, because two traditions by different writers are interwoven in the account. David is now perceived as having been a shepherd in the hills, who brought food to his older brothers on Saul's battlefield against the Philistines.[14]

247

It was on this visit to his warrior brethren that David was said to have become a great hero among the Israelites for slaying the giant Philistine champion, Goliath of Gath. We are told that Goliath's height was 'six cubits and a span' — that is something approaching 10 feet (c.3 m) tall.[15] But in spite of his physique and the enormity of his sword, it seems that David slew him with a well aimed stone to the forehead,[16] and was subsequently made a commander against the Philistines.

Goliath had issued a challenge to settle the battlefield conflict by way of a single combat between himself and the Israelite champion. But, there was none in Saul's army who dared to stand against him until David appeared on the scene and accepted the challenge. Goliath presented himself in readiness for a duel but, instead of entering into close combat as expected, David slew the man with a sling-shot before any fight had begun. This scene has often been questioned in terms of David's dubious integrity, but the story was not unique to Israelite legend. It was a folklore standard in many cultures, deriving originally from the Egyptian *Adventures of Sinuhe* in about 2000 BC. In much the same way as David, the young Prince Sinuhe had accepted an open challenge from the mighty champion of the tribes of Tenu. When the warrior arrived with his spear in readiness for combat, Sinuhe simply shot a bolt from his bow into the man's neck and killed him.[17]

Apart from David's heroic prestige, he also married Saul's daughter Michal, and became a close friend of her brother Jonathan. Nonetheless, King Saul vowed that he would kill David in order to secure the kingship within his own family.[18] In the knowledge of this, Jonathan warned his friend, who duly took his army into the hills of Engedi to await the King's assault. Saul eventually came with 3,000 men but, in separating him from his troops, David forgave the man and set him free.

Shortly afterwards Samuel died and, without his seer, Saul consulted the wise woman of Endor to determine his fate. She duly conjured the ghostly shade of Samuel, who advised Saul that he and his son would soon fall in battle against the Philistines. And so it was that, when Jonathan was slain on the field of Mount Gilboa, Saul knew that his hour of humiliation had come. Not wishing to be killed by the enemy, he elected instead to fall upon his own sword.[19]

Historically, what little information exists concerning Samuel indicates that his figure has been greatly exaggerated in the Bible. He was never a judge of the Israelite nation, and his operational domain was actually quite small, centring on Ramah where he was the resident seer and presided over the sacrificial altar. From there, his authority extended over the Canaanite altars of Gigal and Mizpah, where he would host local feasts and broadcast his prophecies.[20]

Obedience to the Lord

There is a good deal of talk about God in the biblical story of King Saul (sacrifices, prayers and such), but he makes no physical appearance. This is explained as being because 'The word of the Lord was precious in those days; there was no open vision'.[21] In this context, we have now entered an historical era that is many centuries removed from the old Mesopotamian and Canaanite texts, wherein the High God, by whatever name, appeared as an 'on the ground' character. Henceforth, he is encountered only as an entity by way of the visions of prophets and seers. He is no longer perceived as dwelling at Bêth-El, but in an inexplicable dimension called Heaven, from where he conducts his reign of judgement: 'The adversaries of the Lord shall be broken to pieces; out of heaven shall he thunder upon them. The Lord shall judge the ends of the earth'.[22]

Although Moses was said to have experienced the presence of God in Sinai, where the spirit of the Lord surmounted a pavement like sapphire stone, it is not since the days of Abraham (more than 800 years before Samuel) that we have any indication of God being in any way material. He has now moved into a realm of belief and tradition — a figure of dreams, visions and mystical experience. In this respect, God is said to have communed with Samuel, and to have been the source of his prophetic wisdom.

But the predominant message of the piece is that God turned against Saul because he was disobedient from the outset of his kingly installation.

Samuel had told Saul that the Lord commanded an invasion of the Amalekites, and that he should 'utterly destroy all that they have, and spare them not; but slay both man and woman, infant and suckling, ox and sheep, camel and ass'.[23] Consequently, Saul launched the campaign with devastating success, but seemingly failed to kill some of the sheep and oxen, and had not managed to slay the Amalekite king. This lack of attention to detail provoked God's anger, and Samuel was obliged to tell Saul that 'Because thou hast rejected the word of the Lord, he hath also rejected thee from being king'.[24]

Once again, in this instance and throughout the narrative, everything is geared towards the necessity for total and absolute obedience to the Lord, whose dictates must be followed to the letter. In an attempt to appease the godly displeasure, Samuel sent for the Amelekite king, and 'hewed Agag in pieces before the Lord'.[25] But God was not appeased, and Samuel was instructed to tell Saul that 'the Lord hath rent the kingdom out of thine hand, and given it to thy neighbour, even to David'.[26] From that point, David's right to kingship was divinely assured, and the Royal House of Judah was subsequently proclaimed. Then, paving the way for the manner in which Jesus was regarded in the New Testament gospels, the Lord was reckoned to have said of David, 'I will be his father, and he shall be my son'.[27]

* * *

Just as in all previous instances, the biblical accounts of the period of the judges identifies no good reason why the Israelites would have chosen to worship Yahweh. Whether forcing Jephthah to sacrifice his own daughter, or instigating campaigns of mass slaughter and destruction, God is constantly depicted as a brutal and violent dictator. To this point, from the time of Adam and Eve, there has been absolutely nothing endearing about his character in the Bible. We should remember, nevertheless, that the scriptures were not written until after the Babylonian Captivity in the 6th century BC and, for the most part (certainly from the time of Moses), the elements of specific detail have no originally documented source that has ever been discovered.

The invasion of Canaan was a particularly savage period in Israelite history. But, by portraying those decades of barbarous occupation as being the 'Will of God', the Israelite scribes were enabled to relinquish their nation's responsibility for the past genocide. Thus, although it might be seen that Yahweh emerges as a despotic psychopath, the chances are that his involvement was wholly invented by the Bible writers of much later times. That said, the biblical accounts are the only supportive record of God's presumed existence during this period. All first-hand contemporary writings concerning him, whether as El or Ilû, had terminated in about 1400 BC.

King of Judah

To begin (c.1008 BC), David's kingship was territorially limited. He was anointed as King of the Israelites and of their lands in the newly dubbed region of Israel, but they were still a good way north of Jerusalem and the Palestinian strongholds in southern Canaan.

With the Ark back in action, David defeated the Philistines in a series of battles, moving southwards towards Mount Moriah with a mustered force of 30,000 men. The Ark was transported throughout on a specially made cart but, when it swayed during the journey, Uzzah the carter inadvertently touched it and was killed on the spot.[28] David was concerned that only the Levites, with their special clothing and training, could handle the sacred relic, when he (even as their king) could not. He donned a priestly *ephod* (a girdled tunic)[29] and danced before the Ark, but knew that despite everything he could never touch it for fear of his life. At length, he and the Israelites reached Mount Moriah, and Zadok the high priest led the Ark into the old Canaanite settlement of Uru-Shālem (Jerusalem), where the Davidic court was established and the king enthroned. As a result of David's leadership, Philistine domination was at an end in southern Canaan, and the land to the south of Israel was renamed Judah.

There is no mention in any of this of the Canaanite succession from Abd-khiba, who had governed Jerusalem around the time of Moses, and historically it is not clear who was running Uru-Shālem prior to David's arrival.[30] The said timing of David's kingly installation in Judah is interesting, however, since it occurred when things were in a state of flux all around. With the Ramesside period at an end, Egypt had moved into a downhill era in which the nation was virtually bankrupt. The south (Upper Egypt)[31] was governed by a ruling class of Theban priests, while the north (Lower Egypt) was separately managed by non-dynastic kings at Tanis in the Nile delta. Meanwhile, the Mesopotamians and Syrians were not especially interested in Canaan, and had avoided the region after the Palestinian conquest. Babylonia was in a state of some decline, and the rise of Assyria had not yet begun. Having defeated the Philistines, David was therefore in a good position not to be challenged from outside, and even made his own inroads into other lands: 'And David smote Hadarezer king of Zobah unto Hanath as he went to stablish his dominion by the river Euphrates'.[32]

What we do not know, however, is the actual name of the character who became recorded as King David. The name was introduced into the biblical scripture, but had never been used as a personal name before that time. It appears to have derived from a titular distinction, and tablets from the palace of Mari use the term *Dâvîdum* (Commander) in much the same way that the style of *Caesar* was used in Rome to denote an imperial figurehead. This being the case, then David, Solomon and their successors might all have been considered *Dâvîdums*, even though only the first king of the dynasty was personally granted the name for posterity in scriptural terms.[33]

Having subjugated the regions of Edom, Ammon and Moab, along with bordering Aramaean centres such as Damascus and the Canaanite conclaves of Megiddo and Bethshean, David is portrayed as having been more of an emperor than a king.

He established trading relations with the Phoenicians of Hamath, Tyre and Sidon, and constructed his court on the traditional Egyptian model of his ancestors. It was administered by appointed officials, with a military commander, a chancellor and a chronicler.[34] Additionally, there were two chief priests (Zadok and Abiathar) and a vizier, just as retained by the pharaohs. David also had his own harem in the style of other Eastern monarchies. In this regard, his primary wives are given as being Michal (the daughter of Saul), Ahinoam of Jezreel, Abigail, Maacah, Haggith, Abital, Eglah and Bathsheba.

Although David was greatly revered as a national hero and one of the most significant biblical figures, he is not always flatteringly portrayed. An example of his devious nature is given in respect of his adultery with Bathsheba who, before marrying David, was the wife of Uriah the Hittite. Beginning at 2 Samuel 11:2, the story relates that when David discovered that he had caused Bathsheba's pregnancy, he recalled Uriah from the battle-field to spend some time with his wife. In his attempt to avoid personal responsibility for Bathsheba's condition, David's plan was that Uriah would consider the conception ultimately to be of his own doing. But Uriah declined the invitation since it was not considered honourable practice for a soldier to visit his wife in times of battle. Consequently, David arranged that Uriah should be placed in the battlefield front line, where he knew the man would likely be killed. Then, following Uriah's death as antici-pated, Bathsheba was free to join the royal household.[35]

David's reign was not without its turmoils, and at one point his eldest son, Absalom, led a revolt against his father, only to be killed in the process — resulting in the lament, O Absalom, My Son.[36] A struggle for succession then erupted, with the Judah faction supporting David's next eldest son, Adonijah, and the Jerusalem faction backing the younger Solomon. When David eventually died, Solomon's supporters were by far the more powerful, having in their number Zadok the priest, Nathan the prophet and Benaiah, captain of the palace guard. They had Adonijah executed,[37] his supporters exiled, and Solomon became the new King in Jerusalem.

Fakes, Forgeries and Relics

In researching this period of Israelite history, we encounter a major problem because of the dearth of records from Canaan. There is very little documentary evidence to support the biblical portrayal of the emergent Royal House of Judah. But, at the same time, nothing has been found that obviously contradicts it.

Whereas thousands of inscribed tablets have been unearthed from earlier periods, methods of record keeping changed significantly from around 1000 BC, at about the time of David's accession. Previously, the Canaanites had written by way of etching with a stylus into subsequently baked clay tablets, but the Israelites introduced the use of ink in the Egyptian style. Papyrus (a high quality paper made from reeds, as used in Egypt) was not easily available and, in any event, constituted an expensive import, so a new style of document evolved. They were called ostraca[38] — hard clay or earthenware tablets on which ink could be used. The problem was that their written surfaces were not suited to longevity. Although many of these ostraca have been discovered, very few are legible. The majority cannot be read since their ink has been eradicated by up to 3,000 years of underground damp.

Among some of the more useful discoveries, a large number of ostraca, found in the Negev at Arad, deal with the administration of the region in the 8th to the 6th centuries BC. Others, found at the Judah site of Lachish, date to around 600 BC, and are letters that discuss military preparations relative to the Babylonian invasion. (In about 588 BC, Nebuchadnezzar attacked Lachish before he assaulted Jerusalem.)

When ostraca are discovered archaeologically, their legitimacy is rarely in doubt. But in recent times a large number have appeared in the antiques market with no archaeological provenance, and many have now been proved as fakes. The basic requirement to produce a fake ostracon is simply an ancient clay shard that can be authentically dated, onto which old style Semitic writing is added in traditional iron-carbon ink. Sometimes, instead of ink being used on tablets, ancient pots and shards have been inscribed with writing that has been cleverly eroded and patinated. Such items have been traded for enormous sums in what has become a multi-million dollar industry that has fooled experts at the highest levels.[39]

In December 2004, a Palestinian and four Israelis were indicted on charges of having run a lucrative forgery ring for several decades. The Israel Antiquities Authority and the Israeli police claimed that the defendants had created a series of biblically related fakes, some of which had been bought for high prices and lodged in the prestigious Israel Museum in Jerusalem. Aiding the case for proving various forgeries have been geologists from Tel Aviv University and the Israel Geology Survey, along with epigraphists from Ben-Gurion Universtity and the Hebrew University in Jerusalem. In the light of all this, since some of the most prized museum artefacts of old Judah have now been discredited, doubt has been cast on all relics that exist without archaeological provenance. It is heartening to know, however, that those authorities whom it might be imagined would wish to preserve the myth of such relics of presumed heritage are the very same authorities who are now denouncing their authenticity.

This, of course, leaves us precisely where we began this section in that there is very little documentary evidence to support the biblical portrayal of the early kings of the House of Judah, although nothing has been found that obviously contradicts it. Notwithstanding this, it is evident from ancient documentary studies that what is not recorded in one place will very likely turn up in another. If the House of David was as prominent and influential as the Bible maintains, then surely it would be mentioned in the archives of other neighbouring lands.

In 1993 a discovery was made north of Judah at Tel Dan in the foothills of Mount Hermon, which has become one of the most significant landmarks in the modern State of Israel. Excavations had begun in 1966 under the direction of archaeologist Avraham Biran. After some years of digging, a monumental mud-brick gate was unearthed, with an arch constructed by the Canaanites in around 1800 BC, long before the Israelites arrived in the region. The Dan location was called Leshem,[40] or Laish,[41] and the ancient

Canaanite Gate is now a conservation project of the Israeli Antiquities Authority.

Among the ruins of Leshem, from later times, were found the remnants of a basalt stela — the largest fragment of which is 12.5 x 8.75 inches (32 x 22 cm). On this, thirteen lines of carved Aramaic script are partially preserved from around 825 BC, soon after the time of David's biblical descendant, King Jehosaphat of Judah. The inscription was created by King Hazael of Aram, and it relates to his father, Hadad II, being victorious in battle against Achazvahu of the *Bytdwd*, which is said to translate to House of David.

The kings, Ben-hadad and Hazael, are biblically discussed in 2 Kings 8:7–15, whilst Achazvahu (in Aramaic) is deemed linguistically synonymous with Jehosaphat (in Hebrew). Hence, the Tel Dan relic is now regarded as a national treasure in the Israel Museum, where it is catalogued as the *House of David Inscription*. But, as we have seen above, David did not exist as a personal name in those times, and the inscription would more likely refer to the House of the Dâvìdum, denoting a titular distinction — like House of the Tzar — rather than referencing David as an individual.

Another kingly relic boasting of conflict with the House of David (or *Dâvìdum*) is the Moabite Stone (alternatively known as the *Mesha Stela*) from about 860 BC. This 42 by 24 inch black basalt monument (107 x 61 cm) was discovered in 1868 at Dhiban, twenty miles east of the Dead Sea (across from Engedi), and is now housed in the Louvre Museum, Paris. As reported in *Time* magazine, December 1995, it is the most extensive inscription ever recovered from ancient Palestine.

The Moabite Stone contains 36 lines of Phoenician script which relate to the rebellion of King Mesha of Moab against the Kings of Israel and Judah. This battle is recounted in the Old Testament book of 2 Kings 3:4–27. In 1994, after examining both the Moabite Stone and its papier-mâché impression in the Louvre, the French scholar André Lemaire reported that line-31 of the stela again mentions the *Bytdwd* (House of David), just as on the Tel Dan fragment.[42]

Discovered in 1868 by the German missionary FA Klein, the Moabite Stone caused another battle when the Berlin Museum expressed an interest in removing it to the West. The *Jewish Encyclopedia* relates that, on hearing of this, local Arabs heaved it out of the earth, lit fires around it and doused it with cold water so that it fragmented. Mediation was subsequently conducted by the French Consulate in Jerusalem, whose conservators restored the artefact, while offering enough money to purchase the stone and thereby placate the inhabitants of Dhiban.

18

A TALE OF TWO KINGDOMS

The Rise of Jerusalem

With the introduction of David's son and successor, King Solomon, we have an example of how distinctive titular names were given to the dynasts of Judah as against their actual birth names. Although we do not know David's real name, we are told in 2 Samuel 12:24–25 that the king who became known as Solomon was called Jedidiah.

From the coronation of Britain's King George II in 1727, George Frideric Handel's anthem, *Zadok the Priest*, has been sung at each successive coronation in Westminster Abbey, London. The composition alludes to the majestic anointing ritual of King Solomon, but its grandeur and dignified surroundings are far removed from the biblical portrayal. In a competitive race for the crown against his older half-brother Adonijah, Solomon rode on a mule to the desert spring of Gihon, where he was anointed by Zadok, the high priest, at a hastily improvised outdoor ceremony.[1]

By contrast to his warlike father, Solomon (who reigned c.968–926 BC) was reputed as a prince of peace. Hence the stylized name by which King Jedidiah became known (Solomon meaning 'peaceable').[2] He did not embark on any expansionist campaigns, although he built defensive garrisons for his chariots and cavalry, notably at Hazor, Megiddo, and Gezer. He also erected huge store-centres and appointed twelve regional governors for his administrative districts. Given that (unlike the Philistines) the Israelites had no maritime experience, Solomon forged good relations with the Phoenician merchants, and King Hiram of Tyre helped him build a fleet of ships to operate in the Red Sea. The fleet was based at Ezion-geber, which enabled Solomon to enter the lucrative horse trade, as a result of which he had 40,000 stalls of horses for his chariots and 12,000 horsemen.³ Even his Jerusalem city stable was extensive and, when excavated by the Knights Templars around 2,000 years later (1118–27) after the First Crusade, it was reported that it was 'a stable of such marvelous capacity and extent that it could hold more than 2,000 horses'.⁴

Although perhaps peaceable in terms of his relationships with other nations, Solomon is portrayed as having been a harsh master in his own domain. He placed the non-Israelites of his realm, along with many of the Israelites from the northern territory, into bonded service for his ambitious building projects in Jerusalem, Hazor, Megiddo and Gezer.⁵ There is substantial archaeological evidence for his constructions at Megiddo, where two palaces and other public buildings have been unearthed and dated to Solomon's era. Excavations at Hazor and Gezer have revealed similarly extensive works, with city walls and gates that also date to the same period.⁶ Given that the Jerusalem Temple was demolished, rebuilt, extended and then demolished again through an overall period of around 1,000 years, we shall return to the matter of its archaeology in a later chapter.

Noted for his wisdom, the biblical Solomon is well remembered for his method of judgement when confronted by two women, each claiming to be the mother of a baby boy. With no real evidence to consider, Solomon called for a sword in order to cut the child in two. He said he would give the women half a boy each, but only one of them said she would rather lose the baby to her rival than see him killed. The King therefore judged that she was doubtless the rightful mother.⁷

In terms of philosophical writings, Solomon has been credited with numerous works, including the *Wisdom of Solomon* which appears in the Apocryphal Bible.⁸ He is also reckoned to have written the Old Testament *Canticles* of the Song of Solomon, along with the book of Proverbs. But, in this latter respect (as with the others), the claim is wholly invalid. Not only were the Ten Commandments drawn from entries in the Egyptian *Book of the Dead*, whilst many of the Psalms of David were likewise drawn from hymns of Egyptian origin, but so too were the biblical Proverbs extracted from the wisdom culture of ancient Egypt.

Thirty of them were translated almost verbatim into Hebrew from the writings of an Egyptian sage called Amenemope, which are now held in the British Museum.[9] Verse after verse of the Bible's book of Proverbs can be attributed to this Egyptian original, and it has been discovered that the writings of Amenemope derived from a far older work called the *Wisdom of Ptah-hotep*, which comes from more than 2,000 years before the time of Solomon.[10]

The apocryphal *Wisdom of Solomon* was a much later work which emanated from Alexandria in about 250 BC — some 700 years after the time of Solomon. It was based on Greek philosophies of the era, and was included in the Alexandrian *Septuagint* Bible.[11] Also wrongly attributed is the Old Testament's exotic *Song of Solomon*. This series of love canticles between a king and his bride is distinctly Arabic, with heavy influences from Syria and Mesopotamia. The Syrian royal marriage ceremony (known as the Threshing Floor Ritual) referenced in Song 1:12, with its kingly table and the bridal ointment of spikenard, was repeated in the Christian New Testament when Mary Magdalene anointed Jesus at the table ceremony in Bethany.[12]

The high point of Solomon's fame was the Temple which he built on Mount Moriah (near David's palace on the Rock of Jerusalem) to house the Ark of the Covenant. For this ambitious project, King Hiram of Tyre came again to his aid, supplying designers, craftsmen and materials. The director of operations was another Hiram, also from Tyre, a skilled artificer in metalwork.[13] According to masonic lore, this Hiram was surnamed Abiff, although he is not referred to as such in the Bible.[14] His namesake, King Hiram (c.969–936 BC), was at that time one of the most notable figures in the Middle East. In a dynasty that began with his father Abi-baal, Hiram's extensive building and civil engineering works transformed Tyre from a small coastal settlement into the richest and most influential trading port in the Mediterranean world.[15]

The Jerusalem Temple, as portrayed in the scripture, was partly modelled on aspects of Phoenician tradition. At its entrance (and in line with contemporary temple custom) were two free-standing pillars, one referred to as *Jachin* (denoting 'establishment'), and the other *Boaz* (meaning 'in strength'), the name of the great-grandfather of David. Traditional masonic ritual tells that these bronze pillars were hollow constructions which contained the constitutional Rolls of the Craft. The Temple walls and ceiling were lined with Lebanon cedar, and decorated with cherubim, palms, pomegranates and lilies. The doors and floor were made of olive and pine — and all of this, from floor to ceiling, was overlaid with gold.[16] Central to the overall theme was the designated *Holy of Holies*, which housed the Ark of the Covenant, guarded by two giant cherubim.[17]

Palace of Gold

Paramount in the story of Solomon is the great wealth of gold that he accumulated: 'Now the weight of gold that came to Solomon in one year was six-hundred threescore and six talents'.[18] 'And all King Solomon's drinking vessels were of gold:

> And King Solomon made two hundred targets of beaten gold; six hundred shekels of gold went to one target[19] ... And he made three hundred shields of beaten gold; three pounds of gold went to one shield[20] ... Moreover the king made a great throne of ivory, and overlaid it with the best gold'.[21]

The list of golden artefacts for Solomon's palace is seemingly endless — and all this was additional to the extensive use of gold in the construction and furnishings of his Temple.

With aid from King Hiram of Tyre, a good amount of Solomon's gold was obtained from the mines of Ophir, near Sheba,[22] from where the Queen also came, bringing more wealth to the Jerusalem court. 1 Kings 10:1–13 relates that the Queen of Sheba arrived with a great caravan, bringing spices, gold and precious stones for the King of Judah,[23] whose unparalleled wisdom was renowned far and wide.[24]

The land of Sheba (correctly, Sāba) is referenced in the Assyrian inscriptions of King Tiglath-pileser III (c.745–727 BC), and of Sargon II (c.720–705 BC). These writings explain that Sāba was the land of the Sābaeans (the *Sāba'aa*), and the latter inscription (from around 707 BC) associates a prevailing Queen Samsé of Aribû with King It'amara of Sāba. His realm was to the far south of Palestine and Jordan in the Arabian Peninsula which now includes Yemen. Bordering the eastern flank of the Red Sea above the Gulf of Aden, the Semitic rendition of the name Sāba was Sheba.[25]

The land of Sheba was certainly noted for its spices and gold, just as portrayed. But as for the Queen, there is no mention in the Bible of her age, her looks, nor anything about her. And yet there is a compelling romance in the mystique of the woman with the wealth-laden camel-train that has led artists and writers to develop a colourful mythology of her over the centuries. By contrast, her biblical presence is very limited, spanning just a dozen short verses which set an appropriate scene for the portrayal of Solomon's own prestige. How better for the scribes to demonstrate the wisdom and wealth of the mighty King than to have the Queen of an historically great trading nation confide, 'Thy wisdom and prosperity exceedeth the fame which I heard'.[26]

God of the Dreams

At the outset of Solomon's reign, God is said to have appeared to him in a dream at Gibeon. Yet again we have a 'vision' of God, rather than a real presence, and the story of this dream is another repeat of an Egyptian original. In the earlier Egyptian version, the Sphinx of Giza appeared to Pharaoh Tuthmosis IV, confirming his right to the kingly succession. Afterwards, Tuthmosis offered sacrifices and was granted a promise of great wisdom. Precisely the same sequence of events occurs in the Solomon account.[27]

All was not well, though, between God and Solomon. In typical Old Testament style, Solomon managed to upset the Lord without trying. When he had completed the seven-year Temple project, God appeared to him in another dream. This time, and with no satisfactorily given reason, God threatened to cast the Israelites from his sight if Solomon should attempt to worship other gods. Once more we have this biblical acknowledgement of 'other gods',[28] and the confirmation that Yahweh was still reckoned to be fearful of his competitors. The concept of there only being One God is still not a feature of the biblical text — only that this particular God remained persistent in his threatening demands for individual loyalty from the Israelites.

In the event, it was primarily to the goddess Ashtoreth (the consort of El Elyon) that Solomon turned his attention, along with the Ammonite god Milcom and the Moabite god Chemosh. He established sanctuaries to these deities on the Mount of Olives near Bethany.[29] Milcom (or Molech, relating to a prince or lord) appears to have been an alternative name for Baal, and Chemosh was the Semitic name of the Mesopotamian god Shamash, the grandson of Enlil/El Elyon.

The blame for Solomon's behaviour in this regard is laid very firmly at the feet of his 700 wives and 300 concubines who, according to the scribes, 'turned away his heart after other gods'. He was said to have 'loved many strange women' and, in his attempts to appease their various requirements, 'Solomon did evil in the sight of the Lord'.[30]

Given that no such claims exist in any other document yet discovered outside the Bible, it seems rather odd that the writers of the book of Kings should have thought to criticise the mightiest of their monarchs in such a way. Their criticism does, nonetheless, serve two purposes. In the first place (after the short interlude with the seemingly delightful Ruth), it brings women generally back into the sinfully manipulative frame that was built around Eve, and which persists through most of the Old Testament. It also serves to prepare the path for the Israelites' Babylonian captivity, which is now just a few generations ahead. Someone had to take the rap for the dreadful treatment of the Israelites by Yahweh, and who better than the kings of their governing dynasty. In this respect, Solomon was not alone and, for the next 300 years, others of his succession are said to have done such evil as to frustrate Yahweh by their constant reverence towards other gods.

In real terms, from long before this stage of the scriptural proceedings, we have no indication that God was actually a part of anything. For a good while now, he has appeared only in the dreams and visions of certain scribally selected figures. He has no physical presence and has become no more than a figment of tradition within an overall culture that still subscribes to the notion of a wider pantheon in which the distant memory of him resides. What this tradition provided, however, was a very effective way of relinquishing responsibility and, at all times when things did not go well for the Israelites, their misfortunes could be attributed to the unfathomable Will of God. But someone still had to shoulder the overall blame and, since the scribes were not willing to discuss the petulant nature of El-Yahweh himself, the kings were perfectly suited to be held responsible for his perceived harshness towards the people.

Fear and Trepidation

In the wider scheme of things, it was undoubtedly felt by the Bible writers — and presumably by the Israelites at large during the post-captivity era — that to have faith in God necessarily meant that one had to suffer pain and hardship. It was somehow taken for granted that suffering was itself a requisite of divine action. In a perpetuation of his *Torah* portrayal, God is seen always as a demanding and opinionated taskmaster. He is never described with the colour and romance of other gods, neither with any sense of fairness or humour. The Old Testament (which is the recognized history of God) grants him no aptitude for mercy or compassion except in certain cases where he has pushed his subjects to their limits of suffering in order to test their loyalty.

A good example in this regard is the story of Job, which appears to have no other purpose than to convey the message that true righteousness can only exist by way of intimidation and blind obedience. The chances are that the biblical accounts of

Job's misfortunes are fictional. But they are literally used in an attempt to cement God's position at a time when many Israelites were losing interest in a deity who actually seemed not to like them very much.

Job enters the scene as a wealthy and successful man, who regularly offered sacrifices to the Lord. With a large family, much livestock and a splendid household, he was said to be 'the greatest of all the men of the east'.[31] In this regard, he has long been identified with Jobab, the Lord of Edom.[32] His adversity begins when the sons of God are in conference with Yahweh, who suggests to one of them that Job's loyalty should be put to the test.[33] This particular son of God is a character called Satan (meaning 'accuser'),[34] and they enter into a bet as to whether or not Job's faith can be destroyed.

Job is then subjected to a series of unjust trials and persecutions in order to measure his virtue. In succession, he bears six great temptations with heroic patience and without the slightest complaint against God, nor any wavering in obedience to him. In the course of these tests, Job loses all of his wealth, the support of his children, then his health, and is finally abandoned by his wife. Riddled with disease and boils, he is stripped and cast onto a rubbish tip, where he faces taunt and torment from the inhabitants of the city.

Eventually, his three friends, Eliphaz, Baldad and Sophar, come to console him, but their visit becomes the seventh and greatest trial. They conclude that Job must be a terrible sinner from whom God has withdrawn his blessing. They deduce that since God is sovereign and in control of all that happens, it must naturally follow that he will only bless those who are obedient and faithful. Hence, Job is convinced that he must be dreadfully unworthy, but has no idea how or why; he knows only that he is sick, destitute and thoroughly confused. Ultimately, when Job's anguish has taken him to the very depths of misery and despair, he learns that it was all a hideous practical joke. He is then restored to his former wealth and station, reunited with his family, and is reckoned to have learned about the mysterious ways of God!

For want of knowing how best to interpret this lengthy story of some 20,000 words, both the Jewish and Christian establishments settled long ago on the conclusion that it provides an example of the magnificent grace and benevolence of God, who saw fit to restore Job to his original position because he remained obedient despite all adversity! In reality, the story proves only that, in the perception of the Israelite scribes, this God was rather more interested in serving his own ego than in being a kindly shepherd to his flock. In Exodus 20:5, he stated: 'I the Lord thy God am a jealous God, visiting the iniquity of the fathers upon the children unto the third and fourth generation of them that hate me' — and at every conceivable turn we are reminded of this malicious aspect of his nature. In Job's case, however, the malice has nothing to do with anyone hating God; the man was known by all to have been a faithful servant. The purposeful cruelty inflicted on Job in this story is immense, and is levelled without any justification. It constitutes a significant pointer to the fact that the actual content of the Bible bears little relationship to the use that is made religiously of the holy book. There is hardly an instance where Yahweh shows any kindness or sympathy for anyone who does not tread his designated and very restrictive path, and he is even portrayed as victimizing those who do.

What we do not know is whether there is any historical merit to this story. Everything points to the fact that it was entirely fabricated when written in the 5th century BC. What we do know, however, is that it was part of a social reconstruction process whereby the Israelites were brought into line with new homeland doctrines after the Babylonian Captivity. In this regard, the priests introduced concocted stories that would instil fear into the community. Without any king to consider at that stage of Israelite history, the priests had become the self-appointed bridges between God and the people. They were the perceived regulators of his wrath, but it was rather more a case of subjecting the Israelites to the rule of the priestly hierarchy than to the actual Will of God.

In terms of biblically documented record, the physical appearances of God had terminated long before in the days of

Abraham and El Shaddai. There were some hints of a godly presence during the Mosaic era but, as we have seen, God becomes wholly theoretical and a product of visions thereafter. From the time of the Davidic Kings of Judah, and onwards through the balance of the Old Testament, Yahweh has become celestial, unreal and mythological. There is no contemporary text outside the Bible that makes any reference to him in those times, and his biblical image is constantly designed to engender fear and trepidation.

The scripture itself also becomes more threatening as it moves towards the era when it was written — a period of oppression when the Israelites were subservient to authoritarian figures who were reckoned to be God's representatives on Earth. Notwithstanding anything that previously had been extracted from Mesopotamian, Canaanite or Egyptian records, the perceived character of Yahweh was scribally modelled to suit political requirement. It was the birth of enforced monotheistic religion by way of psychological entrapment — a process of obedience to dictatorial priests whose institutional law became the accepted path of righteousness.

It was by virtue of the inherent anomalies and unpleasantries in God's biblical portrayal that philosophical Judaism evolved. This began in Alexandria during the period between the Testaments, when the Greek scholarly pursuit of 'theonogy' (the genealogy of the gods) gave way to 'theology' (an analysis of theistic religious faith). This led, in one of its Judaean branches, to the revised godly perception of the Nazarenes, and to the emergent, redefined God of later Christianity.

A Divided Nation

By the end of Solomon's reign, the Tribes of Israel were very much settled in their own particular regions of the once land of Canaan. To the north (where the Israelites had originally gained occupation), were the tribes of Asher, Naphtali, Zebulun and Issachar, whilst Gad, East Manasseh and Reuben were located in the

Transjordan sector. Centrally situated were the tribes of West Manasseh, Ephraim, Dan and Benjamin, with Judah and Simeon occupying the southern country to the west of the Dead Sea. The capital of the Davidic kingdoms inherited by Solomon was Jerusalem in the tribal area of Judah, which name was given to the southern territory, while the north remained classified as Israel.

Judah, by that time, had enveloped theoretically the maritime plain of Palestine including Gaza, Askelon, Ashdod, Ekron and Gath. But, despite some wishful thinking by the Old Testament scribes, the historical Philistines did not succumb to rule from Jerusalem. Holding out against invasion attempts from Egypt, Assyria and Macedonia, they managed to retain their own independence with a succession of recorded kings until Roman occupation in the 1st century BC.[35]

When Solomon's son Rehoboam acceded to the throne in about 926 BC, the Israelite residents of the north appealed for some better treatment than his father had given them with his bonded service and punitive levies. They requested social equality with the Judaeans of the south, but Rehoboam dismissed their pleas, stating, 'My father made your yoke heavy, and I will add to your yoke; my father chastised you with whips, but I will chastise you with scorpions'.[36]

In consequence, the northern tribes united against the Jerusalem monarchy. They stoned Rehoboam's regional governor, Adoram, to death, and appointed their own king in the person of Jeroboam, a son of Solomon's erstwhile courtier Nabat. The united monarchy established by David was thus divided, and the apparent solidarity of the Mosaic exodus into the Promised Land was shattered as the children of Israel set themselves regionally against each other. From that time, their loyalties were split through the middle, and separate successions of kings reigned in the realms of Israel and Judah.

Soon afterwards, the capital of the northern kingdom of Israel was established at a newly built citadel called Samaria.[37] In later times (c.720 BC) this city was conquered by Sargon II of Assyria, whose incoming Mesopotamian tribes occupied much of the surrounding region. They became known as Samaritans and, although integrating with the Israelite communities, their dominion placed a geographical wedge between Israel and Judah, with the central land being renamed, after its capital, Samaria.

If the original kingdom of David and Solomon was ever expected to become a viable empire, such hopes were dashed from the competitive reigns of Rehoboam and Jeroboam. From that moment, the Israelite nation was so fiercely divided that it became a constant prey to outside powers, notably the Babylonians and Assyrians, who were each attempting to dominate the region at that time. The blood of Israel and Judah was shed in three centuries of civil war between the once tribal cousins, and a massive walled fortress was built by the Judaeans a few miles north of Jerusalem, at Mizpah, to guard the frontier. The American excavation of this defensive structure by William F Bade of the Pacific School of Religion in 1927–35 revealed an enclosure wall 26 feet thick (c.7.9 m).[38]

It was during the early stages of this Israelite civil war in the fifth year of Rehoboam's reign, that Shishak, the King of Egypt, seized his opportunity to enter Jerusalem, 'And he took away the treasures of the house of the Lord, and the treasures of the king's house ... And he took away all the shields of gold which Solomon had made'.[39]

Shishak has never successfully been identified since there is no record of this Egyptian raid outside the Bible. The French Egyptologist, Jean François Champollion (who deciphered the hieroglyphic code in 1822), speculated that Shishak was most probably Pharaoh Sheshonq I, founder of the 22nd dynasty. Whether or not this pharaoh actually invaded Jerusalem is unknown, but he certainly assaulted other Judaean settlements. A relief carving at the Egyptian temple of Karnak depicts Sheshonq leading 156 manacled prisoners out of Megiddo, where his name has been found inscribed in the ruins.[40]

19

THE IMPLACABLE LORD

Annals of the Kings

The given biblical reason for the division of the kingdoms was that God had been displeased with Solomon for acknowledging Ashtoreth, along with the other gods and goddesses of his wives. Solomon's son Rehoboam was therefore granted kingship over the tribe of Judah, while all other tribes were made subject to Jeroboam, the new King of Israel. Notwithstanding the apparent inequity of this arrangement, Rehoboam retained Jerusalem and the Temple for the House of David in descent from Judah, although the priests in descent from Judah's brother Levi came under the auspices of Jeroboam. The balance of the story, as it moves through successive generations, is therefore one of conflict between the two royal houses, during which it seems that loyalties to God were divided.

To begin, we are told how Jeroboam feared that, since the Temple was in Jerusalem, his people might go there to worship and thereby claim Rehoboam as the senior king. So he established his own bases at Bêth-El and Dan, where he placed two golden calves as Aaron had once made in Sinai. These, he announced, were to be the new gods of the Israelites,[1] whereas Yahweh was henceforth the God of the Judaeans.

From that juncture, it becomes clear (in biblical terms at least) that God's said choice to separate the kingdoms was not the wisest of moves. Israel and Judah became warring nations and, during the early years, Rehoboam's successor, King Abijah of Judah, took Bêth-El and other Israelite places from Jeroboam.[2] And so the battles continued through the generations, while at the same time the Israelite lands were constantly under threat from Philistines, and from the Aramaeans of Syria whose capital was at Damascus. Meanwhile, the Levite priests of Israel ignored

Jeroboam's idols and pledged their allegiance to the House of Judah which commanded the Temple.

Much of the narrative in the books of Kings and Chronicles is taken up with accounts of the ongoing dispute, and has very little to do with God except for some brief mentions that occur in the course of the action. One of the best remembered among these is the story of King Ahab of Israel, who erected altars and planted groves to venerate Baal when he was seduced into following 'the wicked ways' of his wife Jezebel, a Phoenician princess of Sidon.[3] In this regard, Ahab joined Jeroboam and the list of other Israelite kings who were said to have 'done evil in the sight of the Lord'.

Omri, the father of Ahab and fifth in the succession from Jeroboam, is the first of the northern kings with known historical references outside the Bible. He is mentioned on the *Mesha Stela* of the Moabite Stone from around 860 BC, and also features in Assyrian inscriptions. One of these is a text of the Assyrian king Tiglath-pileser III (c.745–727 BC), which describes Israel as the *bit hu-um-ri-a* — the House of Omri.[4] Jehu, a successor of Omri, is discussed and pictured on an obelisk of Shalmaneser III (c.840 BC) as having paid tribute to the Assyrian king.

There is little doubt that Omri and other Israelite kings made a considerable impression on the rulers of neighbouring domains, even though the Kings of Israel were a succession, but not a continuous family dynasty as was the case in Judah. Between them, Omri and Ahab greatly improved the towns of Hazor and Megiddo, constructing their magnificent water systems, whilst rendering the city of Samaria virtually impregnable by way of massive fortifications. But none of these works of enterprise has any space in the Bible because of the scribes' overwhelming intent to promote the rather less influential House of David in Jerusalem. King Omri's son Ahab is also cited honourably in Assyrian inscriptions but, as far as the scriptures are concerned, he was a worshipper of Baal, and was therefore evil.

Following the reigns of 19 kings in 200 years, the Israelite capital of Samaria eventually fell to the armies of Sargon II of Assyria in 722 BC. The Assyrian records state that some 27,290 Israelites were sent into exile by Sargon, and at that point in history the northern kingdom of Israel came to an end.[5] It was this event which led to the speculative mythology concerning the said Lost Tribes of Israel. But although the names of ten tribes (excluding those of Judah, Benjamin and a Levite faction) were not individually referenced in Jewish literature from that moment in time, 27,290 exiles hardly constituted anything remotely close to the whole Israelite nation, and the majority remained, having simply lost their tribal regions to Assyrian control.

During this same period, only ten kings and a queen had reigned in Judah. Since this smaller, more southerly realm, did not suffer the same empire-building assaults from Syria and Assyria, it is not so well recorded outside the Bible. There are, as we have seen, some references to kings of the House of David in Syrian and Moabite inscriptions, but the first King of Judah to be fully identifiable in historical record was Hezekiah. This report emanates from soon after the Assyrian conquest of Samaria, when the forces of Sennacherib set their sights on the Judaean and Palestinian lands of the south. There appears to be no doubt of Hezekiah's potential strength, even though he could not withstand the Assyrian onslaught. In 715 BC Sennacherib wrote:

> Hezekiah the Jew did not submit to my yoke; I laid siege to forty-six of his strong cities, walled forts and to the countless small villages in their vicinity, and conquered them by means of well-stamped ramps and battering rams, combined with the attack by foot soldiers ...
> I drove out 200,150 people young and old, male and female ... Himself I made a prisoner in Jerusalem, his royal residence, like a bird in a cage.[6]

This historical account, which undoubtedly confirms the Davidic royal capital in Jerusalem, continues with details of gold, silver, precious stones and other riches that were given as tribute offerings to Sennacherib by Hezekiah, much as scripturally related in 2 Kings 18:13–16. Not only had the Israelite kingdom been decimated, but ruin was about to befall the southern kingdom of Judah. These were the lands of God's said 'chosen people' in descent from Abraham — the very tribes he had supposedly promised to defend and protect. The Bible explains the anomaly of Israel, however, by claiming that its kings each 'did evil in the sight of the Lord', and none more so than Ahab, who appears to have provoked a lasting anger because of his marriage to Jezebel. And the Lord said:

> Behold, I will bring evil upon thee, and will take away thy posterity ... And will make thine house like the house of Jeroboam the son of Nebat, and like the house of Baasha the son of Ahijah, for the provocation where-with thou hast provoked me to anger, and made Israel to sin ... The dogs shall eat Jezebel by the wall of Jezreel.[7]

As against Ahab and the other Kings of Israel, what had Hezekiah of Judah done to fire the Lord's anger against himself and his posterity? The answer, it appears, is absolutely nothing. The fault was said to have been that of his father Ahaz, who had made a copy of an altar that he admired in Damascus, and had placed it in the Temple of Jerusalem.[8] This was perceived as an act of defilement which somehow proved that Ahaz had turned against the Lord. The result was that God allowed the Assyrians to invade Jerusalem, so that Hezekiah became a vassal of Sennacherib.

Plainly, this interpretation of events in Judah (as with those that preceded in Israel) was a mind-set of the biblical scribes rather than an aspect of history. Someone had to be blamed for the treatment the Israelites were receiving, and the demise of their kingdoms was said, at all stages, to have been the fault of kings who consistently managed to upset God. In laying these various blames, the scriptural depictions of Yahweh present him as being ferocious and resentful, but he was never once criticised by the scribes. In fact, quite the reverse; his dictatorial rule was biblically upheld at all times.

What the Chronicles and Kings writers were heading towards in their scene-setting was the eventual sacking of Jerusalem by Nebuchadnezzar of Babylon. Meanwhile, although Hezekiah had

THE ORIGIN OF GOD

become a vassal of Assyria, the kingdom of Judah remained under his deputized authority. Something far worse than a Syrian altar now had to be introduced in order to pave the way for God's total abandonment of his people, and the king who took the scribal rap for this was Hezekiah's son Manasseh. It was written that he caused the ultimate revenge of the Lord by openly introducing pagan practices. In apparent contrast, contemporary Assyrian texts claim that Manasseh ruled well in Jerusalem as a vassal of the empire,[9] and it seems that he managed to govern a stable society by way of affording some religious toleration. In this respect, he allowed the Assyrian and Samaritan incomers to worship their own gods within his realm — not that he really had much choice in the matter since they were invaders who did whatever they wanted. But in conceding this element of freedom, Manasseh managed to widen the field of his government into regions that previously had been removed from his family's control, and a period of comparative peace prevailed in Judah.

According to the Israelite scribes, however, there was no room for any religious toleration, and Yahweh had said, 'I am the Lord thy God ... Thou shalt have no other gods before me'.[10] Manasseh might well have been a dutiful servant of Yahweh, but he allowed others to think differently if they wished, and that was enough for the scribes to condemn him. The same applied to Amon, his son and successor, who was said to have 'abandoned the Lord'. This all led to a fearful rage from Yahweh. Beginning with a reminder that he had chosen the tribe of Judah as his own special favourite from all those of the Israelite nation, Yahweh is said to have launched his most fearsome and punitive verbal attack:

> They have hearkened not, and Manasseh seduced them to do more evil than did the nations whom the Lord destroyed before the children of Israel. Because Manasseh, King of Judah, hath done these abominations, and hath done wickedly above all the Amorites did ... I am bringing such evil upon Jerusalem and Judah that whosoever heareth of it, both his ears shall tingle ... And I will wipe

Jerusalem as a man wipeth a dish ... And I will
forsake the remnant of mine inheritance, and
deliver them into the hand of their enemies because
they have done that which was evil in my sight,
and have provoked me to anger since the day their
fathers came forth out of Egypt.[11]

Subsequent to that, Amon's son Josiah was said to have endeavoured to enforce the veneration of Yahweh throughout the realm.
The Mosaic *Book of the Law* was recorded as being discovered in
the Temple during his reign,[12] and Josiah did his best to implement its teaching. But it was to no avail; God's wrath had been
kindled and, soon after Josiah's death in 609 BC, his successors
were faced with military opposition from the west and the east.

The trouble began when Pharaoh Necho II of Egypt gained a
foothold in Syria and the Israelite lands, while Assyria was losing
control in Mesopotamia to the developing empire of Babylonia.
Necho seized King Josiah's son Jehoahaz and carried him off to
Egypt, where he died. His half-brother Eliakim was installed in
his stead by the pharaoh, who gave him the alternative name
Jehoiakim. Necho was a close ally of the Assyrians, but
Nebuchadnezzar II of Babylon defeated the Egyptians at
Carchemish on the Euphrates, and brought the hitherto Assyrian
territories under his own control.

In 596 BC, having subjugated much of Canaan, the troops of
Nebuchadnezzar laid siege to Jerusalem. The book of 2 Kings 24:6
relates that Jehoiakim died before this event, but his son
Jechoniah was carried off to Babylon with 'all of Jerusalem, and
the princes, and all the mighty men of valour, even ten thousand
captives, and all the craftsmen and smiths; none remained save
the poorest sort of people of the land'.[13] At the loss of Jechoniah,
his uncle Mattaniah acceded to the throne of Jerusalem, taking the
name Zedekiah. But a few years later he was also removed to
Babylon where he was blinded and his sons murdered.[14]

In historical terms, the whole of this was a consequence of the
collapse of Assyria and the simultaneous rise of Babylonia as one
empire fell to another. The Bible writers viewed it rather

differently however. To them, their many decades of bonded servitude resulted from a personally addressed act of God's vengeance, and they wrote that Nebuchadnezzar ravaged Jerusalem and Judah, destroying the Temple of Solomon 'at the commandment of the Lord ... for the sins of Manasseh, according to all that he did'.[15]

This explanation might be sufficient to satisfy theological requirement, but in practical terms it makes little sense. Nebuchadnezzar was not a servant of Yahweh, and would certainly not have masterminded such an incursion to appease the god of a foreign nation. His reason for taking so many hostages must, therefore, have been substantially different from the scenario as biblically portrayed. He could easily have overthrown Jerusalem and taken control in Judaea without the inconvenience of seizing such a vast number of captives. In the longer term, they might well have contributed to the Babylonian economy, but in the short term it would have been an expensive and unnecessary exercise.

What had happened was that, between 612 and 609 BC, the mighty Assyrian state of King Ashurbanipal collapsed in ruins at the hands of the neighbouring Babylonians and Medes, who became the new masters of Mesopotamia. The primary palace of Nineveh had been looted and razed to the ground,[16] and what followed was a colossal new building programme with Babylon becoming the largest and most impressive city in the Middle East.[17] In a relatively short space of time, it became the world centre of a great literary and architectural renaissance. Not least among Babylon's stunning features were the reintroduced Hanging Gardens (repeating one of the *Seven Wonders* of the ancient world) and the exquisitely glazed Ishtar Gate, one of eight monumental entrances to the new city. The immediate requirement was for a substantial workforce of many tens of thousands — either to serve directly in the extensive building project, or to supplement the businesses and trades of those Babylonians who were seconded to it. To satisfy this, Nebuchadnezzar did not have to look very far, and he elected to obtain the necessary manpower from nearby Judaea.

A Loss of Integrity

From 586 BC, more than 10,000 Israelites were held in Babylon — princes, priests, prophets and all. According to Jeremiah 29:5-7, they lived freely in their own homes, ran their own farms and businesses, generally conducting their lives as normal. Some of their hitherto governors might have been badly treated but, despite their hostage status, the people appear to have been well maintained. Their descendent families remained there until the first group of 50,000 returned to Jerusalem in 536 BC. It was, however, in the reclaimed palace libraries of old Babylon that the Israelite scholars discovered the records of their original Mesopotamian heritage — the stories of the Creation, of Adam and Eve, of the *Anannage* lords and the Flood. This was the land from which their great ancestor Abraham had emerged with his family 1,400 years ago, and they began to record the ancient events concerning   Ilû Kur-gal, the god of their Hebrew ancestors. It was during this lengthy period of bondage in Babylon that the book of Genesis was born.

In the course of this and subsequent writings, the scriptural perception of Yahweh became gradually more corrupted to the point of eventual abstraction. To begin, the Mesopotamian records were clear enough in citing Ilû Kur-gal (Enlil) as an 'on the ground' figure in Sumer, at Nippur, and in the environment of Kharsag — just as God is portrayed in the early chapters of Genesis. As president of the Grand Assembly (the Bible's Congregation of the Mighty), he was the key figurehead at the time of Abraham's departure into Canaan, where he was known as El Elyon (El Shaddai in Hebrew and Assyrian texts).

Enlil was not generally cited in ancient record as the primary god of Creation. In the Babylonian *Enûma elish* that role was applied to Marduk, whereas in the Sumerian epic from 1,000 years earlier[18] the god of man's creation was Enlil's brother Enki. By contrast, however, the even older *Chronicles of Kharsag* (c.2800 BC) do indeed refer to Enlil as the 'Father of mankind'.

In their attempt to forge a One God culture to take back to Jerusalem, the Genesis writers of the Captivity dismissed Enki, and concentrated on the Enlil-Ilû figure who was eventually to become known as Yahweh. But Enki, Marduk and others could not be wholly ignored and, as we have seen, this led to a great deal of confusion in that the plurality of 'gods' in the old documents gave rise to a similar plurality in the Old Testament. Yahweh could not be portrayed as the only God because all other traditions contradicted this. At best he could be portrayed as the one God that mattered to the Hebrews and later Israelites, albeit he was constantly depicted as an implacable taskmaster who was impossible to please.

The biblical portrayals of Yahweh (El Shaddai) are such that, throughout the Old Testament scriptures, he is seen as being selfish, vindictive and unforgiving. His actions, even at a very personal level, are often appalling, as in his treatment of the loyal servant Job; in his testing of Abraham when inducing him to slay his own son Isaac, and when compelling Jephthah to sacrifice his daughter. From the way that Yahweh is biblically presented, it might justifiably be wondered why on earth he became the undeserving subject of Israelite veneration. It cannot be claimed by anyone that it was because he was the 'one and only' God as many would perhaps like to believe. The Bible makes it very clear that he was not, as do other documents of the era when the scriptures were written. As is identified numerous times in the Old Testament, Yahweh was not even the generally favoured God of the Israelites, and for many centuries they were inclined towards Baal, Tammuz and others, including the traditional goddesses Ashtoreth and Anath. The reason why Yahweh appears ultimately to have gained individual favour was based on the Israelites' absolute fear of his continued retribution in the aftermath of the Babylonian Captivity. In historical terms, and as conveyed in the scriptures, Yahweh was never the individually adopted God of the Israelites until after this event in the 6th century BC.

It is evident from the scriptures that the Bible writers were convinced that their promoted God was a jealous and vengeful character, and they made no attempt to present him in any other light. By virtue of this, the inclusion of his judgemental pronouncements in the text enabled the Temple authorities to subject the rank and file to subservience when they returned to Jerusalem. The priests were designated as the authorized bridges between Yahweh and the people. Consequently, the Israelites lived in an environment of dread, and were strategically brought under the rule of the priests, whose self-appointed rights of communion with God were beyond challenge.

* * *

Once the old texts of the Mesopotamians and Canaanites had been scoured for information concerning the *Elohim*, the scribes worked to create a continuing image of Yahweh that was so vague and abstract that all practical connection with humankind was lost. In Mesopotamian thought, the world, the heavens, the gods and the people were perceived as reflections of Nature. But, to the Israelites, Nature was reckoned to be a servant of Yahweh, who was said to have created everything:[19] 'The heavens declare the glory of God, and the firmament sheweth his handiwork'.[20]

In the event, Yahweh's character was scripturally contrived so that he transcended Nature, as a result of which the harmony of people and Nature was forfeit. In erstwhile Mesopotamian, Canaanite and Egyptian thought, the inexplicable divine was always thought to be manifest within Nature, and Nature enveloped both the gods and society. But this belief was shattered for all time by the priests and biblical compilers, who forsook harmony in favour of subservience. Hence, the balance of relationship between humankind and the phenomenal world was destroyed, and what was ultimately lost was integrity.

Flight of the Angels

Once we move into the annals of the kings, there is not only a noticeable change in the way that God is presented as a more obscure character, but there are also fewer references to angels. In fact, there are no biblical mentions of any angel through the whole of the 400-year Egyptian period from Joseph's era down to the time of Moses, when 'the angel of the Lord appeared unto him in a flame of fire out of the midst of a bush'.[21] Subsequent to that, an angel was said to have accompanied the pillar of cloud that the Israelites followed into Sinai.[22]

Angels appear far less frequently in the scriptures than might be imagined from the prominence they achieved in Christian art portrayals of the Old Testament in much later times. The first biblical mention of an angel appears in Genesis 16:7, when Hagar had been banished by Abraham's wife Sarah, and 'the angel of the Lord found her by a fountain of water in the wilderness'. Soon after that we have the two angels who visited Lot's house in Sodom, 'and he did bake unleavened bread, and they did eat'.[23] An angel appeared to Abraham when he prepared to sacrifice his son Isaac at Moriah,[24] and Abraham was later advised by 'the angel of the Lord' that God 'will multiply thy seed as the stars of the heaven'.[25]

The next mention of angels is entirely visionary, when Abraham's grandson Jacob 'dreamed, and behold a ladder set up on the earth, and the top of it reached to heaven; and behold the angels of El ascending and descending on it'.[26] After that, there are no more angelic citations until Moses' brief encounter at the burning bush, and not until Numbers 22–23 is there another episode when the Israelites had reached the River Jordan near Jericho. In this account, a man called Balaam set out with his ass to join the Moabites in their confrontation of the Israelite invaders. But an angel stepped into his path, sword in hand, and stopped him, whereupon Balaam struck his animal with a stick, and a strange conversation about maltreatment ensued between Balaam and the ass. In the event, the angel allowed Balaam to continue his journey so long as he promised to convey the words of God to the King of Moab. He was to advise him that the Israelites were God's chosen people, who should be blessed, not molested — and so Balaam eventually did as instructed. But it was all to little avail for, when the Israelites and Moabites finally got together, many of the Israelites elected to worship the gods of Moab, at which 'the anger of the Lord was kindled against

Israel' and, in his usual retaliatory style, he pronounced that they should all be executed:

> And the Lord said unto Moses, Take all the
> heads of the people, and hang them up
> before the Lord against the sun, that the
> fierce anger of the Lord may be turned away
> from Israel.[27]

When Gideon was a judge of the Israelites, an angel sat with him beneath an oak tree to discuss military strategy against the Midianites.[28] Shortly afterwards, an angel appeared to the wife of Manoah, saying 'Behold now, thou art barren and bearest not, but thou shalt conceive and bear a son.[29] This is the first instance in which there is any reference to an angel perhaps having a name. But, when Manoah asked him, the angel responded, 'Why asketh thou thus after my name, seeing it is secret?'[30] There are actually no names given to any angels in the Old Testament.

To this point, the few angels who have appeared in the narrative are all seen to have been straightforward 'messengers', which is precisely what the old Greek word *aggelos* means. There is no hint of them being winged celestial creatures and, apart from the angel who confronted Balaam with a sword, they have not appeared in any way aggressive. Their literary image changes, however, from the time of King David when God had a further bout of anger against the Israelites. First he 'sent pestilence upon Israel; and there fell of Israel seventy thousand men', and then 'God sent an angel unto Jerusalem to destroy it ... And David lifted up his eyes, and saw the angel of the Lord stand between the earth and the heaven, having a drawn sword in his hand stretched out over Jerusalem'.[31]

Some generations later, in the reign of King Ahab of Israel, the prophet Elijah was approached by an angel, who wakened him from sleep in the wilderness and brought food for the man.[32] Then, in contrast to documentary record, when Sennacherib of Assyria defeated King Hezekiah of Judah, 2 Kings 19:35–36 reports:

> The angel of the Lord went out, and smote in the camp of the Assyrians an hundred fourscore and five thousand: and when they arose early in the morning, behold, they were all dead corpses. So Sennacherib King of Assyria departed, and went and returned, and dwelt at Nineveh.[33]

There is no explanation of how the Assyrians could possibly have awakened to find themselves dead. But, given that Sennacherib survived, presumably there were others who also lived to discover the slaughter. Nevertheless, this wholly fictional account of an otherwise well-documented historic battle in which Sennacherib was victorious, provides another account of how some biblical angels were reckoned to have amazing powers of destruction.

From the time of Elijah (c.880 BC), the angels move into a realm where they are henceforth communicators with the prophets. The word *nabi*, as translated to 'prophet', more correctly refers to a 'spokesman',[34] although the *nabis* were also presented as divinely inspired seers.

Relating to about 580 BC, during the early Babylonian Captivity, the book of Daniel provides the first scriptural reference to a character named Gabriel. There is no direct angelic association here (as is the case for Gabriel in the New Testament), but it might perhaps be inferred since the *Gabri-el* distinction was indicative of a 'bright one'. Daniel (a young Judaean nobleman) is attempting to understand a vision when the said Gabriel arrives to judge his interpretation. In this regard, the name 'Daniel' appears to have been tactically contrived by the scribes in order to support the briefly given story, with *Dani-el* (having the same *el* suffix as *Gabri-el*) implying to be 'judged by a bright one'.

As we saw in chapter 6, certain Mesopotamian figures were styled *Gabri-el* by way of individually applied rank as the highest level diplomatic negotiators. From the outset of the first Eden project in about 9500 BC they were the Governors of the Garden at Kharsag,[35] and a primary duty of a *Gabri-el* was that of estate management.

In the more lately written prophetic books of the Old Testament, a newly styled biblical phenomenon appears — a daunting, albeit envisioned, category of airborne devices that were said to rise above the earth by mechanical means. They were never once called angels, and generally these blazing spectacles had wheels, as in Daniel 7:9: 'His throne was like the fiery flame, and his wheels as burning fire'. In Isaiah 6:1–2 there is a similar account of an airborne throne, and 'above it stood the seraphims: each one had six wings'. Yet another reference to such an apparatus occurs in Ezekiel 1, where the whole scenario is entirely in keeping with the others, including fire, wheels and noisy rotating rings. Ezekiel subsequently refers to these phenomena as 'cherubims' which, as we saw in chapter 15, were likened to chariots or mobile thrones. The text relates: 'The sound of the cherubims' wings was heard even to the outer court, as the voice of the Almighty God when he speaketh'.[36] In respect of the 'seraphims', Isaiah 6:1–2 states, when discussing the throne of the cherubim: 'Above it stood the seraphims: each one had six wings; with twain he covered his face, and with twain he covered his feet, and with twain he did fly'.

There is mention of a similar vehicle in 2 Kings 2:11, when Elijah is taken up in a chariot of fire, and there are further descriptions of a like conveyance in the Mesopotamian *Epic of Gilgamesh*. Flaming seraphims also appear with regularity in ancient documents. That they were 'fiery' is consistent with the etymology of the word *seraph*, which is related to an old Hebrew stem meaning 'flame'.[37] They feature also in another of God's vengeful attacks, when a large proportion of Israel died after the Lord sent seraphims (fiery serpents) among them.[38]

These wheeled spectacles, with their lights and noisy rotating wings, appear in all respects like flying machines — a concept which is extremely difficult to reconcile. Even though they are presented as appearing only in dreams and visions, the very notion of such airborne conveyances being imagined in those far distant times is quite remarkable.

By contrast, the winged celestial beings that finally emerged in Christian artwork were most likely inspired by the carved reliefs of Assyria from the 1st millennium BC. Here, in the north of Mesopotamia, the great palace gardens and allotments were cultivated and tended by master agriculturalists of a most ancient and sacred tradition. They were revered as *Elohim* geniuses with advanced scientific intellect, and were called *Apkallu*.

The impressive stone slab portrayals of the braid-bearded *Apkallu* (sometimes depicted with eagle, griffin or fish head-dresses) are now to be found in the world's most prestigious museums. Generally clasping pine-cone purifiers (*mullilû*) and situla buckets (*banduddû*), these sages of genetic understanding were deemed to transcend the competence of regular men, in which respect the royal sculptors depicted them each with four wings.

Many of the finest *Apkallu* reliefs were unearthed by British Assyriologists in the middle 1800s at the Nimrud palace of King Ashurnasirpal II, who reigned 883–859 BC,[39] and at the Khorsabad palace of Sargon II (720–705 BC).

In rather more distant Kharsag and Sumerian times, these revered 'bright farmers of the enclosure' were originally styled *Apkarlu* or *Abgallu*. Seven were appointed at Eridu by the *Anannage* lord Enki (*c*.4000 BC), and were recorded as being named Uan-adapa, Uan-dugga, Enme-duga, En-megalanna, Enme-buluga, An-enlilda, and Utu-abzu.

Part VIII

God of Religion

20

BETWEEN THE TESTAMENTS

The Hidden Ark

In discussing his celestial vision of the Lord, Ezekiel explained that the great cherubim had a crystal firmament that contained 'the likeness of a throne ... and upon the likeness of the throne was the likeness as the appearance of a man above upon it ... This was the appearance of the likeness of the glory of the Lord'.[1] Recounting another visionary episode, the book of Daniel similarly relates that, when the throne was descended, 'the Ancient of Days did sit, whose garment was white as snow ... His throne was like the fiery flame, and his wheels as burning fire.[2]

As we discovered in chapter 15, the terms 'cherub' and 'cherubim' derive from the old Semitic verb *kerûb*, meaning 'to ride'. Both 2 Samuel 22:11 and Psalm 18:10, state that the Lord 'rode upon a cherub and did fly'. And in discussing the Ark of the Covenant's Temple abode, 1 Chronicles 28:18 directly associates the cherub guardians with 'chariots'. With regard to the further association of cherubs with thrones, the Bible additionally relates that, on occasions, the Lord sat on the mercy seat of the Ark: 'He sitteth between the cherubims'.[3] It is also confirmed that he communed with Moses from this throne: 'He heard the voice of one speaking unto him from off the mercy seat'.[4] Philosophical Judaism has long perceived the Ark to represent a celestial throne, and the omnipotent presence of God was reckoned to dwell between the cherubim.[5] The Ark was therefore considered to be 'a dangerous trust' for its Levite bearers.[6]

From the time that the Temple of Jerusalem was built by King Solomon, the Ark was housed within its innermost sanctuary called the *Kadosh Hakadashim* (the Holy of Holies).[7] During the next generation of Rehoboam's reign in Jerusalem, a dynastic change occurred in Egypt, when a Libyan chief named Sheshonq married the Egyptian heiress and became the new pharaoh. This ex–commander of the *Meshwesh* (a Libyan police force) decided to reinstate Egypt's dominion over Palestine in accordance with the *Israel Stela*. Sheshonq is therefore reckoned to be the 'Shishak' of the Bible, who launched an assault against Rehoboam and surrounded Jerusalem.[8] He is said to have removed many portable items from the Temple to prove his supremacy over the King of Judah, and then turned his sights northwards against the Israelite kingdom of Jeroboam, who duly fled across the Jordan.[9] A composite record of the campaign was later inscribed on the wall of the temple of Amun at Thebes. The Ark of the Covenant was not listed in Sheshonq's table of plunder, and it remained in Jerusalem throughout the generations until at least the reign of Hezekiah (the 12th lineal descendant from Solomon), who was said to have prayed before the Ark.[10]

In the subsequent reigns of Manasseh and Amon, the Ark was removed to a Levite sanctuary during a period of disturbance and sectarian conflict in Jerusalem. Later, when recalling the era of Hezekiah's great–grandson, King Josiah, 2 Chronicles 35:3 relates how Josiah decreed that the Ark should be returned to its proper abode in the Temple. He 'said unto the Levites that taught all Israel, which were holy unto the Lord, Put the holy Ark in the house which Solomon the son of David king of Israel did build; it shall not be a burden upon your shoulders'. This was over 360 years after Solomon built the Temple, and shortly before the first invasion of Jerusalem by Nebuchadnezzar in around 596 BC.

At that time, the high priest of Jerusalem was Hilkiah. It was he who was said to have found the *Book of the Law*,[11] which the *Damascus Document* (discovered among the Dead Sea Scrolls at Qumrân) explains had been concealed from the time of Moses in the Ark of the Covenant.[12] Shortly before Nebuchadnezzar's invasion, Hilkiah's son Jeremiah secreted the Ark in a place of safety, where it might be lost to the invaders. In this respect, the Bible and other Jewish annals are consistent in stating that the Ark was eventually hidden in the Temple vaults during the reign of Josiah, so as not to be seized by the Babylonians.[13] The book of Jeremiah records: 'The ark of the covenant of the Lord; neither shall it come to mind, neither shall they remember it, neither shall they visit it'.[14] According to the Hebrew *Talmud*, it was secreted below ground near the *Holy of Holies*.[15] Consequently, the Ark does not appear in the inventory of Nebuchadnezzar's looting before the Temple was demolished,[16] and the book of 2 Chronicles 5:9 (compiled around 275 BC, long after the replacement Temple was built) states in respect of the Ark, 'There it is unto this day'.

A Period of Conquest

Just as the Assyrian domains had fallen to the Babylonians, so the empire of Babylon eventually fell to the Persians. Cyrus II, the Great, had united the separate kingdoms of Persia (Iran) in the middle 500s BC to become the overall Shah, and in 539 BC he took his troops into Babylon, overthrowing Nabonidus, the fourth successor of Nebuchadnezzar. On taking control in the region, Cyrus permitted the descendent Israelite exiles to return to Judah. Of those who elected to leave what effectively had become their new homeland, the first wave travelled to Jerusalem with Jechoniah's descendant, Zerubbabel, in about 536 BC.[17] Around twenty years later, a new Temple was completed on the old site, but there were to be no more reigning kings of the House of Judah. Henceforth their overlords were Darius I and his successors of the Persian Empire, whilst they were locally ruled by Persians such as Sheshbazzar, the appointed Governor of Judah.

With the repatriated Israelites under Persian command, and their own reigning dynasty at an end, they also became subject to the official Aramaic imperial language. The high priest of the new Temple became the head of a culture that was wholly centered on religion, and their newly defined *Law of God* became the recognized law of the land.[18]

A second major wave of descendent exiles returned from Babylon in 458 BC under the leadership of Ezra the priest.[19] He was responsible for Israelite religious affairs within the Persian administration. It was subsequently related in the book of

Ezra that, although the Israelites had been exiled and bonded at the command of God, he had now 'extended mercy unto us in the sight of the kings of Persia, to give us a reviving, to set up the house of our God, and to repair the desolations thereof, and to give us a wall in Judah and in Jerusalem'.[20]

With the Persian government prevailing thereafter for two centuries, it is at this point that the Old Testament comes to an end. Just as happened between the books of Genesis and Exodus, there is now a period of something approaching 400 years before the Christian New Testament begins.

* * *

The intervening era between the Jewish and Christian scriptures began with the rise to power of Alexander the Great of Macedonia, who defeated Shah Darius III in 333 BC. Destroying the city of Tyre in Phoenicia, he then moved into Egypt and built his citadel of Alexandria. With full control of the hitherto Persian Empire, Alexander then pressed on through Babylonia, moving ever eastwards, until he finally conquered the Punjab. At his early death in 323 BC, his generals took control. Ptolemy Soter became Governor of Egypt, Seleucus ruled Babylonia, while Antigonus governed Macedonia and Greece. By the turn of the century, Palestine (as the Holy Land had become known) was also enveloped within the Alexandrian domain.

A powerful new military-led force then gathered momentum in Europe: the Republic of Rome. In 264 BC the Romans ousted the Carthaginian rulers of Sicily, also capturing Corsica and Sardinia. The Carthaginian general, Hannibal, then retaliated by seizing Saguntum in Spain. He advanced with his troops across the Alps, but was checked by the Romans at Zama. Meanwhile, Antiochus III (a descendant of the Macedonian general Seleucus) became King of Syria. By 198 BC he had rid himself of Egyptian influence to become the master of Palestine. His eldest son, Antiochus IV Epiphanes, then occupied Jerusalem — an action that promptly gave rise to a fierce Jewish revolt under the Hasmonaean priest Judas Maccabaeus. He was killed in battle against the Seleucids, but the Maccabees were victorious and finally achieved Israelite independence in 142 BC.[21]

Owing to the historical void between the Old and New Testaments, the history of Judas Maccabaeus and the Hasmonaean Maccabees is not found in the Bible. It is detailed at length, however, in the 1st–century writings of Flavius Josephus, who was himself of Hasmonaean birth.[22] Their story is also told in the apocryphal books of the Maccabees, which were added to the *Septuagint* Bible. But the final Hebrew canon was established without them because they were not directly concerned with the affairs of God.[23]

Judas, known as 'the Hammerer' (*Maqqaba*), was a son of the priest Mattathias of Modin, near Jerusalem. As a result of his nickname, his successors became known as Maccabees and were dubbed with the surname Maccabaeus. In broader terms, they were known as Hasmonaeans, after their ancestor Hasmon (Asmonaeus), the great–grandfather of Mattathias.

In the footsteps of his father, Judas Maccabaeus took up arms against the Seleucid kings of Syria, who had overrun Jerusalem. They were the successors of Alexander the Great's Macedonian general Seleucus, and consequently imposed Greek culture and religion on the people of Judaea (as old Judah had become known). The main Seleucid antagonist of the era was King Antiochus IV, who had become allied with brothers of the Aaronite high priest of Jerusalem. They usurped their family's legacy to side with the invader, while introducing Greek gods and worship to the Temple. To emphasise this requirement, *Torah* scrolls were soaked in pig fat and burned, circumcision was banned, and the Greek language was made compulsory on pain of death.

With the wayward Jerusalem priests supporting the insurrection against their own Jewish culture, Mattathias of Modin initially took up the challenge with a guerrilla force that was later inherited by his son Judas. Over a number of years, Judas defeated several Syrian armies in great battles with many thousands of men on each side. In the course of all this, Jerusalem was wrecked but, on the 25th day of *Kislev* 165 BC,[24] Judas finally ousted the towering Greek statue of Zeus and rededicated the Temple to the Jewish faith. The city's Menorah was lit to begin an eight–day festival of celebration, and the annual feast of *Hanukkah* was born.[25]

That was not the end of the Hasmonaean Revolt, for there were still Syrians to defeat in the hills and surrounding country. However, it was the incident which led to a new priestly culture in Jerusalem under Judas' brother Jonathan. To expedite this, the Hasmonaeans gained the military backing of Rome (the new rising power in the Mediterranean world), thereby achieving Judaean independence from 142 BC.

Victorious as the Maccabees had been against the Seleucids, a good deal of social damage had been done because the arduous campaign had necessitated fighting on the Sabbath. A core group of ultra-pious Jewish devotees, known as the *Hasidim*, strongly objected to this, and when the triumphant House of Hasmon took control, setting up their own dynasty in Jerusalem, the *Hasidim* not only voiced their opposition, but marched *en masse* out of the city. Eventually, they established their own community in the wilderness region of Qumrân by the Dead Sea. According to the *Copper Scroll*, Qumrân was at that time called Sekhakha.

The books of Maccabees relate how Simon Maccabaeus, the brother of Judas and Jonathan was installed as the first Hasmonaean prince of Jerusalem. He was followed by his nephew John Hyrcanus, who was succeeded by his sons Aristobulus and Alexander, then by Alexander's sons Hyrcanus II and Aristobulus II, followed by his son Antigonus. At last, there was a reigning dynasty again in Judaea.

* * *

During this era of change, the Roman armies destroyed Carthage and formed the new province of Roman North Africa. Further campaigns brought Macedon, Greece, and Asia Minor under Roman control. But disputes raged in Rome because the Carthaginian (or Punic) wars had ruined the Italian farmers, whilst simultaneously enriching the aristocracy, who built large estates utilizing slave labour. The Democrat leader Tiberius Graccus put forward proposals for agrarian reform in 133 BC, but was murdered by the Senatorial Party. His brother took up the farmers' cause and he too was murdered, with the Democrat leadership passing to the military commander Gaius Marius.

By 107 BC Gaius Marius was Consul of Rome. But the Senate found its own political champion in Lucius Cornelius Sulla, who eventually deposed Marius and became Dictator in 82 BC. A horrifying reign of terror then ensued until the Democrat statesman and general, Gaius Julius Caesar, gained popularity and was elected to primary office in 63 BC.

In that same year, Roman legions marched into the Holy Land, which had moved into a state of sectarian turmoil. The Pharisees, who observed strict ancient Jewish laws, had risen in protest against an evolving Greek-influenced liberal culture. In so doing, they also opposed the priestly caste of the Sadducees, and the unsettled environment rendered the region ripe for invasion. Seeing their opportunity, the Romans, under Gnaeus Pompeius Magnus (Pompey the Great), subjugated Judaea and seized Jerusalem, having annexed Syria and the rest of Palestine.

Meanwhile, the Roman hierarchy was undergoing its own upheavals. Julius Caesar, Pompey and Crassus formed the first Triumvirate in Rome, but their joint administration suffered when Caesar was sent to Gaul and Crassus went to supervise matters in Jerusalem. In their absence, Pompey changed political camps, deserting the Democrats for the Republican aristocrats, whereupon Caesar returned and civil war ensued. Caesar was victorious at Pharsalus in Greece, and eventually gained full control of the imperial provinces when Pompey fled to Egypt.

Until that time, Queen Cleopatra VII had been ruling Egypt jointly with her brother Ptolemy XIII. But then Caesar visited Alexandria and conspired with Cleopatra, who had her brother assassinated and began to rule in her own right. Julius Caesar went on to campaign in Asia Minor and North Africa but, on his return to Rome in 44 BC, he was murdered by Republicans. His nephew Gaius Octavius (Octavian) formed a second Triumvirate with General Mark Antony and the statesman

Marcus Lepidus. Octavian and Mark Antony defeated the foremost of Caesar's assassins, Brutus and Cassius, at Philippi in Macedonia. But Antony then deserted his wife Octavia (Octavian's sister) to join Cleopatra. At this, Octavian declared war on Egypt, and was victorious at the Battle of Actium, following which Antony and Cleopatra committed suicide.

Palestine, at that juncture, was composed of three distinct provinces: Galilee in the north, Judaea in the south, and Samaria between. Julius Caesar had installed Antipater the Idumaean as Procurator of Judaea, with his son Herod as the Governor of Galilee. It was soon after this that the House of Hasmon came to an abrupt end when their princess Mariamme married Herod. The adventurous story of this marriage and the surrounding intrigue of Antony and Cleopatra is told at length by Flavius Josephus in his *Wars of the Jews* and *Antiquities of the Jews*.[26] But the net result was that, when Antigonus died in 37 BC, the sole Hasmonaean heiress was his niece Mariamme. As a consequence of this, her husband Herod was summoned to Rome for appointment as the new King of Judaea.

This was the harsh environment into which Jesus was born: a climate of oppression controlled by a puppet monarchy and a highly organized military occupational force. The Hebrew elders in Jerusalem were content to hold lucrative high-priestly positions within the new regime. But elsewhere, the Jews were more generally desperate for a Messiah (an Anointed One, from the Hebrew verb *maisach*: 'to anoint') — a forceful liberator to secure their freedom from the Roman overlords.

Qumrân and the Temple

The period of formal occupation at Qumrân commenced in about 130 BC, with the Essene therapeutics consolidating the settlement in around 100 BC.[27] The Essenes were a philosophical Israelite healing community that was significantly influenced by the Greco-Egyptian culture. Jewish chronicles describe a violent Judaean earthquake around seventy years later in 31 BC,[28] which caused an evacuation of the settlement. This is confirmed at Qumrân by a break between two distinct periods of habitation.[29] In the *Wars of the Jews*, Josephus explains that the Essenes were practiced in the art of healing and received their medicinal knowledge from the ancients.[30] Indeed, the term 'Essene' refers to this expertise, for the Aramaic word *asayya* meant physician and corresponded to the Greek word *essenoi*.

Other Jewish sects which had evolved in Jerusalem as opposers of the Maccabees were the Pharisees and Sadducees. The essential difference between these groups and the Essenes was that, as Josephus explained, the Essenes 'live the same kind of life as do those whom the Greeks call Pythagoreans'.[31] The community cultures of these three main philosophical sects were distinctly different in many respects, and Josephus described that the Essenes had 'a greater affection for one another than the other sects have'.[32] The Pharisees and Sadducees were strictly regulated in the Hebrew tradition, whereas the Essenes were far more liberal and westernized. The Pharisees observed ancient Jewish laws and, although the Sadducees had a more modern outlook, they were largely non-spiritual, whereas the Essenes were culturally inspired and inclined towards Hellenic mysticism.

The second residential period at Qumrân began during the reign of Herod the Great. Apart from the evidence of the *Dead Sea Scrolls*, a collection of coins has also been amassed from the Qumrân settlement.[33] These relate to a time-span from the Hasmonaean ruler John Hyrcanus (135–104 BC) to the Jewish Revolt of AD 66–70 against the Romans. Many relics of the era have since been discovered and, during the 1950s, more than a thousand graves were unearthed at Qumrân. A vast monastery complex from the second habitation was also revealed, with meeting rooms, plaster benches, huge water cisterns and a maze of water conduits. In the scribes' room there were inkwells and the remains of tables on which the Scrolls had been written — some more than 17 feet (*c*.5 m) in length.[34] It was confirmed by archaeologists and scholars that the original settlement had been damaged in the earthquake and rebuilt by the Essenes in the later Herodian era. The white-robed Essenes were, in principle, the old aristocrats of the land who longed for a return to the influential days of Judah and the Royal House of David.[35] It was they, and their associate Nazarenes, who mostly prophesied and awaited the coming of a liberating Messiah.

During the reign of Herod the Great (37–4 BC) vast sums of money were expended in Jerusalem in the wake of a disaster which beset the kingdom in 25 BC. In that year the rains failed, and there was no harvest in Palestine or Syria.[36] There was neither seed nor corn, and all the goats and sheep had died. Josephus commented that, to feed the people in the face of this adversity, Herod stripped all the wealth of gold and silver from his palace, sending it to Petronius, the Prefect of Egypt, for supplies from the pharaonic granaries. These, along with clothing and other needs, were distributed freely throughout the realm in exceptional quantity.[37] After two years the crisis was over, but the Jerusalem coffers were completely bare. Herod had saved the nation from catastrophe, but had become completely broke in the process.

Within a short time, however, Herod was conducting his economy on an amazingly lavish scale. His donations and bequests were enormous — far in excess of the calculable tax revenues. On top of that, he extended and restored the Temple of Jerusalem so that, within a new complex of over 35 acres, it was bigger than the Acropolis in Athens and, according to Josephus, was the most magnificently appointed construction of the era. Thousands of masons worked on the colossal project over many years. History has it that, from his bankrupt starting base, Herod accumulated much of the new wealth of Jerusalem from joint ventures with his mother's wondrous rock-cut city of Petra in South Jordan below the Dead Sea. With its valuable spice and marble trades, Petra was an extremely wealthy centre governed by the Nabataean ruler, King Aboud. Petra's engineers were noted far and wide as experts in hydraulic systems, and this unique expertise was another of the city's famed exports, for which lucrative trade King Herod of Jerusalem provided raw materials and introduced trading contacts within the Roman Empire.

It seems that, despite the biblical black mark against Herod for his supposed slaying of the infants when Jesus was born, history actually records him as a competent and well-regarded king. In fact, his slaying of the infants appears in no historical chronicle of the era, not even in the annals of his enemies; it features only in the Christian New Testament gospel of Matthew and appears to have no basis of authenticity. Herod even converted to a form of Judaism in order to aid his acceptance by the people, although he had ten wives and upheld other customs of his Arab upbringing. In all respects, he appears to have been popular enough with the Israelites, and there is no record of him being blamed by them for the generally oppressive Roman regime. But his son Herod II Antipas was of a different nature. He was very much a part of the occupational machine, and equally cruel, to become notorious in the Gospels as the Herod who beheaded John the Baptist. It was during the early reign of Herod-Antipas that, from their base at Qumrân, the vehemently aggressive Zealot movement against the Roman overlords emerged under the warlord Judas the Galilean. Born of Hasmonaean stock from John Hyrcanus, Judas took the same guerrilla route as his ancestral namesake Judas Maccabaeus. Eventually, two generations later in the reign of Herod-Agrippa II, the Zealots fronted a fierce campaign against the governors of Jerusalem, and this led to a full scale Jewish revolt against the Romans in AD 66.

The four-year revolution was ultimately unsuccessful and, following the Roman destruction of Jerusalem and the Temple by General Titus in AD 70, the inhabitants scattered, leaving the city a desolate ruin for over six decades. In AD 132 Emperor Hadrian began a rebuilding scheme, with a temple dedicated to Jupiter planned for the old Temple Mount. This prompted a further unsuccessful Jewish revolt under the guerrilla leader Shimon Bar-Kockba, at the end of which the surviving Jews were banished or sold into slavery. Henceforth, Jewish study and worship were considered punishable offences, and Jerusalem was renamed Aelia Capitolina by the Romans.[38]

After the 5th-century collapse of Imperial Rome, Jerusalem came under full control of the Byzantine authorities from

Constantinople. It was later conquered by Persians, and then by the forces of the lately established Islāmic faith under Caliph Umar ibn Al-Khattab in AD 638. He constructed a mosque (later called the *Al-Aqsa* Mosque) on the old Temple site, and soon afterwards the Dome of the Rock shrine (now the foremost Jerusalem landmark) was built nearby on the Rock of David.[39]

Although King Herod's Temple is often referred to as the third construction on the site, it was actually a mammoth extension of the Temple that previously existed. Following the destruction of Solomon's original building by Nebuchadnezzar, the second Temple had been completed by Zerubbabel's masons in about 520 BC. Subsequently, a fortified platform was built by the Seleucid Kings in 186 BC.[40] A further extension was added by the Hasmonaean Maccabees in 141 BC and, in due course, this was substantially enlarged by Herod the Great. From the days of Solomon to the time of Herod, the foundation increased dramatically in size, making it the largest man-made building platform in the classical world.[41] Herod's final construction occupied a space of some 144,000 square metres, compared with 30,000 for the Acropolis in Athens.[42] It had an outer wall that was 16 feet thick (nearly 4.9 m) and many of its stones weighed as much as 80 tons. In his awestruck, first-hand description of the edifice, Flavius Josephus used such words as 'incredible', 'immense' and 'amazing'.[43] The Roman senator Cornelius Tacitus recorded in *The Histories* that water was supplied to the enclosure by an ever-flowing spring, with a series of tanks for collecting rainwater.[44] Additionally, the *Middoth* tractate of the *Mishnah* (an early rabbinic codification of Jewish Law from about AD 200) relates that there was a great wheel, which drew water from the underground Golah Cistern.[45]

* * *

Prior to being concealed from Nebuchadnezzar of Babylon at the time of King Josiah, the Ark of the Lord was located in the Temple's *Holy of Holies* where, as stated by King Solomon in 1 Kings 8:21, 'I have set there a place for the Ark'. In complete accord with the Hebrew Bible, this location has been physically identified by way of its still visible setting in the floor of the once *Holy of Holies* — an inset depression of 53 x 31 inches facing the entrance.[46] Interestingly, this rectangular floor-setting indicates that the Ark was placed with its short side forward to the approach, not lengthwise as is often portrayed. The *Holy of Holies* was only 20 cubits square and, as given in the *Talmud*, the Ark's carrying shafts were 10 cubits in length,[47] so they would have needed the entrance space in order to be withdrawn once the Ark was lowered into position.[48]

Since the destruction of Jerusalem, there have only been two excavations beneath the *Al-Aqsa* Mosque. The first was that of the Knights Templars in 1118–27, after the Crusade forces had retrieved Jerusalem from Turkish Muslim occupation, and they carried away many of the Temple treasures and documents which had been secreted in ancient times.[49] Much later, in the 1860s, the British explorer Sir Charles Warren conducted extensive excavations beneath Temple Mount for the Palestine Exploration Fund.[50] The related photographic and art collections (currently held by the Fund) are very revealing. To begin, Warren's team dug a number of vertical shafts down to the bedrock, and then opened lateral tunnels between them to reveal the walls of the earliest foundations and their subsequent extensions. Having achieved that, they went even deeper into the limestone rock itself, where they discovered an astonishing subterranean labyrinth of winding corridors and passages. Branching off these were large storage facilities and a virtual fairyland of cleverly engineered caves and water cisterns.[51] They even found a number of Templar relics from the earlier dig in the 12th century.

It was during the course of these excavations that the square foundation of King Solomon's first Temple was found. Its lower retaining walls were intact, and their structure was quite different from that of the second Temple. That this exploration took place when it did was truly fortuitous because, apart from a mapping survey by British military engineers in 1894, the underground area has since become inaccessible by virtue of Muslim political and religious sensibilities.[52]

21

THE IMAGE OF GOD

A Split Personality

Nothing concerning the above detailed history of the Holy Land between the Testaments is to be found in the Bible. Consequently, nothing is known about God's supposed activities through a period of nearly 400 years. His tradition does not surface again in canonical scripture until the Herodian era, when Nazarene writings introduced the figure of Jesus during the period of Roman occupation. In this regard, God emerges with an entirely new image. Although some of the Old Testament scriptures were written as late as the 2nd century BC, they still relate to events that took place before the 5th century BC. Consequently, they are of little value in determining how it was that, in the minds of many Judaeans, the image of God changed during the period before the Gospel era of the Christian New Testament.

Fortunately, in this respect, we have the texts of the *Dead Sea Scrolls* as produced by the Essene scribes of Qumrân during the intervening years. As we have seen, the Essene culture differed somewhat from mainstream rabbinical opinion, and was in many ways contrary to the more traditional Hebrew philosophies of the Pharisees and Sadducees, who were the upholders of Jewish law in Jerusalem. It was nevertheless from the community spirit of the Essenes that Christianity was born, and it is therefore within the *Dead Sea Scrolls* that we should expect to find the newly defined Christian God emerging.

It has to be remembered that, although Christianity became increasingly divorced from Judaism in the 2nd century AD, and was quite separately identified from the 4th century, it was originally the product of a particular Jewish sect that was said to have been led by Jesus the Nazarene. By virtue of this, the God of emergent Christianity was seen to be synonymous with the earlier recorded God of the Israelites. In the way that things transpired, however, this was not necessarily the case in all respects because the Christian God was perceived to have a quite different personality. Some of the differences were so striking that even Jesus was criticized by certain factions of the later Christian movement because his views were considered too Jewish to be viable aspects of the newly evolving faith.

Among the earliest of all gospels, although not selected by the 4th-century Church Fathers for the New Testament canon, was the *Gospel of the Nazarenes*. This ground-breaking Jewish text was written in Hebrew, and the date of its composition is reckoned to be the middle of the 1st century when Christian-style concepts were first being collated.[1] Later, in about AD 177, Irenaeus, the Christian Bishop of Lyon in Gaul, challenged the writings of the early Nazarenes, and even went so far as to suggest in his treatise, *Adversus Haereses* (Against Heresies), that Jesus had himself been practising the wrong religion![2]

Confirmation that Nazarene Christianity was born out of Essene Judaism is emphasized in a Qumrân scroll fragment known as the *Aramaic Apocalypse*. This text relates to a prophesied Messiah, who (like King David) would be 'proclaimed', 'designated' and 'called' the son of God,[3] although he would in reality be the son of man. It is also the case that certain teachings of Jesus, such as those of his Sermon on the Mount, were directly based on the Qumrân model. His famous series of eight *Beatitudes*, each beginning 'Blessed are ...'[4] can be seen to emanate from the sentiments of the *Beatitudes Wisdom Scroll* of the Essenes.[5]

The concept of an anticipated Messiah (an 'anointed one' who was expected to redeem Israel from oppression by the nation's enemies) had been vaguely alluded to in the Old Testament book of Daniel.[6] This was written around the time of the first Maccabaean Revolt against the Syrians in *c.*165 BC, but was narratively related to earlier events during the Babylonian Captivity. The later Essenes of Qumrân applied this messianic prophecy to the anticipated overthrow of Roman occupation in Judaea, and it was in this regard that John the Baptist sent his disciples to ask Jesus, 'Art thou he that should come, or do we look for another?'[7]

Although it can justifiably be said that, by way of ultimate Roman Church intervention, the original philosophies of Jesus were corrupted to form the basis of a newly devised hybrid religion, it is equally clear that Jesus' own message was based on the lore of the Essenes. In respect of Jesus, the *Jewish Encyclopedia* makes the point that, although not an overt law breaker, he was persistently inclined to flout regulations in an attempt to have changes made within the rigid legal structure. It is stated that 'in making these pretensions he was following a tendency which, at the period of his career, was especially marked in the ways of the Essenes'.[8]

Jesus' views on matters such as wealth, marriage and baptism were in no way commensurate with the 1st-century Hebrew culture of the Pharisees and Sadducees, nor even in agreement with the scribes of Temple Law. His views all stemmed from Essene tradition as referenced in the *Dead Sea Scrolls*. Throughout the gospels, Jesus makes his position perfectly clear:

> Woe unto you, scribes and Pharisees; hypocrites! You compass sea and land to make one proselyte,[9] and when he is made, you make him twofold more the child of hell than yourselves.[10]

He openly criticised the Pharisee rabbis and the Sadducee priests, advising that his own disciples should not follow their examples of preaching one thing and doing another.[11]

As we saw in chapter 2, there was no consolidated Hebrew Bible as such in the Gospel era. There were individual books that made their way into the Old Testament canon, and some Aramaic *Targums* were produced, but there were also various other texts that were not considered finally acceptable, and many of these emanated from the Essene community at Qumrân. Such writings formed the basis of the Nazarene style of Judaism practised by Jesus and his apostles, and it is within these documents that the perception of a better side of God is first suggested.

A long-standing puzzle which has confronted all biblical research is the anomaly of God's distinctly split personality. In the

New Testament he is portrayed as a paternal shepherd calling his loyal sheep to his side. But throughout the Old Testament he is depicted as launching fire and brimstone even on his own supporters. Such descriptions of his ferocious behaviour have led many theologians to wonder how it is that God would have allowed so many of history's atrocities to have occurred. But the Old Testament is clear in its interpretation that God 'allows' nothing. On the contrary, everything is reckoned to be of his doing. In the book of Isaiah 45:7 God is quoted as saying, 'I make peace and create evil'. And in Amos 3:6 it is asked, 'Shall there be evil in a city, and the Lord hath not done it?'

Atonement and Penance

A key difference between the God of the Old Testament and the God of later Nazarene theology is evident in the nature of forgiveness. The God of the original scriptures was entirely unforgiving, as was plainly indicated when Moses asked him to forgive the Israelites for having made a golden calf in Sinai. God's answer to this request was negatively direct: 'And the Lord said unto Moses, Whosoever hath sinned against me, him will I blot out of my book'.[12] Later, when addressing the Israelites after the death of Moses, Joshua reconfirmed this to the Israelites, stating that forgiveness was not an aspect of God's nature: 'And Joshua said unto the people, Ye cannot serve the Lord, for he is an holy God; he is a jealous God; he will not forgive your transgressions, nor your sins'.[13]

This appears somewhat contrary to the notion of repentance for sins as represented by the annual Day of Atonement (*Yom Kippur*), which occurs on the 10th day of *Tishri* (30 days within September–October) in the Jewish calendar. This concept was laid down in the laws of Leviticus 16,[14] even though God had asserted that he was personally unforgiving. In this regard, however, the wording of the rule is explicitly defined: 'In the seventh month, on the tenth day of the month, you shall afflict your souls, and you shall not do any work ... For on that day shall the priest make an atonement for you to cleanse you from all your sins before the Lord'.[15] It was therefore recognized that, although God might not acknowledge the atonement, the priests would offer forgiveness to the people on behalf of God if they repented for their sins and made the proper sacrifices.

This was an aspect of early Judaism that greatly appealed to the eventual hierarchy of the Catholic Church when they introduced the Sacrament of Penance. In this sacrament, commonly known as Confession, forgiveness of sins committed after baptism is granted through the priests' absolution to those who confess their sins and promise to repent by way of imposed reparations.[16] Irrespective of any involvement by God, both Atonement and Confession afford extreme powers of control to the priests who, in granting absolution and imposing satisfaction, are accepted as being those who are ordained to pronounce judgment and sentence.

Unlikely Forgiveness

Despite the great number of 'God said ...' references in the Old Testament, there are only two such entries in the New Testament. One of these occurs in a parable,[17] and is not a direct statement; the other occurs in recounting what the Lord had once said to King David.[18] In fact, God does not feature directly as a player in any part of the New Testament, except by way of implication through the teachings of Jesus, who refers to him as the Father. In these respects, he uses the terminology 'thy Father', 'your Father', 'our Father' and 'my Father'.[19] These teachings, however, embrace throughout the ideal of forgiveness, even to the extent of the well-known Lord's Prayer: 'And forgive us our debts, as we forgive our debtors'[20] — adding as an emphasis, 'If ye forgive not men their trespasses, neither will your Father forgive your trespasses.[21] The question that arises therefore is: From where did Jesus obtain the notion that God would forgive anyone for anything when the Israelite biblical scriptures made it quite clear that he was wholly unforgiving?

The concept of God's uncharacteristic forgiveness occurs specifically in the *Damascus Document*, found among the *Dead Sea Scrolls* of the Essenes. To begin, the document states:

> Listen now all you who know righteousness, and consider the works of God; for he has a dispute with all flesh and will condemn all those who despise him ... Hear now, my sons, and I will uncover your eyes that you may see and understand the works of God; that you may choose that which pleases him and reject that which he hates.[22]

The text subsequently relates to variously familiar incidents when God punished and persecuted the people of his own creation — biblical stories from the great Flood to the Babylonian Captivity. But, in contrast to the Hebrew scriptures, it is ultimately stated:

> Yet they wallowed in the sin of man and in the ways of uncleanliness, and they said, 'This is our way'. But God, in his wonderful mysteries, forgave them their sin and pardoned their wickedness.[23]

In discussing the priestly Levites and Zadokites, it is claimed in the *Damascus Document* that 'they were the first men of holiness whom God forgave'. Then referring to 'all the righteous who enter after them' and 'according to the covenant which God made with their forefathers, forgiving their sins, so shall he forgive their sins also'.[24]

What emerges from this is that, whereas mainstream Israelite society had created a religion based on fear of the wrath of the Lord after the Babylonian Captivity, the Essenes had developed a rather different ideal. They conceded that perhaps their ancestors had indeed been sinful and deserved all the punitive hardships that were thrust upon them. But, since God was all-powerful and could have destroyed them all as he once did in the days of the

Flood, they felt that he must have a merciful side in that he had actually allowed some of them to live. The text maintains that, for those he deemed righteous or in some manner worthy,

> God had built them a sure house in Israel, whose like has never existed from former times until now; those who hold fast to it are destined to live forever, and all the glory of Adam shall be theirs.[25]

Not only had the scribes of this document determined the nature of God's imagined forgiveness and the route to it, they also introduced the concept of everlasting life for those who followed the Essene rule of *The Way*. Such writings as these would have been very familiar to Jesus and his fraternity, who were raised in a Nazarene environment beyond the rigid structure of the Jerusalem priests. Although not in line with conventional rabbinical teaching, such theories became mainstays of Jesus' mission, which also incorporated the unorthodox healing methods of the Essene therapeutics.

According to the Gospels, a precept that Jesus fronted, in opposition to the Temple priests, was that he promoted the universality of God. As far as the Hebrew regulators were concerned, the Jews were God's chosen people, and their personal God was not available to those of other races. At that time, however, Judaea was under Roman occupation, and Jesus appears to have recognized that Rome could never be defeated while extremes of competitive doctrine existed within the Jewish community itself. His vision was straightforward, and was based upon the logic that a split Jewish nation could never overcome its plight whilst maintaining a separatist stance against the native non-Jews, whom the New Testament classifies as Gentiles. His ambition was for an harmonious, integrated society, but he was more than frustrated by the unbending Jews of rigid Hebrew principle. They considered that God belonged to them. But Jesus put forward a concept of sharing God with the Gentiles in a way that did not require them to take on all the trappings of orthodox

Judaism. He also applied his medical expertise to the said unworthy and unclean communities. Much to the disapproval of the priests, he did not restrict his aid to Jewish society alone as the Pharisees and others would have preferred.

A Race Apart

We can now begin to understand some of the apparent anomalies of the Old Testament in terms of how God was portrayed by the Israelite scribes as seemingly condemning certain activities on the one hand, whilst actively promoting them on the other.

The supposed Ten Commandments of the *Decalogue*, as listed in the books of Exodus 20:2–17 and Deuteronomy 5:6–21 (with a few variations), actually number fourteen in all, given that certain of the ten contain more than one directive. The commandment, 'Thou shalt not kill'[26] is blatantly contradicted by the instruction given to the Israelites in respect of Hittites, Amorites, Canaanites, Amalekites and various other nations:

> And when the Lord thy God shall deliver them before thee, thou shalt smite them, and utterly destroy them; thou shalt make no covenant with them, nor show mercy unto them.[27]

> Spare them not; but slay both man and woman, infant and suckling, ox and sheep, camel and ass'.[28]

The commandments: 'Thou shalt not steal'[29] and 'Thou shalt not covet thy neighbour's house'[30] are completely ignored when the Mosaic Israelites, on entering the Promised Land, are told to take possession from the Canaanites of their

> great and goodly cities which thou buildedst not, and houses full of all good things which thou filledst not, and wells digged which thou diggedst not, vineyards and olive trees which thou plantedst not.[31]

In these and other such instances, it becomes clear that the laws not to kill, steal or covet relate explicitly to the all important description of 'neighbours'. That is to say, the rules of the Ten Commandments applied only to the Israelites' treatment of other Israelites; they were not considered to be codes of conduct towards those of other races, tribes or nationalities.

As previously discussed, the Commandments were extracted from the Negative Confessions of the pharaohs as laid down in the Egyptian *Book of the Dead*. We do not, therefore, have to consider them as any form of original words from God, to whom they were spuriously attributed by the biblical scribes. It is the case nevertheless that, since the codes were seen to be applicable to the treatment of Israelites alone, this would not have made it easy for Jesus and his followers to share the Jewish God with the Gentiles. To them, Yahweh was perceived as a mercenary and aggressive deity, who actually hated everyone but the Israelites, and had treated them badly in any event. The only consolation was to be found in Exodus when, having stated, 'I the Lord thy God am a jealous God, visiting the iniquity of the fathers upon the children unto the third and fourth generation of them that hate me',[32] God was said to have added, 'And showing mercy unto thousands of them that love me, and keep my commandments'.[33] Although there was no sign of any such mercy in the Old Testament, the Commandments were brought into play by Jesus as a possible way to circumvent God's apparent dislike of the Gentiles. And Jesus said, 'Keep the commandments ... Thou shalt do no murder, Thou shalt not commit adultery, Thou shalt not steal, Thou shalt not bear false witness'.[34]

From this starting base, Jesus is seen to have developed the theme by introducing an item from the laws of Leviticus, which relates, 'Love thy neighbour as thyself'. What the Gospels veil, however, is the full extent of the Levitical ruling, which actually states, 'Thou shalt not avenge, nor bear any grudge against the children of thy people, but thou shalt love thy neighbour as thyself'.[35] Once again, the ruling concerning 'neighbours' was only applicable to 'the children of thy people': the Israelites. But Jesus reinterpreted this by adding a new principle of his own:

'I say unto you, Love your enemies, bless them that curse you, do good to them that hate you, and pray for them which despitefully use you, and persecute you'.[36]

Another concept which Jesus emphasized was the notion of loving God instead of fearing him, as was the norm in Israelite society. In this regard, Jesus said, 'Thou shalt love the Lord thy God with all thy heart, and with all thy soul, and with all thy mind. This is the first and great commandment'.[37] In reality, this was not the first commandment, which actually states, 'I am the Lord thy God ... Thou shalt have no other gods before me'.[38] But it did stem from the thankful words of Moses in Deuteronomy after Yahweh had aided the Israelite exodus from Egypt.[39]

For the Israelite God to become universally acceptable, it was necessary for him to appeal to the Gentile races as well as the Jews and, in this respect, he had to be newly portrayed as a more kindly and benevolent figure. There was very little in the Israelite texts to facilitate this endeavour, but there were some entries that could be reinterpreted as applicable to people at large, rather than just the Jewish nation. And there were some items that could be extracted and used to create a more gentle fatherly image — as for example, 'The Lord is my shepherd ...' from Psalm 23.

The precepts, 'love God', 'love thy neighbour' and even 'love thine enemy' became the underpinners of Jesus' mission to unite the people of Judaea. But since the Pharisees and Sadducees of the Temple hierarchy and the Sanhedrin Council of Jerusalem elders did not approve of this newly styled God-sharing, those of the traditionally strict Hebrew faith held themselves apart. Jesus might well have been a Jew, as were many of his followers, but his Nazarene movement was not a matter of racial heritage; it was a product of social, religious and political expediency, which began to rise in parallel with conventional Judaism.

The New Religion

Christianity had not yet been determined as a separate faith from Judaism and, since baptism was an aspect of the Jewish faith, it was contrary to customary doctrine that Gentiles should be baptised unless they were proselyte converts. In such cases, those of rigid Hebrew principle determined that the males should also be circumcised. This led to a good deal of debate and dispute concerning the ranks of Jesus' Gentile followers. By accepting Yahweh as their God, and in some cases being baptised according to choice, they were deemed to be acknowledging Jewish beliefs, in which case they should also be circumcised — a matter over which even Jesus' closest apostles were divided in opinion. Nearly three decades after the crucifixion of Jesus, the matter was still being discussed, and a Council was convened in Jerusalem to officiate. The Council, as detailed in Acts 15, was chaired by Jesus' brother James as the prevailing Nazarene bishop in Jerusalem.

This particular dispute had been sparked by a confrontation in Antioch: 'And certain men which came down from Judaea taught the brethren, and said, Except ye be circumcised after the manner of Moses, ye cannot be saved'.[40] The disciples Paul and Barnabus disputed this, claiming that circumcision had nothing to do with salvation. But in Jerusalem a group of Pharisees insisted that 'it was needful to circumcise them, and to command them to keep the law of Moses'.[41] The apostle Peter retaliated, maintaining that pure hearts and a belief in God were the important factors, and that Gentiles willing to commit to such faithful undertakings should not be subjected to a ritual that was a characteristic mark of the Hebrew race, not a necessity of godly commitment.[42] Ultimately, James found a compromise in judging that, although circumcision would not be rendered compulsory, the converts should uphold certain other Jewish rites, and should 'abstain from pollutions of idols, and from fornication, and from things strangled, and from blood' in the manner of the synagogue teachings.[43]

What was beginning to happen here was the emergence of a new style of monotheistic religion, but within a few years the AD 66 revolt against the Romans erupted. Just four years later, Jerusalem was destroyed and many other towns of Judaea were left in ruins. Taking up new lives in other countries, the so-called *Christus Jews* and Gentiles of the Nazarene movement retained their religious platform, but dropped the specifically Jewish aspects such as attending synagogues and abstaining from certain meats. Differing from the Jewish regime of their old homeland, they adopted the ways of their new environments and attracted many newcomers to their belief structure in other countries. As distinct from anything that Jesus might have envisioned in his God-sharing plan, he had unwittingly sown the seeds of a wholly new religion that was eventually to become divorced from its Judaic heritage under the adopted style of Christianity.

In its original form, Christianity was born from the peaceful ideals of Jesus' mission: 'love God', 'love thy neighbour' and 'love thine enemy'. In such respects, he even went so far as to denounce certain precepts of Jewish instruction as laid down in the *Torah* books of Exodus and Leviticus — e.g. 'Thou shalt give ... eye for eye, tooth for tooth, hand for hand, foot for foot ... burning for burning, wound for wound, stripe for stripe ... breach for breach'.[44] In direct contrast Jesus preached, 'Ye have heard that it hath been said, An eye for an eye, and a tooth for a tooth; but I say unto you that ye resist not evil, but whosoever shall smite thee on thy right cheek, turn to him the other also.[45] The true extent of Jesus' belief in this pacifist extreme of thought is unknown, especially when weighed against such instructions to his apostles as 'He that hath no sword, let him sell his garment and buy one'.[46] The overall attempt, nevertheless, seems to have been to create the image of a God who was gracious and forgiving, as distinct from the merciless Yahweh of Israelite tradition.

Christianity, as we have come to understand it, is based on the life and mission of Jesus, who has in essence become the individual godhead of the faith. Originally, however, Christianity was about people's relationships with God and their neighbours. Jesus was its instigator and its proponent, but he was not the object of personal religious veneration. His plan was to make God accessible to all, and indeed to present him in a way that the Old Testament and synagogue teachings did not. But this revised, agreeable image of God would not have been easy for the early Christians to accept because the inexorable Yahweh of the Old Testament was still evident in the scriptures.

22

A MATTER OF BELIEF

God of Israel

In pursuing the evolutionary story of the Judaeo-Christian God to this point, we have considered the biblical text of the Old Testament by way of a flowing précis of its chronological content. There is actually no other way to learn how the God *Yahweh* came to exist as a venerated cultural entity, since the Bible is the recognized document of record from which all related teachings are drawn. God, in the way he is religiously understood, was primarily featured in the Bible, which remains the base reference work for all theistic writings that have emanated in the millennia since its composition. As we have seen, however, the Old Testament is not actually a book about God; it is a generational account of a patriarchal strain which became the Israelite nation. It is a story of individuals, families and kings, of hardships and successes. In the course of this narrative, God plays a major role at the outset, making a few personal and semi-personal appearances down to the post-Abrahamic era (*c*.1750 BC). He then moves into physical obscurity and, from around 1350 BC, becomes almost incidental to the plot from the time of Moses.

What the Bible does not do, neither does it attempt at any stage, is to prove the existence of God. His reality is taken as read from the outset. In this regard, the *Jewish Encyclopedia* states:

> The existence of God is presupposed throughout the Bible, no attempt being anywhere made to demonstrate his reality.[1]

In clarifying the fact that (as portrayed by individually given names throughout the Old Testament) there were indeed other recognized gods and goddesses of the era, it is further explained:

> The books of the Prophets never treat of the
> fundamental problems of God's existence or
> non-existence; but their polemics are directed
> to prove that Israel (ready at all times to accept
> and worship one or the other god) is under the
> obligation to serve *Yhwh* and none other.

Albeit the Christian interpretation of later times forged a visual image of God, the Bible does not presume to describe him. Even though God appears as a physical presence in the garden of Eden and at the tent of Abraham, he is more generally regarded as being incorporeal, and thereby not composed of matter with a physically tangible existence.

The Christian perception derives, however, from the Genesis statement that man was made in God's image.[2] On that basis, the presumption is that God must look like a man, although clearly a wise, elderly man. In a way, although necessarily symbolic, this perception is odd since God is said to be 'consistent and ever-lasting', by virtue of which he would not age; neither would he be subject to the human normality that wisdom increases with age. He was, nevertheless, described as the 'Ancient of Days',[3] and is regarded within Christianity as 'the Father'. Thus, an elderly depiction is in line with the image of a paternal guardian.

The Bible, in contrast (at least from when his physical appearances terminate), relates rather more to God's spirit than to his material presence.[4] Notwithstanding the reference to man being made in God's image, the Bible states that his incorporeality cannot be likened to any living thing or to any person.[5] In line with later Islāmic understanding, the Jewish expression of God relies on his attributes rather than his person. It is said that 'He is One' and that none shares supremacy with him. 'His decisions will always come to pass; he is unchangeable from the first, and will prevail at the last'. Furthermore, 'God is not like man, for his knowledge is too high for man, although his wisdom is the source of human understanding. He judges the world in righteousness, punishes the wicked and turns their world upside down'.[6] Above all, God is said to be omnipresent: 'He is everywhere, watching everyone, and possesses an immediate knowledge of all people's secrets, feelings, and innermost thoughts'.

The first Jewish writer to attempt any proof of God's existence was the Alexandrian philosopher Philo (20 BC – AD 50). He stated that God's reality was entirely understandable because it could not be understood! Hence, he claimed, this proves that there exists something bigger than man's understanding. Man is capable of having ideas, wrote Philo, but those ideas must emanate from something bigger than himself: 'Since God determines and therefore knows all that will come to pass, then clearly man's ideas and actions must derive from God's predetermined plan. Therefore God must exist'.[7]

Actually, there is no proof of any sort offered here. What we have in the whole of Philo's lengthy exposition is simply an assumption that whatever might be thought, said or done by anyone has to be the result of those thoughts, words and actions emanating from a predestined schedule of events as determined by a supreme instigator, who must be God. In this regard, all results and occurrences are subjected to the pre-emptive questions, How? and Why? — to which the answer is always 'God'. Plainly, however, such a nondescript answer does not address the questions. It is simply an attempt to close the door on further scientific, theological or philosophical inquiry and, unfortunately, this has been a constant endeavour of religious instruction through the ages.

This restrictive type of attitude appears to stem from the root of all religious control (whether Jewish, Christian or Islāmic) when it was discovered that bringing God into any contentious arena was an effective method of pulling people into line. Beginning with Jewish interpretation, as later adopted by the other faiths, this strategy relates to the early days of lawgiving. That is to say it relates to the requirement of individuals or groups (elected or otherwise) who implement rules to govern the lives of others. It was ascertained in very early times that an expedient method of enforcement was to present man-made regulations as being the Laws of God or the Will of God, and that God's decrees must be accepted and obeyed without question.

Such expressions of divine supremacy rendered the laws of man (whether good or bad) quite beyond challenge, especially when they were said to have been divulged by God to prophets, priests and saints. If not laws, the same happened with matters of opinion in that unpopular reasoning could strategically be reinforced by explaining it as being God's Will. Given that the monotheistic religions are of such combined influence on the world stage, it is evident from all documented record that the tactical usage of the terms God's Law, God's Will and the Word of God have been largely instrumental in dominating governmental affairs throughout history on a wide international scale.

The Christian View

Turning now to the Christian perspective, the *Catholic Encyclopedia* also reiterates the same point that is made in the *Jewish Encyclopedia*. It states: 'Nowhere in the Bible do we find any elaborate argumentation devoted to proving that God exists'. But it is then added: 'This truth is rather taken for granted'.[8] Unlike the Jewish entry, this Christian item is unnecessarily dogmatic in its use of the word 'truth'. There is no room left here for discussion — i.e. The Bible does not seek to prove the existence of God because it is an accepted fact. An attempt is then made to further reinforce this argument by the nonsensical assertion that, because God's existence is not demonstrable by way of any proof, this itself provides the proof that his existence must be real because it cannot be explained!

Within Christian writings outside the Bible we can find a number of variable propositions that endeavour to explain and prove the existence of God. One school of thought suggests that the answer can be reduced to one or other of two propositions:

> 1. That we have naturally an immediate consciousness or intuition of God's existence, and may therefore dispense with any attempt to prove this truth.

> 2. That if we cannot prove it in such a way as to satisfy the speculative reason, we can, nevertheless, and must conscientiously believe it on other than strictly intellectual grounds.[9]

Either way, much the same is being stated: 'We do not need to prove it because we know it and, even though we cannot prove it, we should believe it anyway'. Overall, the point is made that God's existence is not a matter of proof, but a matter of belief which requires no evidence. However, since the mechanism of belief relies on the ability to choose, then the existence of God, by way of these propositions, can only be regarded as a matter of opinion, not as a matter of fact.

Revered among the foremost theologians of the Catholic Church was St Thomas Aquinas (1225–74). In his treatise *Summa Theologica* he advanced five particular arguments to prove the existence of God. Many scholastic writers have followed his lead to the extent that these so-called 'five proofs' have achieved classical status.[10] They are:

> 1. Motion: The passing from power to act, as it takes place in the universe, implies a first unmoved mover, who is God; else we should postulate an infinite series of movers, which is inconceivable.

Nothing can move without having a 'mover'. And since movers can move, there must ultimately be a primary mover, who must be God.

> 2. First Cause: Efficient causes, as we see them operating in this world, imply the existence of a first cause that is uncaused and possesses in itself the sufficient reason for its existence; and this is God.

Since everything that exists has been caused to exist, then there must have been a 'first cause' that existed but was not itself caused. Everything had to be created, and the creator must therefore have been God.

3. Existence: The fact that contingent beings exist, whose non-existence is recognized as possible, implies the existence of a necessary being, who is God.

Given that physical things exist and are necessarily created, then their creator must be an entity that is not physical and existed before material existence. This can only be God.

4. Degrees: The graduated perfections of 'being', actually existing in the universe, can be understood only by comparison with an absolute standard that is also actual — an infinitely perfect being, which is God.

All mundane qualities differ by degrees — as in good or bad, honest or false, healthy or sick — and since people have the ability to vary within these parameters, it follows that there must be a base standard of perfection which is unchangeable. This is God.

5. Design: The wonderful order or evidence of intelligent design, which the universe exhibits, implies the existence of a supramundane designer, who is no other than God.

Everything that exists was originally designed. It follows that there must be an ultimate designer, a supreme architect who exists but was not designed, and this is God.

In consideration of these said 'five proofs', it is evident that, even if the presumption that universal nature embodies motion along with a prior cause and a form of creation is valid, it does not follow that inquiry into these matters terminates automatically with God. The use of God as a manner of concluding any such inquiry is simply an arbitrary judgement which proves absolutely nothing.[11]

In postulating such judgements, St Thomas and other venerable churchmen added their own definitions of primary cause, and have called it God. But in no case has God been cemented as an ultimate personal reality who controls all matter and phenomena. If it is deemed necessary to terminate every subject of inquiry with a single pronouncement that results from an infinite regress, then it could equally be deduced that Nature constitutes the first cause of existence. Vague and indistinct as this might be as a conclusive answer, it is more comprehensible than invoking the figure of God. This has become evident in numerous recently conducted surveys which enquire of people: 'Do you believe in God?' The hesitant, and almost apologetic, response in so many cases is 'Yes, but not in the way he is generally understood'. What these people are saying is that they find it acceptable to recognize some form of universal motivation that is perhaps beyond our present understanding, but that they cannot comprehend this prevailing force to be a God figure. Hence, their answers are generally qualified by adding such further statements as 'What I mean is that I don't believe in an old man who sits in the clouds'.

It might be wondered why these people do not simply answer 'No' in the first instance, thereby dismissing God before addressing what they actually do believe. There appear to be two main reasons for this, both of which relate to matters of conditioning. A straightforward atheist would of course answer 'No' without reservation. But a great many people would rather give the impression that they are open minded and, to some extent, spiritually inclined even though not conventionally religious. Such people are often sensitive to an indoctrinated social requirement which leads to the second reason for their guarded responses. By way of their conditioning, even though they might not believe in the biblical God, they do not wish to offend others within an environment that is to a large extent religiously motivated. This results in a compromise answer, which asserts no particular opinion one way or the other. But when pressed further on the matter these same people often profess their belief in an inexplicable cosmic force, which they reckon might as well be called *God* as by any other name.

For reasons that have never satisfactorily been defined, it is widely understood that religious faith must be respected, whereas it is not in any way incumbent on religious people to respect or even tolerate the views of non-believers. Because there are no proofs of God's existence, religious society is especially vulnerable. As a result, it becomes instinctively defensive to the extent that objective discussion is rarely possible. Religious stalwarts think nothing of expressing their views in any company as if those views were matters of unchallengeable fact that must be accepted. But when a non-believer attempts to expound his or her contrary opinion, it is regarded as a disrespectful blasphemy. This generally results in doubters and non-believers keeping their opinions to themselves, while at the same time having politely to endure all that emanates from the other camp.

The matter of assumed offence by virtue of a challenge or difference of opinion is not just the product of belief versus disbelief; it also exists between the differing monotheistic faiths, and even between denominational or cultural sects within individual religions: Sunni versus Shi'a Muslims, Catholic versus Protestant Christians, and so forth. Each of the respective groups considers that the others are misguided in the interpretation and application of their faiths, and yet ultimately they all believe in the same God. Thus, the contentious issue of 'whether' one believes in God is paralleled by the equally inconsequential dispute about 'how' one believes in God. The divergence of opinion leads not only to heated disagreement, but to outright hatred on a world scale, and history is filled with the violent consequences of such narrow-minded intolerance.

Atheists do not care if someone else believes in God; their right to do so is accepted even if not understood. Believers, on the other hand, cannot accept that the contrary opinions of others should likewise be acknowledged. As stated above, 'belief' is by all definition a matter of choice, not a matter of proven substance. We saw earlier that the old Greek word for 'choice' was *hairesis*, from which derived the term 'heresy' — a denial of free will and the right to choose. Christians determine that atheists are heretics; Muslims think that Christians are heretics. And so it progresses, with each faction enacting their own right to choose and thereby form dogmatic opinions that deny the rights of others to make their own choices and form their own opinions.

Unfortunately for rational Christians, there are plenty of fundamentalist and evangelical groups, especially in the USA, whose hierarchy seek to instil fear of disbelief through television broadcasts and Internet postings. For example:

> God's terrible wrath is revealed against those who claim that He does not exist. Many people who consider themselves intelligent, educated members of society do not believe in God. This is because they think they are cleverer than God ... Such people have no idea what a great sin it is not to believe in God.[12]

Statements such as this do not come from the Bible, nor from any legitimate doctrine. They are the product of dogma enforcement by way of a control endeavour based on scriptural ignorance.

There is little so arrogant and socially destructive as these persistent attempts to enforce unsubstantiated opinions as if they were matters of irrefutable fact. There is nothing wrong with a belief in God; there is nothing wrong with not believing in God. But there is everything wrong with conceited judgements that one's own rights of choice and opinion in this regard are somehow superior to those of someone else. In effect, this is seemingly what the Gospels describe that Jesus preached in his expanded version of the 'love thy neighbour' doctrine. Social harmony through toleration and mutual regard must be preferable to divisive, discriminatory practice.

Fortunately, there is at least one layer of consensus within a generally unhealthy religious environment in that fanatics and extremists of any religion are not well regarded by their own mainstream establishments. But it is not so readily understood by the mainstream networks that even they are inclined towards pompous, antagonistic behaviour when confronted by opposition banners. Maybe this is what Jesus was referring to when he suggested turning the other cheek if a matter of potential dispute is irrelevant and pointless. There might be plenty of good causes that are worth fighting to uphold, but hostility over 'whether' or 'how' one's neighbour might believe in God is not one of them.

The Wager

In 1670 a work entitled *Pensées – Apologie de la religion Chrétienne* (Thoughts – Defence of the Christian Religion) was published a few years after the death of its author. He was the French mathematician, physicist and philosopher Blaise Pascal (1623–62). The approach that Pascal took towards the question of whether or not to believe in God was based on an applied form of mathematical odds that became known as *Pascal's Wager*. In determining what to him appeared a sensible approach, Pascal maintained that, although we are incapable of knowing whether or not God exists, we must wager one way or the other: 'Reason cannot settle which way we should incline, but a consideration of the relevant outcomes supposedly can'. He continued:

> Since you must choose, let us see which interests you least. You have two things to lose, the true and the good; and two things to stake, your reason and your will, your knowledge and your happiness. And your nature has two things to shun, error and misery. Your reason is no more shocked in choosing one rather than the other, since you must of necessity choose ... If you gain, you gain all; if you lose, you lose nothing. Wager then, without hesitation, that 'God is'.[13]

The theory is a simple one. Even if the odds are heavily in favour of God's non-existence, there remains an outside chance that perhaps he does exist. If one decides to believe in God, there is everything to gain if that is the right choice, but there is nothing to lose if it is wrong. Alternatively, if one decides to believe that God does not exist, there is equally nothing to lose if that is the right choice. But there is a loss of everything in terms of heavenly salvation if it is wrong. The safest approach therefore, said Pascal, is to wager that God does exist.

It does rather seem that, whether knowingly or not, this is precisely the thought process that might result in some of the answers given to the survey question as mentioned above:

'Do you believe in God?' Many of those who answer, 'Yes, but not in the way that he is generally understood', might actually prefer to state that they are unconvinced, but do not do so because (in view of the unprovable nature of God's existence or his non-existence) they elect to hedge their bets. What if they were to answer 'No' and then it turned out that God did exist?

An obvious error in Pascal's judgement, however, is the starting premise: 'Since you must choose'. There is, in fact, no reason why anyone 'must' make any decision in this regard; there are plenty of people who have never given the matter any thought. But when Pascal addressed the question in the 17th century, the concepts of Heaven and Hell were far more dramatically cemented in people's minds than they are today. And this was reason enough for him to suggest that a decision should be made in God's favour, just in case he does exist.

Vaguely logical as this might appear at first consideration by way of its bet-hedging stance, it is actually quite illogical since it is not possible to believe in something on the basis that a potential threat is posed by disbelief. At best, *Pascal's Wager* is an argument for a pretence — a feigning of belief by way of outward appearance. A naturally committed believer would never be confronted by the problem in the first place, and those who are faced with the dilemma are actually doubters — in which case God (if he were to exist as the omnipotent presence that religion presumes) would see through the deception anyway.[14] One can 'choose' to believe by way of informed or considered opinion, but one cannot simply 'decide' to believe in something because it seems the better bet. That is not belief; it is a contrived attempt at self delusion which, owing to the very nature of its premise, would be ineffectual in any event.

A Rapid Decline

The *Catholic World News* reported recently that, on an international scale, church attendance is now declining faster than ever before. Even in Italy, a report from Rome indicates that the number of Catholics who attend Mass each week has dropped steadily since 1993. A survey by the Italian National Statistics Office has revealed that only 35% of Catholics attend church every week, and 14% said they never go to church.[15] The Anglican Church, the Dutch Reform Church and others have expressed similar Protestant concerns, and the highest levels of decline are in Britain, North America, Western Europe and Australia.

Overall, the figures reveal internationally that only one in every ten listed Christians now attends church with any form of regularity. The year 2004–05 saw a 20% fall in congregations, following a similar decline in the previous year, and a majority of average congregations now occupy less than a quarter of the pews. The 2005 *English Church Census*, carried out by the independent Christian Research Organization, found that in the previous six years half a million people stopped going to church on Sundays. Evidently, the figure was lower than expected because about a million left the congregations of England in the nine years before that. It appears, however, that the rate of decline had been lessened by virtue of immigrant Christians from Africa who boosted the Pentecostal and Evangelical movements. Overall, just 6% of the presumed Christian population in Britain now attends church on an average Sunday. This compares with the 10% international average as cited above.[16]

As an adjunct to the falling congregational figures in Britain, a *Daily Telegraph* poll has revealed that the proportion of people who believe in God is actually declining at a faster rate than church attendance. This contradicts the common perception that people 'believe without belonging'. 'People see themselves as being Christian', it was stated, 'in much the same way as they are British. When filling in forms, they tag themselves with the religious environment of their upbringing, but this has nothing whatever to do with their current beliefs'. Since, to a large extent, children inherit religion from their parents, it is already known that the next adult generation will be even less inclined towards church involvement.[17]

Amid all this, and especially in America, the Christian flag has been waved more vehemently than ever by political leaders at a time when cosmopolitan society in general is at its highest level of ethnic and religious dissemination. Unlike Britain, where the monarch is, by tradition, the designated Head of the Anglican Protestant Church, the United States *Constitution* specifically affirms that there is no tie between the Federal State and any particular religion. And yet, in a New Orleans address before the 2005 flood disaster, Republican President George W Bush called for people to embrace the miracle of Christian Salvation.[18] The United States is, by definition, 'One Nation under God' but, far from acting as the leader of a multicultural, multi-religious nation, the President's address was phrased emphatically in the language of Evangelical Christianity.

A 2006 Gallup poll in the United States discovered that 46% of Americans believe the Federal Government 'should advocate Christian values', whereas 54% thought otherwise.[19] Around 90% of those polled (including Jews and Muslims) said they believed in God, although a quarter of those deemed Christian preferred the nondescript 'cosmic force' concept rather than the biblical and generally recognized clerical interpretation. Overall, the nation-wide result was that around two-thirds of the population believed in the biblical God. This is markedly higher than in Britain, but the United States national average is considerably enhanced by a significant *per capita* belief among zealous Christians in the Southern and Midwestern States. Elsewhere, especially in the major cities, there is an ongoing decline in accordance with Britain, Australia and the European countries.[20]

As each country follows a progressive move from being an individual 'nation state' to the newly required role as a global 'market state', the traditional influence held by religion in society is being overwhelmed by the greater corporate influence, which is led by competition rather than cooperation.[21] As against earlier days, people now spend more time with their fellow workmates than with their residential neighbours. Consequently, the sharp decline in local community involvement is reflected in the downturn of local church attendance.

Many reasons have been put forward for the current religious decline and the rise of a more secular society, but the most common reason given in surveys is that people now see religion as something sinister — something to avoid and of which to be afraid. Religion is now perceived by many as a realm of fanatics, terrorists and manipulative political leaders. Fundamentalism in all religions and creeds has risen to a point which the leaders of mainstream religious establishments consider to be a level of crisis.

Another reason for a generally waning belief in God is that scientific awareness is closing many of the doors that have long been theologically guarded. Professor Charles Coulson (1910–74), a theoretical chemist at Oxford University and vice president of the Methodist Conference, made the point that God had been inserted into so many gaps of understanding that could not be explained scientifically. He had become traditionally a 'God of the Gaps', but scientific discovery was gradually pushing God out of the gaps.[22] This has made the arguments in favour of God's relevance far more difficult to sustain, whilst lessening the need to believe in God in order to be well informed.

In practice, however, it is not so much the notion of God that is being undermined by science, but the inaccuracies of a customary Church teaching which has not evolved in step with other fields of educational advancement.

As we have seen, scriptural teaching is not based so much on biblical content, but rather more on clerical interpretations of that content — interpretations that have persisted for centuries despite the changing environment in which they exist. Modern secular society is largely based, through advertising and other marketing strategies, on providing solutions to requirements and needs. If a genuine 'need' is not readily apparent, then it is commercially generated, via the press, media and Internet, on the basis that people react possitively to the offer of 'benefits'. It is therefore a natural instinct for people these days to ask, 'Why do I need to believe in God?' If that question is not answered satisfactorily with the prospect of an attractive 'benefit', then there is no reason why they should give the matter any further thought, and it is clear from the surveys that this attitude is increasingly becoming more prevalent.

Individual Choice

Throughout the course of this investigation, we have seen that God has never been an historical constant; he is the result of an ancient concept that has been developed as a progressive theme within different cultures. Dr Rowan Williams, the Archbishop of Canterbury, made reference to the continual 'reinvention' of God in his 2003 New Year address. He also mentioned that, although God has no definable image, 'that hasn't stopped us down the ages inventing millions of pictures of him — human images of our own devising, to help us try to grasp the divine'.[23] This, of course, only applies in the Christian tradition since the making of such deiform portrayals is forbidden in the Jewish and Islāmic faiths.

Following our documentary trail of the variously recorded gods from the earliest Mesopotamian accounts, written from the 3rd millennium BC, reports of their said activities were continued and paralleled in Canaanite texts during the 2nd millennium BC. Quite how far the godly tradition goes back is impossible to determine; we know of them only from the time that *cuneiform* writing evolved into a literary story-telling form. At the other end of the chronological line, the subsequently relevant Canaanite writings terminate in around 1400 BC. Onwards from that date the accounts were continued in Assyria and elsewhere, but they were not presented as being contemporary with the gods they discuss. The writings deal, in the main, with ongoing traditions of a pantheon that was introduced in earlier times. They treat the deities as if they still exist, but do not relate to their personal presence in the manner that previous literature had described them. Given that the opening sequences of the Jewish *Torah* were constructed with the more ancient Mesopotamian and Canaanite tablets as source references, we find that precisely the same occurs in the Bible.

To begin, from the time of Adam and Eve, God is presented and encountered as a physical entity; he walks in the garden of Eden, meets later at Mamre with Abraham, and has vaguely described relationships with Isaac and Jacob. Then, moving swiftly through the centuries (with a 400-year lapse between the books of Genesis and Exodus), we pass through the 1400 BC literary deadline, when the first-hand Canaanite texts expire. Emerging on the latter side of that date in the biblical era of Moses, God's presence is seen to have transformed into a series of spiritual experiences. His voice is heard from a burning bush; he moves in a pillar of cloud, and appears thereafter in dreams and visions. It is subsequently explained: 'The word of the Lord was precious in those days; there was no open vision'.[24] God is no longer perceived as dwelling in person at Bêth-El, but has become a figure of celestial imagery who resides in an inexplicable dimension beyond the material domain. Experienced mainly by prophets and seers, God has moved from an ostensibly real environment into a realm of belief and tradition.

* * *

Whoever the original overlords of the *Anannage* Grand Assembly might have been, and from wherever they came, there is no particular reason to doubt their existence. The ancient tablets, from various neighbouring regions through thousands of years, are consistent in their portrayals and appear to have been written with as much sincerity as any historical record. But in the final analysis, it is not explained that the various descendent godly figures died or removed to some other place. The documentary perception simply changed in about 1400 BC, as if by way of a dimensional shift, from one of actual physical presence to that of mysterious spiritual presence. The once 'on-the-ground' figures departed the literary arena prior to the Mosaic era when the prevailing El-Yahweh-Elyon (as one of their number) also became wholly inscrutable in the Bible. If he and the other gods truly existed at any time down to the middle 2nd millennium BC, we might well ask: What happened to them after that? But the answer remains an untold mystery, and brings us full circle to another question with which we began this research: In line with the belief of a great many people worldwide, does the God of emergent monotheism actually exist in some form today?

In intellectual terms, as admitted and confirmed in both Jewish and Christian theology, there is absolutely no proof, nor even circumstantial evidence, that can be cited in this regard. We are left, therefore, with precisely the same situation that Blaise Pascal confronted around 350 years ago. God can only be said to exist as an optional concept based on individual choice. He is a subject of unsubstantiated belief, not of certainty, and whether one elects to believe or disbelieve remains purely a matter of conjecture and personal opinion.

NOTES AND REFERENCES

INTRODUCTION

1 'The Asian Tsunami', Dr Rowan Williams, *Sunday Telegraph*, 2 January 2005.

2 'Atrocities', Dr Rowan Williams at the Genocide Memorial, Tsitsernakaberd in Yerevan, Armenia, 25 September 2007.

3 'Where most people see a Weather System, some see Divine Retribution', Alan Cooperman, *Washington Post*, 4 September 2005.

4 'The Terrorist Katrina', Editorial, *New York Sun*, 2 September 2005.

5 'Where was God?' Nancy Gibbs, *Time*, 15 September 2005.

6 Re. President George W Bush in *Dayton Daily News*, Dayton, OH, 15 January 2004.

7 'Tsunami', David Rosenberg, Channel 4 UK television, December 2005.

8 'Where most people see a Weather System, some see Divine Retribution', A Cooperman.

9 'Tsunami', David Rosenberg.

10 'Where most people see a Weather System, some see Divine Retribution', A Cooperman.

11 'Where was God?' Nancy Gibbs.

12 Lecture: 'We Few; We happy few; We band of brothers', Prof J Andrew Thomson, Athiest Alliance International Congress, Washington, DC, 27–30 September 2007. In the period 1981–90, suicide bombings worldwide were recorded at an average of 4.7 per annum. From 1991 to 2000 the average was 16 per annum. In the year 2001 alone the figure rose to 81, increasing annually to 460 suicide bombings in the year 2005.

13 'Where most people see a Weather System, some see Divine Retribution', A Cooperman.

14 'Where was God during the Virginia Tech Shootings?' Lillian Kwon, *Christian Post*, 19 April 2007.

15 'Thought for the Day', Dr Rowan Williams, BBC Radio 4, *Today*, 8 July 2005.

16 'Statement on London Terrorist Attacks by the Archbishop of Canterbury', Dr Rowan Williams, Lambeth Palace, 7 July 2005.

17 News: 'Lets make peace', and Comment: 'Half the world', *The Times*, 12 October 2007.

18 'Where was God during the Virginia Tech Shootings?' Lillian Kwon.

Part I – God of Creation

Chapter 1: THE CREATION DEBATE

1 'Adam and Eve in the Land of the Dinosaurs', Edward Rothstein, *New York Times*, 24 May 2007.

2 'So what's with all the dinosaurs?' Stephen Bates, *The Guardian*, 13 November 2006.

3 'Creationist display creating controversy', Jim DeBrosse, *Dayton Daily News*, 26 May 2007.

4 *Ibid.*

5 'Protests planned for grand opening of Creation Museum', Doug Huntington, *Christian Post*, 27 April 2007.

6 The female skeleton, dubbed *Lucy*, and other hominoid bones of 13 individuals (together called the 'First Family') were unearthed in 1974 by Donald Johanson, an archaeologist from the University of Chicago, in excavations at Hadar in Ethiopia. The *Turkana Boy* was discovered in 1984 by Kamoya Kimeu, a member of a team led by the Kenyan palaeontologist Richard Leakey, at Nariokotome near Lake Turkana in Kenya. *Peking Man* was discovered during the 1923–27 excavations at Zhoukoudian (Choukoutien) near Beijing (Peking) in China.

7 According to a survey in the journal *Scientific American* in March 2002, 45% of Americans think that God created life some time in the past 10,000 years, even though scientists believe that life on earth began around 4 billion years ago.

8 'Matter of Faith', Leader, *The Guardian*, 9 March 2002.

9 'A Scientist's View', Richard Dawkins, *The Guardian*, 9 March 2002.

10 At an average individual production cost of £25 million, this modern, state-of-the art type of school (called a City Academy) relies on an initial £2 million investment from a private source. In return, the sponsor and appointed headteacher are granted autonomy in control of decisions over the curriculum, admissions and ethos of the school. The concept arose from the Learning and Skills Act, 2000.

11 'Ofsted OK creationism in college', Polly Curtis, *The Guardian*, 24 May 2002.

12 'Fresh threat to Darwin in Ohio schools', Duncan Campbell in Los Angeles, *The Guardian*, 12 March 2002.

13 'US school in eye of creationist storm', Julian Borger in Washington. *The Guardian*, 13 January 2005.

14 'Georgia schools to remove creationist stickers from textbooks', Polly Curtis, education correspondent, *The Guardian*, 14 January 2005.

15 'Intelligent design opponents invoke US Constitution', Donald MacLeod, *The Guardian*, 18 October 2005.

16 'From Our Own Correspondent', Justin Webb in Washington, BBC World Service, 26 November 2005.

17 'Intelligent design lessons ruled unconstitutional', *Daily Telegraph*, 21 December, 2005. Also 'Keep the divine out of biology lessons, Federal judge rules', Harry Mount, *Daily Telegraph*, 21 December 2005.

18 'School board delivers blow to creationism', Suzanne Goldenberg in Washington, *The Guardian*, 15 February 2006.

19 'Academics fight rise of creationism at universities', Duncan Campbell, *The Guardian*, 21 February 2006.

20 'Archbishop: Stop teaching creationism', Stephen Bates, Religious Affairs correspondent, *The Guardian*, 21 March 2006.

21 'Revealed: rise of creationism in UK schools', James Randerson, science correspondent, *The Guardian*, 27 November 2006.

22 'How Genesis crept back into the classroom', Graeme Paton, Education Correspondent, *The Daily Telegraph*, 28 November 2006.

23 'Ministers to ban creationist teaching aids in science lessons', James Randerson, science correspondent, *The Guardian*, 7 December 2006.

Chapter 2: GATEWAY OF THE LORD

1 Discovered in the excavations of Gerald Lankester Harding (director of the Department of Antiquities of Jordan) and Père Ronald de Vaux (a French Dominican priest), who began their work at Qumrân in 1949.

2 The 22-character Aramaic alphabet was the ancestor of both the Hebrew and Arabic alphabets. From the time of Darius I (*c.*500 BC) it was the official language of the Persian Empire and it overshadowed Hebrew as the main language of the Jews for about 1,000 years from that time.

3 There are *Targums* to all the canonical books except Daniel, Ezra, and Nehemiah; for some books of the Bible there are several *Targums*. As regards age and linguistic character they may be divided into three classes: (1) *Targum of Onkelos* and *Targum of Jonathan*; (2) *Jerusalem Targums*; (3) *Targum on the Hagiographa*.

4 JW Etheridge, *The Targums of Onkelos and Jonathan Ben Uzziel on the Pentateuch with the fragments of the Jerusalem Targum from the Chaldee*, Longman Green, London, 1862.

5 Information concerning the origin of the Septuagint comes from a document of the era known as the *Letter of Aristeas*. It tells of how the pharaoh Ptolemy Philadelphus (285–247 BC) was advised by his librarian to have the laws of the Jews translated for his library, and that Aristeas was

commissioned to ask the high priest, Eliezer, to send a body of scholars to translate their sacred scriptures into Greek.

6 *Tanakh* is an acronym that identifies the Hebrew Bible. It is based on the initial letters of each of the text's three parts: (i) The *Torah* : (the Law, Teaching or Instruction) – also called the *Chumash*, meaning: 'The five' (the books of Moses). In Greek, the *Pentateuch*. (ii) The *Nevi'im*, relating to the 'Prophets'. (iii) The *Ketuvim* or *Hagiographa*, meaning 'Writings'.

7 Jewish Encyclopedia, Funk & Wagnalls, New York, NY, 1906, under Deuteronomy.

8 2 Kings 23:12.

9 2 Kings 21:14–15.

10 2 Kings 24:3.

11 Alongside the Hanging Gardens of Babylon, the other Seven Wonders were the Great Pyramid of Giza, the Statue of Zeus at Olympia, the Temple of Artemis at Ephesus, the Mausoleum of Maussollos at Halicarnassus, the Colossus of Rhodes, and the Lighthouse of Alexandria.

12 James Hastings (ed), *Dictionary of the Bible*, T&T Clark, Edinburgh, 1909, under Babylon. The term 'Gateway of the God' is sometimes used for *Bāb-ilû* since *ilû* has a ommon deiform connotation. The Mesopotamian term relates however to 'bright' or 'shining' – stemming from *êl* ('to shine') and *êllu* ('to be bright').

13 2 Kings 24:14.

14 Genesis 1:1–2:4.

15 Genesis 1:28, 2:20.

16 Christian and Barbara Joy O'Brien, *The Genius of the Few*, Dianthus, Cirencester, 1999, ch 2, p 27.

17 JW Jack, *The Ras Shamra Tablets – Their Bearing on the Old Testament*, T&T Clark, Edinburgh, 1935, ch 3, p 15.

18 Genesis 1:26.

19 Genesis 3:5.

20 Genesis 3:22.

21 Genesis 17:1.

22 El Shaddai: 31 times in Job. First used in Genesis 17:1, 2. Also Genesis 31:29, 49:24, 25, Ruth 1:20, 21; Proverbs 3:27; Micah 2:1, and Isaiah 60:15, 16, 66:10, 13.

23 Genesis 14:18; Numbers 24:16; Deuteronomy 26:19, 32:8; Psalms 7:17, 18:13, 56:2, 78:35, 97:9; Daniel 7:25, 27, and Isaiah 14:14.

24 The name El Shaddai is retained however in the Latin *Vulgate* Bible, translated and produced by St Jerome in AD *c*.382.

25 Jack Miles, *God – A Biography*, Vintage, New York, NY, 1995, ch 2, p 51. *See* also J Hastings, *Dictionary of the Bible*, under God.

26 For *Ilû* (Enlil) *see* Thorkild Jacobsen, *The Treasures of Darkness – A History of Mesopotamian Religion*, Yale University Press, New Haven, CT, 1976, ch 4, p 117. Also *see* Samuel Noah Kramer, *Sumerian Mythology*, Harper Bros, New York, NY, 1961, ch 2, p 59, referencing Ilû as the 'great mountain'.

27 JW Jack, *The Ras Shamra Tablets*, ch 3, p 13.

28 *Ibid*, ch 3, p 15. Bêth-El is rendered in modern texts as Bethel.

29 Genesis 35:6–7.

30 *Septuagint* entry for Psalm 82:1.

31 For example, in Genesis 7:1, 28:3, 35:11; Numbers 23:22; Joshua 3:10; 2 Samuel 22:31, 32; Nehemiah 1:5, 9:32; Isaiah 9:6, and Ezekiel 10:5.

Part II – God of the Records

Chapter 3: HERITAGE OF THE PATRIARCH

1 For an overview of the rise of Sumer, and Mesopotamian history, *see* Georges Roux, *Ancient Iraq*, George Allen & Unwin, London, 1964.

2 *Tell al Mugayyar* = Mound of Pitch. Sir Charles Leonard Woolley, *Ur of the Chaldees*, Ernest Benn, London, 1930, intro, p 13,

3 In 1923, the archaeologist Sir Charles Leonard Woolley, with a joint team from the British Museum and the University of Pennsylvania, began excavations at Ur. This dig is detailed more fully in Woolley's above mentioned book.

4 The *Lament* is discussed in T Jacobsen, *The Treasures of Darkness*, ch 3, pp 87–91, and in SN Kramer, *Sumerian Mythology*, intro, p 14. Also *see* Samuel Noah Kramer, *Lamentation Over the Destruction of Ur* (Assyriological Studies, 12) Chicago University Press: Chicago, 1940, pp 16–17.

5 G Roux, *Ancient Iraq*, ch 10, pp 146–49.

Michael Wood, *Legacy: A Search for the Origins of Civilization*, BBC Network Books, London, 1992, ch 1, p 34.

7 Benny J Peiser, Trevor Palmer and Mark E Bailey, *Natural Catastrophes During Bronze Age Civilizations*, Archaeopress, Oxford, 1998, pp 78–81.

8 Thorkild Jacobsen, *The Sumerian King List* (Assyriological Studies 11), University of Chicago Press, Chicago, 1939.

9 G Roux, *Ancient Iraq*, ch 7, p 97.

10 Samuel Noah Kramer, *History Begins at Sumer*, Thames & Hudson, London, 1958, ch 20, pp 214–15.

11 Henri Frankfort, *Kingship and the Gods*, University of Chicago Press, Chicago, 1948, ch 16, p 224.

12 The term *Chaldee* derives from *Kaldû*, which eventually became a generic term for Babylonians. *See* Dr William Smith, *Smith's Bible Dictionary* (1868 revised), Hendrickson, Peabody, MA, 1998.

13 J Hastings, *Dictionary of the Bible* – under Chaldaea.

14 In 1853 Britain's foremost Assyriologist, Sir Henry Creswicke Rawlinson, first announced in his address to the Royal Asiatic Society that the *cuneiform* writings of ancient Sumer and Akkad had evolved from a script introduced into the region from ancient Scythia. *See* Sir Charles Leonard Woolley, *The Sumerians*, WW Norton, London, 1965, ch 1, p 20.

15 Carlo Suarès, *The Cipher of Genesis*, Samuel Weiser, York Beach, ME, 1992, 'Ha-Qabala', p 21, 20:155.

16 Sir CL Woolley, *Ur of the Chaldees*, ch 5, pp 168–69.

17 Rev George H Schodde (trans), The *Book of Jubilees*, Capital University, Columbus, OH (EJ Goodrich edn), 1888; reprinted Artisan, CA, 1992. The Hebrew *Book of Jubilees* was written by a Pharisee scribe in the 2nd century BC during the Maccabaean reign of John Hyrcanus in Jerusalem.

18 G Roux, *Ancient Iraq*, ch 10, pp 137, 146–48 and chart appendix.

19 David M Rohl, *A Test of Time: The Bible from Myth to History*, Century, London, 1995, ch 9, p 200.

20 J Hastings, *Dictionary of the Bible*, under Eber.

21 Genesis 11:14–17.

22 Genesis 11:27.

23 Genesis 11:31.

24 Werner Keller, *The Bible as History*, (trans, William Neil), Hodder & Stoughton, London, 1956, ch 5, p 63.

25 The archaeology of Mari is discussed at length in Daniel E Fleming, *Democracy's Ancient Ancestors*, Cambridge University Press, Cambridge, 2004.

26 Lavinia and Dan Cohn-Sherbok, *A Short Reader in Judaism*, Oneworld, Oxford, 1997, ch 1, p 13. For a detailed account of the Ebla discoveries, *see* Giovanni Pettinato, *Archives of Ebla: An Empire Inscribed in Clay*, Doubleday, New York, NY, 1981.

27 Genesis 13:10.

28 *An-unna-ki* ('Heaven came to earth'). Recommended books concerning the *Anannage* are Christian and Barbara Joy O'Brien, *The Shining Ones*, Dianthus, Cirencester, 1997, and *The Genius of the Few*.

29 M Wood, *Legacy: A Search for the Origins of Civilization*, ch 1, p 34.

30 According to Oxford etymology, the Old English and Teutonic word 'god' derived from other Western equivalents such as *got, cot, guo, gut,* and *gude* – each referring to 'one who is worshipped'.

31 J Hastings, *Dictionary of the Bible*, under Abraham.

32 Watson E Mills (ed), *Lutterworth Dictionary of the Bible*, Lutterworth Press, Cambridge, 1994, under Abraham.

33 Genesis 14:12.

34 The names of these regional kings were found recorded on tablets presented to the Congress of Orientalists in 1894. *See* Theophilus G Pinches, *The Old Testament in the Light of the Historical Records and Legends of Assyria and Babylonia*, SPCK, London, 1902, ch 6, pp 222–23.

35 Genesis 14:18–19.

36 Matthew 26:26–28.

37 *Scroll of The Rule*, Annex II, 17–22. For details of the *Messianic Rule, see* Geza Vermes, *The Complete Dead Sea Scrolls in English*, Penguin, London, 1997, pp 157–60.

38 Artists such as Dieric Bouts the Elder (1415–75), Peter Paul Rubens (1577–1640), Franz Franken II (1581–1642), Giovanni Benedetto Castiglione (1610–70), Giovanni Battista Tiepolo (1696–1770).

39 EA Speiser, *The Anchor Bible – Genesis* (translation from Hebrew text), Doubleday, Garden City, NY, 1964, ch 17, p 108.

40 G Vermes, *The Complete Dead Sea Scrolls in English*, p 500.

41 2 Samuel 8:17.
42 Genesis 14:18.

43 JW Jack, *The Ras Shamra Tablets*, ch 3, p 21.

44 Genesis 33:20. These various Genesis entries are cited, along with others, in *Ibid*, ch 3, p 14.

Chapter 4: GODS AND GODDESSES

1 Genesis 15:7.

2 Genesis 17:7–8.

3 JW Jack, *The Ras Shamra Tablets*, ch 5, pp 38–41.

4 H Frankfort, *Kingship and the Gods*, ch 17, pp 235–36.

5 Zecharia Sitchin, *The 12th Planet*, Avon, New York, NY, 1978, ch 5, p 48.

6   EA Speiser, *The Anchor Bible – Genesis*, ch 12, pp 75–76.

7   Sir Ernest A Wallis Budge, *Babylonian Life and History* (1886), rep. Dorset Press, New York, NY, 1992, ch 3, p 73.

8   Genesis 11:17.

9   Genesis 11:9.

10 Sir EAW Budge, *Babylonian Life and History*, ch 3, p 61.

11 M Wood, *Legacy: A Search for the Origins of Civilization*, ch 1, p 34

12 For example: Allesandro Allori, William Blake, Sir Edward Burne-Jones, Frans Franken, Jusepe de Ribera, Tintoreto, Georgio Vasari.

13 Genesis 28:12–13.

14 Genesis 28:17.

15 JW Jack, *The Ras Shamra Tablets*, ch 3, pp 1–15.

16 C and BJ O'Brien, *The Shining Ones*, ch 3, p 66.

17 Genesis 3:9.

18 Genesis 35:7

19 Genesis 35:10

20 Raphael Patai, *The Hebrew Goddess*, Wayne State University Press, Detroit, IL, 1967, ch 5, p 117.

21 Elath (Elat) is the feminine form of El. *See* William Foxwell Albright, *Yahweh and the Gods of Canaan*, Athlone Press, University of London, London, 1968, ch 4, p 165. The port of Elath on the Red Sea's Gulf of Aqaba was named after her. Also, the son of Leah's maid Zilpah (by Jacob) was named Asher after Lady Asherah, *see* Genesis 10:13.

22 Referenced in 2 Kings 14:22 and 16:6.

23 Once in Exodus, once in Jeremiah, once in Micah, twice in Isaiah, three times in Deuteronomy, four times in 1 Samuel, five times in Judges, and twenty-seven times in the books of Kings and Chronicles.

24 William L Reed, *The Asherah in the Old Testament*, Texas Christian University Press, Fort Worth, TX, 1949, ch 1, p 2.

25 In strict terms, Baalim and Ashtaroth are titular plurals of Baal and Ashtoreth.

26 For example, Judges 2:11.

27 Such as Judges 2:13 and 10:6.

28 1 Samuel 7:4.

29 In 1 Kings 18:19 it is stated that there were 400 priests of Asherah (Priests of the Groves, as Asherah's cult was called) at the table of Jezebel of Tyre, the wife of King Ahab of Israel, c.876 BC.

30 Jeremiah 7:18, 44:17–19, 25.

31 2 Kings 23.

32 W Robertson Smith, *The Religion of the Semites*, Adam & Charles Black, London, 1894, ch 5, p 211. (The term Anathoth means 'Images of Anath'.)

33 Jeremiah 1:1.

34 Kabbalah is neither an intellectual discipline, nor a rational exegesis of Jewish Law like the *Talmud*. It is essentially a code of practice and a way of life, fully integrated with Judaism as a whole. *See* Perle Epstein, *Kabalah – The Way of the Jewish Mystic*, Shambhala Publications, Boston, MA, 1988, p xvii. Also *see* Lewis Browne (ed), *The Wisdom of Israel*, Michael Joseph, London, 1948, p 13, under Cabala. The most important work of the Kabbalah is *Sefer ha Zohar* (The Book of Splendour, or Radiance) – close to a million words of applied scriptural philosophy based on ancient Jewish traditions and written in a form of literary Aramaic. It was compiled in 1286 by Moses de Leon in Castile, Spain, and its content was attributed to the 2nd-century Palestinian mystic Shimeon ben Yohai. For an overview on traditional Kabbalah, *see* Gershom G Scholem, *Major Trends in Jewish Mysticism*, Thames & Hudson, London, 1955.

35 R Patai, *The Hebrew Goddess*, ch 4, pp 97–99.

36 Exodus 36.

37 In Hebrew, the Tabernacle, constructed by Moses in Sinai, is known as the *Mishkan* (the Tent of Meeting).

38 Steve Davies, 'The Canaanite Hebrew Goddess' in C Olson (ed), *The Book of the Goddess Past and Present*, Crossroad Publishing, New York, NY, 1989, p 77.

39 Exodus 21:23–24.

40 Forbidden to own land in Europe, the Jews had turned to trade and banking, but money-lending was subsequently prohibited by the Church of Rome. King Edward I Plantagenet had all Jews expelled from England in 1209, with the exception of skilled physicians.

41 In respect of God's wrath, Numbers 21:14 actually mentions the ancient *Wars of the Lord*, a book which does not appear in the Old Testament canon – *see* EA Speiser, *The Anchor Bible – Genesis*, Intro, p xxxix. Other texts, which are cited but not included, are the *Book of the Lord* (Isaiah 34:16) and the *Book of Jasher* (Joshua 10:13, 2 Samuel 1:18).

2 GG Scholem, *Major Trends in Jewish Mysticism*, lecture 6, p 229.

43 S Davies, 'The Canaanite Hebrew Goddess' in C Olson (ed), *The Book of the Goddess Past and Present*, p 78.

44 The Battle of Karkar in 853 BC, when Shalmaneser III of Assyria recorded his opponent as King Ahab of Israel.

45 For a good general overview on these chronological matters, *see* the *Times Atlas of Archaeology (Past Worlds)*, Times Books, London, 1988.

46 Jeremy Black and Anthony Green, *Gods, Demons and Symbols of Ancient Mesopotamia*, British Museum Press, London, 1992, intro, p 11.

47 Sir CL Woolley, *The Sumerians*, ch 1, p 20

48 In 1853, the Assyriologist, Sir Henry Rawlinson, announced to the Royal Asiatic Society that he had found an interesting pre-Sumerian script in Babylonia – a non-Semitic writing which he proffered was probably of Scythian origin from Central Europe. But his colleagues were not convinced and they decided to call this early script Akkadian (Akkad being the older name for Babylonia). At this, Rawlinson made the point that the ancient Scythians (a transient kingly tribe who first domesticated the horse before 4000 BC) were indeed the early occupiers of Akkad in pre-Sumerian times. Notwithstanding this, the matter was dropped and there was deemed to be no connection between this script and the emergent Sumerian cuneiform. *See* Samuel Noah Kramer, *The Sumerians*, University of Chicago Press, Chicago, IL, 1963, ch 1, p 20.

In support of Rawlinson's theory, a form of writing, identical to that found in Akkad, has been unearthed in the Transylvanian village of Tartaria in the Balkans. In the 1940s three small clay tablets were found in an ash-filled dedication pit and, as detailed in the journal *Scientific American* of May 1968, their markings are in many ways similar to later symbols emanating from Crete in about 2000 BC. Perhaps more surprisingly, they are of precisely the same style as that which preceded *cuneiform* in Mesopotamia, and the symbols relate directly to those found at Jemdat Nasr, near Babylon, by the Oxford Assyriologist Stephen Langdon in 1925.

49 SN Kramer, *Sumerian Mythology*, intro, p 21.

50 Recommended reading on ancient Sumer, apart from Sir Charles Leonard Woolley's *The Sumerians* (above), includes Thorkild Jacobsen's *The Treasures of Darkness*, Georges Roux's, *Ancient Iraq* and SN Kramer, *The Sumerians*.

51 Genesis 17:7–8.

52 Genesis 17:19.

Chapter 5: IN THE BEGINNING

1 Flavius Josephus, *The Works of Flavius Josephus*, including *The Antiquities of the Jews*, *The Wars of the Jews* and *Against Apion*, (trans, William Whiston), Milner & Sowerby, London, 1870.

NOTES AND REFERENCES

2 Charles Darwin was not the first in the field of evolutionary research. The French naturalist, George, Comte de Buffon, Keeper of the *Jardin de Roi*, published *Epochs of Nature* in 1778. The Scottish physician James Hutton (the acclaimed founder of geology) published his *Theory of the Earth* in 1785. The French anatomist Baron Georges Cuvier (father of palaeontology) published his *Tableau éleméntaire de l'histoire naturelle des animaux* in 1798. This was followed by his great work, *Le règne animal*. The French naturalist, le Chevalier de Jean Baptiste de Monet Lamark, Professor of Zoology at the University of Paris, published his *Philosophie Zoologique* in 1809. This was followed by the *Histoire naturelle des animaux sans vertebrates*. The Scotsman Sir Charles Lyell published his *Principles of Geology* in the early 1830s. Charles Darwin published his *On the Origin of Species by Means of Natural Selection* in 1859. This was followed by *The Descent of Man* in 1871.

3 Genesis 1:28.

4 Intelligent Design research is fronted by the Discovery Institute, 1511 Third Ave, Suite 808, Seattle, WA 98101.

5 'Creationism, Intelligent Design, and other claims of supernatural intervention in the origin of life or of species are not science' in Committee for Science and Creationism, *Science and Creationism: A View from the National Academy of Sciences*, 2nd edition, National Academy of Sciences, National Academies Press, Washington, DC, 1999.

6 This was ascertained in 1997, when a team led by Dr Svante Pääbo of the University of Munich managed to extract DNA (deoxyribonucleic acid) from a Neanderthal upper armbone fragment. Mitochondrial DNA is passed down, unchanged, from mothers to their children, and, apart from the odd random mutation, all today's humans have very similar sequences. It transpired that the 40,000 year-old Neanderthal DNA was so significantly different that it had to be that of an entirely separate species. The scientists announced that, without question, the Neanderthal race was a 'biological dead end' and that there is no indication of any crossbreeding with Cro-Magnon *homo sapiens*. It was possible, they said, that Neanderthalers and *homo sapiens* had some form of common ancestor about 600,000 years ago, but this could not be proven and was of little relevance. *The Times*, 11 July 1997, from a report in the scientific journal *Cell*.

7 'Leg bone yields DNA secrets of man's Neanderthal Eve', Ian Sample, science correspondent, in *The Guardian*, Friday August 8 2008.

8 For further reading on Intelligent Design, *see* Michael Behe, *Darwin's Black Box*, Free Press, Simon & Schuster, New York, NY, 1996.

9 Genesis 2:2.

10 Alexander Heidel, *The Babylonian Genesis*, University of Chicago Press, Chicago, IL, 1942, ch 1, p 16.

11 *Ibid*, ch 1, p 14.

12 G Roux, *Ancient Iraq*, ch 6, p 86.

13 A Heidel, *The Babylonian Genesis*, ch 1, p 1.

14 These waters were called *Apsû* (male) – the 'sweet waters'; Mummu (male) – the 'veiling mist', and *Tiâmat* (female) – the 'salt waters'. *See* G Roux, *Ancient Iraq*, ch 6, p 86.

15 Genesis 1:2.

16 Robert Graves and Raphael Patai, *Hebrew Myths – The Book of Genesis*, Cassell, London, 1964, ch 2, p 31.

17 Genesis 1:14.

18 A Heidel, *The Babylonian Genesis*, ch 1, p 46.

19 Genesis 3:22.

20 James M Robinson (ed), *The Nag Hammadi Library*, Coptic Gnostic Library: Institute for Antiquity and Christianity, EJ Brill, Leiden, 1977, 'On the Origin if the World', p 163.

21 The word *ruah*, which was wrongly translated in Genesis as 'spirit', actually meant 'wind'. *See* R Graves, and R Patai, *Hebrew Myths – The Book of Genesis*, ch 2, p 31.

22 SN Kramer, *Sumerian Mythology*, ch 2, p 69.

23 *Ibid*, ch 2, p 74.

24 *Ibid*, ch 2, pp 73–74

25 Robert Winston, *The Story of God*, Bantam, London, 2005, ch 4, p 115.

26 SN Kramer, *Sumerian Mythology*, Intro, p 21.

27 The Sumerians were not so called because they lived in Sumer. The reverse was the case: the land was called Sumer because the Sumerians settled there. The Sumerians gained their own descriptive name directly from their unique language, which was itself called *Sumerian*. Hence, they are more correctly defined as 'Sumerian speaking people'. *See* G Roux, *Ancient Iraq*, ch 5, p 75.

28 Sir CL Woolley, *Ur of the Chaldees*, ch 1, p 19.

29 G Roux, *Ancient Iraq*, ch 5, p 75.

30 Details of Sumerian schools are given in SN Kramer, *History Begins at Sumer*, ch 1, pp 35–41.

31 Z Sitchin, *The 12th Planet*, ch 2, p 22.

32 T Jacobsen, *The Treasures of Darkness*, ch 3, p 86.

33 Apsû, and Tiâmat were regarded as having had a son called Mummu, whose brothers and sisters were born as two male and female pairs. The first were Lahmu and his sister Lahâmu, and then Anshar and his sister

Kishar. In due course, Anshar and Kishar produced a son who was to reign overall. This son was An, Lord of the Sky.

34 David Day, *Tolkien's Ring*, HarperCollins, London, 1994, ch 3, p 31.

35 *Ibid*, ch 1, pp 13–14.

36 As well as their Sumerian names, the *Anannage* also became known by alternative Semitic names in Akkad and Babylonia. In this regard, Antu was also called Nammu, and Ki was called Urash.

37 T Jacobsen, *The Treasures of Darkness*, ch 4, p 117.

38 Nîn-kharsag (or Nîn-khursag) was also known as Nîn-mah, the Great Lady.

39 Z Sitchin, *The 12th Planet*, ch 4, p 102,

40 T Jacobsen, *The Treasures of Darkness*, ch 1, p 17.

41 C and BJ O'Brien, *The Genius of the Few*, ch 2, p 27.

42 G Roux, *Ancient Iraq*, ch 6, p 83.

43 T Jacobsen, *The Treasures of Darkness*, ch 1, p 17.

44 Genesis 15:7.

45 Genesis 17:1.

46 Genesis 28:13.

47 Genesis 35:1.

48 Genesis 46:3.

49 Genesis 48:3.

50 Exodus 3:6.

51 Exodus 3:15.

52 Exodus 6:3.

53 WE Mills (ed), *Lutterworth Dictionary of the Bible*, under God, Names of.

Part III – God of the Enclosure

Chapter 6: THE EDEN PROJECT

1 Woolley's digs in Iraq were largely funded by the wealthy English crime novelist Agatha Christie who, in 1930, married Woolley's assistant Max Mallowan.

2 G Roux, *Ancient Iraq*, ch 4, p 62.

3 SN Kramer, *Sumerian Mythology*, ch 2, p 51,

4 SN Kramer, *Sumerian Mythology*, ch 2, p 53, and ch 5, p 115, note 53.

5 SN Kramer, *History Begins at Sumer*, ch 14, pp 164–65.

6 G Roux, *Ancient Iraq*, ch 4, p 62.

7 In practice, we remain today within the final throes of the Ice Age until the ice-sheet polar remnants of Greenland and Antarctica have finally dispersed and the current Holocene period becomes fully interglacial.

8 Steve Gagné, *The Energetics of Food*, Spiral Sciences, USA, 2006, ch 38, p 445.

9 *Ibid*, ch 38, pp 452–60.

10 *Ibid*, ch 37, p 426.

11 *Ibid*, ch 37, p 438.

12 *Ibid*, ch 37, p 430–32.

13 'Tapping Crops' Genetic Wealth' in *Scientific American*, August 2004, pp 28–33.

14 S Gagné, The Energetics of Food, ch 13, p 87.

15 Daniel Zohary and Maria Hopf, *Domestication of Plants in the Old World: The Origin and Spread of Cultivated Plants in West Asia, Europe and the Nile Valley*, Oxford University Press, Oxford, 2001.

16 The Patrick Foundation – http://www.goldenageproject.org.uk/ *Golden Age Project*.

17 EA Speiser, *The Anchor Bible – Genesis*, ch 2, p 16. The Akkadian variant of the word was *edin*.

18 The Patrick Foundation *Kharsag Research Project* – http://www.goldenageproject.org.uk/kharsagresearch.html

19 Charles Hapgood, *The Earth's Shifting Crust*, Pantheon Books, New York, NY, 1958.

20 Charles Hapgood, *Maps of the Ancient Sea Kings*, Chilton Books, Philadelphia, PA, 1966.

21 Charles Hapgood, *The Path of the Pole*, Chilton Books, Philadelphia, PA, 1970.

22 The *Piri Reis Map* was discovered in 1929 when Topkapı Palace, Istanbul, was being converted into a museum. It is the extant western third of a world map drawn on gazelle skin in 1513 by the Ottoman-Turkish admiral and cartographer Piri Reis.

23 Paul A LaViolette, *Earth Under Fire*, Starburst, Schenectady, NY, 1997, ch 12, p 314.

24 Richard B Alley (2000), 'The Younger Dryas cold interval as viewed from central Greenland' in *Quaternary Science Reviews* 19 (1), pp 213–26.

25 Richard Firestone, Allen West and Simon Warwick-Smith, *The Cycle of Cosmic Catatrophes*, Bear, Rochester, VT, 2006, ch 11, pp 132–148.

26 DS Allan and JB Dellair, *Cataclysm*, Bear, Rochester, VT, 1997, chs 8–9, pp 191–95.

27 Derek S Allan, 'An Unexplained Arctic Catastrophe – Part II: Some Unanswered Questions', in *Chronology & Catastrophism Review*, Society for Interdisciplinary Studies, September 2005.

28 Fragments from the *Book of Noah* were found preserved among the Dead Sea Scrolls in Qumrân Cave-1, and two large fragments found in Cave-4. Some fuller extracts from the *Book of Noah* were, however, interpolated into a parallel *Book of Enoch* (also found in part at Qumrân) – from a translated section of which the given extract is taken. *See* Richard Laurence (trans 1881), *The Book of Enoch the Prophet*, DeVorss, Camarillo, CA, 1995, ch LXIV, p 78.

29 Robin McKie, science editor, *The Observer*, Sunday 20 May 2007.

30 O Bar-Yosef and A Belfer-Cohen, 'Facing environmental crisis. Societal and cultural changes at the transition from the Younger Dryas to the Holocene in the Levant', in René TJ Cappers and Sytze Bottema (eds), *The Dawn of Farming in the Near East*, Oxbow, Oxford, 2002, pp 55–66.

31 John Punnett Peters, *Nippur or Explorations and Adventures on the Euphrates: The Narrative of the University of Pennsylvania Expedition to Babylonia in the Years 1888–1890*, GP Putnam's Sons, New York, NY, 1897.

32 Clarence S Fisher, *Babylonian Expedition of the University of Pennsylvania, Part II, Excavations at Nippur: Plans, Details and Photographs of the Buildings, with Numerous Objects Found in Them During the Excavations of 1889, 1890, 1893–1896, 1899–1900*. University of Pennsylvania, Philadelphia, PA, 1905.

33 HV Hilprecht, *The Excavations in Assyria and Babylonia, The Babylonian Expedition of the University of Pennsylvania Series D: Researches and Treatises*, Department of Archaeology of the University of Pennsylvania, Philadelphia, PA, 1904.

34 *Annual Report of the Provost to the Board of Trustees, September 1st, 1901, to September 1st, 1902*, Elibron Classics, Adamant Media, Boston, MA, fac. rep. 2004, pp 140–41.

35 JA Halloran, *Sumerian Lexicon: A Dictionary Guide to the Ancient Sumerian Language*, Logogram Publishing, Los Angels, CA, 2006

36 C and BJ O'Brien, *The Genius of the Few*, ch 3, p 35.

37 George A Barton, *Miscellaneous Babylonian Inscriptions*, Yale University Press, New Haven, CT, 1918, Introductory Note.

38 *Ibid*, cylinder text no.1 (collection no. 8383), p 5.

39 SN Kramer, *Sumerian Mythology*, ch 1, p 44.

40 *Ibid*, Intro, p 18.

41 Golden Age Project – *The Genius of the Few*
http://www.goldenageproject.org.uk/genius.html

42 C and BJ O'Brien, *The Genius of the Few*, ch 3, p 39.

43 GA Barton, *Miscellaneous Babylonian Inscriptions*, no 4, p 34.

44 *Ibid*, ch 3, p 43.

45 C and BJ O'Brien, *The Genius of the Few*, ch 6, p 139.

46 Today's aptly named 'Eden Project' in England is the world's largest greenhouse complex. Nestling within a giant crater, 50 metres deep, near St Austell Bay in Cornwall, are two gigantic geodesic conservatories. One is a majestic rainforest cathedral; the other is host to the fruits and flowers of the Mediterranean, South Africa and California –
http://www.edenproject.com

47 Kharsag: Latitude 33° 30' 4" N. Longitude 35° 50' 22" E.

48 G Vermes, *The Complete Dead Sea Scrolls in English*, (4Q201), pp 513–14.

49 1 Enoch 6:6 in RH Charles (trans), *The Book of Enoch* (revised from Dillmann's edition of the Ethiopic text, 1893), Oxford University Press, Oxford, 1906 and 1912.

50 C and BJ O'Brien, *The Genius of the Few*, ch 2, p 28.

51 *Ibid*, ch 4, p 116.

52 Alexander Heidel, *The Gilgamesh Epic and Old Testament Parallels*, University of Chicago Press, Chicago, IL, 1949, pp 137–38.

53 *Ibid*, ch 6, p 126.

54 *Ibid*, ch 8, pp 167–72.

Chapter 7: DAWN OF THE EARTHLINGS

1 Genesis 1:27 and 2:7.

2 Genesis 3:20.

3 Robert Alter, *Genesis*, WW Norton, New York, NY, 1996, ch 1, p 5.

4 Genesis 2:7.

5 R Alter, *Genesis*, intro, p xii.

6 F Josephus, *Antiquities of the Jews*, bk I, ch I:2.

7 EA Speiser, *The Anchor Bible – Genesis*, ch 2, p 16.

8 Z Sitchin, *The 12th Planet*, ch 12, p 348.

9 *Ibid*, ch 2, p 357.

10 T Jacobsen, *The Treasures of Darkness*, ch 4, p 107.

11 In about 2100 BC, King Gudea of Babylon recorded that Nîn-kharsag was the 'Mother of all children'. *Ibid*, ch 4, p 106.

12 TG Pinches, *The Old Testament in the Light of the Historical Records and Legends of Assyria and Babylonia*, ch 2, p 70.

13 SN Kramer, *Sumerian Mythology*, ch 2, p 73.

14 Samuel Noah Kramer, *Mythologies of the Ancient World*, Anchor Books, Garden City, NY, 1961, p 103.

15 *Ibid*, p 122.

16 Genesis 2:15.

17 T Jacobsen, *The Treasures of Darkness*, ch 4, pp 113–14.

18 Z Sitchin, *The 12th Planet*, ch 12, pp 349–50.

19 SN Kramer, *Sumerian Mythology*, ch 2, p 71.

20 Enki and Nîn-kharsag are identified in the *Atrahasis Epic* by their Akkadian names, Ea and Nîn-igiku.

21 *Atrahasis Epic*, tablet fragment IV, column 4.

22 T Jacobsen, *The Treasures of Darkness*, ch 4, p 108.

23 Z Sitchin, *The 12th Planet*, ch 12, p 351.

24 G Roux, *Ancient Iraq*, ch 7, p 95.

25 *Ibid*, ch 12, p 349.

26 *Adapa Tablet*, Fragment I.

27 *Ibid*, Fragment IV. *See* A Heidel, *The Babylonian Genesis*, pp 152–53

28 T Jacobsen, *The Sumerian King List*, part II, pp 15–23. Kish was a Sumerian region to the east of Babylon, between the Tigris and Euphrates rivers.

29 T Jacobsen, *The Treasures of Darkness*, ch 5, p 159.

30 Mark 14:36; Romans 8:15; Galatians 4:6.

31 H Frankfort, *Kingship and the Gods*, ch 15, p 215.

32 Genesis 3:6.

33 G Roux, *Ancient Iraq*, ch 7, pp 95–96.

34 R Alter, *Genesis*, ch 3, p 15.

35 F Josephus, *Antiquities of the Jews*, bk I, ch I:2.

36 Genesis 2:21–23 relates that Eve was formed by God from a rib taken out of Adam's side.

37 SN Kramer, *History Begins at Sumer*, ch 19, p 210. Also *see* SN Kramer, *The Sumerians*, ch 4, p 149.

38 Genesis 3:7.

39 Genesis 3:21.

Chapter 8: RISE OF THE GUARDIANS

1 Genesis 3:3–6.

2 Genesis 2:17.

3 Genesis 3:17.

4 Jubilees 3:28. Elda is referred to as 'the land of their creation', and was presumably somewhere in Sumer, although the place is not identifiable by that name.

5 Genesis 3:22–24.

6 Genesis 3:16–19.

7 Genesis 3:16.

8 Genesis 1:25.

9 The Koran (*Al-Qur'an*), a collection of individually written remembrances of God's Word by Muhammad and others, was collated during the 2nd caliphate of Umar, and authorized by his successor, Uthmān (AD 644–56).

10 Hippo is now Annaba in Algeria.

11 Genesis 3:14.

12 Genesis 3:22.

13 SN Kramer, *Mythologies of the Ancient World*, p 123.

14 Z Sitchin, *The 12th Planet*, ch 13, p 371.

15 C and BJ O'Brien, *The Genius of the Few*, ch 6, p 136.

16 Genesis 3:3–4.

17 Genesis 3:24.

18 GA Barton, *Miscellaneous Babylonian Inscriptions*, item I, p 9.

19 Robert D Biggs, et al (eds), *The Assyrian Dictionary*, Oriental Institute of the University of Chicago, IL, 1999.

20 JB Pritchard, *Ancient Near Eastern Texts Relating to the Old Testament*, Princeton University Press, Princeton, NJ, 1954, pp 114–18.

21 Psalm 90:2.

22 Psalm 102:25–28.

23 Ivan Engnell, *Studies in Divine Kingship in the Ancient Near East*, Basil Blackwell, Oxford, 1967, ch 2, p 29, note 2.

24 J Maddox, 'Big bang not yet dead but in decline' in *Nature*, vol 377, 1995.

25 Willis Barnstone (ed), *The Other Bible*, HarperSanFrancisco, San Francisco, CA, 1984, 'Haggadah', pp 14–38.

26 *Ibid*, 'Secrets of Enoch', pp 3–9.

27 EA Speiser, *The Anchor Bible – Genesis*, ch 7, p 44.

28 F Josephus, Flavius, *Antiquities of the Jews*, bk I, ch III:1.

29 Z Sitchin, *The 12th Planet*, intro, p vii.

30 1 Enoch 6.

31 1 Enoch 10:16.

32 Daniel 4:13.

33 Daniel 4:23.

34 Jubilees 4:16–18.

35 Jubilees 8:3.

36 1 Enoch 20:20.

37 André Dupont-Sommer, *The Essene Writings from Qumrân* (trans, Geza Vermes), Basil Blackwell, Oxford, 1961, ch 5, p 167.

38 *Ibid*, ch 5, p 124. *Damascus Document*, Manuscript A, 2:17–19.

39 C and BJ O'Brien, *The Genius of the Few*, ch 5, p 97.

40 C Suarès, *The Cipher of Genesis*, ch 16, p 137.

41 T Jacobsen, *The Sumerian King List*, notes, p 142.

42 *Ibid*, ch 16, pp 140–41.

43 *Ibid*, ch 16, p135.

44 Genesis 25:31–34.

45 Genesis 4:10.

46 Genesis 4:11–16.

47 EA Speiser, *The Anchor Bible – Genesis*, ch 4, p 31.

48 R Graves and R Patai, *Hebrew Myths – The Book of Genesis*, ch 16, pp 96–97.

49 I Engnell, *Studies in Divine Kingship in the Ancient Near East*, ch 2, p 37.

50 AM Hocart, *Kingship*, Oxford University Press, Oxford, 1927, ch 8, p 103.

51 Although the *Book of Jubilees* (The history of the division of the days of the Law) was excluded from the Old Testament canon, it does form part of the Jewish *Midrash* (Inquiry), a rabbinical interpretation of biblical text.

52 Jubilees 4:8.

53 Rutherford H Platt (ed), *The Forgotten Books of Eden*, New American Library, New York, NY, 1974, '2 Adam and Eve', LXXIV, p 53.

54 The *Talmud* ('teaching') is essentially a commentary on the Mishnah, compiled originally in Hebrew and Aramaic and deriving from two independently important streams of Jewish tradition: the Palestinian and the Babylonian. The *Mishnah* – or Repetition – is an early codification of Jewish law, based on ancient compilations and edited in Palestine by the Ethnarch (Governor) Judah I in the early 3rd century AD. It consists of traditional law (*Halakah*) on a wide range of subjects, derived partly from old custom and partly from biblical law (*Tannaim*) as interpreted by the rabbis (teachers).

55 Genesis 4:17–18.

56 Genesis 4:26, 5:1–25.

57 EA Speiser, *The Anchor Bible – Genesis*, ch 5, pp 35–36. Also *see* J Hastings (ed) *Dictionary of the Bible*, under Lamech.

58 Genesis 4:19–22.

59 T Jacobsen, *The Sumerian King List*, part V, p 181. Also *see* G Roux, *Ancient Iraq*, ch 8, p 117.

Chapter 9: ANNALS OF THE DELUGE

1 Genesis 6:5–7.

2 Genesis 7:2–3.

3 Genesis 6:17.

4 In contrast to the Bible, the Koran does give a reason for Noah's particular selection by Allāh, and Noah is of great importance to Islām. Muhammad identified himself most of all with Noah, whom he listed among the great prophets. The Koran explains that Allāh chose Noah (an

ordinary man without any special powers) because he was a true believer, unlike the other elders whose unconditional belief in the will of Allāh was found wanting. Koran 23:31–40. *Al-Qur'an of Mohammed*, Chandos/Frederick Warne, London (undated).

5 Genesis 9:1.

6 A Heidel, *The Gilgamesh Epic and Old Testament Parallels*, p 81, Epic of Gilgamesh, Tablet XI.

7 *See* T Jacobsen, *The Sumerian King List*, part III, p 76.

8 SN Kramer, *History Begins at Sumer*, ch 20, pp 214–19.

9 A Heidel, *The Gilgamesh Epic and Old Testament Parallels*, ch 4, p 224. Also *see* SN Kramer, *Sumerian Mythology*, ch 4, p 97.

10 A Heidel, *The Gilgamesh Epic and Old Testament Parallels*, ch 4, pp 224–25.

11 T Jacobsen, *Treasures of Darkness*, ch 4, pp 116–21.

12 Correctly entitled *Sa nagba imurur*: 'He who saw everything'. Also *see* Leonard Cottrell, *The Land of Shinar*, Souvenir Press, London, 1965, p 42.

13 A Heidel, *The Gilgamesh Epic and Old Testament Parallels*, ch 1, p 15.

14 *Ibid*, ch 2, p 105.

15 *Epic of Gilgamesh*, Tablet XI:19–31.

16 Genesis 4–9.

17 EA Speiser, *The Anchor Bible – Genesis*, ch 5, p 36.

18 Jubilees 11:1–4.

19 R Alter, *Genesis*, intro, p xii.

20 R Graves, and R Patai, *Hebrew Myths – The Book of Genesis*, ch 14, p 85.

21 W Keller, *The Bible as History*, ch 2, p 40.

22 Roy Norvill, *Giants – The Vanished Race of Mighty Men*, Aquarian Press, Wellingborough, 1979, p 58.

23 Sir CL Woolley, *Ur of the Chaldees*, ch 4, pp 137–38.

24 *Ibid*, ch 1, p 25.

25 *Ibid*, ch 2.

26 T Jacobsen, *The Sumerian King List*, part V, p 181.

27 G Roux, *Ancient Iraq*, ch 8, p 117.

28 T Jacobsen, *The Sumerian King List*, part III, p 93.

29 J Hastings (ed), *Dictionary of the Bible*, under Cain.

30 *Ibid*, under Tubalcain.

31 A cylinder-seal inscription denotes that Mes-kalam-dug 's wife was Nîn-banda. *See* G Roux, *Ancient Iraq*, ch 8, p 117.

32 Sir CL Woolley, *Ur of the Chaldees*, ch 1, p 26.

33 W Keller, *The Bible as History*, ch 3, p 50.

Part IV – God of the Covenant

Chapter 10: INTO CANAAN

1 Genesis 9:20–27.

2 Genesis 9:24.

3 Genesis 5:32, 6:10. Some English-language Bibles use the word 'younger' (instead of 'youngest) to lessen the anomaly, but the Hebrew text does not yield this meaning.

4 Genesis 9:25–26.

5 Genesis 17: 8.

6 Alexander the Great of Macedonia, who defeated the Persian Emperor Darius in 333 BC. Destroying the city of Tyre in Phoenicia, he then moved into Egypt and built his citadel of Alexandria.

7 A Dupont-Sommer, *The Essene Writings from Qumrân*, ch 8, p 284.

8 *Ibid*, ch 8, p 285.

9 *Ibid*, ch 8, p 283.

10 Genesis 11:32.

11 Genesis 12:4.

12 Mary Ellen Chase, *Life and Language in the Old Testament*, Collins, London, 1956, ch 3, pp 32–39.

13 Genesis 5:27.

14 Genesis 17:10–13.

15 Genesis 17:5.

16 Genesis 17:15. Sarai and Sarah etymology from the *Oxford Bible Readers Dictionary and Concordance*, Oxford University Press, Oxford (undated).

17 Genesis 11:30.

18 Genesis 25:21.

19 Genesis 29:31.

20 Genesis 12:2.

21 Genesis 16:1–16.

22 Genesis 16:19–21.

23 Genesis 21:14–18.

24 Genesis 17:15–16.

25 Genesis 17:19.

26 Genesis 25:1–2.

27 Genesis 17:18–21.

28 Genesis 22:16.

29 'Hammurabi' – Akkadian, *Khammurabi*, from the Amorite *Ammurapi*, meaning 'The Kinsman is a Healer' (*Ammu*: paternal kinsman + *Rapi*: to heal) – also transliterated as Ammurapi, Hammurapi, or Khammurabi. He was the sixth king of Babylon. Achieving the conquest of Sumer and Akkad, and ending the last Sumerian dynasty of Isin, he was the first king of the Babylonian Empire.

30 D Winton Thomas (ed), *Documents from Old Testament Times*, Harper Torchbooks, New York, NY, 1958, p 32.

31 Genesis 16:6.

32 Nuzi Tablet number 67.

33 Susa, in ancient Elam, is now in Khuzestan, Iran, to where the stela had been taken as plunder by the Elamites in the 12th century BC.

34 Of seven ancient Law Codes so far discovered, four (including the Hammurabi stela) are royal codes which date from the Sumerian era. They are the *Code of Ur-Nammu of Ur* (*c.*2100 BC), the *Code of Lipit-Ishtar of Isin* (19th century BC) and the *Code of the Kingdom of Eshnunna* from the same period. Others are *Middle-Assyrian Laws* from the 12th century BC, *Hittite Laws* from Asia Minor (14th century BC), and the *Laws of the Neo-Babylonian Empire* (*c.*600 BC).

35 Sigmund Freud, *Moses and Monotheism*, Hogarth Press, London, 1939, II, ch 3, pp 44, 49. (Freud previously published his work concerning Moses in the 1932 German *Imago* magazine of psychoanalysis, under the title 'Moses, an Egyptian'.) Also *see* A Osman, *Stranger in the Valley of Kings*, ch 3, p35.

36 R Alter, *Genesis*, ch 17, p 73.

37 Flavius Josephus, *Against Apion*, ch I:22 in *The Works of Flavius Josephus*.

38 Genesis 15:18.

39 Genesis 12:12–15.

40 Genesis 20:12.

41 *M'ãrath Gaze*, published as: Sir Ernest A Wallis Budge (trans), *The Book of the Cave of Treasures*, Religious Tract Society, Manchester, 1927.

42 Amenemhet's other wives were Dedyet, who may also have been his sister, and Sobek'neferu.

43 A Dupont-Sommer, *The Essene Writings from Qumrân*, ch 8, p 286.

44 EA Speiser, *The Anchor Bible – Genesis*, ch 14, p 89; and R Alter, Genesis, ch 12, p 53. As an adjunct to this, both the Hebrew and English texts – when referring to the later period of Sarah's time in the company of King Abimalech of Gerar (Genesis 20:1–6) – make the point that 'Abimalech had not come near her'. But no such statement is made in respect of her relationship with the pharaoh.

45 Genesis 17:16.

46 Genesis 18:1.

47 Genesis 18:3.

48 Genesis 18:17.

49 *Ibid*, ch 23, p 138, note xix.

50 Genesis 19:1.

51 Genesis 19:2–16.

52 Genesis 19:17–38.

53 EA Speiser, *The Anchor Bible – Genesis*, ch 23, p 142. Another suggestion is that bitumen, which abounds in the region, was somehow ignited. *See* J Hastings (ed) *Dictionary of the Bible*, under Cities of the Plain.

54 The title relates to Noah's eldest son, Shem.

55 Coptic was a language of Egypt in the early centuries AD.

56 JM Robinson (ed), *The Nag Hammadi Library*, VII, 1:29.

57 Nag Hammadi III–2: 60:10. Also *see* Jean Doresse, *The Secret Books of the Egyptian Gnostics* (trans, Philip Mairet), Hollis & Carter, London, 1960, ch 6, p 298.

58 Barbara Thiering, *Jesus the Man*, Transworld/Doubleday, London, 1992, appx II, p 312.

59 The first mention of Lake Asphalt is in F Josephus, *Antiquities of the Jews*, bk I, ch IX:1.

60 W Keller, *The Bible As History*, ch 7, p 90.

61 The Dead Sea contains 25% of solid ingredients, mostly sodium chloride (cooking salt), as against 4.6% in most ocean water.

62 W Keller, *The Bible as History*, ch 7, p 96. Information concerning Sanchuniathon is derived from the works of Philo of Byblos (AD *c*.100). Excavations at Ras Shamra (ancient Ugarit) in Syria in 1929 revealed Phoenician documents supporting much of the information in Sanchuniathon's Phoenician and Canaanite histories.

63 BJ Peiser, T Palmer and ME Bailey, *Natural Catastrophes During Bronze Age Civilizations*, pp 79–80.

Chapter 11: STRATEGY OF SUCCESSION

1 C Suarès, *The Cipher of Genesis*, 'Ha-Qabala', p 21.

2 Sometimes rendered as the *Tablet of Destinies* – symbols of concept without nominal expression that formed a cosmic bond between the heavens and the lower world. *See* J Black and A Green, *Gods, Demons and Symbols of Ancient Mesopotamia*, p 173.

3 *See* J Hastings (ed), *Dictionary of the Bible*, under Jewels and Precious Stones – items: sapphire and jacinth. The term originally used in old texts was *sappir*, whereas the word generally related to 'sapphire' in biblical writings was *leshem*.

4 Raziel was Raguel the Holy Watcher, one of the seven archangels of 1 Enoch 20:4. Note: *Raziel ha Malach* has nothing whatever to do with a spurious and currently available work, entitled *The Book of Raziel*, first published in Amsterdam in 1701.

5 Rabbi Yehuda Berg, *The Power of Kabbalah*, Hodder & Stoughton, London, 2003, p 232.

6 Sir Isaac Newton's laws were first published in his *Philosophiae Naturalis Principia Mathematica*, 1687. This work is currently published as: Isaac Newton, *The Principia*, Prometheus, Amherst, NY, 1995.

7 EA Speiser, *The Anchor Bible – Genesis*, ch 14, p 88.

8 Genesis 24:10.

9 Genesis 15:2.

10 Genesis 23:19.

11 Genesis 25:8.

12 Genesis 25:16.

13 R Alter, *Genesis*, ch 24, p 114.

14 BSJ Isserlin, *The Israelites*, Thames & Hudson, London 1998, ch 3, p 68.

15 W Keller, *The Bible as History*, ch 16, p 168.

16 EA Speiser, *The Anchor Bible – Genesis*, ch 31, p 175.

THE ORIGIN OF GOD

17 Genesis 25:25.

18 R Alter, *Genesis*, ch 25, p 129. Also *see* R Graves and R Patai, *Hebrew Myths – The Book of Genesis*, ch 39, p 191.

19 It is possible that the word *se'ar*, which was translated to 'hairy', should perhaps have been *seir*, a synonym for *adom*. EA Speiser, *The Anchor Bible – Genesis*, ch 33, p 195. Also *see* R Alter, *Genesis*, ch 25, p 127.

20 Genesis 25:27.

21 T Jacobsen, *The Treasures of Darkness*, ch 7, p 197. Also *see* EA Speiser, *The Anchor Bible – Genesis*, ch 33, p 196.

22 L and D Cohn-Sherbok, *A Short Reader in Judaism*, ch 1, p 13.

23 Genesis 35:10

24 Genesis 25:27.

25 EA Speiser, *The Anchor Bible – Genesis*, ch 33, p 195.

26 Genesis 25: 30–34.

27 The Nuzi tablets are held at The Oriental Institute, Chicago University; The Harvard Semitic Museum; The Yale University Babylonian Collection; The Hearst Museum, Berkeley; The Louvre Museum, Paris; The British Museum, London, The Iraq Museum, Baghdad, and The Hermitage Museum, St Petersburg. Also *see* A Osman, *Stranger in the Valley of Kings*, ch 3, p 39. The ancient city of Nuzi is now called Yoghlan Tepe.

28 Genesis 17:16.

29 Genesis 26:1–6.

30 EA Speiser, *The Anchor Bible – Genesis*, ch 34, p 200.

31 Genesis 26:7–24.

32 Genesis 27:1–41.

33 Genesis 26:34 gives Esau's wives as Judith (daughter of Beeri the Hittite) and Bashemath (daughter of Elon the Hittite). Genesis 28:9 cites the wife Mahalath (daughter of Ishmael, sister of Nebajoth). Genesis 36:1–3 has Esau's wives as Adah (daughter of Elon the Hittite), Aholibamah (granddaughter of Zibeon the Hivite) and Bashemath (daughter of Ishmael, sister of Nebajoth).

34 Genesis 36:3.

35 Genesis 36:10.

36 Genesis 36:17.

37 Genesis 36:31 and 1 Chronicles 1:43.

356

38 R Alter, *Genesis*, ch 36, p 204.

39 Genesis 17:20.

40 Genesis 28:13.

41 Genesis 29:16–30.

42 Genesis 29:31 – 30:9.

43 Genesis 31:13.

44 R Alter, *Genesis*, ch 31, p 169.

45 Genesis 31:17–52.

46 Genesis 35:11.

47 Genesis 34:24.

48 Genesis 34:25–29.

49 Genesis 34:30.

50 Genesis 25:16.

51 Genesis 37:3.

52 R Alter, *Genesis*, ch 37, p 209.

53 JR Porter, *The Illustrated Guide to the Bible*, Duncan Baird, London, 1995, p 48.

54 EA Speiser, *The Anchor Bible – Genesis*, ch 49, p 290.

55 This is now the site of *Tell Dothan* at the southern extremity of the Valley of Jezreel in Samaria, a little south of Jenin. The site was used from the Neolithic to the Hellenistic periods.

56 For details concerning the writers, *see* EA Speiser, *The Anchor Bible – Genesis*, ch 49, p 292.

57 Genesis 37:24–28.

58 Genesis 37:36.

59 Alternatively *Teima* or *Temâ* (Tamar), as mentioned in Ezekiel 47:19.

60 *The Koran* (*Al-Qur'an of Mohammed*), Chandos/Frederick Warne, London (undated), Intro, p 4.

61 2 Samuel 13:1.

62 2 Samuel 14:27.

63 The name Pharez derives from the Hebrew perets, meaning to 'breach' or 'burst forth'.

Part V – God of Tradition

Chapter 12: YAHWEH THE INEFFABLE

1 Genesis 41:43.

2 Genesis 41:50–52. On marrying Asenath, It is explained in Genesis 41:45 that Joseph was dubbed Zaphnath-paaneah. This is said by the Israeli Bible scholar, Moshe Weinfeld of the Hebrew University of Jerusalem, to mean something akin to 'God speaks – he lives' [in reference to the Israelite God in Egypt]. An alternative translation comes from the German Egyptologist, Georg Steindorff, who relates that the name means 'The god speaks – May he live'.

3 W Keller, *The Bible as History*, ch 8, p 103.

4 Genesis 39:7–18.

5 A Osman, *Stranger in the Valley of Kings*, Tuya app, p 160.

6 *Ibid*, ch 8, pp 99–100.

7 The name Goshen (Gosen) relates to a particular type of soil, similar to that found in parts of Galilee. *See* WF Albright, *Yahweh and the Gods of Canaan*, ch 4, pp 134–35.

8 Genesis 46:3.

9 *Ibid*, ch 8, pp 104–05. (The *Bahr Yusuf* was largely engineered from the 12th dynasty of Egypt onwards.) *See* also Peter A Clayton, *Chronicle of the Pharaohs*, Thames and Hudson, London, 1994, pp 82, 84.

10 *Ibid*, pp 115–16. The books of Exodus 13:19 and Joshua 24:32 each relate to the bones of Joseph, claiming that the Israelites took them out of Egypt for burial at Shechem. But this is inconsistent with Genesis 50:26, which states that the body of Joseph the vizier was embalmed in Egypt. If any bones were removed by the Israelites, they might perhaps have been the bones of the original Joseph or someone of his era, but they could not possibly have been those of Joseph the vizier, whose mummy is now in the Cairo Museum.

11 Ahmed Osman, *The House of the Messiah*, HarperCollins, London, 1992, p 2.

12 Cyril Aldred, *Akhenaten, King of Egypt*, Thames & Hudson, London, 1988, ch 19, p 220.

13 PA Clayton, *Chronicle of the Pharaohs*, p 115.

14 Ibid, p 123.

15 EA Speiser, *The Anchor Bible – Genesis*, ch 53, p 314.

16 A Osman, *Stranger in the Valley of Kings*, ch 12, pp 124–25.

17 JH Breasted was the founder of The Oriental Institute at the University of Chicago in 1922. Also *see* PA Clayton, *Chronicle of the Pharaohs*, pp 109–10.

18 Genesis 15:18.

19 A Osman, *Stranger in the Valley of Kings*, ch 12, p 122.

20 The alternative, *adonai*, meant 'my lord'. Adon is used biblically as a name of God and also as a description of mundane lords: Exodus 4:11; Judges 6:15; 2 Samuel 7:18–20; Psalm. 8, and 114:7, 135:5, 141:8, 109:21–28, plus numerous times in Ezekiel and Daniel.

21 Ahmed Osman, *Moses, Pharaoh of Egypt*, Grafton/Collins, London, 1990, ch 37, p 167.

22 James Baikie, *The Amarna Age*, A&C Black, London, 1926, p 91.

23 Pi-Ramesses is often said to have been a grain storehouse centre, but this description has now been overturned. The concept arose because an inscription relating to a public official was translated to define him as an 'overseer of granaries'. It now transpires that the correct translation is 'overseer of foreign lands'. *See* A Osman, *Stranger in the Valley of Kings*, ch 10, pp 111–12. Also TE Peet, *Egypt and the Old Testament*, ch 4, p 84.

24 Excellent studies of individual women in the Old and New Teatament scriptures are found in John Baldock, *Women in the Bible*, Arcturus, London, and Foulsham, Slough, 2006.

25 Genesis 46:27.

26 Individual tribal and sectional numbers are detailed in the book of Numbers. The *Sunday Times* reported, 30 November 1997, that research by Colin Humphreys, Professor of Materials Science at Cambridge University, revealed that the actual number of Israelites was substantially smaller than reported because of translatory misunderstandings of the Hebrew word *lp* (*elep*). This was taken to mean 1,000, but apparently meant 'troop'. However, even if a designated troop was less than 1,000 men, the overall number of Israelites would still be tens of thousands, if not hundreds of thousands, and remains quite inequitable against the original seventy Israelites of only three generations before.

27 WR Smith, *The Religion of the Semites*, ch 1, p 1.

28 I Velikovsky, *Ages in Chaos*, ch 1, p 10, note 18.

29 Numbers 1:41.

30 DM Rohl, *A Test of Time: The Bible from Myth to History*, ch 4, p 116.

31 I Velikovsky, *Ages in Chaos*, ch 1, p 10. Also *see* T Eric Peet, *Egypt and the Old Testament*, Liverpool University Press, Liverpool, 1922, ch 5, p 124. (There were *Aperu/Habirû* in Egypt as late as the reign of Rameses IV.)

32 *Lifelines* magazine, Lifelines Trust, Honiton, July 1997.

33 Exodus 10:22–23. As featured in the journal *Nature*, Macmillan, London, summer 1997.

34 I Velikovsky, *Ages in Chaos*, ch 1, p 27.

35 Exodus 12:40.

36 In F Josephus, *Antiquities of the Jews*, bk II, ch XV:2. Josephus claims that the said 430 years related to the period 'from the time Abraham first came into Canaan', with only 215 of those years being the sojourn in Egypt. It appears that Josephus obtained the essence of this information from the Greek *Septuagint*, which states: 'And the sojourning of the children of Israel, that is which they sojourned in the land of Egypt and in the land of Canaan, was four hundred and thirty years'. However, the Greek text does not refer to Abraham in this context, as does Josephus; it refers specifically to the 'children of Israel', who were the descendants of Abraham's grandson Jacob-Israel.

37 Genesis 12:7, 33:20.

38 Genesis 35:14.

39 Genesis 31:54, 46:1.

40 Exodus 26–27.

41 As, for example, in Genesis 7:1, 28:3, 35:11; Numbers 23:22; Joshua 3:10; 2 Samuel 22:31, 32; Nehemiah 1:5, 9:32; Isaiah 9:6, and Ezekiel 10:5.

42 Genesis 14:18; Numbers 24:16; Deuteronomy 26:19, 32:8; Psalms 7:17, 18:13, 56:2, 78:35, 97:9; Daniel 7:25, 27, and Isaiah 14:14.

43 First used in Genesis 17:1, 2, and in 31:29, 49:24, 25; Ruth 1:20, 21; 31 times in Job; Proverbs 3:27; Micah 2:1, and Isaiah 60:15, 16, 66:10–13.

44 Including 32 times in Genesis 1. Also Genesis 6:18, 9:15, 17:7, 50:24; 1 Kings 8:23; Jeremiah 31:33; Isaiah 40:1, along with numerous mentions in Ecclesiastes, Daniel and Jonah.

45 Genesis 31:42, 54.

46 R Alter, *Genesis*, ch 31, pp 174, 176.

47 Leviticus 14–16.

48 2 Kings 21:3.

49 Robert Graves, *The White Goddess*, Faber & Faber, London, 1961, ch 16, p 287.

50 J Hastings, *Dictionary of the Bible*, under God.

51 Exodus 6:3, Psalms 83:18, Isaiah 12:2, Isaiah 26:4.

52 Exodus 20:4.

53 Psalm 90:2.

54 Psalm 102:25–28.

55 T Jacobsen, *The Treasures of Darkness*, ch 7, pp 217–18.

56 Exodus 3:14–16.

57 Exodus 19:5.

58 Exodus 19:9.

59 Leviticus 9:23.

60 Numbers 12:4–10.

Chapter 13: THE MOSES REVELATION

1 Exodus 2:1.

2 Exodus 6:20.

3 Exodus 1:7.

4 Exodus 2:2–10.

5 Exodus 2:11.

6 G Roux, *Ancient Iraq*, ch 9, p 128.

7 S Freud, *Moses and Monotheism*, I, ch 1, pp 12–13.

8 A Osman, *Moses, Pharaoh of Egypt*, ch 6, p 66.

9 James Henry Breasted, *The Dawn of Consciousness*, Charles Scribner's Sons, New York, NY, 1934, p 350. Also *see* A Osman, *Moses, Pharaoh of Egypt*, ch 6, p 66.

10 WF Albright, *Yahweh and the Gods of Canaan*, ch 4, p 144.

11 Exodus 2:21.

12 Exodus 3:1.

13 Genesis 36:4.

14 Exodus 11:3.

15 F Josephus, *Against Apion*, bk I, chs XXVI–VII.

16 F Josephus, *The Antiquities of the Jews*, bk II, ch X:2.

17 It was the mitochondrial DNA of the matrilineal succession that was important to the dynasties. Although mitochondria is inherited from mothers by both sons and daughters, it is only passed on by the daughters,

361

since this DNA resides within the female egg cells. *See* Steve Jones, *In the Blood: God, Genes and Destiny*, HarperCollins, London, 1996, ch 2, p 93.

18 A Osman, *Moses, Pharaoh of Egypt*, ch 6, p 61.

19 Nefertiti's mother is often said to be unknown, although it is recognized that she was raised by Tey, the wife of Yusuf-Yuya and Tjuyu's son Aye. *See* PA Clayton, *Chronicle of the Pharaohs*, p 121. Nefertiti was, however, the daughter of Amenhotep III and Sitamun, and it was by way of marriage to Nefertiti that Amenhotep IV (Akhenaten) secured his right to the throne. *See* A Osman, Moses, *Pharaoh of Egypt*, ch 6, p 62.

20 In 1955 it was reported in the *Journal of Near Eastern Studie*s that, since Nefertiti was the designated 'Great Royal Wife' of Akhenaten, she was doubtless of superior royal blood. *See* 'King Aye and the Close of the Amarna Age' in the *Journal of Near Eastern Studies*, vol 14, 1955, pp 168–80. A boundary stela of Akhenaten specifically denotes her as the royal heiress, calling her 'Mistress of Upper and Lower Egypt – Lady of the Two Lands'. *See* C Aldred, *Akhenaten, King of Egypt*, ch 19, p 222.

21 Amenhotep IV was also called Amenemhat IV, Amenemes IV and Akhenaten.

22 DM Rohl, *A Test of Time: The Bible from Myth to History*, ch 9, p 197.

23 S Freud, *Moses and Monotheism*, II, ch 2, p 35.

24 A Osman, *Moses, Pharaoh of Egypt*, ch 10, p 105.

25 PA Clayton, *Chronicle of the Pharaohs*, p 122.

26 A Osman, *Moses, Pharaoh of Egypt*, ch 12, p 121.

27 DM Rohl, *A Test of Time: The Bible from Myth to History*, ch 9, p 199.

28 Exodus 6:20.

29 A Osman, *Moses, Pharaoh of Egypt*, ch 19, p 184.

30 *Oxford Bible Readers Dictionary and Concordance*, under Amram.

31 Exodus 2:1.

32 J Baikie, *The Amarna Age*, p 241.

33 A Osman, *Moses, Pharaoh of Egypt*, ch 6, pp 63–64.

34 PA Clayton, *Chronicle of the Pharaohs*, pp 128–34.

35 Exodus 2:15 – 3:1.

36 The sons are named in Exodus 18:4.

37 Exodus 3:6.

38 Exodus 3:13–14.

39 Exodus 6:3

40 Exodus 4:1–9.

41 Exodus 4:14.

42 Exodus 7:10–12.

43 A Osman, *Moses, Pharaoh of Egypt*, ch 18, pp 178–79.

44 PA Clayton, *Chronicle of the Pharaohs*, p 120.

45 It was from Gaedheal (Gael), the son of Prince Niul and Princess Scota, that the original Scots Gaels of Ireland were said to have descended.

46 Geoffrey Keating, *The History of Ireland* (trans, David Comyn and Rev PS Dinneen) 1640, reprinted by Irish Texts Society, London 1902–14, vol II, pp 20–21.

47 *Ibid*, vol II, p 17 and vol I, p 233.

48 Ray Winfield Smith, *The Akhenaten Temple Project*, Aris & Phillips, Warminster, 1976, p 22.

49 DM Rohl, *A Test of Time: The Bible from Myth to History*, app E, p 397.

50 PA Clayton, *Chronicle of the Pharaohs*, p 126.

51 The reason given for this theory is that some contemporary depictions of Akhenaten show him with an unusually rounded pelvic structure. But 'Amarna Art', as it has become known, was particularly unique and incorporated many physical eccentricities, such as the exceptionally long neck on the famous bust of Nefertiti. The only extant textual fragments indicate that the tomb was prepared for a royal female and, although the inscriptions are badly damaged, the occupant's name certainly has a feminine ending.

52 Akhenaten's alabaster canopic chest (with four compartments for the jars that would contain his vital organs) has also been found, but this too was empty, unstained and quite unused; it had simply been placed in the tomb in readiness to receive the jars, as was the preparatory custom. A Osman, *Moses, Pharaoh of Egypt*, ch 14, p 134 and pp 138–47.

53 1 Samuel 3:1.

Part VI – God of the Exodus

Chapter 14: NO OTHER GOD

1 PA Clayton, *Chronicle of the Pharaohs*, pp 140–41.

2 Exodus 4:19.

3 A Osman, *Moses, Pharaoh of Egypt*, ch 6, p 64.

4 Exodus 13:17.

5   Exodus 13:20 – 14:31.

6   A Osman, *Moses, Pharaoh of Egypt*, ch 4, p 43.

7   PA Clayton, *Chronicle of the Pharaohs*, p 142.

8   I Velikovsky, *Ages in Chaos*, ch 1, p 7.

9   Around 350 tablets have been unearthed from the Amarna cache, but a large number are badly damaged.

10 TE Peet, *Egypt and the Old Testament*, ch 5, p 115.

11 *Ibid*, ch 5, p 109.

12 PA Clayton, *Chronicle of the Pharaohs*, p 157.

13 Exodus 14:22.

14 Exodus 16:1, 18:1.

15 W Keller, *The Bible as History*, ch 11, pp 127–28.

16 Numbers 12:10, 15.

17 Numbers 20:1.

18 C Aldred, *Akhenaten, King of Egypt*, ch 18, pp 203–04.

19 J Hastings (ed), *Dictionary of the Bible*, under Miriam.

20 C Aldred, *Akhenaten, King of Egypt*, ch 20, p 234.

21 Exodus 6:23.

22 A Osman, *Moses, Pharaoh of Egypt*, ch 19, p 185.

23 Numbers 25:11–13.

24 Arthur Weigall, *The Life and Times of Akhenaten*, Thornton Butterworth, London, 1910, pp 138–39.

25 Exodus 20:2-3.

26 Sir WM Flinders Petrie, *Researches in Sinai*, John Murray, London, 1906, ch 9, pp 126–27.

27 *Ibid*, ch 9, p125.

28 Sir WMF Petrie, *Researches in Sinai*, ch 6, p 85.

29 For a full report on the discovery of the temple, *see Ibid*. Details of individual reliefs and inscriptions are given in Jaroslav Cerny (ed), *The Inscriptions of Sinai*, Egypt Exploration Society, London, 1955. Also for additional information concerning specific activities at the temple, *see* Laurence Gardner, *Lost Secrets of the Sacred Ark*, HarperElement, London 2003, ch 1 *passim*.

30 A Osman, *Moses, Pharaoh of Egypt*, ch 17, p 172.

31 Exodus 19:18.

Chapter 15: THE WILDERNESS YEARS

1 Leviticus 14–16.

2 Deuteronomy 6:3.

3 Deuteronomy 6:10–11.

4 Deuteronomy 6:13–15.

5 Deuteronomy 7:1–2.

6 Deuteronomy 7:6.

7 Deuteronomy 20:1.

8 Deuteronomy 12:3.

9 Judges 3:5–6.

10 Exodus 20:3.

11 Exodus 18:11.

12 Exodus 17:6.

13 Exodus 17:11–14.

14 Exodus 34:27.

15 W Keller, *The Bible as History*, ch 11, p 134.

16 Exodus 19:20–25.

17 Exodus 20:1–17.

18 Exodus 24:4.

19 Exodus 24:12.

20 Exodus 31:18.

21 Exodus 32:15–19.

22 Exodus 34:1.

23 Exodus 34:27–28.

24 Jasher 14:10–33.

25 The *Book of the Dead* is alternatively known as the *Papyrus of Ani* (a royal scribe). This 18th-dynasty document from Thebes was acquired by the British Museum in 1888. It is is extensively illustrated and around 76 feet (over 23 m) in length.

26 Sir Ernest A Wallis Budge (trans 1895), *The Book of the Dead*, Gramercy, New York, NY, 1999, ch CXXV, pp 576–82.

27 BSJ Isserlin, *The Israelites*, Thames & Hudson, London, 1998, ch 2, p 53

28 Barbara Watterson, *Gods of Ancient Egypt*, Sutton, Stroud, 1996, p 122.

29 Numbers 20:5–13.

30 Numbers 20:28.

31 Deuteronomy 34:5.

32 Numbers 32:13.

33 Judges 13:1.

34 B Thiering, *Jesus the Man*, app I, pp 177, 196.

35 Matthew 1:1–16.

36 Genesis 25:20–21.

37 Genesis 26:34.

38 In much later Islämic times, the mosque and Mosaic shrine of *Il Nebi Musa*, west of Madaba in Transjordan, was named in order to establish a geographical Mount Nebo site in compliance with the scripture.

39 Alfred Jeremias, *The Old Testament in the Light of the Ancient Near East*, Williams & Norgate, London, 1911, vol 2, ch 18, p 93.

40 Sir EAW Budge, *Babylonian Life and History*, ch 6, p 105.

41 Exodus 40:20.

42 Exodus 35:31–33

43 Exodus 37:1–2. Before that, it was explained that Bezaleel (assisted by Aholiab) was specially chosen by the Lord for the commission (Exodus 31:2–11).

44 The cubit was a variable measurement, sometimes given as 22 inches. The Ark could therefore have been 55 inches long, by 33 inches in height and width (c.140 x 84 x c.84 cm). Whatever the case, the precise width/height-to-length ratio is given as 1:1.666.

45 Acacia trees still flourish in the Serâbît valley. *See* J Cerny (ed), *The Inscriptions of Sinai*, vol 2, p 5. Isaiah 4:19 refers to the *shittah* tree as the singular of *shittim*. The place called Abel-shittim (Meadow of the acacias), mentioned in Numbers 33:49, was identified by Josephus as Abila, about six miles east of Jordan, near Jericho. *See* J Hastings, *Dictionary of the Bible*, under Shittim.

46 Exodus 20:4.

47 Exodus 32:20–21.

48 J Robinson (ed), *The Nag Hammadi Library*, 'On the Origin if the World', p 166.

49 *Catholic Encyclopedia*, Robert Appleton Co, New York, NY, 1908, under Cherubim.

50 The books of 1 and 2 Chronicles were originally known in Greek as the *Paralipomenon* (Things passed over), and in old Hebrew as *Dibhere Hayyamim* (Acts of the Days). *See* in *Catholic Encyclopedia*, under Paralipomenon.

51 F Josephus, *The Antiquities of the Jews*, bk VI, ch II:5. At much the same time, the Jewish philosopher Philo (30 BC – AD 45) wrote that, whatever the Ark's cherubim might have looked like, he rather felt they were in some way symbolic of knowledge. *See* R Patai, *The Hebrew Goddess*, ch 3, pp 75–6.

52 *Merkabah*, in Hebrew, literally means 'chariot'.

53 Ezekiel 10:9–16.

54 Ezekiel 1:26–28.

55 As per the *Concise Oxford English Dictionary*, Oxford University Press, Oxford, 9th edn, 1995, under Cherub.

56 Psalm 99:1.

57 Numbers 7:89.

58 Joshua 3:3–17, 6:6–13.

59 Leviticus 10:1–2 and 2 Samuel 6:6–7.

60 1 Samuel 5.

61 Leviticus 10:1–2.

62 Louis Ginsberg, *Legends of the Jews*, John Hopkins University Press, Baltimore, MD, 1998, vol 3, p 187.

63 1 Chronicles 13:10–11.

64 Exodus 28:4–38.

65 Exodus 30:21.

66 Exodus 33:7–11. *See* also L Ginsberg, *Legends of the Jews*, vol 3, p 229. For details of the mechanical and scientific natures of the Ark, *see* L Gardner, *Lost Secrets of the Sacred Ark*.

67 The designation 'E' was adopted because this particular scribe wrote a good deal about the Elohim.

68 J Hastings (ed), *Dictionary of the Bible*, under Tabernacle, 1 & 9.

69 The Tabernacle is detailed intermittently from Exodus chapters 26–40.

70 The Bible gives all its related measurements in cubits – a loose standard based upon a forearm's length from elbow to fingertip. The measurement was therefore a variable, ranging from 18 inches to 22 inches. Within this range, there were differences between Egyptian, Hebrew, and Sumerian cubits, while there were also Royal, Sacred, and Angelic cubits.

71 J Hastings (ed), *Dictionary of the Bible*, under Tabernacle, 5c.

72 Prior to King Solomon's Temple dedication in Jerusalem, 1 Chronicles 15:1 explains that his father, King David, had pitched a new tent for the Ark.

73 Genesis 22:17.

Part VII – God of the Battles

Chapter 16: THE CONQUEST

1 Numbers 31:8–10.

2 Numbers 10:33–36.

3 Numbers 11:1.

4 Jericho is the oldest continuously inhabited city on earth, first settled in about 8500 BC as a salt trading centre.

5 As in Joshua 10:1–32. Lachish was excavated by Tel Aviv University 1973–87.

6 Joshua 11:10. Hazor excavations were begun in 1990 by the Hebrew University of Jerusalem.

7 J Hastings (ed), *Dictionary of the Bible*, under Philistines and Caphtor. Also *see* W Keller, *The Bible as History*, ch 17, p 174.

8 The great battle between Rameses III and the Philistines is depicted as a stone relief in the Egyptian temple of Medinet Habu. It was the greatest victory in all the history of the Nile.

9 Chiam Herzog and Mordechai Gichon, *Battles of the Bible*, Greenhill Books, London, 1997, ch 4, p 80.

10 Mentioned in Jeremiah 47:4 and Amos 9:7.

11 J Hastings (ed), *Dictionary of the Bible*, under Caphtor.

12 G Roux, *Ancient Iraq*, ch 14, pp 190–91.

13 W Keller, *The Bible as History*, ch 15, pp 157–58.
14 Joshua 3:3–4.

15 Joshua 3:13–4:24.

16 Joshua 6:12–20.

17 Joshua 6:21–25.

18 The first excavations were those of the German-Austrian expedition led by professors Ernst Sellin and Karl Watzinger from 1907. British excavations commenced in 1930 under Prof John Garstang, followed by those of Dr Kathleen Kenyon in 1953.

19 For details of the Ark in operation, *see* L Gardner, *Lost Secrets of the Sacred Ark*, ch 7, pp 106–7.

20 C Herzog and M Gichon, *Battles of the Bible*, ch 2, p 51.

21 Joshua 8:15–20.

22 Joshua 1:9.

23 Joshua 10:40.

24 2 Kings 21:14–15.

25 J Hastings (ed), *Dictionary of the Bible*, under Jesus.

26 Joshua 24,

27 As cited, for example, in Judges 2:13 and 3:7.

28 Judges 21:19–25.

29 Judges 3:15–23.

30 W Keller, *The Bible as History*, ch 16, p 167.

31 Judges 5. A good account of the military tactics used in this conflict is given in C Herzog and M Gichon, *Battles of the Bible*, ch 3, pp 66–71.

32 Judges 6:5.

33 BSJ Isserlin, *The Israelites*, ch 3, p 68.

34 W Keller, *The Bible as History*, ch 16, p 168.

35 Judges 7:16–22.

36 Judges 11:1–8.

37 Judges 11:30–31.

38 Judges 11:32–39.

39 Judges 13:3–5.

40 Judges 15:15.
41 Judges 16:3.

42 Judges 16:4–19.

43 Judges 16:20–30.

44 For an account of similar character traditions in lore and legend, *see* A Jeremias, *The Old Testament in the Light of the Ancient Near East*, vol 2, ch 23, pp 161–73.

45 Judges 2:14, 2:20, 3:8, 10:7.

46 Judges 17:6.

Chapter 17: THE ROAD TO MORIAH

1 Ruth 4:18–21.

2 Biblical spelling differences such as Amminadab/Aminadab, Naashon/Nahshon, Ram/Amram, and Salmon/Salma occur because of variations between Greek and Hebrew language sources.

3 Ruth 4:21–22.

4 Exodus 18:3–4.

5 Numbers 12:1.

6 The name Nahshon derives from the consonantal stem *nhsh*, which means 'to decipher' or 'to find out'.

7 *Midrash Sifre* on Numbers 47. Jacob Neusner (trans), *Sifre to Numbers*, Scholars Press, Atlanta, GA, 1986.

8 John Rogerson, *Chronicle of the Old Testament Kings*, Thames & Hudson, London, 1999, p 60.

9 W Keller, *The Bible as History*, ch 18, p 177.

10 1 Samuel 4:17.

11 1 Samuel 5:1–6:16.

12 1 Samuel 22:18–19.

13 1 Samuel 16:21–23.

14 1 Samuel 17:12–20.

15 There have been such warriors in our modern age. The post-War German wrestler, Kurt Zehe, was 8 feet 4 inches, and the Rotterdam colossus of the ring, Rhinehardt, stood at 9 feet 6 inches. *See* Sir Atholl Oakeley, *Blue Blood on the Mat*, Stanley Paul, London, 1971, ch 18, p 159.

16 1 Samuel 17:4–51.
17 A Jeremias, *The Old Testament in the Light of the Ancient Near East*, vol 1, ch 13, p 325–27.

18 1 Samuel 19:1.

19 1 Samuel 28:7 – 31:4.

20 JR Porter, *The Illustrated Guide to the Bible*, p 76.

21 1 Samuel 3:1.

22 1 Samuel 2:10.

23 1 Samuel 15:3.

24 1 Samuel 15:23.

25 1 Samuel 15:33.

26 1 Samuel 28:17.

27 2 Samuel 7:14

28 2 Samuel 6:6–7.

29 2 Samuel 6:13–15. The ephod was sleeveless, bibbed and girdled. *See* F Josephus, *The Antiquities of the Jews*, bk III, ch VII:5. In later times the garment became a badge of the Levite guardians of the Ark, with its bib folded down over the girdle to form a small flapped apron. *See* J Hastings (ed), *Dictionary of the Bible*, under Dress, item: Apron. It is represented today by the short apron of masonic regalia.

30 Israel Finkelstein and Neil Asher Silberman, *The Bible Unearthed*, Touchstone, New York, NY, 2002, ch 9, pp 239–40.

31 Although geographically ambiguous, the Upper and Lower distinctions of Egypt were not conventionally related to north and south, but to the reaches of the north-flowing River Nile.

32 1 Chronicles 18:3.

33 W Keller, *The Bible as History*, ch 19, pp 191.

34 *Ibid*, ch 19, pp 189–90.

35 2 Samuel 11:12–27.

36 2 Samuel 18:33.

37 1 Kings 2:13–25.

38 From the Greek, meaning 'shell' or 'sherd'. Quite often fragments of pots were used for everyday notes. Also *see* W Keller, *The Bible as History*, ch 5, pp 190–92.

39 Criminal File 482/04, District Court of Jerusalem. For a full report on variously identified forgeries and the related court case, with named defendants, *see* 'The Other Shoe' in *Biblical Archaeology Review*, Biblical Archaeology Society, Washington, DC, March/April 2005, pp 58–69.

40 Joshua 19:47.

41 Judges 18:27.

42 *Biblical Archaeology Review*, May/June 1994, pp 30–37. Lemaire had to supply one destroyed letter, the first 'D' in '[D]avid' to decode the wording. Other scholars found that no other letter produced a reading that made any sense, although Baruch Margalit of Haifa University attempted to discredit Lemaire's conclusion (*see* Baruch Margalit, 'Studies in NW Semitic Inscriptions' in *Ugarit-Forschungen, Ugarit Verlag*, Münster, 1994, vol 26, p 275). In the 14 years since, however, his criticism has not attracted any significant support in scholarly publications.

Chapter 18: A TALE OF TWO KINGDOMS

1 1 Kings 25:38–39.

2 *The Oxford Bible Readers Dictionary and Concordance*, and J Hastings (ed), *Dictionary of the Bible* – each under Solomon.

3 1 Kings 4:26.

4 Louis Charpentier, *The Mysteries of Chartres Cathedral*, Research Into Lost Knowledge Organization and Thorsons, Wellingborough, 1992, ch 7, p 55–56.

5 1 Kings 9:20–21.

6 J Rogerson, *Chronicle of the Old Testament Kings*, pp 88–89.

7 1 Kings 3:15–27.

8 *The Bible* – Authorized King James Version with Apocrypha, Oxford University Press, Oxford, 1998, 'The Wisdom of Solomon', pp 93–112.

9 Proverbs 22:17 – 24:22.

10 JH Breasted, *The Dawn of Consciousness*, pp 371, 377–78.

11 JR Porter, *The Illustrated Guide to the Bible*, pp 127–27, 132.

12 John 12:3. Also in Matthew 26:6–13 and Mark 14:3–9, with a previous anointing by Mary in Luke 7:36–50 as referenced again in John 11:2. Bridal anointing was a conferral of Messianic status and transferral of property rights. *See* WE Mills (ed), *Lutterworth Dictionary of the Bible*, under Anoint. Spikenard is a fragrant, sweet-smelling ointment compounded from the Himalayan nard plant. Growing only at heights of around 15,000 feet (*c*.4,570 m), it was very expensive. *See* expanded details of the ritual in Laurence Gardner, *The Magdalene Legacy*, HarperElement, London, 2005, ch 10, pp 155–61.

13 1 Kings 7:13–14.

14 The name Abiff does not appear in the 1390 *Regius Manuscript* of Masonic Constitution, but does appear in the 1550 *Downland Manuscript*. For detailed information concerning Hiram Abiff in Freemasonry, *see* Laurence Gardner, *The Shadow of Solomon*, HarperElement, London, 2006, ch 2, pp 19–34, ch 8, pp 122–39.

15 For recommended reading in respect of ancient Tyre, *see* HJ Katzenstein, *The History of Tyre*, The Bialik Institute, Jerusalem, 1997, and Maria Eugenia Aubet, *The Phoenicians and the West: Colonies, Politics and Trade* (trans, Mary Turton), Cambridge University Press, Cambridge, 2001.

16 1 Kings 6:20–30.

17 1 Kings 8:6–7.

18 1 Kings 10:14. This is about 30 tons: today's value *c*.£134 million (*c*.$250 million). One talent of gold = 108 pounds *avoirdupois*: J Hastings (ed), *Dictionary of the Bible*, under Money. One ton = 2,240 pounds.

19 1 Kings 10:16.

20 1 Kings 10:17.

21 1 Kings 10:18.

22 1 Kings 9:27–28. Re. the location of Ophir, *see* J Hastings, *Dictionary of the Bible*.

23 Repeated in 2 Chronicles 9:1–12.

24 1 Kings 10:10 specifies that she brought Solomon 120 talents (about 5.5 tons) of gold.

25 J Hastings (ed), *Dictionary of the Bible*, under Sheba, and under Sheba, Queen of. The location also confirmed in BBC2 television documentary, *Queen of Sheba: Behind the Myth*, 18 May 2002.

26 1 Kings 10:7.

27 1 Kings 3:5–15.

8 1 Kings 9:6.

29 2 Kings 23:13.

30 1 Kings 11:1–6.

31 Job 1: 1–3.

32 J Hastings (ed), *Dictionary of the Bible*, under Job – from the writings of Aristeas and Eusebius – as note appended in the *Septuagint* Bible. *See* also the *Catholic Encyclopedia*, vol VIII, under Job.

33 Job 2:1–6.

34 The Hebrew word *satan* (accuser) is equivalent to the Greek *diabolos* (aggressor).

35 J Hastings Hastings (ed), *Dictionary of the Bible*, under Philistines.

36 1 Kings 12:14.

37 1 Kings 16:24.

38 W Keller, *The Bible as History*, ch 6, p 222.

39 1 Kings 14:25–26. Also detailed in 1 Chronicles 12:2–9

40 W Keller, *The Bible as History*, ch 6, pp 223–4.

Chapter 19: THE IMPLACABLE LORD

1 1 Kings 12:28–29.

2 2 Chronicles 13:1–22.

3 1 Kings 16:31–33.

4 J Rogerson, *Chronicle of the Old Testament Kings*, p 101.

5 *Ibid*, p 121.

6 *Ibid*, p 141.

7 1 Kings 21:21–23.

8 2 Kings 16:10–11.

9 J Porter, *The Illustrated Guide to the Bible*, p 106.

10 Exodus 20:2–3.

11 2 Kings 21:7–15.

12 2 Kings 22:8.

13 2 Kings 24:14.

14 Jeremiah 39:6–7, 52:10–11.

15 2 Kings 24:3.

16 The first *Enûma elish* tablets to be discovered in recent times were unearthed in the 1848–76 excavations of Sir Austen Henry Layard, from the Assyrian library of King Ashurbanipal at Nineveh.

17 G Roux, *Ancient Iraq*, ch 23, p 310.

18 SN Kramer, *Sumerian Mythology*, ch 2, p 69.

19 Henri Frankfort, *Before Philosophy*, Penguin, London, 1951, ch 8, pp 240–48.

20 Psalm 19:1.

21 Exodus 3:2.

22 Exodus 14:19, Numbers 20:16, Judges 2:1.

23 Genesis 19:1–3.

24 Genesis 22:11.

25 Genesis 22:15–17.

26 Genesis 28:11–12.

27 Numbers 25:4.

28 Judges 6:11–12.

29 Judges 13:2–3.

30 Judges 13:18.

31 1 Chronicles 21:14–16. Also 2 Samuel 24:15–16.

32 1 Kings 19:5–6.

33 This account is repeated in Isaiah 37:36–37.

34 J Porter, *The Illustrated Guide to the Bible*, p 94.

35 C and BJ O'Brien, *The Genius of the Few*, ch 6, p 139.

36 Ezekiel 10:5.

37 J Hastings (ed), *Dictionary of the Bible*, under Seraphim.

38 Numbers 21:16.

39 Excavated in 1845 by the English diplomat, Sir Austen Henry Layard. Subsequently, Britain's foremost Assyriologist, Sir Henry Creswicke Rawlinson, also unearthed the great library of King Ashurbanipal a little north of Nimrud at Nineveh.

Part VIII – God of Religion

Chapter 20: BETWEEN THE TESTAMENTS

1 Ezekiel 1:26–28.

2 Daniel 7:9.

3 Psalm 99:1.

4 Numbers 7:89.

5 1 Samuel 4:4, 2 Samuel 6:2, 1 Chronicles 13:6, Psalm 80:1, Psalm 99:1, Isaiah 37:16.

6 L Ginsberg, *Legends of the Jews*, vol 3, p 228.

7 In the 1300s, an anonymous Ethiopic book appeared, entitled *Kebra Nagast* (Glory of the Kings). It suggested that Menelek, a fictitious son of Solomon and Sheba, had stolen the Ark from the Temple and taken it to Abyssinia. The work is translated as Sir EA Wallis Budge, *Kebra Nagast*, Oxford University Press, Oxford, 1932. Amazingly, the legend lives on to this day, encouraged by the Ethiopian Orthodox Church and the Axum tourist industry. The relic is said to be kept in a crudely erected 1960s chapel to which entry is prohibited, and no one (not even the Patriarch) has ever seen it. A full account of the Ethiopian tradition is given in Graham Hancock, *The Sign and the Seal*, Heinemann, London, 1992.

8 1 Kings 14:25.

9 PA Clayton, *Chronicle of the Pharaohs*, pp 185–86.

10 2 Kings 19:15.

11 2 Kings 22:8, 2 Chronicles 34:15.

12 G Vermes, *The Complete Dead Sea Scrolls in English*, p 130. The *Damascus Document* was written in about 100 BC. *Ibid*, p 127.

13 Alan Unterman, *Dictionary of Jewish Lore and Legend*, Thames & Hudson, London, 1997, under Ark of the Covenant.

14 Jeremiah 3:16.

15 For a discussion of various hiding places, *see* Roderick Grierson and Stuart Munro-Hay, *The Ark of the Covenant*, Weidenfeld & Nicolson, London, 1999, ch 8, pp 106–27.

16 2 Kings 25:13–17, Jeremiah 52:17–23.

17 Ezra 2:2–64.

18 Ezra 7:23–26.

19 Ezra 8:1–20.

20 Ezra 9:9.

21 The Hasmonaeans were a distinguished and priestly family, prominent in Jerusalem in the 2nd century BC. At the time of Antiochus IV, the head of the household was the high priest Mattathias, who initiated the Jewish Revolt. Before he died, he nominated his third son Judas (nicknamed Maccabaeus) to be the movement's military commander. Judas was in turn succeeded by his brothers Jonathan and Simeon who, along with all their followers, were thereafter known as Maccabees.

22 F Josephus, *The Antiquities of the Jews*, bks XII and XIII.

23 1 Maccabees and 2 Maccabees in *The Bible* – Authorized King James Version with Apocrypha, pp 180–248.

NOTES AND REFERENCES

24 *Kislev*: the 10th month of the Jewish calendar, which corresponds to 29 or 30 days within the Gregorian calendar months of November and December. The names of the Jewish months are of Babylonian origin. It is based on the Babylonian astronomical calendar, hence for example the 4th month of *Tammuz* as originally dedicated to the Mesopotamian god Dumuzi. The monthly names were introduced by the returning Israelite exiles to Jerusalem at the time of Ezra the scribe. For descriptions of the Jewish calendar and its history, *see* http://www.jewfaq.org/calendar.htm

25 *Hanukkah* – the Jewish festival of lights, which commemorates this event in 165 BC.

26 F Josephus, *The Wars of the Jews*, bk I, and The Antiquities of the Jews, bk XV.

27 André Dupont-Sommer, *The Jewish Sect of Qumrân and the Essenes*, Vallentine Mitchell, London, 1954, p 169.

28 F Josephus, Flavius, *The Antiquities of the Jews*, bk XV, ch V:2.

29 JT Milik, *Ten Years of Discovery in the Wilderness of Judaea* (trans, J Strugnell), SCM Press, London, 1959, ch 3, pp 51–53.

30 F Josephus, *The Wars of the Jews*, bk II, ch VIII:6.

31 F Josephus, *The Antiquities of the Jews*, bk XV, ch X:4.

32 F Josephus, *The Wars of the Jews*, bk II, ch VIII:2.

33 John Allegro, *The Dead Sea Scrolls*, Penguin, London, 1964, ch 5, p 94.

34 *Ibid*, ch 5, p 93.

35 B Thiering, *Jesus the Man*, ch 7, p 34.

36 Stewart Perowne, *The Life and Times of Herod the Great*, Hodder & Stoughton, London, 1956, ch 17, pp 135–36.

37 F Josephus, Flavius, *The Antiquities of the Jews*, bk XV, ch IX:1–2.

38 'Aelia' in honor of the Emperor Hadrian, whose full name was Publius Aelius Hadrianus. 'Capitolina' after the Capitoline triad, Jupiter, Juno, and Minerva, who were to be the patrons of the new city. The triad was worshipped on the Capitoline Hill in Rome.

39 The Dome of the Rock was not always golden as it is today. Its 80 kilos of gold plating was a recent undertaking by the late King Hussein of Jordan, who sold one of his London houses to help fund the project.

40 Seleucid I to Seleucid VI: Kings of Syria from 301 to 93 BC. Seleucid IV (also called Soter, 187–176 BC) sent his chancellor, Heliodorus, to plunder the Temple of Jerusalem (2 Maccabeees 3:1–40). However, as the result of an apparition, he was prevented from fulfilling the task and murdered Seleucus instead.

41 Leen and Kathleen Ritmeyer, *Secrets of Jerusalem's Temple Mount*, Biblical Archaeological Society, Washington, DC, 1998, ch 5, p 57.

42 Shimon Gibson and David M Jacobsen, *Below the Temple Mount in Jerusalem*, Tempus Reparatum, Oxford, 1996, pref, p vii.

43 F Josephus, *The Antiquities of the Jews*, bk XV, ch XI:5.

44 Cornelius Tacitus, *The Histories* (trans, Kenneth Wellesley), Penguin, London, 1995, V:12, p 287.

45 Middoth 5:5.

46 L and K Ritmeyer, *Secrets of Jerusalem's Temple Mount*, ch 6, p 108.

47 *Talmud*, Yoma 54a.

48 L and K Ritmeyer, *Secrets of Jerusalem's Temple Mount*, ch 6, pp 109–10.

49 For details of this 12th-century Templar excavation, *see* L Gardner, *Lost Secrets of the Sacred Ark*, ch 15, pp 217–22.

50 Palestine Exploration Fund, 2 Hinde Mews, Marylebone Lane, London, W1U 2AA.

51 L and K Ritmeyer, *Secrets of Jerusalem's Temple Mount*, ch 5. pp 71–77.

52 *Ibid*, ch 5, p 83.

Chapter 21: THE IMAGE OF GOD

1 Willis Barnstone, (ed), *The Other Bible*, HarperSanFrancisco, San Francisco, CA, 1984, p 334.

2 Irenaeus, *Adversus Haereses*, AD *c*.175, vol I, bk I, ch 26:2. *See* also the *Catholic Encyclopedia*, vol V, under Ebionites.

3 G Vermes, *The Complete Dead Sea Scrolls in English*, Scroll 4Q246, pp 576–77.

4 Matthew 5:3–12.

5 *Ibid*, Scroll 4Q525, p 424.

6 Daniel 9:25.

7 Luke 7:19–20.

8 *Jewish Encyclopedia*, under Jesus.

9 Proselytes were Gentile converts to Judaism.

10 Matthew 23:15.

11 Matthew 23: 2–4.

12 Exodus 32:31–33.

13 Joshua 24:19.

14 Also *see* Exodus 30:10; Leviticus 23:27–31, 25:9; Numbers 29:7–11.

15 Leviticus 16:29–31 and 23:27–28. Settled always on a Sabbath, the precise date for *Yom Kippur* varies slightly each year between latter September and early October in the Gregorian calendar. For example:
2005 (Jewish Year 5766) from sunset 12 October to nightfall 13 October.
2006 (Jewish Year 5767) from sunset 1 October to nightfall 2 October.
2007 (Jewish Year 5768) from sunset 21 September to nightfall 22 September.
2008 (Jewish Year 5769) from sunset 8 October to nightfall 9 October.
2009 (Jewish Year 5770) from sunset 27 September to nightfall 28 September.

16 *Catholic Encyclopedia*, vol XI, under Sacrament of Penance.

17 Luke 12:20.

18 Matthew 22:44 This is repeated in Mark 12:36, Luke 20:42 and Acts 2:34.

19 All as in Matthew 6:6, Matthew 6:8, Matthew 6:9 and Matthew 7:21, along with like references in the other gospels.

20 Matthew 6:12.

21 Matthew 6:15.

22 'The Exhortation' in G Vermes, *The Complete Dead Sea Scrolls in English* – Damascus Scroll fragments 4Q265–73, 5Q12, 6Q15, p 127–28.

23 *Ibid*, p 129.

24 *Ibid*, p 130.

25 *Ibid*, p 129.

26 Exodus 20:13, Deuteronomy 5:17.

27 Deuteronomy 7:1–2.

28 1 Samuel 15:3.

29 Exodus 20:15, Deuteronomy 5:19.

30 Exodus 20:17, Deuteronomy 5:21.

31 Deuteronomy 6:10–11.

32 Exodus 20:5.

33 Exodus 20:6.

34 Matthew 19:17–18.

35 Leviticus 19:18.

36 Matthew 5:44.

37 Matthew 22:37–38.

38 Exodus 20:2–3.

39 Deuteronomy 6:5, 11:13, 11:22, 13:3, 19:9, 30:6, 30:16, 30:20.

40 Acts 15:1.

41 Acts 15:5.

42 Acts 15:7–11.

43 Acts 15:19–21.

44 Exodus 21:23–25. Leviticus 24:19–20.

45 Matthew 5:38–39.

46 Luke 22:36.

Chapter 22: A MATTER OF BELIEF

1 *Jewish Encyclopedia*, under God.

2 Genesis 1:26.

3 Daniel 7:9, 13, 22.

4 For example, Genesis 1:2, Numbers 14:22, Isaiah 12:2, Zechariah 4:6.

5 Jeremiah 10:6–7.

6 *Jewish Encyclopedia*, under God.

7 *Ibid.*

8 *Catholic Encyclopedia*, under The Existence of God.

9 *Ibid.*

10 *Ibid*, from Thomas Aquinas, *Summa Theologica*, part I, items 1, 2, 3.

11 Richard Dawkins, *The God Delusion*, Bantam, London, 2006, ch 3, pp 77–79.

12 The Evangelical Media Group – http://www.god.com/index.php?site=lectures/bit/bit3&lg=en

13 The subject is fully covered in Jeff Jordan, *Pascal's Wager: Pragmatic Arguments and Belief in God*, Clarendon Press, Oxford, 2006.

14 R Dawkins, *The God Delusion*, ch 3, p 104.

15 'Church attendance dropping in Italy', *Catholic World News*, 18 October 2001.

16 'Migrants fill empty pews as Britons lose faith', *The Daily Telegraph*, London, 19 September 2006.

17 'Religious belief falling faster than church attendance', *The Daily Telegraph*, London, 17 August 2005.

18 Re. President George W Bush in *Dayton Daily News*, Dayton, OH, 15 January 2004.

19 *USA Today*, McLean, VA, 12 September 2006. The poll was analyzed by sociologists from Baylor University's Institute for Studies of Religion, Waco, Texas.

20 Also *see* 'Fundamentalism and the Decline of Christianity' *New York Times Magazine*, NY, 2 April 2005.

21 This point was emphasized by Dr Rowan Williams, Archbishop of Canterbury, in his 'Dimbleby Lecture' at Westminster School, London, 19 December 2002.

22 David Wilkinson, *God, Time & Stephen Hawking*, Monarch, Grand Rapids, MI, 2001, ch 8, pp 126–27.

23 Dr Rowan Williams, Archbishop of Canterbury, New Year Message, 31 December 2002.

24 1 Samuel 3:1.

BIBLIOGRAPHY

Albright, William Foxwell, *The Archaeology of Palestine and the Bible*, Fleming H Revel, New York, NY, 1932.

— *Archaeology and the Religion of Israel*, John Hopkins University, Baltimore, MD, 1942.

— *Yahweh and the Gods of Canaan*, Athlone Press, University of London, London, 1968.

Alcuin, Flaccus Albinus, Abbot of Canterbury (trans), *The Book of Jasher*, Longman, London, 1929.

Aldred, Cyril, *Akhenaten, King of Egypt*, Thames & Hudson, London, 1988.

— *Egypt to the End of the Old Kingdom*, Thames & Hudson, London, 1992.

Allan, DS, and JB Dellair, *Cataclysm*, Bear, Rochester, VT, 1997.

Allegro, John, *The Dead Sea Scrolls*, Penguin, London, 1964.

Al-Qur'an of Mohammed, Chandos/Frederick Warne, London (undated).

Alter, Robert, *Genesis*, WW Norton, New York, NY, 1996.

Anati, E, *Palestine Before the Hebrews*, Jonathan Cape, London, 1963.

Armstrong, Karen, *A History of God*, Ballantine, New York, NY, 1993.

— *In the Beginning*, HarperCollins, London, 1997.

Aubet, Maria Eugenia, *The Phoenicians and the West: Colonies, Politics and Trade* (trans, Mary Turton), Cambridge University Press, Cambridge, 2001.

Bade, William F, *The Old Testament in the Light of Today*, Houghton Mifflin, Boston, MA, 1915.

Baikie, James, *The Amarna Age*, A&C Black, London, 1926.

Baldock, John, *Women in the Bible*, Arcturus, Foulsham, Slough, 2006.

Barnstone, Willis (ed), *The Other Bible*, HarperSanFrancisco, San Francisco, CA, 1984.

Barton, George Aaron, *A Sketch of Semitic Origins*, Macmillan, London, 1902.

— *Miscellaneous Babylonian Inscriptions*, Yale University Press, New Haven, CT, 1918.

— *The Royal Inscriptions of Sumer and Akkad*, Yale University Press, New Haven, CT, 1929.

Behe, Michael, *Darwin's Black Box*, Simon & Schuster, New York, NY, 1996.

Berg, Rabbi Yehuda, *The Power of Kabbalah*, Hodder & Stoughton, London, 2003.

Bertholet, Alfred, *A History of Hebrew Civilization* (trans, AK Dallas), George G Harrap, London, 1926.

Biggs, Robert D, *et al* (eds), *The Assyrian Dictionary*, Oriental Institute of the University of Chicago, IL, 1999.

Black, Jeremy, and Anthony Green, *Gods, Demons and Symbols of Ancient Mesopotamia*, British Museum Press, London, 1992.

Box, GH, *Judaism in the Greek Period*, Oxford University Press, Oxford, 1932.

Breasted, James Henry, *The Dawn of Consciousness*, Charles Scribner's Sons, New York, NY, 1934.

Brenton, Sir Lancelot CL (trans), *The Septuagint*, Samuel Bagster, London, 1851.

Browne, Lewis (ed), *The Wisdom of Israel*, Michael Joseph, London, 1948.

Budge, Sir Ernest A Wallis (trans), *The Book of the Cave of Treasures*, Religious Tract Society, Manchester, 1927.

— *Kebra Nagast*, Oxford University Press, Oxford, 1932.

— *Babylonian Life and History* (1886), rep. Dorset Press, New York, NY, 1992.

— *The Book of the Dead* (trans 1895), Gramercy, New York, NY, 1999.

Burney, CF, *The Book of Judges*, Rivingtons, London, 1930.

— *Israel's Settlement in Canaan*, Oxford University Press, Oxford, 1919.

— *Notes on the Hebrew Texts of the Books of Kings*, Clarendon Press, Oxford, 1903.

Cappers, René TJ, and Sytze Bottema (eds), *The Dawn of Farming in the Near East*, Oxbow, Oxford, 2002.

Carlyon, Richard, *A Guide to the Gods*, Quixote, London, 1981.

Cassuto, Umberto, *The Goddess Anath* (trans, Israel Abrahams), Magnes Press, Hebrew University, Jerusalem, 1971.

Catholic Encyclopedia, Robert Appleton Co, New York, NY, 1908.

Cerny, Jaroslav (ed), *The Inscriptions of Sinai*, Egypt Exploration Society, London, 1955.

Charles, RH (trans), *The Book of Enoch* (revised from Dillmann's edition of the Ethiopic text, 1893), Oxford University Press, Oxford, 1906 and 1912.

Charpentier, Louis, *The Mysteries of Chartres Cathedral*, Research Into Lost Knowledge Organization and Thorsons, Wellingborough, 1992.

Chase, Mary Ellen, *Life and Language in the Old Testament*, Collins, London, 1956.

Chiera, Edward, *They Wrote on Clay*, University of Chicago Press, Chicago, IL, 1938.

Childe, Gordon, *New Light on the Most Ancient Near East,* Routledge & Kegan Paul, London, 1934.

Church, Rev Leslie F (ed), *Matthew Henry's Commentary on the Whole Bible*, Marshall Pickering, London, 1960.

Clayton, Peter A, *Chronicle of the Pharaohs*, Thames and Hudson, London, 1994.

Cohn-Sherbok, Lavinia and Dan, *A Short Reader in Judaism*, Oneworld, Oxford, 1997.

Collon, Dominique, First Impressions – *Cylinder Seals in the Ancient Near East*, British Museum Press, London, 1987.

Committee for Science and Creationism, *Science and Creationism: A View from the National Academy of Sciences*, Second Edition, National Academy of Sciences, National Academies Press, Washington, DC, 1999.

Concise Oxford English Dictionary, Oxford University Press, Oxford, 9th edn, 1995.

Cook, Stanley A, *The Religion of Ancient Palestine in the Light of Archaeology* (from the 1925 Schweich Lectures of the British Academy), Oxford University Press, Oxford, 1930.

Cornhill, CH, *History of the People of Israel* (trans, WH Carruth), Open Court, Chicago, IL, 1898.

Corteggiani, Jean Pierre, *The Egypt of the Pharaohs at the Cairo Museum*, Scala, London, 1987.

Cottrell, Leonard, *The Land of Shinar*, Souvenir Press, London, 1965.

Coulborn, Rushton, *The Origin of Civilized Societies*, Princeton University Press, Princeton, NJ, 1959.

Cruden, Alexander, *Complete Concordance to the Old and New Testaments and the Apocrypha*, Frederick Warne, London 1891.

Curtis, John (ed), Early Mesopotamia and *Iran: Contact and Conflict 3500–1600 BC*, British Museum Press, London, 1993.

Danby, Herbert (trans), *The Mishnah*, Oxford University Press, Oxford, 1933.

Daniel, Glyn, and Paintin, Elaine (eds), *The Illustrated Encyclopedia of Archaeology*, Macmillan, London, 1978.

Darwin, Charles, *On the Origin of Species* (1872), New York University Press, New York, NY (6th edn), 1988.

David, Rosalie and Anthony, *A Biographical Dictionary of Ancient Egypt,* Seaby, London, 1992.

Davies, Norman De Garis, *The Rock Tombs of El-Amarna*, Egypt Exploration Society, London, 1906.

Dawkins, Richard, *River Out of Eden*, Basic Books, New York, NY, 1995.

— *The God Delusion*, Bantam, London, 2006.

Day, David, *Tolkien's Ring*, HarperCollins, London, 1994.

Doresse, Jean, *The Secret Books of the Egyptian Gnostics* (trans, Philip Mairet), Hollis & Carter, London, 1960.

Driver, GR, *Canaanite Myths and Legends*, T&T Clark, Edinburgh, 1956.

Dupont-Sommer, André, *The Jewish Sect of Qumrân and the Essenes*, Vallentine Mitchell, London, 1954.

— *The Essene Writings from Qumrân* (trans, Geza Vermes), Basil Blackwell, Oxford, 1961.

Durán, Fray Diego, *Book of the Gods and Rites, and the Ancient Calendar* (trans, F Horcasitas and D Heyden), University of Oklahoma Press, Oklahoma City, OK, 1971.

Eisenman, Robert, *Maccabees, Zadokites, Christians and Qumrân*, EJ Brill, Leiden, 1983.

— *The Dead Sea Scrolls and the First Christians*, Element Books, Shaftesbury, 1996.

Engnell, Ivan, *Studies in Divine Kingship in the Ancient Near East*, Basil Blackwell, Oxford, 1967.

Epstein, Perle, *Kabalah – The Way of the Jewish Mystic*, Shambhala Publications, Boston, MA, 1988.

Etheridge, JW, *The Targums of Onkelos and Jonathan Ben Uzziel on the Pentateuch with the fragments of the Jerusalem Targum from the Chaldee*, Longman Green, London, 1862.

Farbridge, Maurice H, *Studies in Biblical and Semitic Symbolism*, EP Dutton, London, 1923.

Finkelstein, Israel, and Neil Asher Silberman, *The Bible Unearthed*, Touchstone, New York, NY, 2002.

Firestone, Richard, Allen West and Simon Warwick-Smith, *The Cycle of Cosmic Catatrophes*, Bear, Rochester, VT, 2006.

Fisher, Clarence S, *Babylonian Expedition of the University of Pennsylvania*, Part II, 'Excavations at Nippur: Plans, details and photographs of the buildings, with numerous objects found in them during the excavations of 1889, 1890, 1893–1896, 1899–1900', University of Pennsylvania, Philadelphia, PA, 1905.

Fleming, Daniel E, *Democracy's Ancient Ancestors*, Cambridge University Press, Cambridge, 2004.

Frankfort, Henri, *Cylinder Seals*, Macmillan, London, 1939.

— *Kingship and the Gods*, University of Chicago Press, Chicago, IL, 1948.

— *Before Philosophy*, Penguin, London, 1951.

— *The Birth of Civilization in the Near East*, Williams & Norgate, London, 1954.

Freud, Sigmund, *Moses and Monotheism*, Hogarth Press, London, 1939.

Gadd, CJ, *The Fall of Nineveh*, British Academy & Oxford University Press, Oxford, 1932.

— *The Stones of Assyria*, Chatto & Windus, London, 1936.

Gagné, Steve, *The Energetics of Food*, Spiral Sciences, USA, 2006.

Gardiner, Alan, *Egyptian Grammar*, Griffith Institute, Ashmolean Museum, Oxford, 1957.

Gardner, Laurence, *Lost Secrets of the Sacred Ark*, HarperElement, London, 2003.

— *The Magdalene Legacy*, HarperElement, London, 2005.

— *The Shadow of Solomon*, HarperElement, London, 2006.

Garstang, John, *The Foundations of Bible History: Joshua and Judges*, Constable, London, 1931.

Geden, Alfred D, *Studies in the Religions of the East*, Charles H Kelly, London, 1913.

Gelb, IJ, *A Study of Writing*, University of Chicago Press, Chicago, IL, 1952.

Gibson, Shimon, and David M Jacobsen, *Below the Temple Mount in Jerusalem*, Tempus Reparatum, Oxford.

Ginsberg, Louis, *Legends of the Jews*, John Hopkins University Press, Baltimore, MD, 1998.

Goff, Beatrice, *Symbols of Prehistoric Mesopotamia*, Yale University Press, New Haven, CT, 1963.

Gordon, Cyrus H, *The Loves and Wars of Baal and Anat*, Princeton University Press, Princeton, NJ, 1943.

Graves, Robert, *The White Goddess*, Faber & Faber, London, 1961.

— and Raphael Patai, *Hebrew Myths – The Book of Genesis*, Cassell, London, 1964.

Gray, John, *The Canaanites*, Thames & Hudson, London, 1964.

Grierson, Roderick, and Stuart Munro-Hay, *The Ark of the Covenant*, Weidenfeld & Nicolson, London, 1999.

Grimal, Nicholas, *A History of Ancient Egypt*, Basil Blackwell, Oxford, 1992.

Guthrie, HH, *God and History in the Old Testament*, SPCK, London, 1961.

Halloran, JA, *Sumerian Lexicon: A Dictionary Guide to the Ancient Sumerian Language*, Logogram Publishing, Los Angeles, CA, 2006.

Hancock, Graham, *The Sign and the Seal*, Heinemann, London, 1992.

Hapgood, Charles, *The Earth's Shifting Crust*, Pantheon Books, New York, NY, 1958.

— *Maps of the Ancient Sea Kings*, Chilton Books, Philadelphia, PA, 1966.

— *The Path of the Pole*, Chilton Books, Philadelphia, PA, 1970.

Harris, ZS, A Grammar of the Phoenician Language, American Oriental Society, New Haven, CT, 1936.

Hastings, James (ed), *Dictionary of the Bible*, T&T Clark, Edinburgh, 1909.

Heidel, Alexander, *The Babylonian Genesis*, University of Chicago Press, Chicago, IL, 1942.

— *The Gilgamesh Epic and Old Testament Parallels*, University of Chicago Press, Chicago, IL, 1949.

Herzog, Chiam, and Mordechai Gichon, *Battles of the Bible*, Greenhill Books, London, 1997.

Hilprecht, HV, *The Excavations in Assyria and Babylonia*, The Babylonian Expedition of the University of Pennsylvania, Series D: Researches and Treatises, Department of Archaeology of the University of Pennsylvania, Philadelphia, PA, 1904.

Hinz, Walther, *The Lost World of Elam*, Sidgwick & Jackson, London, 1972.

Hocart, AM, *Kingship*, Oxford University Press, Oxford, 1927.

Holy Bible, Authorized King James Version with Apocrypha, Oxford University Press, Oxford, 1998.

Holy Scriptures of the Old Testament, The (Hebrew and English), The British & Foreign Bible Society, London, 1925.

Hooke, SH, *The Origins of Early Semitic Ritual* (from the 1935 Schweich Lectures of the British Academy), Oxford University Press, Oxford, 1938.

Isserlin, BSJ, *The Israelites*, Thames & Hudson, London, 1998.

Jack, JW, *The Ras Shamra Tablets – Their Bearing on the Old Testament*, T&T Clark, Edinburgh, 1935.

Jackson, FJ Foakes, *The Biblical History of the Hebrews*, Heffer, London, 1909.

Jacobsen, Thorkild, *The Sumerian King List* (Assyriological Studies 11), University of Chicago Press, Chicago, IL, 1939.

— *The Treasures of Darkness – A History of Mesopotamian Religion*, Yale University Press, New Haven, CT, 1976.

James, EO, *The Nature and Function of Priesthood*, Thames & Hudson, London, 1955.

— *Prehistoric Religion*, Thames & Hudson, London, 1958.

— *The Cult of the Mother Goddess*, Thames & Hudson, London, 1959.

Jeremias, Alfred, *The Old Testament in the Light of the Ancient Near East*, Williams & Norgate, London, 1911.

Jewish Encyclopedia, Funk & Wagnalls, New York, NY, 1906.

Jones, AMH, *The Herods of Judaea*, Clarendon Press, Oxford, 1938.

— *The Decline of the Ancient World*, Longman, London, 1966.

Jones, Steve, *In the Blood: God, Genes and Destiny*, HarperCollins, London, 1996.

Jordan, Jeff, *Pascal's Wager: Pragmatic Arguments and Belief in God*, Clarendon Press, Oxford, 2006.

Josephus, Flavius, *The Works of Flavius Josephus*, including *The Antiquities of the Jews*, *The Wars of the Jews* and *Against Apion* (trans, William Whiston), Milner & Sowerby, London, 1870.

Katzenstein, HJ, *The History of Tyre*, The Bialik Institute, Jerusalem, 1997.

Kaufmann, Yehezkel, *The Religion of Israel*, University of Chicago Press, Chicago, IL, 1969.

Keating, Geoffrey, *The History of Ireland* (trans, David Comyn and Rev PS Dinneen), 1640, reprinted by Irish Texts Society, London 1902–14.

Keil, KF, *Manual of Biblical Archaeology* (trans, Peter Christie), T&T Clark, Edinburgh, 1888.

Keller, Werner, *The Bible as History*, (trans, William Neil), Hodder & Stoughton, London, 1956.

Kennett, RH, *Deuteronomy and the Decalogue*, Cambridge University Press, Cambridge, 1920.

Kenyon, Kathleen, *Amorites and Canaanites* (from the 1963 Schweich Lectures of the British Academy), Oxford University Press, Oxford, 1966.

King, LW, *The Letters and Inscriptions of Hammurabi*, Luzak, London, 1898.
— *A History of Babylonia and Assyria*, Chatto & Windus, London, 1910.
— *A History of Sumer and Akkad*, Chatto & Windus, London, 1910.

Kitchen, Kenneth Anderson, *Ramesside Inscriptions*, Basil H Blackwell, Oxford, 1975.

Knappert, Jan, *The Encyclopedia of Middle Eastern Religion and Mythology*, Element Books, Shaftesbury, 1993.

Kramer, Samuel Noah, *Lamentation Over the Destruction of Ur* (Assyriological Studies, 12) Chicago University Press: Chicago, 1940.

Kramer, Samuel Noah, *History Begins at Sumer*, Thames & Hudson, London, 1958.
— *Sumerian Mythology*, Harper Bros, New York, NY, 1961.
— *Mythologies of the Ancient World*, Anchor Books, Garden City, NY, 1961.
— *The Sumerians*, University of Chicago Press, Chicago, IL, 1963.
— *The Sacred Marriage Rite*, Indiana University Press, Bloomington, IN, 1969.

Kuhl, C, *The Prophets of Israel*, Oliver and Boyd, London, 1960.

Lambert, WG, *Babylonian Wisdom Literature*, Clarendon Press, Oxford, 1960.
— *Enûma Elis*, Clarendon Press, Oxford, 1966.

Langdon, Stephen H, *Tammuz and Ishtar*, Clarendon Press, Oxford, 1914.

Laurence, Richard (trans 1881), *The Book of Enoch the Prophet*, DeVorss, Camarillo, CA, 1995.

LaViolette, Paul A, *Earth Under Fire*, Starburst, Schenectady, NY, 1997.

Leick, Gwendolen, *A Dictionary of Ancient Near Eastern Mythology*, Routledge, London, 1991.

Lloyd, Seton, *Foundations in the Dust*, Penguin, London, 1955.

Mellersh, HEL, *The Ancient World – Chronology 10,000 BC to AD 799*, Helicon, Oxford, 1976.

Mertz, Henrietta, *Gods From the Far East*, Ballantyne, New York, 1975.

Miles, Jack, *God – A Biography*, Vintage, New York, NY, 1995.

Milik, JT, *Ten Years of Discovery in the Wilderness of Judaea* (trans, J Strugnell), SCM Press, London, 1959.

Mills, Watson E (ed), *Lutterworth Dictionary of the Bible*, Lutterworth Press, Cambridge, 1994.

Montgomery, James Alan, and Zellig S Harris, *The Ras Shamra Mythological Texts*, American Philosophical Society, Philadelphia, PA, 1935.

Moorey, PRS, *The Ancient Near East*, Ashmolean Museum, Oxford, 1987.

Neumann, Erich, *The Great Mother* (Princeton University Bollingen Series), Routledge, London, 1963.

Neusner, Jacob (trans), *Sifre to Numbers*, Scholars Press, Atlanta, GA, 1986.

Newton, Isaac, *The Principia*, Prometheus, Amherst, NY, 1995.

Norvill, Roy, *Giants – The Vanished Race of Mighty Men*, Aquarian Press, Wellingborough, 1979.

Noth, Martin, *The History of Israel* (trans, S Godman), Adam & Charles Black, London, 1960.

Oakeley, Sir Atholl, *Blue Blood on the Mat*, Stanley Paul, London, 1971.

Oates, Joan, *Babylon*, Thames & Hudson, London, 1986.

O'Brien, Christian and Barbara Joy, *The Shining Ones*, Dianthus, Cirencester, 1997.

— *The Genius of the Few*, Dianthus, Cirencester, 1999.

Olson, C (ed), *The Book of the Goddess Past and Present*, Crossroad, New York, NY, 1989.

Oppenheim, A Leo, *Ancient Mesopotamia – Portrait of a Dead Civilization*, University of Chicago, Chicago, IL, 1964.

Osman, Ahmed, *Moses, Pharaoh of Egypt*, Grafton, London, 1990.

— *The House of the Messiah*, HarperCollins, London, 1992.

Osterley, WOE, *Hebrew Religion – Its Origin and Development*, Macmillan, New York, NY, 1937.

Oxford Bible Readers Dictionary and Concordance, Oxford University Press, Oxford (undated).

Patai, Raphael, *The Hebrew Goddess*, Wayne State University Press, Detroit, IL, 1967.

Peet, T Eric, *Egypt and the Old Testament*, Liverpool University Press, Liverpool, 1922.

Peiser, Benny J, Trevor Palmer and Mark E Bailey, *Natural Catastrophes During Bronze Age Civilizations*, Archaeopress, Oxford, 1998.

Perowne, Stewart, *The Life and Times of Herod the Great*, Hodder & Stoughton, London, 1956.

— *The Later Herods*, Hodder & Stoughton, London, 1958.

Peters, John Punnett, *Nippur – or Explorations and Adventures on the Euphrates* – The Narrative of the University of Pennsylvania Expedition to Babylonia in the Years 1888–1890, GP Putnam's Sons, New York, NY, 1897.

Petrie, Sir WM Flinders, *Researches in Sinai*, John Murray, London, 1906.

Pettinato, Giovanni, *Archives of Ebla: An Empire Inscribed in Clay*, Doubleday, New York, NY, 1981.

Pinches, Theophilus G, *The Old Testament in the Light of the Historical Records and Legends of Assyria and Babylonia*, SPCK, London, 1902.

Platt, Rutherford H (ed), *The Forgotten Books of Eden*, New American Library, New York, NY, 1974.

Porter, JR, *The Illustrated Guide to the Bible*, Duncan Baird, London, 1995.

Postgate, Nicholas, *The First Empires*, Elseiver, Oxford, 1977.

Pritchard, JB, *Ancient Near Eastern Texts Relating to the Old Testament*, Princeton University Press, Princeton, NJ, 1954.

Reade, Julian, *Assyrian Sculpture*, British Museum Press, London, 1983.

— *Mesopotamia*, British Museum Press, London, 1991.

Redford, Donald B, *Akhenaten, the Heretic King*, Princeton University Press, Princeton, NJ, 1984.

Reed, William L, *The Asherah in the Old Testament*, Texas Christian University Press, Fort Worth, TX, 1949.

Rhode, James Montague (ed), *The Apocryphal New Testament*, Clarendon Press, Oxford, 1924.

Ritmeyer, Leen and Kathleen, *Secrets of Jerusalem's Temple Mount*, Biblical Archaeological Society, Washington, DC, 1998.

Roaf, Michael, *Cultural Atlas of Mesopotamia and the Ancient Near East*, Equinox, Oxford, 1990.

Rogerson, John, *Chronicle of the Old Testament Kings*, Thames & Hudson, London, 1999.

Rohl, David M, *A Test of Time – The Bible from Myth to History*, Century, London, 1995.

Roux, Georges, *Ancient Iraq*, George Allen & Unwin, London, 1964.

Rowley, HH, *From Moses to Qumrân*, Lutterworth Press, Cambridge, 1963.

Saggs, HWF, *The Greatness that was Babylon*, Sidgwick & Jackson, London, 1988.

Schaeffer, Claude FA, *The Cuneiform Texts of Ras Shamra-Ugarit* (from the 1936 Schweich Lectures of the British Academy), Oxford University Press, Oxford, 1939.

Schodde, Rev George H (trans), *The Book of Jubilees*, Capital University, Columbus, OH (EJ Goodrich edn), 1888; reprinted Artisan, CA, 1992.

Scholem, Gershom G, *Major Trends in Jewish Mysticism*, Thames & Hudson, London, 1955.

Segal, JB, *The Hebrew Passover from the Earliest Times to AD 70*, Oxford University Press, Oxford, 1963.

Sitchin, Zecharia, *The 12th Planet*, Avon Books, New York, NY, 1978.

Smith, Dr William, *Smith's Bible Dictionary* (1868 rev), Hendrickson, Peabody, MA, 1998.

Smith, George, *The Chaldean Account of Genesis*, Sampson Low & Marston, London, 1876.

Smith, Ray Winfield, *The Akhenaten Temple Project*, Aris & Phillips, Warminster, 1976.

Smith, Sidney, *Early History of Assyria*, Chatto & Windus, London, 1928.

Smith, W Robertson, *The Religion of the Semites*, Adam & Charles Black, London, 1894.

Speiser, EA, *The Anchor Bible – Genesis* (translation from Hebrew text), Doubleday, Garden City, NY, 1964.

Sollberger, Edmund, *The Babylonian Legend of the Flood*, British Museum Press, London, 1984.

Sparks, HFD (ed), *Apocryphal Old Testament*, Clarendon Press, Oxford, 1984.

Strommenger, E, *The Art of Ancient Mesopotamia*, Thames & Hudson, London, 1964.

Strong, James, *The Exhaustive Concordance of the Bible*, Abingdon Press, New York, NY, 1890.

Suarès, Carlo, *The Cipher of Genesis*, Samuel Weiser, York Beach, ME, 1992.

Tacitus, Cornelius, *The Histories* (trans, Kenneth Wellesley), Penguin, London, 1995.

Teisser, Beatrice, *Ancient Near Eastern Cylinder Seals from the Marcopoli Collection*, University of California Press, Berkeley, CA, 1984.

Thiering, Barbara, *Jesus the Man*, Transworld, London, 1992.

Thomas, D Winton (ed), *Documents from Old Testament Times*, Harper Torchbooks, New York, NY, 1958.

Times Atlas of the Bible, Times Books, London, 1987.

Times Atlas of Archaeology (Past Worlds), Times Books, London, 1988.

Unterman, Alan, *Dictionary of Jewish Lore and Legend*, Thames & Hudson, London, 1997.

Vaux, Roland de, *The Early History of Israel to the Period of the Judges*, Darton, Longman & Todd, London, 1978.

Vermes, Geza, *The Complete Dead Sea Scrolls in English*, Penguin, London, 1997.

Walker, CBF, *Cuneiform*, British Museum Press, London, 1987.

Ward, William Hayes, *The Seal Cylinders of Western Asia*, Carnegie Institute, Washington, DC, 1910.

Watterson, Barbara, *Gods of Ancient Egypt*, Sutton, Stroud, 1996.

Weigall, Arthur, *The Life and Times of Akhenaten*, Thornton Butterworth, London, 1910.

Wellhausen, J, *Prolegomena to the History of Israel*, Scholars Press, Atlanta, GA, 1994.

Wigram, WA, *The Cradle of Mankind*, A&C Black, London, 1914.

Wilkinson, David, *God, Time & Stephen Hawking*, Monarch, Grand Rapids, MI, 2001.

Winston, Robert, *The Story of God*, Bantam, London, 2005.

Wood, Michael, *Legacy – A Search for the Origins of Civilization*, BBC Network Books, London, 1992.

Woolley, Sir Charles Leonard, *Ur of the Chaldees*, Ernest Benn, London, 1930.

— *The Development of Sumerian Art*, Faber & Faber, London, 1935.

— *A Forgotten Kingdom*, Max Parish, London, 1959.

— *The Sumerians*, WW Norton, London, 1965.

Zohary, Daniel, and Maria Hopf, *Domestication of Plants in the Old World – The Origin and Spread of Cultivated Plants in West Asia, Europe and the Nile Valley*, Oxford University Press, Oxford, 2001.

INDEX

Compiled by Walter Schneider

INDEX

411

CPSIA information can be obtained at www.ICGtesting.com
Printed in the USA
LVOW061201280712

291970LV00002B/4/P